Globalisation, Information and Libraries

CHANDOS
INFORMATION PROFESSIONAL SERIES

Series Editor: Ruth Rikowski
(email: rikowski@tiscali.co.uk)

Chandos' new series of books are aimed at the busy information professional. They have been specially commissioned to provide the reader with an authoritative view of current thinking. They are designed to provide easy-to-read and (most importantly) practical coverage of topics that are of interest to librarians and other information professionals. If you would like a full listing of current and forthcoming titles, please visit our web site **www.chandospublishing.com** or contact Hannah Grace-Williams on email info@chandospublishing.com or telephone number +44 (0) 1865 884447.

New authors: we are always pleased to receive ideas for new titles; if you would like to write a book for Chandos, please contact Dr Glyn Jones on email gjones@chandospublishing.com or telephone number +44 (0) 1865 884447.

Bulk orders: some organisations buy a number of copies of our books. If you are interested in doing this, we would be pleased to discuss a discount. Please contact Hannah Grace-Williams on email info@chandospublishing.com or telephone number +44 (0) 1865 884447.

Globalisation, Information and Libraries

The implications of the World Trade Organisation's GATS and TRIPS Agreements

RUTH RIKOWSKI

Chandos Publishing

Oxford · England

Chandos Publishing (Oxford) Limited
Chandos House
5 & 6 Steadys Lane
Stanton Harcourt
Oxford OX29 5RL
UK
Tel: +44 (0) 1865 884447 Fax: +44 (0) 1865 884448
Email: info@chandospublishing.com
www.chandospublishing.com

First published in Great Britain in 2005

ISBN:
1 84334 084 4 (paperback)
1 84334 092 5 (hardback)

© Ruth Rikowski, 2005

British Library Cataloguing-in-Publication Data.
A catalogue record for this book is available from the British Library.

Cover images courtesy of Bytec Solutions Ltd (*www.bytecweb.com*) and David Hibberd (*DAHibberd@aol.com*).

Printed in the UK and USA.

Dedication

I am dedicating this book to my late Aunt Sophia Lovice Olivia White (née Vickery), who all the family lovingly knew as 'Olive' (1910–1993). Without my Aunt Olive I would never have become what I am today. Dear Aunt Olive – your inspiration, your love, your strength, your depth, your warmth – these qualities have been and always will be unforgettable and will remain with me throughout the whole of my life. Your love of books, your search for an alternative world and your sense of humour will remain with me forever. Dear Aunt – thank you for giving me so much, for understanding me, for listening to me, and for giving me the love and confidence as a child to set me on my path, which made it possible for me to become what I have now become. I will love you forever.

Contents

Foreword

Anders Ericson

My first contact with Ruth Rikowski was through her writing. This should not surprise anyone, since she writes a lot. My first reading was an article entitled 'The Corporate Takeover of Libraries', which can still be found at the significant website and journal *Information for Social Change*, of which Ruth is today co-editor.

It was June 2002. For some time I had been searching the Web for material on the commercialisation of public services, in particular libraries. I had with some effort gathered some bits and pieces from here and there, but all of a sudden I found myself reading the lead of this 42-page article by Ruth Rikowski. That was almost exactly what I had been looking for! We librarians tend to make jokes about stupid students who expect books to be easily available on just any topic their teachers may cook up for their homework papers. Thus, my discovery of Ruth's article was like finding the tailor-made book I didn't quite believe in. I have returned to and quoted from this article more than any other article throughout my whole professional career.

Today it is a pleasure to find that Ruth's article has become part of a printed book, namely this debut of hers between two covers. A revised version of 'The Corporate Takeover' is a central part. Here it comes together with a lot of other very valuable material and the author's own analysis. She has deepened her study of GATS from her 2002 version, and her examination of TRIPS (Trade-Related Aspects of Intellectual Property Rights) will be remembered as an unquestionable pioneer work.

This is important stuff indeed. As a former librarian and today a freelance journalist and consultant, the future of libraries takes most of my time. My editors and employers (e.g. library authorities and organisations, mostly in Scandinavia) are fully aware of the impact of ICT, of the Internet, etc. on the future of libraries and librarianship, but only very few ask me to write or talk about the fact that there are companies out there with piles of venture capital who are already moving into library-like knowledge services and are even considering getting involved in running actual libraries. We have had examples of both commercial virtual reference services and pay-per-view e-book libraries. Their limited success so far does not mean they will never make a breakthrough. If general politics continues developing in the present direction maybe just a generation from now governmental support of today's libraries may wither enough not only to open the way for commercial solutions, but to make people demand them. How soon is hard to tell, but what we know, and what Ruth Rikowski clearly shows among other things, is that private companies who run library services will give priority to the parts that make not only profit, but the most profit.

The more social theoretical parts of this book are essential to fully understand why the author seems so confident about her message. I personally found the conclusive chapters with the Open Marxist approach very challenging and enlightening. The opening 'fact' chapters can be read alone or in conjunction with the more theoretical chapters.

Again, Ruth Rikowski has used much of her spare time to spread her ideas of what she is convinced are some of our most urgent needs. Hopefully a majority of the library and knowledge communities will take her message seriously as her book is reviewed and quoted and Ruth herself and others follow it up in smaller formats and in speeches and debates.

Anders Ericson
Moss, Norway
31 October 2004

Acknowledgements

I would like to thank a large number of different people and organisations for their help, ideas, support and enthusiasm which all played some part in helping to make it possible (either directly or indirectly) for me to write this book.

First, I would like, in particular, to thank my husband, Glenn Rikowski, for his continued inspiration, encouragement, devotion and patience during the writing of this book, and indeed, in general. In particular, it was during the reading of his book *The Battle in Seattle: Its Significance for Education*, that I originally became interested in the topic of globalisation.

Following on from this, the idea of considering the topic of globalisation and information specifically was first suggested to me by John Pateman from *Information for Social Change* (ISC), which led to me editing a special issue of ISC on the topic. So, I would like to thank John for his support during the editing of the special edition, and indeed for his continued support in general. I would also like to thank Matthew Mezey, the News Editor of *Library and Information Update*, for his support and useful advice. I would also like to thank the other members of the ISC Editorial Board: Gill Harris, Martyn Lowe and John Vincent. I would also like to thank Rory Litwin for all the webmaster work he did for ISC and, in particular, for putting the *Globalisation and Information* issue onto the ISC website.

I would also like to thank Graham Coult, the editor of *Managing Information*, and Paul Pedley, regular columnist in *Managing Information* (the Aslib monthly journal), for their continued support in regard to my writing in general. Also, for the interest they have taken in regard to my work on the GATS and TRIPS, in particular.

Many thanks go to Clare Joy, the Campaigns Officer at the World Development Movement, for the interest she has taken in the GATS and libraries issue specifically, and for the article that she wrote on the GATS for the special ISC issue on *Globalisation and Information*. Also, for providing me with the opportunity to speak on the *You and Yours* programme on Radio 4, on the GATS.

I would like to thank those who contributed articles to the *Globalisation and Information* issue, namely Bill Lehm, Clare Joy, Fiona Hunt, Glenn Rikowski, Anneliese Dodds, Shahrzad Mojab, Victor Rikowski, Alex Nunn, Patrick Ainley and Jonathan Rutherford.

In addition, I would like to thank all the people that spoke at the fringe meeting that I organised at the International Federation of Library Association and Institutions (IFLA) Conference in Glasgow in 2002 on the topic of the GATS and libraries. These were: Steve Rolfe, Paul Whitney, Frode Bakken, Glenn Rikowski and Anneliese Dodds. I would like to thank Gill Harris for her support during the organisation of the meeting. I would also like to thank the UK Chartered Institute of Library and Information Professionals (UK CILIP) for providing me with the funding and for making it possible for me to attend the IFLA conference; and for Jill Martin's support in particular. I would also like to thank all the people that came to the meeting and participated in the event so enthusiastically.

I would like to thank the past and present members of the European Bureau of Library, Information and Documentation Associations (EBLIDA) World Trade Organisation (WTO) Working Group, for the work they have undertaken and continue to undertake with regard to the GATS and libraries issue. The TRIPS is now also included in their remit. Also, for the support that they have given me personally. In particular, I would like to thank Frode Bakken (who invited me to be an observer on the EBLIDA WTO Working Group), Teresa Hackett, Kjell Nilsson, Toby Bainton, Maria Pia González Pereira and Britt-Marie Häggström. I would also like to thank Barbara Schleihagen, from the German Library Association, and past president of EBLIDA, for the interest she has shown in my work on the GATS and libraries.

It was great that the Association for the Taxation of Financial Transactions (ATTAC) gave me the opportunity to speak at one of their meetings at the London School of Economics (LSE) on the GATS and libraries. I would like to thank them also for enabling a one-day event to take place at LSE on the GATS and public services in the UK. As part of the ATTAC WTO Working Group I helped to organise this event and we invited a variety of speakers from different public sectors to speak. I would like to thank all these speakers: Niaz Alam, Benjamin Geer, Markus Krajewski, Sally Ruane, Francois Ogliaro, Emanuele Lobina, Hugo Lowe, Les Levidow, Glenn Rikowski, Sylvie Gosme and Kat Fletcher. I would also like to thank, in particular, the following members of ATTAC for their support, solidarity and help in regard to the organisation of this event and in general: Francois Ogliaro, Markus Krajewski, Helena Kotkowska, Matti Kohonen, Ben Geer, David Whiting and Emma Dowling. I would also like to thank all the people that came to the seminar and participated so enthusiastically.

I would like to thank Anna Weschke, a member of the World Development Movement and People and Planet, for organising a very successful evening session on the GATS and public services at Sussex University. Also, for inviting me to speak at this event, on the topic of the GATS and libraries.

I would also like to thank the editors of various journals who published my different articles on the GATS and TRIPS and who gave me the opportunity to develop my ideas in print. These include Stephen Parker, the editor of the *IFLA Journal*; Tim Owen, the editor of *Business Information Review*; Debby Raven, the editor of the *Public Library Journal* (the journal of the Public Library Group of CILIP); and Ann Irving, the editor of *Focus* (the journal for the International Library and Information Group of CILIP). Also, Massimo de Angelis, the editor of the *Commoner* (a left activist e-journal); Andrew Martin, the Chief Editor of *Relay* (the journal of the University College and Research Group of CILIP); Gill Harris, the editor of *Link-Up: The Newsletter of LINK: A Network for North–South Library Development*; Michael Peters, co-editor of *Policy Futures in Education*; Lennart Wettmark, the editor of *BIS* (*Bibliotek i Samhaelle* – a Swedish left library journal); and Graham Coult, the editor of *Managing Information*.

I would also like to thank Jane McKenzie, who at the time was the News Editor for the *Big Issue*, for writing a piece in the *Big Issue* on the GATS and libraries, for referencing my work and for raising awareness about this important topic. I would also like to thank Anders Ericson, a freelance journalist and librarian from Norway, for his enthusiasm and support for my work. Also, for coming over to England to interview me about my work on the GATS and libraries, for raising awareness further about this topic and for the piece he wrote subsequently, which was published in the Norwegian library journal *Bok og Bibliotek* (*BOB*). I would also like to thank George Monbiot, columnist in the *Guardian*, and Susan George for the interest they have taken in my work and for all the work that they have undertaken on globalisation. I would also like to thank Mikael Böök for the enthusiastic interest he has taken in my work on the GATS and TRIPS. Also, for inviting me to speak at the World Social Forum (WSF) in India in 2004, on the workshop on the

'Democratisation of Information: Focus on Libraries' (even though, unfortunately, I was not able to attend!).

Many people provided me with the opportunity to speak on the topics of the GATS and TRIPS at various events, and these experiences sharpened my analyses of these WTO Agreements. On this score, I would like to thank Paul Sturgess, from Loughborough University, for inviting me to speak on the GATS and libraries at the CILIP Umbrella Conference, in 2003, and Jonathan Davidson for inviting me to speak on TRIPS and Libraries at the Library and Information Show, at Excel, Docklands in 2003. I would also like to thank Bob Roberts for inviting me to speak to a group of MSc students at Kingston University on TRIPS in 2003.

I would also like to thank David Marzella, a Unison shop steward from Greenwich public libraries, for the interest he has taken in my work on the GATS and for inviting me to speak and liaise with some other shop stewards in Greenwich public libraries on the topic. I would also like to thank Deian Hopkin, the Vice-Chancellor of London South Bank University, for the interest he has taken in my writing. Thanks also go to George Bell, a lecturer at London South Bank University for the interest he has taken in this book and for inviting me to give a talk on it at London South Bank University. I would also like to thank David Gurteen for organising Knowledge Cafes and knowledge e-mail newsletters. This helped me to develop some of my ideas further in regard to the knowledge revolution, the significance of value and how this links to the GATS and TRIPS. Also, for providing me with the opportunity to speak at one of the Knowledge Cafes on the topic of knowledge management (KM) and value.

There are a number of people that I have liaised with in regard to the GATS in general, and the threat it poses to public services in particular. I would like to thank them for their exchange of ideas and thoughts on the GATS issue in general, and for the interest they have taken in the GATS and libraries issue specifically. These include: Sally Ruane, Linda Kaucher, Steve Kelk, James Cemmell, John Hilary, Tom Lines, Les Levidow, Anne Gray, David Weston, Chris Keene, Hilary Wainwright, Stuart Hodkinson and Polly Jones.

A number of writers have particularly inspired me during the writing of this book. These include George Monbiot, Martin Khor, Denise Nicolson, Inge Kaul, Nick Cohen, Steve Shrybman, Stuart Hamilton and Moishe Postone. There are many others, but I would like to acknowledge these authors in particular.

Special thanks go to a number of other people that have taken a particular interest in my work on globalisation. These include: Lee Rose, Charles Oppenheim, Bernard Naylor, Stuart Hamilton, Bob Bater, Kingsley Oghojafor, Dinesh Gupta, Natalie Pollecutt, Keith Nockells, Sue Brown, Graeme Hawley, Al Kagan, Andrew Coburn, Emma Farrow, Jon Sims, Jerry Power, John Lindsay, Mike Martin, Katriona Higgins, Rob Bleijerveld, Robin Rice, Maurice Line, Julian Samuels, Mark Vera, Mark Rosenzweig and Mark Perkins.

I would also like to thank a number of other people that I have liaised with on topics that are important to me in general, and who have given me support, encouragement, food-for-thought, etc., including Paula Allman, Peter McLaren, Rachel Gorman, Corinna Lotz, Paul Feldman, David Black, Chris Ford and David Harvie. There are many others who have taken an interest in my work – too many to mention – but I would like to thank all of them as well!

I would also like to thank a number of different organisations for raising the topics of the GATS and TRIPS. These include:

- Information for Social Change – for providing a platform for alternative views in the library and information world.
- ATTAC – for raising and debating the GATS.
- Canadian Library Association – for being one of the first library associations to raise the issue of the GATS and for the support they gave me in regard to the IFLA fringe meeting on the GATS that I organised. Also, for commissioning Steve Shrybman to write his important report about the GATS and public sector libraries in 2001, and for commissioning Ellen Gould to update this in 2004. Also for helping to organise the research that is currently being undertaken on the TRIPS and libraries in Canada by Myra Tawfik of the University of Windsor, Canada.
- British Columbia Library Association (BCLA) – for first raising the topic of the GATS and libraries, and informing the library and information profession about it.
- World Development Movement – for contributing an article to the special issue on *Globalisation and Information,* for providing me with the opportunity to speak on a radio programme and for providing a speaker for the IFLA fringe meeting. Also, for providing a wealth of very useful literature, and for all the very good work they have undertaken in general in regard to raising awareness about the topic of the GATS.

- European Bureau of Library, Information and Documentation Associations (EBLIDA) – for inviting me to be an observer on the EBLIDA WTO working group and for the work that it has done and continues to do in regard to raising awareness about these WTO agreements.

- International Federation of Library Associations and Institutions (IFLA) – for raising awareness about these WTO agreements, for making it possible for me to be able to organise a fringe meeting at an IFLA conference on the topic, for including sessions at its conference on trade agreements and for publishing my articles in the *IFLA Journal*.

- Association for Information Management (Aslib) – for providing me with the opportunity to raise the topics of the GATS and TRIPS through its monthly journal, *Managing Information*.

- Chartered Institute of Library and Information Professionals (CILIP) (UK) – for giving me funding to enable me to attend the IFLA Conference in Glasgow, 2002; for inviting me, through the International Library and Information Group of CILIP, to speak at the CILIP Umbrella Conference in 2003, on the GATS; for including news items about the GATS in *CILIP Update* – CILIP's monthly professional journal; for providing the facility to enable me to talk about the *Globalisation and Information* issue at CILIP HQ (through the International Library and Information Group of CILIP) and for contributing some money towards the production of the special ISC issue. Also, for enabling groups within CILIP to thrive. In particular, for enabling my work to be published in journals of three of its groups – namely, the International Library and Information Group, the Public Library Group, and the University College and Research Group.

- British Broadcasting Corporation (BBC) – for inviting me to speak on the BBC Radio 4 programme, *You and Yours*, on the GATS and libraries.

- Link, an organisation in liaison with CILIP that connects with library workers in the developing world – for providing general support, and for publishing some of my articles and other material on the GATS and libraries in its journal *Link-up*.

- People and Planet – for raising awareness about the GATS, for providing very useful literature and support in general.

- House of Lords – for publishing a very important and useful report on *Globalisation* in general and for publishing my article on *Globalisation and Libraries* in particular.

- Commission on Intellectual Property Rights (UK) – for raising and debating the important topic of intellectual property rights, which included TRIPS in its remit. They held a series of meetings, commissioned working papers, held workshops and organised a very useful and informative conference, in 2002, which debated how intellectual property rights could benefit the developing world more, which I attended. Also for producing a very informative and interesting report entitled *Integrating Intellectual Property Rights and Development Policy*.

- London South Bank University, School of Business, Computing and Information Management – for taking an interest in my work on globalisation, libraries and information.

- Other library associations and cultural organisations (not previously referred to) – for passing resolutions and/or issuing statements and/or showing concern/interest in some other way, about the GATS, libraries and cultural issues. These include – the American Library Association, Australian Library and Information Association, Australian Coalition for Cultural Diversity, Australian Writers' Guild, Professional Associations from the Cultural Milieu, the Writers' Guild of America, West and the Library Association of Ireland.

- Other non-governmental organisations – that have taken an interest in and/or have undertaken some work and have participated in demonstrations and events in regard to various trade issues. These include organisations such as Oxfam and War on Want.

On a personal note, I would also like to pay tribute to my three children – Alexander, Victor and Gregory – for either their help or their hindrance during the writing of this book! They have been, and always are, a great motivating factor and I love them all dearly. I would also like to thank my friend Elaine, my Aunt Jean and her family, my cousin Helen, my friends Frances, Tina, Margaret, Clive and Alison and my elderly friend John, for always being there and being ready and willing to talk and listen to me!

List of abbreviations

ACCD	Australian Coalition for Cultural Diversity
ACP	African, Caribbean and Pacific Group (WTO)
Aids	acquired immune deficiency syndrome
ALA	American Library Association
ALIA	Australian Library and Information Association
Aslib	Association for Information Management
ASU	Australian Services Union
ATTAC	Association for the Taxation of Financial Transactions (UK)
A-V	audio-visual
AWG	Australian Writers' Guild
BBC	British Broadcasting Corporation
BCLA	British Colombia Library Association
BIBSAM	Swedish Royal Library, Department for National Coordination and Development
BIS	*Bibliotek i Samhaelle* (Swedish library journal)
BOB	*Bok og Bibliotek* (Norwegian library journal)
BV	Best Value (UK)
CBD	Convention on Biological Diversity
CBI	Confederation of British Industry
CCA	Center for the Creative Community (USA)
CDPA	Copyright, Designs and Patents Act 1988 (UK)
CGL	Community Grid for Learning (UK)
CILIP	Chartered Institute of Library and Information Professionals (UK)

CIP	Community Initiative Partnership (UK)
CLA	Canadian Library Association
CLM	Copyright and Other Legal Matters Committee (IFLA)
COL	Committee on Legislation (ALA)
COSATU	Congress of South African Trade Unions
CPC	Central Product Classification (UN)
DCMS	Department for Culture, Media and Sport (UK)
DETR	Department for the Environment, Transport and the Regions (UK)
EBLIDA	European Bureau of Library, Information and Documentation Associations
EC	European Communities (for legal reasons the name of the EU in WTO business)
EU	European Union
FAIFE	Committee on Free Access to Information and Freedom of Expression
FOIA	Freedom of Information Act 2000 and 2005 (UK)
FTA	Free Trade Agreement
FTAA	Free Trade Agreements of the Americas
GATS	General Agreement on Trade in Services
GATT	General Agreement on Tariffs and Trade
GDP	Gross Domestic Product
ICT	information and communications/computer technology
IFLA	International Federation of Library Associations and Institutions
IMF	International Monetary Fund
IP	intellectual property
IPC	Intellectual Property Committee
IPR	intellectual property right
ISC	Information for Social Change (UK)
IT	information technology

KM	knowledge management
LA	Library Association (now CILIP) (UK)
LDC	Least Developed Country Group (WTO)
LISWA	Library and Information Service of Western Australia
LMG	Like-Minded Group (WTO)
MAI	Multilateral Agreement on Investment
MFAT	Ministry of Foreign Affairs and Trade (New Zealand)
MLA	Museums, Libraries and Archives Council (formerly Resource)
MNC	multinational corporation
NAFTA	North Atlantic Free Trade Association
NAPLE	Danish National Library Authority
NGO	non-governmental organisation
NOF	New Opportunities Fund (UK)
OECD	Organisation for Economic Cooperation and Development
P2P	person-to-person
PBR	People's Biodiversity Register (India)
PC	personal computer
PFI	Private Finance Initiative (UK)
PhRMA	Pharmaceutical Research and Manufacturers of America
PIC	'prior informed consent' (CBD)
PSP	payment service provider
RAFI	Rural Advancement Foundation International
SCONUL	Society of College, National and University Libraries (UK)
SPS	Sanitary and Phyto-sanitary Agreement (WTO)
SSCL	Services Sectoral Classification List
TINA	There Is No Alternative
TK	traditional knowledge
TOLIMAC	Total Library Management Concept (UK)

TRIM	Trade-Related Investment Measures (WTO)
TRIPS	Trade-Related Aspects of Intellectual Property Rights
UCC	Universal Copyright Convention
UN	United Nations
UNCTAD	United Nations Conference on Trade and Development
UNESCO	United Nations Educational and Cultural Organisation
USTR	US Trade Representative
W3C	World Wide Web Consortium
WDM	World Development Movement
WGA	Writers' Guild of America, West
WIPO	World Intellectual Property Organisation
WTO	World Trade Organisation

About the author

Ruth Rikowski is a well-known author and academic with 25 years' experience as an information professional. Ruth is an observer on the EBLIDA (European Bureau of Library, Information and Documentation Associations) WTO Working Group. She is currently a Visiting Lecturer at London South Bank University and the University of Greenwich and is also the Series Editor for the Chandos Series for Information Professionals.

The author may be contacted at:

E-mail: *rikowski@tiscali.co.uk*   or   *rikowskigr@aol.com*

Introduction

In many ways our world can seem strange, although also often exciting – everything is on the move; speed is of the essence; information technology is here to stay; information appears to flow freely; and everything is happening, we are led to believe, within the notion of a 'happy global family'. We all live together in a globalised world, which is ultimately for the good of everyone. This is the rhetoric that we are fed.

How, though, have we come to believe in this naive notion? It is rather like fairyland or heaven. We like the idea of a utopian world, and so the thought that this can be accomplished simply through the economic, political and social system in which we all currently live is appealing. So we fool ourselves that we can all live happily and healthily within global capitalism. Clare Short, the then International Development Secretary in the UK, said in December 2000, for example, that we need to harness the 'forces of globalisation' to reduce world poverty (Atkinson and Elliott, 2000: 13), thus naively believing (let us be charitable!) that it is possible to reduce world poverty significantly in this way. Meanwhile, Jawara and Kwa consider the World Trade Organisation (WTO), which is an institution that is harnessing and extending globalisation. They point out that the WTO supporters are of the opinion that the WTO is needed because:

> ... the institutional framework provided by a 'rules-based' international institution at least puts the developing countries in a stronger position to challenge the developed countries than the anarchy of a ruthless system. (Jawara and Kwa, 2003: 302)

However, numerous examples illustrate that this naive view is far removed from reality, and this will be explored further in this book. Developing countries are in a weak position at the WTO, and this rules-based system does not, on the whole, operate in their favour.

Furthermore, we witness death, destruction, suffering and injustice everyday, and globalisation is not reducing these horrors, yet we like to fool ourselves that somehow everything will 'come good' in the end. At the same time, we are led to believe that the search for alternatives is at least fanciful and offers us unrealistic/unrealisable dreams, or at worst is evil. Therefore, apparently, 'TINA rules OK' – the philosophy that preaches 'There Is No Alternative'. Clare Short, it seems, is of this opinion, and says that:

> Globalisation is here to stay; the political challenge is to manage it well. (Short, 2001: 17)

Similarly, with regard to the WTO specifically, Watkins argues that:

> Some anti-globalisers will view any proposal to reform the WTO as ill-conceived. But what are the alternatives? (Watkins, 2003: 33)

Meanwhile, Jack Straw, the British Foreign Secretary, interestingly states that:

> There is nothing inevitable about globalisation. It is created and shaped by the choices and decisions of us all. (Straw, 2001: 13)

However, he then goes on to contradict himself, by saying:

> Since the collapse of the Soviet Bloc, there is no longer a coherent alternative ideology on offer. (Straw, 2001: 13)

Apparently, then, there is only one ideology. Derber sees this 'TINA philosophy' as being depressing and says:

> TINA. There Is No Alternative. These four little words seem the most common in the world today. They are depressing, and they paralyze many people who are deeply uneasy about globalization and would dearly love to help make a better world. I bet you think TINA when you think about 'reinventing globalization'. But the popularity of TINA reflects a terrible ignorance of history. (Derber, 2003: 127)

So, cannot humans, with their great intellect, conceive of a better system? Capitalism emerged from previous economic, social and political systems – it is not a system that the human race has chosen by using its intellect and deciding that it is the best possible. No, instead it has evolved from other systems, such as feudalism and ancient slave-based societies, I would suggest, and now there is an assumption that we must just accept it. It is inevitable apparently – as inevitable and predictable as the fact that the sun will rise and that it will rain. Is this what our intelligence leads us to conclude?

This book will challenge these assumptions and it will do this by tackling 'head on' some of the most significant decisions that are taking place on the global stage; in essence it will do this by examining the WTO. Furthermore, it will look at the implications of some of the decisions that are taking place at the WTO for the library and information world in particular, as I am an Information Professional/Librarian and an academic and come from a library/information background. Indeed, I entered the profession because I wanted to try to improve the world in some small way. Thus the time has come for a book to be written on this very important topic that still relatively few people know about.

The book will begin by considering the meaning of 'globalisation' itself. It is a term that is becoming very much part of everyday vocabulary, but often the precise meaning of it is given scant regard. More accurately, in fact, it should be referred to as 'global capitalism' rather than 'globalisation'. Following on from this, it will examine the World Trade Organisation itself. This will include a brief historical analysis of the WTO as well as an examination of some of its main practices, procedures, administrative and decision-making processes and groupings.

It will focus in particular on two of the agreements that are being developed at the WTO that are likely to have particularly significant implications for libraries and information – namely, the General Agreement on Trade in Services (GATS) and the Agreement on Trade-Related Aspects of Intellectual Property Rights (TRIPS). These agreements will be considered and analysed in general, followed by an examination of how they are likely to impact on the library and information world in particular within an international perspective. Some work on writing, analysing and raising awareness has been undertaken within the library and information profession on these important agreements and this will be considered, but more work still needs to be done. With this in mind, I am currently an observer on the European Bureau of Library, Information and Documentation Associations (EBLIDA)

WTO Working Group. I also attended the International Federation of Library Associations and Institutions (IFLA) Conference in Glasgow held in 2002 to raise awareness about the GATS, and organised a meeting with a variety of speakers. I have also been involved in various other activities that will be considered further in this book.

The chapters on the GATS, TRIPS, libraries and information will consider a number of areas. These will include: public goods, private goods and commodities; which countries have signed up their library services to the GATS; the position of various library associations and other cultural bodies internationally with regard to the GATS; and practical examples of how the GATS is impacting on libraries in the United Kingdom. It will highlight, in particular, the fact that many different library associations have made statements against the GATS. This will be followed by an examination of TRIPS and copyright, which will include an historical analysis of copyright and moral and economic rights in copyright. TRIPS, patents, traditional knowledge, information and libraries in the developing world will then be considered along with the implications of TRIPS for libraries and information within an international perspective. It will demonstrate how TRIPS threatens principles embedded in the library and information profession such as the balance in copyright and how it is particularly disadvantageous for those in the developing world.

From here, the book will argue that to understand and explain globalisation, or more accurately global capitalism, we need to develop relevant, credible and rigorous social scientific theory, and that, as far as I am concerned, this involves developing Marxist theory. In particular, I am developing an Open Marxist theoretical analysis of value (R. Rikowski, 2003g, 2003h, 2004), focusing on the work of Moishe Postone (Postone, 1996), and this will be explored at a preliminary level in the last part of this book (Part 4, Chapters 11 and 12).

My position in brief is that the continued success of capitalism is dependent upon the continued creation and extraction of value from labour, and that only labour can ever create value. Capitalism goes through various phases, such as the agricultural revolution and the industrial revolution, but now we are moving into the knowledge revolution. In the industrial revolution, value was largely extracted from manual labour and the production of manufactured goods, whereas in the knowledge revolution, value is increasingly being extracted from intellectual labour, which is then embedded in intangible goods/ commodities. Meanwhile, the production of manufactured goods is increasingly taking place in the developing world rather than in the developed world.

Thus it becomes necessary to examine areas such as intellectual property rights, services, knowledge, information, brand names, white-collar and intellectual work, skills, human capital, intellectual capital, ideas and brainpower. Therefore the WTO is playing a crucial role in ensuring the continued development of the knowledge revolution, and thus ensuring the continuation and perpetuation of global capitalism itself. This is being achieved in particular by transforming intellectual property rights (through TRIPS) and services (through the GATS) into international tradable commodities. Then, value from intellectual labour is embedded in these commodities, and from this value profits are derived, which benefits companies and ensures the continuance of global capitalism in general.

Thus, in my future published works, I will be analysing an Open Marxist theoretical analysis of value and the commodity in some depth and then relating this theory specifically to the GATS and TRIPS. The true nature and horror of global capitalism can only ever be fully understood and exposed by adopting such a grounded, theoretical approach, I would suggest, and then relating it to practical considerations. By such an approach, we can become proactive, rather than just waiting for evolutionary processes to take their course. From such a position, we can then start to conceive of and work towards a better, a fairer and a kinder world. As Marx said:

> The philosophers have only interpreted the world, in various ways: the point, however, is to change it. (Marx, 1845: 30)

So we need to analyse the world and then seek to change it.

The book will conclude by drawing all these strands together and demonstrating in particular how the developing world will continue to suffer as a result of the WTO, while rich countries and large corporations reap most of the benefits. Much traditional knowledge in the developing countries is being appropriated by large corporations and is then being turned into intellectual property rights and thus commodified. It can then be traded in the marketplace, through TRIPS, while the creators of this knowledge are often given no or little recompense. Furthermore, poor people in the developed world will also suffer more as a result of the agreements. The GATS, for example, threatens the state-funded provision of many of the services in the developed world. This includes public library provision. In the future, members of the local community might find themselves visiting a local public library that is owned by a private company and having to pay to go into the library. Such a scenario is clearly likely to be disadvantageous for the poor in the community, who might not be able to afford to pay these fees. Therefore decisions that are taking place so far from home can, and I feel sure will, have serious and worrying implications, in particular for the poor, the deprived and various minority groups. Let us, then, seek to try to change the tide.

Part 1
Globalisation and the World Trade Organisation

Globalisation and an overview of the WTO

2.1 Globalisation

2.1.1 Historical significance of globalisation

Globalisation is a term that we are all very familiar with today. However, it is sometimes thought to be a modern term, when in fact this is far from the truth. It was first used in the ancient civilisations and then throughout various periods in history after this. The world's first great civilisations, such as Mesopotamia and Egypt, invented the term 'ancient globalisations'. Then the concept of globalisation was taken forward with the Romans. Furthermore, Italian city-states such as Venice and Florence created a merchant-driven 'Renaissance globalisation'. The colonial powers of countries such as Spain, the Netherlands, France and Britain then built a new form of globalisation. Then, finally, over the last 50 years, the USA reinvented a new model of globalisation (Derber, 2003: 217). Amin also notes that:

> The globalisation of the capitalist system is certainly nothing new, but it has undeniably taken a qualitative step forward during the most recent period. (Amin, 1997: 31)

However, what is of particular significance is that 150 years ago Marx and Engels saw that a particular capitalist form of globalisation was developing, saying that:

> All that is solid melts into air ... the need of a constantly ex-panding market for its products chases the bourgeoisie over the whole surface of the globe. It must nestle everywhere, settle

everywhere, establish connections everywhere. (Marx and Engels, 1848: 83)

Thus the concept of globalisation needs to be considered within this broader context.

2.1.2 Definition of 'globalisation'

What exactly is 'globalisation'? Globalisation has been defined in a variety of ways and some of these definitions have been highlighted in a report that was produced by the House of Lords Select Committee on Economic Affairs (2002). The report refers to a cross-government departmental memorandum, for example, which highlights the fact that globalisation has both an economic and a political dimension. In an economic sense, it is concerned with accelerating international trade and capital and information flows, whereas the political dimension includes the diffusion of global norms and values, the spread of democracy and the proliferation of various treaties (Ev 1, p.1, in House of Lords report on Globalisation, 2002: 12).

Meanwhile, the United Nations Conference on Trade and Development (UNCTAD) view on globalisation was that it involves the process of increasing economic integration across different nations, through cross-border flows of goods and resources. Furthermore, within this framework there is a related set of organisational structures to manage this activity (Ev 1: 360, in House of Lords report on Globalisation, 2002: 13).

The House of Lords Select Committee concludes the section noting that it does not offer a simple definition of globalisation, but that:

> ... it is our view that the period of globalisation represents a new departure in world affairs. Partly this is to do with what has been called 'the death of distance', assisted by the absolute and relative decline in transport costs ... we have one world in an economic and cultural sense, which has not existed before. (House of Lords, 2002: 18)

Thus there is a clear recognition here that what we are witnessing and experiencing is something significantly different from what has taken place in the past, albeit that it is building on past happenings, and that the globalisation that we know today did not just materialise out of 'thin air'. The term itself also needs to be given some considerable thought. More accurately, as already stated, we should be referring to 'global capitalism' rather than 'globalisation', but 'globalisation' is the term that is in general popular usage today.

Meanwhile, Clare Short, who at the time (2001) was the UK's Secretary of State for International Development, sees globalisation as the '... growing interdependence and interconnectedness of the modern world.' This includes the increasing ease of movement of goods, services, capital, people and information across different national borders. Such ease of movement is leading towards the creation of a single global economy, she argues. Furthermore, all this is taking place within a technological age in which information technology is playing a key role. She also associates globalisation with the 'spread of democracy', the diffusion of global norms and values and the proliferation of global agreements and treaties. Short argues that it is absurd to say that one is 'for' or 'against' globalisation because 'it is here to stay' – so, once again, we have the 'TINA rules OK' philosophy. She says that if globalisation is to work for poor people, then more investment in education, lifelong learning and skills is necessary (Short, 2001: 17).

Derber (2003: 29) spoke in particular about the connection between globalisation and the Internet and information technology, and argued that some people find it almost impossible to be able to differentiate between the two.

There are also issues related to language. In this globalised world, it would presumably be useful if we were all able to speak the same language. However, there is often an assumption that English is and should be the dominant language. Yet people whose mother tongue is English constitute only 5 per cent of the global population and over 50 per cent of the online population now access the Internet in a language other than English (see Anon., 2001).

From all this, globalisation can be seen to encompass many different factors. These include: exacerbating international trade; enhancing global knowledge and information flows; the increasing interconnectedness of the world and the 'death of distance'; increasing reliance on the Internet and information technology; the spread of democracy; and a global approach to norms and values. All these factors seem to constitute very good news for the development of contemporary society.

However, there are also many contradictory themes with regard to globalisation. At one level, globalisation seems to equate with the desire to have one overriding set of global norms and values, for example, but on another level there is a wish to celebrate diversity and cultural differences. Similarly, globalisation can be seen to equate with notions of the free flow of information, but at another level there is a desire to encapsulate information within intellectual property rights, thus restricting this free flow. Instead, once information is encapsulated in intellectual property rights, through agreements such as the WTO Agreement on Trade-Related Aspects of Intellectual Property Rights (TRIPS), it can then be traded in the marketplace, for a price. Also, while there is much global movement of trade and capital, labour does not have the same level of flexibility and movement (although labour is more mobile than it used to be). Gray emphasises this point, saying that:

> ... while trade and capital move freely across the globe, the movement of labour is strictly limited ... (Gray, 2001: 25)

Thus these contradictions, in themselves, should start to make us somewhat sceptical about the simplistic rosy picture that can sometimes, initially, be drawn when considering globalisation.

2.1.3 The four dimensions of globalisation

Therefore it is actually necessary to consider the meaning of globalisation at a deeper level. Glenn Rikowski has considered some of the complexities and argues that there are four dimensions to the term 'globalisation'. Firstly, there is the cultural dimension. He draws attention to the fact that there are two approaches to the cultural issue, and that they are contradictory. One is the recognition and appreciation of cultural differences, while the other is the homogenisation and the bringing together of different cultures into one overall global culture. He states:

> ... globalisation has been associated simultaneously with the cross-fertilisation and increasing hybridity of cultural forms and identities on the one hand and the homogenisation of culture on the other. (G. Rikowski, 2001a: 8)

The second dimension is concerned with the eroding of the power and significance of nation states in the face of global capital. Instead, transnational organisations are setting the scene, such as the WTO, the International Monetary Fund (IMF) and the World Bank. He argues that these organisations are increasingly taking on world government roles for the interests of capital in general and transnational corporations in particular. These organisations can override many decisions that are taken by governments within nation states. Furthermore, this is also connected to economic factors, such as the deregulation of labour, the growth of e-commerce, the increasing importance of the 'knowledge structure' and the fact that knowledge is now seen to be a leading factor of production (G. Rikowski, 2001a: 9).

The third dimension relates to 'capital's rapid expansion'. The emphasis here is on the commodification of all that surrounds us in this globalised world. G. Rikowski says that:

> ... the processes of capital's expansion ... take over and suck in, like a social vortex, all forms of social life such that they become commodified, become incorporated within capital's social universe. (G. Rikowski, 2001a: 10)

The debate about whether a parent should be able to choose the sex of their child is one good example here. The decision was taken in November 2003 that, at the time, parents would not be able to choose the sex of their child in the UK – there is a fear that this might start to lead to the 'commodification of babies'. Boseley, writing in the *Guardian* newspaper, reported that the organisation Human Fertilisation, which regulates fertility treatment, recommended a ban on sex selection, except for families in which one gender would risk inheriting a serious genetic disorder. She made the point that many would argue that parental love should be unconditional and that children are a gift, not a choice, and that if parents were able to choose the sex of their child, they might then want to select other characteristics in regard to their child (Boseley, 2003a: 1). What if the parent chooses a girl, but she is a tomboy, for example? Does the parent hand the child back? Is a child to be traded like a car? Or would the parents then be offered the opportunity to choose whether or not they wanted their child to have any tomboy characteristics, which might involve further manipulation of genes? Thus there is some awareness of the dangers of the intensification of the commodification process. However, this is the direction in which global capitalism is heading, and indeed inevitably how it *must* move. A Marxist analysis of the commodity and the commodification process is explored in Chapters 11 and 12.

The fourth dimension encapsulates the fact that our labour takes on a particular social form: the value-form.

> The value-form of labour entails the creation of value so that profit can be drawn off from the surplus value created. This is at the core of 'globalisation'. (G. Rikowski, 2001b: 10)

Value is created from labour and it can only ever be created from labour. This value is embedded in the commodity, and from surplus value profits are then generated (value in excess of that incorporated in the wage). Globalisation ensures the intensification of this process, as more forms of life are being transformed into international tradable commodities. As already outlined, I am developing an Open Marxist theoretical analysis of value, and this will be considered further in Part 4, Chapters 11 and 12. Thus these four dimensions immerse us into considering globalisation at a deeper, more theoretical level.

If we want to have a better, more lasting understanding about globalisation, then I suggest that we need to examine globalisation at this deeper level. Then, moving on from this, we can develop a deeper and more meaningful understanding about global capitalism itself. When one examines this within a Marxist analysis of capitalism, then the picture becomes clearer. The contradictory approaches in regard to cultural issues, for example, might at first seem difficult to comprehend, but under a Marxist analysis they become clear, because capitalism itself is based on a set of contradictions. This is in contrast to a functionalist theoretical approach, which argues that systems and sub-systems work together. Under a functionalist approach the contradictions with regard to cultural issues would be more difficult to understand, but not so under a Marxist approach. Global capitalism needs to be viewed within this context.

2.1.4 Globalisation and the World Trade Organisation

Thus there are many facets and aspects to globalisation or global capitalism and various definitions. Since the supposed death of communism, global capitalism now appears to stalk the earth. We are led to believe that it is the accepted order and, indeed, that we should celebrate it. This is why it is termed 'global capitalism', rather than simply 'capitalism', because of its seemingly all-pervading nature, although the preferred terminology is 'globalisation' as this camouflages the true reality to some extent and sounds more pleasant. While it is important to draw the reader's attention to these different facets, global capitalism, with all its complexities, cannot be fully explored in the space of this book. Therefore my analysis will focus, specifically, on the WTO. Michael Moore, the then WTO Director-General, referred to the WTO saying that:

> ... the WTO is fundamentally about international solidarity, interdependence; breaking down barriers between people as well as economies. Prosperity and peace – that to me is what the multilateral system can bring about. (WTO, 1999: 1)

This, then, is Michael Moore's utopian view of the WTO, and the validity of such statements will be explored further throughout this book.

My analysis of the WTO will incorporate the second, third and fourth dimensions of globalisation. It will not, however, include a detailed examination of other areas, such as the World Bank or global cultural issues. In regard to the second dimension, the WTO plays a highly significant part in helping to reduce the power of the nation state. With regard to the third dimension, the agreements that are being developed at the WTO will result in the commodification of more and more forms of social life. This will be illustrated very clearly through an examination of the GATS and TRIPS. The fourth dimension, the creation of value, will be intensified by the continued implementation of these agreements. This is because I am arguing that in the knowledge revolution today, intellectual labour is becoming increasingly important. This intellectual labour creates value and this value is then embedded in commodities. The GATS and TRIPS assist with the extension of this commodification process, as public services (through the GATS) and intellectual property rights (through TRIPS) are being transformed into international tradable commodities. This will be considered further in Part 4, Chapters 11 and 12 of this book.

With regard to the WTO specifically, these WTO agreements were due to come fully into effect in 2005. There has now been some slippage in this regard, but it is highly likely that they will come into force some time in the foreseeable future (possibly in 2007; Williams, 2004). However, if they do not, and even if the WTO itself were to collapse, this does not alter the main gist of my argument. Global capitalism must, by definition, seek new markets everywhere, so even if the WTO were to collapse, the global trade liberalisation agenda would 'rear its head' in another format. There have been other international agreements that existed or were proposed before or in conjunction with the GATS, for example, that had some similarities with the GATS. There was the proposed Multilateral Agreement on Investment (MAI), and before that there was the General Agreement on Tariffs and Trade (GATT). The GATT was one of the key agreements that was established after the Second World War; it came into effect in 1948, and 23 countries signed up to it in the first instance. Derber said about the GATT:

> Before the Uruguay Round, GATT embodied a constitutional compromise favoring First World corporate interests but accepting a small number of global labor standards and the need of poor nations for special protections to promote industrial development and sustain poor farmers. (Derber, 2003: 118)

Meanwhile, the MAI would have applied to the 29 wealthiest Organisation for Economic Cooperation and Development (OECD) nations. It aimed to create a 'level playing field' for investors, by establishing investment guidelines and standardising the way in which foreign investment was treated globally. It would have enabled foreign investors to circumvent domestic legal systems and sue governments as and when they thought appropriate. However, many people protested against the MAI and it never actually came to fruition.

Therefore, if the GATS does not materialise for whatever reason, then it is highly likely that some other similar agreement would take its place, with an agenda for the liberalisation of trade in services. I would argue that this same scenario applies to the WTO itself. Thus, to this extent, this book is timeless, for the duration of capitalist society. It cannot be made redundant and/or irrelevant as a result of any decisions that might be made on the global stage, whether this be a 'softening up' in regard to the WTO agreements, the elimination of the WTO itself, or any other decisions that might on initial inspection seem to significantly change the map.

The important question to ask, therefore, is whether, in an ultimate way, globalisation can actually benefit the world population, enhancing prosperity while at the same time eliminating poverty and starvation. In this book I hope to convince the reader that this is impossible. Instead, we need to need to think outside of this 'globalisation box'. I will do this by examining, specifically, the implications of the GATS and TRIPS agreements for the library and information world.

2.2 Overview of the World Trade Organisation

2.2.1 Historical analysis

The idea of an international monetary and trading system free of the protectionism of the interwar years was formulated towards the end of the Second World War. Different organisations and agreements were established to cement the idea of a 'free' international monetary and trading system. These included organisations such as the World Bank and the IMF. One of the key agreements established after the Second World War was the GATT, and this came into effect in 1948. The GATT provided a legal and international framework for international trade and tariffs until 1995. The participants of the GATT were 'contracting parties' rather than actual members. All participants had to be treated equally, to the extent that when a country reduced trade tariffs for one GATT participant, it had to do so for all.

The idea was that the GATT was to be a charter for the International Trade Organisation (ITO), and that this was to be an agency of the United Nations. The ITO was to become permanent, and the GATT would form a part of it. The ITO was to cover many areas and not just trade. Other areas it was to cover included employment, economic development, competition and restrictive practices. However, from the United States' point of view the ITO conceded too much to workers' rights and third world issues and:

> In 1950, the ITO failed to win ratification in the US Congress and was consigned to history. The GATT, meanwhile, remained in use to regulate international trade. (G. Rikowski, 2001b: 10)

The WTO eventually emerged from the Uruguay Round of GATT negotiations, which lasted from 1986 to 1994. Before the creation of the WTO in 1995, the relevance of trade rules was strictly limited. Negotiations under the GATT were often limited to tariffs on merchandise. However, some of the core principles of the GATT, such as liberalisation and non-discrimination, were transferred to the WTO. Now, though, the remit of the WTO goes far beyond that of the GATT, and as Watkins stated:

> Today, the WTO's remit covers not only trade in goods, but also laws on intellectual property protection, foreign investment, the provision of services and taxation. When governments sign up for membership of the WTO they embrace the whole package ... (Watkins, 2003: 28)

Thus the WTO emerged out of GATT, but it embraces far more than the GATT ever did. It took on the philosophy of the liberalisation of trade, but extended it beyond the trading of goods into many other areas, including the trading of services and intellectual property rights.

2.2.2 Background information on the WTO

Until 1999 relatively few people had heard of the WTO. However, at the WTO Ministerial meeting that was held in Seattle in 1999 masses of people showed their discontent and demonstrated against the WTO. They were concerned, in particular, about the amount of power and influence that large corporations and rich countries wielded at the WTO. As Adam Piore said with regard to the 'Battle in Seattle' (which is what this became known as in many quarters):

> Antitrade protestors were battling police in the streets outside, raising tension among the delegates to unbearable levels. Inside the Seattle Civic Center, their talks were breaking down in screaming matches and tears. Rich nations were at loggerheads with the poor, and with each other, over trade barriers against bananas, software, you name it. (Piore, 2001: 35)

The demonstrations made the headlines and the TV screens, and suddenly many more people knew about the WTO and the philosophy behind it. In Seattle, Derber argued that there was a signpost of a:

> ... Constitutional Movement, a period when the basic rules of the social and political system are rewritten, or written for the first time. In the barricaded streets of Seattle, I saw pictures carried high by WTO protestors of a colorful globe under construction, a potent representation of the real meaning of a Constitutional Movement. (Derber, 2003: 106)

However, many ordinary people are still very ignorant about the shadowy WTO, and yet it is establishing rules that will have a profound effect on their lives. Jawara and Kwa made the point that the WTO is often seen as being an institution that makes trade rules that are 'incomprehensible to the ordinary person on the street ...' and yet it is establishing trade rules that will '... have a major effect on people's livelihoods' (Jawara and Kwa, 2003: 3). They also emphasised how rules established at the WTO often require member countries to change their intellectual property legislation, their industrial and agricultural policies, their service provisions and even sometimes their constitutions.

The WTO is based permanently in Geneva and is controlled by a General Council comprising states' ambassadors. It now has approximately 150 members and this includes members from countries that were previously clearly Communist. China, for example, joined the WTO in December 2001, an event which Derek Brown (2001) described as being 'momentous'. Montagnon, reporting in the *Financial Times* shortly before China joined the WTO, emphasised China's enthusiasm for joining, despite various possible setbacks. He said that nothing seemed to be discouraging China from wanting to join the WTO, not even factors such as the demonstrations in Seattle, the slow pace of negotiations with the European Union and the failure at the time to launch a new round at the WTO Ministerial in Seattle (Montagnon, 2000: 10).

Russia is also likely to join shortly (Williams, 2002a). Speaking about the death of communism and the rise of globalisation in general, Gray stated:

> The West greeted the collapse of communism – though it was itself a Western utopian ideology – as the triumph of Western values. The end of the most catastrophic utopian experience in history was welcomed as a historic opportunity to launch yet another vast utopian project – a global free market. (Gray, 2001: 25)

Thus more and more countries are joining the WTO and we are, it seems, being presented with another 'utopian project': with the notion of a 'global free market'.

Many different agreements are being established at the WTO, such as the Trade-Related Investment Measures (TRIM), the Financial Services Agreement (FSA), the Sanitary and Phyto-sanitary Agreement (SPS), the General Agreement on Trade in Services (GATS) and Trade-Related Aspects of Intellectual Property Rights (TRIPS). Many transnational corporations have permanent staff based in Geneva to lobby the WTO regarding their interests, and corporate representatives sit on many sub-committees and working groups.

Furthermore, the WTO is likely to limit the power that governments will be able to have over their own affairs and thus threatens democracy itself. As Jawara and Kwa stated, the WTO:

> ... brings limitations on the ability of governments to enact policies in the interests of their own populations – even, in some cases, policies that affect trade only indirectly – and effectively gives precedence to trade and international commercial interests over people and international commitments and agreements directed at their benefit. (Jawara and Kwa, 2003: 5)

They emphasised how this would be concerning even if the WTO was a model of democracy and accountability. But as it is, Jawara and Kwa emphasised how commercial interests largely take precedence and the few are favoured over the many.

Meanwhile Clare Joy, the campaigns officer for the World Development Movement speaking about the GATS and the threat it poses to the nation state, said:

> GATS will have an enormous impact on the ability of governments to pursue objectives in their service sector which conflict with the needs of companies trading those services. Perhaps the biggest threat posed by GATS is the threat to democracy. (Joy, 2001: 21)

A thousand meetings take place at the WTO every year, many running in parallel with each other. Ministerial meetings take place at least once every two years and are preceded by a number of mini-ministerial meetings attended by only some members. According to the WTO Conference Office statistics, on the basis of half-day units (a meeting lasting a full day is calculated as two meetings), there were nearly 400 formal meetings of WTO bodies in 2001. There were also over 500 informal meetings and 90 assorted symposia, workshops and seminars under the umbrella of WTO bodies. However, those from the developing countries do not have as many professional staff, so are not able to attend as many of these WTO meetings as those from the developed world. There is much activity taking place (Jawara and Kwa, 2003: 22).

2.2.3 Staffing structure at the WTO

The Marrakesh Agreement of 1994 established the WTO and the staffing structure was laid out in the agreement. This included a Secretariat to help with the work of the WTO. The Secretariat is based in Geneva, has approximately 550 staff and is headed by a Director-General (DG) There are 23 divisions and each division is headed by a Director. There are four Deputy Director-Generals (DDGs) for each division. However, Jawara and Kwa made the point that:

> Both the staff and the budget ... are surprisingly small for an international organization of such influence. (Jawara and Kwa, 2003: 184)

The IMF, in contrast, had 2,633 staff and 343 contractual employees. It is interesting to note that work that will have far-reaching implications on the global stage is being undertaken by a relatively small number of staff.

In principle, the WTO Secretariat does not have any decision-making powers. Instead, decisions about trade should only be made by members of the WTO. However, the Marrakesh Agreement did not define the Secretariat's role, so different Director-Generals have defined the role differently. The last Director-General was Mike Moore and the current one is Supachai Panitchpakdi, and they have both put their own interpretations on the role. Mike Moore, who was once briefly a Prime Minister of New Zealand, headed the WTO for three years, and his style was considered to be '... brash and sometimes abrasive ...' (de Jonquieres, 2002: 18), whereas Supachai Panitchpakdi was a former Deputy Prime Minister of Thailand, and:

> For the first time in the history of the global trade system, its leadership will be entrusted to an official from a developing nation. (de Jonquieres, 2002: 18)

Given that Panitchpakdi comes from the developing world many of the WTO members from the poorer countries are putting their hopes in him and:

> ... regard Mr Supachai as 'their' man and hope he will champion their interests against the handful of wealthy powers that have long

called most of the shots in world trade policy. (de Jonquieres, 2002: 18)

Furthermore, Panitchpakdi is considered to have a '... thoughtful and courteous manner ... [and] ... an open mind ...' (de Jonquieres, 2002: 18). Thus Panitchpakdi is seen to be kinder and generally more caring about the developing world than Moore.

De Jonquieres referred to the Secretariat's role in general, emphasising that no formal powers or resources were attached to the role. Rather, authority largely depends on '... judicious diplomacy [and] skilful deal-broking ...' (de Jonquieres, 2002: 18). In theory, the Secretariat's role should be largely administrative and the Secretariat staff should aim to be neutral, carrying out administrative tasks and providing support and advice to members. However, in reality, as Jawara and Kwa (2003: 186) note, this is often far from the case.

There is also a gross imbalance in the staffing structure between the developed and the developing countries. While four-fifths of the WTO members are from the developing countries, four-fifths of the staff are from the developed countries. In 2001 there were 512.5 posts within the organisation altogether, with an additional 39.5 posts vacant or under recruitment, and 410 of these posts were filled by people from the developed countries. Furthermore, a few developing countries have between 8 and 13 professional staff, but most only have between 2 and 5. In addition, most of the WTO members from the developing world have to represent their countries in over 20 other international agencies based in Geneva as well as the WTO. Hence, this puts a great strain on the developing countries which do not have enough staff working on their behalf.

2.2.4 Democracy – one member one vote at the WTO?

Given that four-fifths of the WTO members are from the developing world, and in theory a one-member-one-vote system is in operation, then WTO members from the developing world should have far more power and influence over decisions that are made than those from the developed countries. De Jonquieres addressed this optimistically:

But developing countries' determination to air their grievances is a sign of their growing assertiveness in the WTO. They account for most of its members and are increasingly aware of, and ready to exert, their bargaining power in a forum long dominated by the US and Europe. (de Jonquieres, 2001: 24)

However, in reality, rich countries and large corporations wield considerably more power and influence at the WTO than those from the developing countries. Indeed, the House of Lords in its report on *Globalisation* says:

> We recognise that member countries of the WTO vary in size and economic power. They vary, therefore, in their capacity to influence decisions in the WTO and, more fundamentally, to maintain a presence at the WTO. It would be naïve to believe that an organisation like the WTO would not be dominated by a small number of rich countries ... we urge the government, with its European Union partners, to consider, first, how to improve the balance of power in the WTO and, secondly, how to ensure that decisions are more transparent. (House of Lords, Select Committee on Economic Affairs, 2002: 10)

The 'arm-twisting' and persuasion that takes place at the WTO meetings by the rich countries and the large corporations makes a mockery of the supposed democracy. When Martin Khor, the Director of the Third World Network, represented the WTO members from the developing countries at the WTO Ministerial meeting at Doha, Qatar, in 2001 he spoke about this. He described in some detail the tactics and manipulation that took place to force those from the developing world to do what the developed world wanted. At Doha the developed world wanted to move on to the 'new issues' in the negotiation process, whereas the developing world still wanted to discuss the current issues that were under negotiation, as they were not happy with many aspects of them. The views of those from the developing world were not being properly listened to. This surely makes a mockery of any notions of democracy. Khor stated:

> ... the Doha meeting was held in conditions of a pressure cooker, in which a set of elite countries, aided by the Secretariat, set upon the majority of developing countries and pressed them to accept major elements of a future work programme which this majority had been rejecting up to the scheduled final day. (Khor, 2002b: 1)

Khor concludes his paper emphasising that, in the end, Doha was very anti-development, despite the fact that they launched a Development Round or a Development Agenda. Furthermore:

> The process before and at Doha, without which the outcome would have been very different, has been undemocratic, discriminatory, deceiving and untransparent, based not on rules but on power-based tactics. What a shame, and a mockery to the supposed principles of the WTO: 'non-discrimination, transparency, rules-based'? It should not be allowed to happen again. (Khor, 2002b: 6)

Meanwhile, the editorial in the *Guardian* when speaking about Doha referred to the arm-twisting that took place and indicated that:

> There was some frenetic arm-twisting and tempting inducements were deployed behind closed doors to prevent a repeat of the Seattle collapse two years ago. (Guardian Editorial, 2001: 23)

Jawara and Kwa also highlight the tactical manoeuvring that goes on and the fact that the 'big players' hold most of the stakes. They say that the WTO is supposed to operate on the principle of 'one country one vote', but although the USA and the European Union (EU) only represent a small minority of the membership, they largely get what they want. As they say:

> The process develops into a game for high stakes, between unequally matched teams, where much of the game is played with few rules and no referee. (Jawara and Kwa, 2003: 50)

Furthermore in theory, the major decisions are supposed to take place by consensus at the large ministerial meetings that have been held at various locations, such as Seattle, Doha and Cancun. However, in reality many of the decisions are made beforehand. There are many conflicting agendas and interests between the different countries and a limited amount of time at the ministerial meetings. This '... creates a boiler room atmosphere at the conferences ...' (Jawara and Kwa, 2003: 50). Thus, because of this, if the WTO is ever to agree on anything, then it becomes necessary to make some of the decisions before the ministerial. However, these pre-ministerial negotiations involve much political manoeuvring behind closed doors. Thus the WTO claims to be democratic and transparent, but this is often far from the truth. Many small meetings are held, at which the most powerful are present and make many of the major decisions. Charlotte Denny, writing in the *Guardian*, also referred to the imbalance at the WTO Ministerial meeting at Qatar:

> Development campaigners have reacted with outrage to the news that American and European corporate lobby groups will out-number organisations from third-world countries at the World Trade Organisation's next summit at Qatar in November. (Denny, 2001: 19)

During the period from February 2002 to August 2002 Jawara and Kwa conducted in-depth semi-structured interviews with some members of the WTO. This involved undertaking research during 33 Geneva-based missions to the WTO across the spectrum of its membership and with 10 WTO Secretariat staff members. Many of the comments made by the inter-viewees are revealing and illustrate the level of discontent that many of them felt with regard to the WTO, particularly those from the developing world. One of the Asian delegates spoke about Mike Moore's (the then Director-General of the WTO) performance at the Doha WTO talks:

> When we came back from Doha, one ambassador said: 'This guy Mike Moore will go down in history as the enemy of the develop-ing countries'. He pretends he is for the developing countries, emphasizing capacity-building and technical assistance. He can-vassed around, played it nicely, got the round started and tagged it a 'development agenda' ... Some ambassadors are very angry at the way he has pulled this through. (Asian WTO delegate, referenced in Jawara and Kwa, 2003: 195)

Clearly, it seems that the supposed democracy at the WTO is a sham. Are we really hoping to build a democratic world order through such an organisation?

2.2.5 The Dispute Settlement Process

The WTO incorporates a complex Dispute Settlement Process and tribu-nals operate in secret to settle disputes between member states. Frances Williams stated:

> The dispute settlement system of the World Trade Organisation is commonly held up as a shining example of how a rules-based system gives small, poor countries the chance to challenge unfair trading practices by the rich and powerful – and win. (Williams, 2002b: 1)

However, Williams pointed out that:

> ... many poor nations ... say the system is stacked against them, and needs radical reform. (Williams, 2002b: 1)

In reality, in this Dispute Settlement Process those from the developing world disadvantaged. Only about a third of approximately 270 cases brought to the WTO in its eight-year history have been filed by developing countries, and about half of these are against developed countries. However, these have been filed by just a dozen developing countries, and:

> No African, or least-developed country has brought a case: they say the system is too expensive and complex, and does not provide adequate remedies if they win. (Williams, 2002b: 8)

The problem is that specialist trade lawyers are required to take cases to industrial tribunals, and this is costly. An Advisory Centre for the WTO was set up in 2001. Funds were provided from nine mainly European governments to provide free or low-cost legal services for developing countries. However, developing countries say that even if they win a case, they can still be at a disadvantage as their economy can be damaged if they find that they are no longer trading with certain countries as a result of the case.

A Dispute Settlement Process, whereby members that are unhappy about certain decisions that have been made can in theory, as a result of their belonging to the WTO, seek to change the situation, may, on paper, seem to be a 'fair' process. However, in reality, it is not fair at all. This is very concerning because ultimately this is the only weapon that WTO members have left at their disposal once they have signed up to the WTO and its agreements. Having agreed and signed up to the agreements they must abide by them, unless a member can take a case to a Dispute Settlement Process and win. Once a WTO member state has agreed to liberalise its library services under the GATS, for example, then it must carry this through, unless it can prove that a particular case in question does not fall under the GATS for whatever reason and win the argument through the Dispute Settlement Process. Thus if the UK (via the European Union) signed up its library service to the GATS, then all the local authorities in the UK could be faced with the possibility that their public library services could be taken over and run by private companies, that is unless they can win the case through the Dispute Settlement Process. Obviously, this is oversimplifying matters, but it describes the direction that the WTO is heading in. This erodes the power of the nation state. At the same time, rich countries can take cases to the Dispute Settlement Process and usually win and force those from developing countries to abide by their wishes, which is likely to further impoverish them.

2.2.6 Country groupings at the WTO

As well as organisation-wide bodies and meetings at the WTO there are also country groupings that are based on geographical regions (Jawara and Kwa, 2003: 22–4). Some countries are members of more than one grouping, while others are not in any at all.

First, there is the 'Quad' (Quadrilateral Group). This includes the US, EU, Japan and Canada, and it is a very powerful and formidable alliance. As Jawara and Kwa say:

> Breakthroughs in difficult negotiations are often a result of the Quad coming to an agreement on how to proceed. (Jawara and Kwa, 2003: 23)

Representatives from the Quad are lobbied heavily by various transnational corporations. These representatives also sit on all the important advisory committees, decide much of the detailed policy and set the agenda (G. Rikowski, 2001b: 12).

Second, there is the European Communities (EC) Group.[1] The 25 member countries of the EU are in this group and individual members coordinate their positions. The group speaks on behalf of all EC WTO members at key WTO meetings, articulating and representing the common position of all EU members.

Third, there is the LDC (Least Developed Country) Group. This group comprises mostly low-income countries defined by the United Nations (UN) as having a low level of economic development. There are 13 WTO members comprising this group. However, 19 least developed countries are not in the WTO at all.

Fourth, there is the ACP (African, Caribbean and Pacific) Group. This group consists of the 56 developing country WTO members in those regions that benefit from the EC trade preferences under EC-ACP Partnership Agreements.

Fifth, there is the Africa Group and this group comprises all the African countries at the WTO. They often produce joint statements and declarations.

Sixth, there is the Like-Minded Group (LMG). This has a diverse membership, and includes WTO members such as Cuba, Egypt, India, Kenya and Jamaica. It meets informally at the WTO.

Finally, there is the Cairns Group. This also has a diverse membership, but members share a common objective in agriculture negotiations as major exporters of agricultural products.

This illustrates some of the complexities of the organisational arrangements with regard to the WTO.

2.2.7 Retain, reform or abolish the WTO?

There are different views about the WTO. Some argue that it is very worthwhile and, ultimately, will benefit everyone, rich and poor alike, as it imposes 'fair' trade rules and prevents anarchy. Others are critical of it, but say that it just needs to be reformed, while others argue that it needs to be abolished altogether.

Legrain argued, for example, that the WTO is better than anarchy and the 'law of the jungle', noting that:

> Of course, the WTO is not perfect. But it is better than the law of the jungle, where might equals right ... if you hate capitalism, you will probably never support the WTO ... but if, like most people, you believe in markets tempered by government intervention, you should think again about the WTO. (Legrain, 2001: 17)

Legrain argues that there are four main charges levied against the WTO – that it:

■ does what big global companies want;

■ undermines workers' rights and environmental issues;

- is harmful to the poor;
- is destroying democracy.

Legrain argued that we should endeavour to address these issues within the framework of the WTO itself, thus suggesting that the WTO in itself is a very worthwhile institution that can ultimately be used for the benefit of all.

However, it can be argued that the WTO as it is currently constituted benefits the rich over the poor. As Kevin Watkins said in regard to the trade round at Doha, for example:

> This is a trade round geared towards the development of rich countries' self-interest and corporate profit – and it will reinforce a pattern of globalisation that is perpetuating mass poverty and inequality. (Watkins, 2002: 19)

Watkins argued that it favours the rich but that it cannot be abolished, thereby suggesting that it needs to be reformed instead. In writing before the WTO meeting at Cancun in September 2003, Watkins said that the WTO rules are '... rigged in favour of the strong. Yet abolition is not an option' (Watkins, 2003: 33). He said that if the WTO were to be abolished, then this would result in rich countries bulldozing poor countries into very unequal trade treaties.

The suggestion here, then, is that we can only reach a fair trade environment by operating through the WTO. However, there is also the point that there has been some suggestion that the USA might want to dispense with the WTO anyway if it does not appear to be working in its favour. George Monbiot writing in the *Guardian* argued that George Bush, the US President, seemed to be interested in destroying the WTO. This is because the trade rules are not unfair enough, and that he '... wants to replace a multilateral trading system with an imperial one' (Monbiot, 2003b: 21) that will benefit the US even more.

On the other hand, Jawara and Kwa said that the notion that global trade liberalisation brings prosperity is an unproven economic theory and that it appears to be far removed from reality. In reality, they argued that the 'rules-based' structure does not benefit the rich and poor countries alike, but instead benefits the rich countries at the expense of the poor, and that '... the WTO has been complicit in reinforcing the interests of the strong.' They also say that it would be very difficult to make the WTO more democratic because of the power structure that is deeply embedded within the WTO and its anti-democratic processes (Jawara and Kwa, 2003: 302–4).

Presumably this leads on to the idea that the WTO needs to be abolished altogether. Derber argued, for example, that we need to restore democracy within nation states, and that this should be seen as an alternative to globalisation. Ordinary citizens should be invested with real control, he argues, rather than global corporations appearing to be the models of democracy (Derber, 2003: 141). Derber argued that we should abolish the WTO because there are various other democratic institutions that are already in place that are carrying out the work of the WTO quite effectively, such as the International Labour Organisation (ILO) and the United Nations Conference on Trade and Development (UNCTAD). These organisations could be given additional resources to enable them to carry out the work that is currently being undertaken by the WTO, he suggests.

Some argue, then, that the WTO is very worthwhile and encourages fair trade and prevents anarchy while others argue that the principles of the WTO are sound but that it needs reforming. There is an alternative view that states that the proceedings of the WTO could be undertaken effectively by other organisations, such as the ILO, and therefore that it should be abolished. Finally, there is the argument that the WTO should be abolished because its basic philosophy is fundamentally wrong. I am of the last persuasion.

However, I would argue that even if the WTO were to be abolished, while we live with global capitalism something similar would come into existence to replace it. This is because the logic of global capitalism is the commodification and marketisation of all that surrounds us. The enforcing of global trade rules and agreements becomes necessary to extend this process. Therefore, we need to think outside of this 'global capitalist' box, and challenge the 'There Is No Alternative' ('TINA') philosophy with regard to globalisation in general. However, this will certainly not be easy. As Derber said, we seem to be obsessed with consumption and consumerism, and with some false sense of liberation in this regard. As he says:

> The culture of globalization is based on the vision of billions of people newly liberated to make their own choices in a market offering dignity and endless delights ... [even though] ... you recognize that it is a fantasy for most of the world's people ... Engrossed shoppers rush around frantically, buying and buying as if making

up for centuries of deprivation and serfdom. It makes you a believer and makes clear that globalization will not disapper until a new, even brighter vision takes root. (Derber, 2003: 58)

Let us then, indeed, look towards a 'brighter vision'.

2.3 Conclusion

Having now considered the meaning of globalisation and provided an overview of the WTO in general, I shall now move on to consider the two agreements that are being developed at the WTO that are likely to have significant implications for libraries and information: namely, the General Agreement on Trade in Services and the Agreement on Trade-Related Aspects of Intellectual Property Rights. As Paul Whitney, City Librarian, Vancouver Public Library, British Columbia, Canada and the Canadian appointee to the Copyright and Other Legal Matters Committee (CLM) of the International Federation of Library Associations and Institutions (IFLA) said with regard to these two agreements:

> The General Agreement on Trade in Services (GATS) and Trade Related Aspects of Intellectual Property Rights (TRIPS) are the two WTO agreements which have the greatest potential to harm public sector libraries. (Whitney, 2003: 2)

Furthermore:

> Librarians must engage in the international debate on international trade treaties to ensure that the government support for public agencies is not undermined, and that governments retain the right to establish and enact laws and regulations which further public policy objectives. Failure to do so will result in what J.K. Galbraith referred to as 'private affluence existing alongside public squalor'. (Whitney, 2003: 3)

Clearly, then, there is a need to consider the implications of these agreements further. I am an information professional/librarian and an academic with a strong social conscience, so bringing these two strands together in a book has been a great ambition of mine.

Note

1. The clarification of this terminology given by the WTO on their official website is as follows:

   For legal reasons, the European Union is known officially as the European Communities in WTO business. The EU is a WTO member in its own right as are each of its 25 member states – making 26 WTO members.

   While the member states coordinate their position in Brussels and Geneva, the European Commission alone speaks for the EU at almost all WTO meetings. For this reason, ... most ... WTO materials refer to the EU or the more legally-correct EC.

   However, sometimes references are made to the specific member states, particularly where their laws differ. This is the case in some disputes when an EU member's law or measure is cited, or in notifications of EU member countries' laws, such as in intellectual property (TRIPS). Sometimes individuals' nationalities are identified, such as for WTO committee chairpersons. (*http://www.wto.org/english/thewto_e/whatis_e/tif_e/org3_e.htm*; see also *http://www.wto.org/english/thewto_e/countries_e/european_communities_e.htm*)

   Furthermore, according to a WTO official (December 2004), '... the EC negotiates on behalf of its members, who themselves coordinate their positions within the Commission, and do not negotiate with other WTO members directly.'

   Thus throughout the text the abbreviation EC has been used solely to refer to the European Communities from the perspective of the WTO, and should not be confused with the European Commission which has been spelled out in full throughout.

Part 2
The General Agreement on Trade in Services

An overview of the GATS

3.1 Introduction

The General Agreement on Trade in Services (the GATS) is one of the agreements that is being developed at the WTO that is likely to have serious implications for libraries and information. The GATS concerns the liberalisation of trade in services, thereby placing more and more service sectors in the marketplace. As such, it threatens public services in general and the state-funded provision of libraries in particular. This includes all types of state-funded libraries, such as public libraries, university libraries, school libraries, college libraries and government libraries. This chapter will provide an overview of the agreement itself, and explain why it threatens the state-funded provision of libraries.

The following chapter will examine the GATS, libraries and information and cultural services from an international perspective and will consider the views and positions of various organisations and individuals from a variety of different countries with regard to this. It will also highlight which countries have signed up their library services to the GATS, and the complexity of this issue in itself.

Chapter 5 will consider the practical implications of the GATS for libraries and information, focusing mainly on public libraries in the UK. This is because I am British and can more easily and readily see the implications for the UK from first-hand experience. Furthermore, during my 25-year experience as an information professional, I have worked in a variety of different libraries in the UK, within both the public and the private sectors, and I will draw on this experience as and when appropriate. However, this chapter will also provide a framework that others can use for analysing the implications of the GATS and libraries in their own countries. Indeed, it will also provide a framework that can be used for analysing different public services, such as education and health, with regard to the GATS. Finally, Chapter 6 will focus on some of the statements and concerns made by various library associations and library, information and cultural bodies internationally with regard to the GATS.

3.2 Historical perspective – GATT and the GATS

The GATS followed on from the previous General Agreement on Tariffs and Trade. GATT, as I have already outlined, was about developing free trade in general, but the GATS focuses on the development of free trade in services in particular. In October 1947 the first round of the GATT resulted in 23 countries signing up to the agreement, which came into effect on 1 January 1948. Under the GATT, national producers could not be favoured over producers from other countries, tariffs were reduced and restrictive practices such as quotas were prohibited. The GATT liberalised international trade and set rules. There were various series of GATT trade negotiations, the purpose of which was to expand trade, and these intensive negotiations were held in what were called the 'Round'. By this method, the aim was to try to coordinate views from different countries, and endeavour to deal with countries that had opposing views. However, as Amin said:

> Supporters of GATT-WTO base their arguments on the simple yet erroneous idea that free trade favours the expansion of trade and that this expansion, in turn, favours growth. History fails to demonstrate the truth of these propositions. (Amin, 1997: 26)

Frode Bakken, a member of the European Bureau of Library, Information and Documentation Associations (EBLIDA) WTO Working Group, the President of the Norwegian Library Association and Chief Librarian of Telemark's University Libraries in Norway, points out the fact that while the GATT was concerned with physical goods, the WTO has a wider remit, and also includes services and intellectual property. As he says:

> GATT was later superseded by the World Trade Organization when WTO was established and the GATS treaty is part of the total WTO mechanisms to promote world trade. While GATT was comprising only goods – physical goods, WTO comprises all kinds of

trade activities in physical goods, services, investment rules and intellectual property. (Bakken, 2002: 2)

The GATS was first formulated in 1994, and became effective from 1 January 1995 with the establishment of the WTO. It is due to be strengthened in 2005, although there has now been some slippage. Throughout this ten-year period various negotiations have been and are still underway. Recently, there has been the 'requests and offers phase', for example, which was initiated after the WTO meeting in Doha, Qatar in November 2001. GATSwatch (undated) reported that on 10 April 2003, 15 WTO member states had filed an initial GATS offer. Under the WTO timetable all requests were supposed to have been completed by the end of June 2002 and all offers by the end of March 2003, but many members did not comply with the timetable. 'Requests' involve WTO members asking/requesting other particular members to offer up certain of their services to liberalisation. 'Offers' are where WTO members offer up some of their particular services for liberalisation. At the WTO Ministerial meeting in Doha, Qatar in 2001 the main activity with regard to trade in services was, indeed, this requests and offers process. However, most of the requests came from the developed countries. Thus this continues the pattern and the relationship that I have outlined in the previous chapter with regard to the developing world and the developed world. The US submitted requests to 141 of the 144 members and the EC to 109 of the other 130 (International Trade Daily, 2002). Some developed countries explicitly said that they wanted developing countries to submit more requests. However, as Jawara and Kwa observe:

> Since most developing countries are not significant exporters of services ... it is extremely difficult (and largely irrelevant) for them to identify their export interests and the barriers preventing access. (Jawara and Kwa, 2003: 260)

In its report GATS: *From Doha to Cancun*, the World Development Movement (2003a) noted that at the beginning of August 2003 only 30 WTO members had replied with initial service offers. Furthermore, most developing countries were not able to submit offers according to the tight negotiation timetable because of a lack of resources. Also, these nations have little to gain from opening up their services in this way.

The GATS negotiations take place at the various WTO meetings, and major decisions are made at the WTO Ministerial meetings. Thus under the philosophy of the GATS more and more services will be liberalised and put into the marketplace.

3.3 What is the General Agreement on Trade in Services?

3.3.1 Introduction

So, what exactly is the GATS? As already stated, the GATS is about the trading of services and the liberalisation of such trade. In general, the international trade in services is expanding quite rapidly. As was noted by the Commission on International Trade and Investment Policy (1999):

> Services are coming to dominate the economic activities of countries at virtually every stage of development ... (Commission on International Trade and Investment Policy, 1999: 1)

In the developed world, services represent over 60 per cent of all trade. On figures from the Commission on International Trade and Investment Policy (1999) services represented 70 per cent of all trade in Australia, for example, 71 per cent in France, 60 per cent in Japan and 72 per cent in the US. Meanwhile, in the developing world services represented about 50 per cent of all trade (Commission on International Trade and Investment Policy, 1999: 1–2). Furthermore, according to Ambani and Birla (2000) more than half of the Gross Domestic Product (GDP) in the major OECD countries is now knowledge based. In addition, about two-thirds of the future growth of the world GDP is expected to come from businesses that are knowledge led. Therefore trade in services is big business today.

One hundred and sixty different services are covered in the GATS agreement, and this includes services that are both within and outside of the public sector. With regard to public services, this includes areas such as health, education, libraries and housing. As Fritz and Fuchs stated:

> A glance at the GATS classification is sufficient to show that it covers all of the services which, in many countries of the world, are carried out by public corporations or for the account of the state,

or which have just recently been (partially) privatized: posts and telecommunications, radio and television, education and health, refuse removal and sewage services, insurance for medical care and pensions, theatres and museums, libraries and archives, and local and intercity transport. (Fritz and Fuchs, 2003: 13)

Maude Barlow pointed out the fact that the GATS will be instrumental in bringing about the privatisation of public services globally, and that this includes libraries:

GATS is paving the way for the privatisation of public services across the world. Nothing will be exempt – education, healthcare, social services, postal services, museums and libraries, public transport; all will be opened up to corporate interests. (Barlow, 2001: 3)

Other services covered (outside of public services) include tourism, financial services and mobile phones.

3.3.2 'Top down' and 'bottom up'

There are two distinct aspects in the agreement: 'top down' and 'bottom up'. The 'top down' part of the agreement is where its clauses apply to all the 160 service sectors thus restricting the power of individual governments to make policies in these sectors. In this way the 'top down' part of the agreement poses a threat to democracy. With the 'bottom up' part there is some flexibility – governments can choose which service sectors to commit to the GATS and can specify limits on these commitments. This works on the basis of 'requests' and 'offers', as described in section 3.2.

3.3.3 Important articles in the GATS – Most Favoured Nation, National Treatment and Market Access

There are a number of articles in the GATS that are particularly important and have far-reaching implications. These include 'Most Favoured Nation' (Article II), 'National Treatment' (Article XVII) and 'Market Access' (Article XVI). Most Favoured Nation means that all trading partners with regard to the GATS must be treated equally and one member must not be favoured over another. National Treatment stipulates that all foreign service providers must be treated as well as domestic ones, and this includes any subsidy a government might give to a particular service area. If a foreign company was interested in taking over running one of the public library services in the UK, for example, then under the GATS they would have to be given the same level of subsidy as the local authority that was currently running the public library service under state control in the UK. Market Access stipulates that no government can create any limitation to market access. Instead, members must open up their domestic markets to all service suppliers from all other members. Thus individual governments cannot legislate to limit any particular aspect of the GATS that it might be unhappy with (unless, of course, it is stipulated in any of the exceptions that it is acceptable to do this). Governments cannot legislate to benefit their own populations if it interferes with open access to trade. If individual governments do introduce such limitations, then they will receive penalties.

3.3.4 Schedule of commitments

The application of the principles of Market Access and National Treatment is set by each member's 'Schedule of Specific Commitments' and only those services that are in the schedules are subject to the GATS disciplines. However, the Most Favoured Nation principle applies to all sectors, irrespective of the content of the schedules of commitments. If individual members want to have certain service sectors exempt from the Most Favoured Nation principle, then this can only be done by having these listed in the exemptions. Thus to find out which service sectors and under which conditions the GATS principles apply, it is necessary to examine a country's schedule of commitments. As I highlight in the next chapter (Chapter 4, section 4.4), some countries have listed their library services in their schedule of commitments while others have not, although this itself is a complex issue. There is not a sector entitled 'Library Services' in the schedules. Instead, library services fall under a variety of other sectors, although main library services fall under Sector 10C: Recreational, Cultural and Sporting Services. It is this sector which I focus on in Chapter 4 when considering which countries have, and which have not, signed up their library services to the GATS.

The service sectors covered by the schedule are set out one by one in the left-hand column of each country's schedule of specific commitments. In the column 'Limitations on Market Access', the member must show any limitations concerning access to its market by foreign service suppliers for the services sector concerned, i.e. any ways in which it will be made difficult for foreign service suppliers to enter the market for a particular service sector. In the column 'Limitations on National Treatment', the member must enter any limitations concerning the treatment of foreign service suppliers which puts them in a less favourable position than domestic services suppliers. In the column 'Additional Commitments', the member must enter any commitments over and above those listed elsewhere. If a member is prepared to improve the treatment it offers to foreign services suppliers in the future by liberalising a services sector from a later date, for example, this must be entered into the 'Additional Commitments' column.

3.3.5 Modes of supply

The commitments are categorised according to the means by which the service is supplied. Under the GATS, services can be supplied in any of four ways. First of all, there is Mode 1, which is 'Cross-border supply'. This concerns the supply of a service from the territory of one member to a consumer in the territory of another. For some services it is necessary for the service supplier to be physically present. Restaurants and hotels, for example, cannot physically be remotely supplied across a border. Therefore no binding commitments can be made. Mode 2 is 'Consumption abroad'. This is where the consumer of the service travels to the service supplier. This is particularly important in tourism, where the consumer is a tourist and is using accommodation and other services abroad. Mode 3, 'Commercial presence', is where the service supplier establishes itself in a foreign market as a legal entity thereby becoming a subsidiary or a branch of the main service supplier in a foreign country. Mode 4, 'Presence of natural persons', covers cases where a foreign service supplier can travel in person to a country to supply a service. General immigration rules still apply here and rules on entry and residence are usually strict. However, many countries have allowed certain types of service suppliers to enter their markets on a temporary basis.

3.3.6 Unbound and horizontal

The level of commitment of a given country is shown in its schedule of commitments by the use of specific GATS terminology. 'Unbound' means that a country has not undertaken any obligations in respect of a particular sector or mode of supply. This means that the country is not bound by any commitment to maintain a certain level of openness in the future, i.e. there is no commitment to liberalise that particular service sector either at the current time or in the future. 'None' means a country is committing itself to ensuring that there are no restrictions which are inconsistent with GATS rules covering participation in the market by foreign service suppliers.

Some existing WTO rules will apply 'horizontally' to all public services, whether or not the area has already been listed within the GATS. One 'horizontal' rule is Most Favoured Nation. This rule will apply to all services, even services that are still protected in some countries, such as health and education. Also, under the horizontal rule, all regulations must be 'Least Trade Restrictive'. This means that all public services will have to operate market mechanisms.

3.3.7 Conclusion

The enthusiasm embedded within the GATS to create a global market environment is self-evident. Other WTO agreements also have these important articles embedded in them. Most Favoured Nation and National Treatment, for example, are included in the TRIPS agreement, and I consider these in Chapter 7. However, the important point to appreciate is the fact that the purpose of these articles is to enhance and exacerbate trade on a global basis.

As can be seen, the GATS is a complex document. I will not be exploring the infinite intricacies of the GATS much further. Rather, my main intention is to demonstrate the philosophy behind the GATS, and within this framework to then show how state-funded libraries are under threat from this agreement.

Note

Information for this section was obtained from the following sources of reference – Background document on the GATS (2000), Barlow (2001), Fritz and Fuchs (2003), Rao and Guru (2003) and World Development Movement (2003b).

3.4 Links between the GATS and the commercialisation, privatisation and capitalisation agenda of state-funded services

3.4.1 Introduction

Many argue that there is no direct connection/link between the GATS and the commercialisation, privatisation and capitalisation agenda of state-funded services. However, in this book I hope to demonstrate that there are clear, definite links. I will establish a framework, which is outlined in Chapter 5, and then give examples to demonstrate the links with practical examples for libraries and information in the UK. However, first I will consider the debate in more general terms and this includes an examination of the meaning of 'services' as outlined in the GATS.

3.4.2 The commercialisation and privatisation agenda and the GATS

The commercialisation and privatisation of many public services has been gathering pace for some years now in the developed world. However, some argue that the GATS is not connected with a privatisation and commercialisation agenda within individual countries. Instead, they argue that the privatisation and commercialisation agenda will continue whether or not agreements are taking place on an international basis. While it is true that the privatisation of services and the commercialisation agenda was taking place before the GATS was introduced, the GATS will give them more weight, will speed up the process and will make it far more difficult to reverse.

However, the point to appreciate is the logic of global capitalism itself, with its drive for continued marketisation and commodification. Therefore, even if, in the unlikely scenario that the GATS does not actually come fully into effect for some reason, it is highly likely that another similar agreement would be developed to replace it. As I have already indicated, there have been other international agreements that existed or were proposed before or in conjunction with the GATS that had some similarities with the GATS. There was the proposed Multilateral Agreement on Investment (MAI), for example, and before that there was the GATT.

However, those driving the GATS forward do not want to cause alarm to those working in and/or caring about the public sector. So, we have various statements that try to reassure us. For example, Richard Caborn MP, the then UK Trade Minister, wrote to the *Library Association Record* (the then monthly professional journal of the UK Library Association, as it was then called) on 8 March 2001, saying that:

> As a major global exporter of services, the UK strongly supports the GATS negotiations and their objective of progressive liberalisation of trade in a fair and predictable way. Despite stories to the contrary, there will be no forced privatisation of libraries or the NHS as a result of the GATS.

Furthermore, Lord Newby argued in the *You and Yours* BBC Radio 4 programme (BBC, 2001a) that our public services are not covered under the GATS and said that:

> My understanding is that services provided by government ... by the public sector, the GATS agreement as it currently stands, are not covered. (BBC, 2001a: 5)

However, although the wording in the GATS is ambiguous, it is now generally recognised that it does indeed pave the way for the privatisation of many of our public services. Let us now explore this further.

3.4.3 The meaning of 'services' in the GATS

The main problem with regard to deciding whether or not our public services fall under the GATS lies in defining the word 'services' as it is used in the GATS. 'Services' are defined in the GATS agreement in Part I, Article I on 'Scope and Definition', in point 3(b) in the following way:

> ... 'services' includes any service in any sector except services supplied in the exercise of governmental authority. (WTO, 1995)

Furthermore, Part I, Article I:3(c) of the agreement indicates that:

> ... 'a service supplied in the exercise of governmental authority' means any service which is supplied neither on a commercial basis, nor in competition with one or more service suppliers.

However, many of our public services today are supplied partly on a commercial basis, and have elements of competition. Therefore, in this way, the GATS will impact on many of our public services. In a document issued by the Trade Policy Directorate on 7 March 2001 it was argued that:

> The GATS excludes from its coverage any service supplied in the exercise of governmental authority. Such services are those 'which [are] supplied neither on a commercial basis, nor in competition with one or more service suppliers'. Our interpretation (and that of the WTO Secretariat) is that this excludes public services such as health and education services (although private sector services would be covered by the GATS) ... however, since the terms have not been tested in WTO jurisprudence, some commentators have suggested that the GATS poses a risk to state provision of these services. We do not believe these fears are justified. (Trade Policy Directorate, 2001)

Under this statement it appears that we are reliant on interpretations of what 'services' means under the GATS. Yet one possible interpretation could be that virtually all our public services would be included under the GATS. It is, to say the least, ambivalent.

However, various legal experts have sought to interpret some of the different agreements that are being developed at the WTO. Markus Krajewski, who at the time of writing was a lecturer in law at King's College, London and now works at the University of Potsdam, Germany, considered the exact meaning of the term 'services supplied in the exercise of governmental authority' (in Article I:3(b)) of the GATS. Krajewski argued that:

> ... this provision is likely to be interpreted narrowly and that most public services will fall within the sectoral scope of GATS. The reason for this finding lies in the definition of governmental services, which emphasizes the non-commercial basis and non-competitive supply of a service. (Krajewski, 2002a: 1)

In another paper Krajewski emphasised that the progressive liberalisation of trade in services is, indeed, the overall object and purpose of GATS (Krajewski, 2002b: 9) – in fact, that it is actually the mandate of GATS to achieve higher levels of liberalisation through progressive rounds of negotiation (as outlined in Article XIX). Therefore he concluded that:

> The goal of these negotiations is to eventually achieve full commitments in all sectors including those sectors where public monopolies still exist. It is therefore safe to conclude that GATS mandates the liberalisation of public monopolies. (Krajewski, 2002b: 21)

Furthermore, representatives of the European Bureau of Library, Information and Documentation Associations (EBLIDA) and the International Federation of Library Associations and Institutions (IFLA) met representatives of the WTO and the European Commission in December 2002 (this is considered further in Chapter 6, section 6.15). Kjell Nilsson, the coordinator of the EBLIDA WTO Working Group wrote a report on the meeting. One of the fundamental questions that they asked the WTO representatives was:

> Are the services of publicly funded libraries included in the scope of GATS, or should they be regarded as 'supplied in the exercise of governmental authority' (Article 1:3c) and therefore by definition be excluded from the treaty?

Kjell Nilsson said that, leading on from what the WTO representatives said, their conclusions were that:

> The services of publicly funded libraries are definitely within the scope of the GATS agreement; only services supplied by public monopolies fall outside. (Nilsson, 2003: 2)

3.4.4 Concluding comment

Therefore it does clearly appear that state-funded library provision falls within the remit of the GATS, as do other public services, and that there are some elements of competition in most forms of public service provision today. Thus the GATS threatens state-funded library provision, in the same way as it threatens many of our other public services. Furthermore, this means that there are clear, definite links between the GATS and the commercialisation and privatisation of our libraries, leading eventually to the capitalisation of libraries, and this will be considered in more detail in Chapter 5. In addition, there are clear, definite links between the GATS and the commercialisation, privatisation and capitalisation of the various public-service sectors in general. There are also various mechanisms that are in place that are *enabling* the GATS to come into effect. Examples of the links and the mechanisms that are in place in the UK for public libraries will all be explored in Chapter 5, section 5.7.

3.5 Summary

In conclusion, the GATS is about the liberalisation of trade in services, and the placing of more and more services in the marketplace. There are, in particular, three very important articles and principles embedded in the GATS. These are Market Access, National Treatment and Most Favoured Nation. The application of these basic GATS principles is set by each member's 'schedule of specific commitments'. There are also two distinct aspects in the agreement – 'top down' and 'bottom up'. The 'top down' part of the agreement is where its clauses apply to all the 160 service sectors, whereas the 'bottom up' part is where members can choose which service sectors to commit to the GATS and can specify limits on those commitments. These are inserted in each member's schedule of commitments. This works on the basis of 'requests' and 'offers'.

Whether or not the GATS threatens the state-funded provision of services in general, and the state-funded provision of libraries in particular, is dependent on the interpretation of the definition of 'services' embedded in the GATS document itself. By a consideration of this definition I have sought to demonstrate that the state-funded provision of services in general, and of libraries in particular, is, indeed, seriously threatened by the GATS. Furthermore, that there are clear, definite links between the commercialisation, the privatisation and the capitalisation agenda of public services and the GATS. Once a public service has elements of commercialisation and competition in it, then it will be much easier to introduce the GATS into that particular service sector. This demonstrates the links. However, it must be remembered that the extension of the commercialisation, privatisation and capitalisation agenda is part of the extension of global capitalism itself, the path which, of necessity, capitalism must go down. The GATS simply represents one of the tools to aid this process. I will now consider some of the responses of various countries to the GATS and libraries issue.

The GATS, libraries, information and cultural services within an international perspective

4.1 Introduction

This chapter will consider some of the reactions of different organisations and individuals in a variety of countries with regard to the GATS and its likely implications for libraries, information and cultural services. Educational services will also be referred to at times. The countries that will be examined will include: Canada, the USA, Japan, Australia, New Zealand, the developing world in general, India, South Africa, Europe, the UK, Chile and Singapore. In this way, something of a global perspective can be achieved, although many countries have also been excluded through time and space considerations. The audio-visual industry and the GATS will also be considered.

However, some countries have not really explored the GATS and libraries at all as a specific issue. This could be for a number of reasons:

- Those countries that are not WTO members might not necessarily be particularly interested, or at least conclude that it will not affect them directly.

- Some countries might not have the necessary resources available to be able to explore the topic.

- Some countries in the developing world have a very poor state-funded library service (if they have one at all). Therefore they might not see the GATS as posing any real threat to their library provision, as it is not possible to take away something not present in the first place! For many countries in the developing world, issues such as water privatisation and how it relates to the GATS are far more urgent.

- Some countries just might not think it is all that important or that the GATS is not likely to impact on libraries very much, arguing that little money can be made out of libraries.

This chapter will also consider the way in which library services fall under the GATS. There is no separate category for 'Library Services' in the GATS schedule of commitments. Rather, main library services fall under Sector 10C: Recreational, Cultural and Sporting Services, and it is on this sector that I shall focus in this chapter, with a consideration of which countries have committed their library services to the GATS. However, library services also fall under Sector 2CJ: Telecommunication Services and Sector 5: Educational Services, and library and library-related services also fall under some other sectors within the schedules. This will be explored further in section 4.3.

Furthermore, this chapter will not consider the practical implications of the GATS for libraries in a number of different countries. That would require another book and much more research would need to be undertaken before such a project could be embarked upon. I found little evidence to suggest that any research had been undertaken on the GATS and libraries, apart from the research that was conducted by Steve Shrybman on the impact of the GATS in public-sector libraries (Shrybman, 2001). This report has recently been updated by Ellen Gould (Gould, 2004) and prepared for the Canadian Library Association.

Instead, I will examine the practical implications of the GATS for libraries in the UK specifically, and this will be covered in Chapter 5. Someone who has a detailed understanding of the workings of the state-funded provision of libraries in other countries is better placed to consider practical local implications.

Before embarking on this international perspective though, I will firstly examine the meaning of a 'public good', which libraries are considered to be, as this is important to the whole debate.

4.2 Public goods, private goods and commodities

4.2.1 Overview

Before considering the GATS and its implications for libraries and information in detail I think it is important to consider the meaning of a 'public good'. This is because, as already stated, it now seems clear that the GATS will indeed impact on public services in general, and public services provide 'public goods'. One of the public goods that the public service provides is libraries, and as IFLA says:

> Libraries are a public good. (IFLA, 2001b: 1)

So, we then need to consider exactly what is meant by a 'public good'.

The distinction between public goods and private goods was first made by Adam Smith in the late eighteenth century. Adam Smith noted the existence of particular products:

> which though they may be in the highest degree advantageous to a great society are, however, of such a nature that the profits could never repay the expenses to any individual or small number of individuals, and which it therefore cannot be expected that any individual or small number of individuals should erect. (Smith, 1994 [1776]: 779)

The market was not able to provide these public goods, so therefore governments must. This was Smith's argument.

However, this was the situation in the eighteenth century, when capitalism was relatively primitive. The picture today is somewhat different. In the eighteenth century capitalism could not deal with many of the economic and social problems caused by capitalism itself. Thus, the responsibility for endeavouring to solve these problems fell upon governments. Capitalism is still not able to deal with many of the problems and resulting misery that it causes, but in the West, governments have now solved some of the most horrific problems. Children no longer work in appalling conditions in advanced capitalist countries, for example, unlike in the period of the industrial revolution when many children worked in dangerous heavy industry, e.g. mining and textiles. In many of the countries in the West the state has also now created a welfare state and an education system. But these are lovely prizes that the private sector would now like to own and control. In effect, governments have played and are playing a 'nanny state' role for private companies, giving them cherry pickings (rather like when various nationalised industries are sold off to private companies for a relatively small amount of money), while in the developing world, these areas are not so appealing. Instead, private companies are keener on moving into areas such as water privatisation and indigenous knowledge.

The essential point to realise here, though, is that the GATS and TRIPS are being introduced as mechanisms to make all this possible – the privatisation of services and the encapsulation of indigenous knowledge into intellectual property rights – and these are then being transformed into international tradable commodities. In essence, public goods are being turned into private goods.

However, historically, the idea of a 'public good' was based on the notion that governments provided certain necessary goods that the private sector could not provide. Let us now consider the definition of public and private goods. This is examined in some detail in the book *Providing Global Public Goods: Managing Globalisation*, edited by Inge Kaul et al. (2003).

4.2.2 Private goods

Private goods can be made excludable and exclusive in consumption and they are associated with clear property rights. The owners of the private goods decide how they want to use them, whether to consume them, lease them or trade them. Private goods are rivals in consumption and have excludable benefits (or costs). The consumption of a private good by one person or group lessens its availability to others. Furthermore, one person or group can exclude others from consuming it. Private goods operate through market transactions and negotiations. Their ownership can be transferred or denied to others, but such transfer takes place on conditional exchange, through the market, usually by paying a price. Thus private goods are an essential part of the market.

4.2.3 Public goods

Public goods are goods that are in the public domain. They are available for everyone to consume and so can affect everyone. A public good is usually defined as being a good with non-excludable benefit and non-rival competition. The market cannot price these goods. They are sometimes seen as being 'market failures' so the government intervenes. Non-excludable means that it is not technically, politically or economically feasible to exclude someone from consuming the good. Furthermore, once a good is provided, everyone can benefit from it. The cleansing of a river, for example, has non-excludable benefits. Non-rivalry means that one person's consumption of the good does not prevent it from being available to others. Also, it can be made available to other users at no or little extra cost. It does not need to be reproduced for each new consumer. Inge Kaul and colleagues said that one example of such a public good is knowledge. They noted, for example, that:

> ... many generations ... have benefitted – and continue to benefit – from indigenously developed medicines in developing countries. (Kaul et al., 2003: 22)

However, as they indicate, and as I have emphasised in the chapters on TRIPS, some types of knowledge also have commercial value and are not in the public domain. Instead, they are made exclusive through intellectual property rights.

Clearly, 'public' itself also needs to be defined. Inge Kaul et al. say that the 'public' includes the general population, civil society organisations and corporate citizens.

4.2.4 Pure and impure public goods

A distinction can also be made between pure and impure public goods. *Pure public goods* possess two characteristics: non-rivalry of benefits and non-exclusion of non-payers. On the other hand, *impure public goods* are those public goods that possess benefits that are partly rival and partly excludable (i.e. excludable at a cost) or both. Most public goods are actually like this. A public good that is completely non-rival but excludable at a very low cost, for example, is pay-per-view television. Drahos and Braithwaite argue that knowledge is an example of an impure public good, and they say that:

> Knowledge is an example of an impure public good because although it is non-rivalrous in consumption it does not always possess the quality of being non-excludable. (Drahos and Braithwaite, 2002: 215)

Furthermore, what is made public and what is private can be a matter of choice and can change over time. As Kaul and Mendoza said:

> ... the properties of public goods can change from being public to private and from private to public. (Kaul and Mendoza, 2003: 80)

4.2.5 Global public goods

The concepts of public goods and private goods take on a new meaning and significance in globalisation. Kaul et al. argued that:

> Managing globalisation depends largely on providing global public goods. (Kaul et al., 2003: 3)

Thus, for Kaul et al., providing global public goods that provide benefits to all is an important part of globalisation. They argue that globalisation is often associated with further 'privateness', but that it is also about increased 'publicness', as people's lives become more interdependent. However, as I have already made clear, I would argue that globalisation is about privatisation, and indeed is ultimately about capitalisation.

Kaul and Mendoza say that most global public goods have arisen from a '... complex, multidimensional, multilayered, multiactor production path' (Kaul and Mendoza, 2003: 101). Meanwhile, Edwards and Zadek made the point that:

> Securing global public goods increasingly requires cooperation between governments and business, international agencies, and civil society organizations. (Edwards and Zadek, 2003: 203)

Thus the successful implementation of global public goods, whereby public goods benefit different populations on a global basis, is partly dependent on greater cooperation between governments and various other organisations on an international basis. However, I would argue that the creation of global public goods will only ever really happen when it seems to be in the interest of global capitalism. The drive for increased trade and marketisation of private goods on a global basis must always take precedence over the creation of global public goods. While the creation and exchange of global public goods is seen to assist with this process, then global public goods will thrive. However, when the connections are not so clear, then the creation and exchange of global public goods will be less predictable.

4.2.6 Goods versus commodities

What is the difference between goods and commodities? I would argue that private goods are commodities whereas public goods are not.

Meanwhile, the logic of capitalism is the commodification of all that surrounds us. Therefore the aim of capitalism is to transfer public goods into private goods, i.e. to turn all goods into commodities. So, as I argue throughout this book, the GATS and TRIPS are mechanisms for transforming public services and intangible assets into internationally tradable commodities. Thus, in essence, the GATS and TRIPS are mechanisms for transforming public goods into commodities.

This also feeds into Marxism. Marx began his analysis of capitalism, in *Capital, Vol. 1* (1887 [1954]) with the commodity. Marx emphasised how the commodity is essential for the capitalist mode of production, saying:

> The wealth of those societies in which the capitalist mode of production prevails, presents itself as an 'immense accumulation of commodities', its unit being a single commodity. Our investigation must therefore begin with the analysis of a commodity. (Marx, 1887: 43)

He also made the point that, on initial inspection:

> A commodity appears ... a very trivial thing and easily understood. (Marx, 1887: 76)

However, in fact, the commodity is a mysterious thing, because of the labour that is embedded in it, which becomes objectified through the abstraction of value.

> A commodity is therefore a mysterious thing, simply because in it the social character of men's labour appears to them as an objective character stamped upon the product of that labour, because the relation of the producers to the sum total of their own labour is presented to them as a social relation, existing not between themselves, but between the products of their labour. (Marx, 1887: 77)

These commodities are then traded in the marketplace in capitalism. This is explored further in Chapter 11 of this book, section 11.7.

4.2.7 Conclusion

In conclusion, within the whole GATS and libraries debate it is important to consider the concept of the 'public good'. In essence, the basic belief with regard to the concept of the 'public good' is that there are certain goods that could and should be provided for the public that cannot be made available through the private sector. Thus these goods are provided by the state. In contrast, private goods operate through market mechanisms and are rivals in consumption and have excludable benefits.

Hence we have public goods that can benefit many different people and that are non-rival, i.e. if one person consumes the good this does not detract from its availability to others. They are also non-excludable, i.e. particular people are not excluded from consuming and benefiting from the good. The adequate provision of public goods in areas such as health and education is clearly essential for any civilised society. Within this framework, libraries are also 'public goods'.

I have considered the difference between public and private goods in some detail in this section, as well as the difference between pure and impure public goods. I have also examined the meaning of global public goods. In this way, we have some clear conceptualisation of the terminology used and some of the issues. However, there is a clear shift away from public goods towards private goods and, as Webster said, there is an:

> ... apparently inexorable shift away from public towards private provision of goods and services throughout society ... it is crucial for librarians to acknowledge the consequences of what has been called the 'neo-liberal consensus' for their long (and short)-term future. (Webster, 1999b: 1)

This process is being aided and abetted by the GATS and TRIPS.

In this book, I am suggesting that more and more forms of life are being commodified, as the extension and intensification of global capitalism continues and takes a hold, apparently into infinity (or rather until we do something about it, as a human race!). So public goods are not commodities – quite the reverse. They represent something outside of this market-driven, capitalist web. Private goods, I would argue, on the other hand, are commodities. Thus the drive is to transform public goods into private goods or commodities. With regard to the GATS and TRIPS specifically, I am arguing that these agreements are involved in the process of transforming public services and intellectual property rights into internationally tradable commodities. This is considered further in Chapters 11 and 12 of this book. A more detailed analysis of the commodity is essential to demonstrate the full horrors of capitalism, and how labour is exploited through the production of value (labour and only labour can create value), which then becomes embedded in the commodity. This will be considered further in Chapter 11, section 11.7 and I will be addressing this topic in much more detail in my future works.

This chapter will now move on to examine 'library services' within the GATS schedule of commitments. It will then consider which countries have signed up their library services to the GATS under Sector 10C. From there it will then explore the reactions of different organisations and individuals in a variety of different countries with regard to the GATS and its likely implications for libraries.

4.3 'Library service' categorisations in the GATS

4.3.1 Introduction

This section will consider 'library service' sectors/categorisations in the GATS. It will highlight the fact that there is not one sector specifically for 'Library Services' in the GATS schedule of commitments. Instead, main library services fall under Sector 10C: Recreational, Cultural and Sporting Services. However, library services also fall under other sectors or categorisations in the schedules. Any full and comprehensive analysis of the GATS and libraries should ideally consider all the different sectors in the GATS schedule of commitments that include library and/or library-related services in some format. However, this is a very ambitious task. It also needs to be remembered that sectors/categories are changing, flexible entities and this will be explored further in this section.

This section will also consider the fact that some organisations and WTO members focus more on the broader categories of cultural services and education services and the GATS rather than library services specifically. Given that there are many overlaps between all these areas it is useful to explore these deliberations within the framework of the libraries and GATS issue.

4.3.2 Sectors in the GATS schedule of commitments that include library services or library-related services

A consideration of library services in the GATS highlights the complexity of the GATS document in general. Services that fall within the GATS are listed in the schedule of commitments, and only those services that are in the schedule are subject to the GATS disciplines, as I emphasise in Chapter 3, section 3.3.4. Thus, when considering which WTO members have committed their library services to the GATS, we need to examine the schedule of commitments. There is not a separate sector for 'library services' within the GATS schedule of commitments. Instead, main library services fall in Sector 10C: Recreational, Cultural and Sporting Services. Hence, when considering which countries have committed their library services to the GATS in this chapter, it is this sector to which I refer (see section 4.4 below).

However, library services also fall under other sectors within the GATS schedule of commitments. EBLIDA has identified three main sectors within the GATS schedule that impact on library services. These are: Sector 2CJ: Telecommunication Services – online information and database retrieval; Sector 5: Educational Services – primary, secondary, higher education, adult and other educational services; and Sector 10C: Recreational, Cultural and Sporting Services – libraries, archives, museums and other cultural services (EBLIDA, 2002b). Thus, while Sector 10C covers the main library services, some also fall within the other two categories. Educational Services includes university libraries, college libraries and school libraries and other libraries that are used for educational purposes. Telecommunications Services includes online information and clearly this sector is likely to increase in the future within library services. However, because of time and space considerations, this book has not included information about which WTO members have committed their library services to these two sectors. It is very important to be aware of these sectors, and any full and comprehensive analysis of the GATS and libraries would need to include an examination of which WTO members have signed up to them as well.

Furthermore, while there are three main sectors for libraries, library services can also fall within other sectors in the GATS schedule of commitments. One of these is Research and Development and, as I explain in section 4.5.6, Canada has made commitments to Research and

Development Services. Thus in this way Canadian libraries could fall within the GATS disciplines, even though they have not been committed in the main category for library services – in Sector 10C. This was considered in the document *GATS and Ontario Public Libraries* (2002). Also, sectors in the GATS schedule of commitments are flexible entities. Thus when representatives from EBLIDA and IFLA met with the WTO, the WTO representatives said that it was possible that online services would go into Sector 2B: Computer and Related Services, and this sector has already been committed by the European Union (EU). Thus, although the EU has not committed its library services to the GATS under Sector 10C, it might find that many of the services now provided by libraries and information, such as online services, do fall within the GATS (Nilsson, 2003). This is particularly concerning given how important online services now are in the library and information world and that money can probably be more easily be made from these services. Thus the library and information profession also needs to be aware of changes in the sectors/categorisations in the GATS.

There are also many other intricacies with regard to categorisations and different sectors in the GATS, how library services can fall within different sectors and how sectors and categorisations are flexible entities. The Central Product Classification (CPC), for example, forms the basis of the GATS treaty and places 'information retrieval from databases' within 'Library Services' (96,311). However, Kjell Nilsson, the coordinator of the EBLIDA WTO Working Group (2003) does not think it will remain there for long. The CPC is 15 years old, so is becoming outdated and is already being supplemented by the WTO Services Sectoral Classification List ('W/120') (Nilsson, 2003). Furthermore, online information retrieval services cannot just be restricted to libraries. Thus, once again, libraries can be classified under various categories and 'library services' today obviously include many facets such as online services.

Thus, considering whether or not a WTO member's library service falls within the remit of the GATS is not as simple and straightforward as it might initially appear to be. To undertake a comprehensive analysis due consideration would need to be given to all the sectors in the GATS schedule of commitments that impact on library services and/or library-related services. This would be a huge task, so in this book I have confined myself to Sector 10C: Recreational, Cultural and Sporting Services and have outlined which of the WTO members have signed up their library services to this sector.

4.3.3 Cultural services, education services and the GATS

In the course of my investigation I have also explored the fact that some organisations focused on the implication of the GATS for cultural services in general, but not for library services specifically. Sometimes, then, I have focused on these broader service sectors when considering the responses of some organisations to the GATS and libraries issue, particularly for cultural bodies such as the Australian Writers' Guild.

It is also useful to consider the broad category of 'cultural services' in general and the fact that 'library services' tend to fall within this broad category in various ways. Indeed this applies to the GATS schedule of commitments itself. As already outlined, the main library services do not have a category of their own, but instead fall under Sector 10C. Meanwhile, the paper *Consultations on Services in the Cultural Sector* (2000) considers the broad category of 'cultural services' and libraries fall within this broad category. In the consultation process that the paper refers to, 'cultural services' are classified as being services that are central to cultural activities (museums, libraries, theatres, etc.) and are included in this classification for the GATS. By combining the Services Sectoral Classification List (SSCL) drawn up for GATS and the definitions contained in the Central Product Classification or CPC (United Nations), an indicative list of services for cultural services was created for the purpose of the consultation exercise. Furthermore, the category of Recreational, Cultural and Sporting Services contained in the SSCL included various sub-sectors and one of these was 'Library, Archive, Museum and other Cultural Services' (CPC 963).

In addition, there are clearly many overlaps between libraries and education, and therefore there are some sections in this chapter that consider the GATS and education agenda in certain countries. In this way I was able to achieve a broader perspective. Thus I consider, in particular, the fact that the liberalisation of education services in Japan, New Zealand and India is gathering pace (see sections 4.7, 4.9 and 4.11, respectively).

4.3.4 Summary

This section has considered 'library services' within the GATS schedule of commitments, and has emphasised how library and/or library-related services can fall under various sectors of the schedules. Also, these sectors or categorisations are flexible entities, thus while a certain sector in the GATS might not include library or library-related services at the current time, it might do so in the future. Therefore the library and information profession needs to remain on its guard and cannot afford to be complacent.

The main library services fall under Sector 10C: Recreational, Cultural and Sporting Services. Library services do not have a sector of their own. When considering which WTO member countries have signed up their library services to the GATS, it is Sector 10C that I am referring to throughout this chapter. For a full and comprehensive analysis of the GATS and libraries though, the other sectors in the GATS schedule of commitments that also include library services and/or library-related services would also need to be examined. It would be particularly important to examine Sector 2CJ: Telecommunication Services and Sector 5: Education Services in this regard.

The section has also highlighted the fact that some organisations focus on the broad categories of cultural services and/or educational services and the GATS rather than library services specifically, and this will be considered further throughout this chapter.

4.4 Countries that have committed their library services to the GATS

In 2002, representatives from EBLIDA met with representatives from the WTO. Dale Honeck, a Counsellor in the Trade in Services Division of the WTO, informed the EBLIDA WTO Working Group that there are now 18 countries that have signed up and committed their library services to the GATS. These countries have committed their library services under Sector 10C: Recreational, Cultural and Sporting Services. The countries that have committed (as of 2004) are: Albania, Austria, Bolivia, Central African Republic, Ecuador, Estonia, Gambia, Georgia, Hong Kong, Iceland, Japan, Jordan, Kyrgyz Republic, Lithuania, Sierra Leone, Singapore, the USA and Venezuela.

This is in contrast to the beginning of the GATS in 1995, when only 13 countries had committed. These were Bolivia, Gambia, Iceland, Sierra Leone, Venezuela, Central African Republic, Japan, Singapore, Ecuador, Hong Kong, New Caledonia and the USA. (Note that New Caledonia has been removed from the latest list because it now falls under France's commitments, and France is a member of the European Union (EU).)

As already stated, the EU is known officially as the European Communities (EC) in WTO business (see note 1 on p. 32), and the EU is a WTO member in its own right, as are each of the 25 member states, making 26 members in all. However, the European Commission speaks for all EU member states at nearly all the WTO meetings (see *http://www .wto.org/english/thewto_e/countries_e/european_communities_e.htm*). Thus it speaks for France and for New Caledonia as the latter now falls under France's commitments. Neither the EU as one entity legally known as the EC nor the 25 countries that it represents have as yet committed their library services to the GATS.

All this demonstrates how the extension of the GATS is already gathering force. It also shows that it is false thinking to be under the illusion that state-funded libraries are excluded from the GATS. Some of the countries that have committed their library services to the GATS under Sector 10C will be considered further below, along with other countries that have not so far committed.

4.5 Canada: libraries and the GATS

4.5.1 Introduction

Canada has not, so far, committed its library services to the GATS under Sector 10C, and has been at the forefront of raising awareness about it. This applies to various service sectors – not just libraries. One of the first books to be published on the impact of the GATS for education, for example, was a Canadian publication entitled *Perilous Lessons: The Impact of the WTO Services Agreement (GATS) on Canada's Public Education System* by Jim Grieshaber-Otto and Matthew Sanger (2002). It was the British Columbia Library Association (BCLA) that first alerted the library community to the GATS, and then the Canadian Library Association took up the issue. First, then, let us look at the BCLA.

4.5.2 British Columbia Library Association

On its website, the BCLA outlines a scenario that could easily occur under the national treatment guidelines of the GATS. They say that an 'informed services' company could go into Canada and offer a similar service to that already being provided by Canadian state-funded libraries. Under the 'National Treatment' clause in the GATS, the company could then claim the same level of government subsidy as that received by the Canadian state-funded library. One way in which the government could avoid this situation from developing would be for it to discontinue the funding that it provides. But then libraries would be forced to generate income or close. This would then lead to a situation where the public would probably have to buy their information from the 'information services company'. The BCLA conclude by saying that:

> If a free flow of information is fundamental in a democratic society, the very basis of our democratic system would be threatened by this scenario. (BCLA, undated:a, under section 'A threatening scenario for libraries')

The BCLA has another short paper on the Web that is entitled *GATS and the Threat to Libraries*. In this document they emphasise that the activities taking place at the WTO could result in the 'eventual elimination of the public sector', and will limit the power of governments. They say that:

> Proposed changes to GATS will open all aspects of the economy to foreign competition including libraries. (BCLA, undated:b, under section 'Introduction', point 2)

So once again, they also note the fact that the GATS threatens democracy. (See also Chapter 6, section 6.3 for further information on the BCLA.)

4.5.3 Canadian Library Association

The Canadian Library Association (CLA) then took up the issue. It voices similar sentiments, saying that:

> Privatization of libraries may result from the proposals for *expansion* [my emphasis] of the GATS Agreement. (CLA, 1999: 'Introduction', Point 2)

It notes that libraries are 'unique social organisations' that provide a range of information and ideas to the public, regardless of age, religion, social status, race, gender and language, and that this could all be threatened by the GATS.

The Canadian Library Association outlines its position clearly, saying that libraries should be exempt from the GATS. It says that:

> CLA supports the creation of an exemption for library services, as the possible outcome of permitting the private sector to compete with libraries ... could be to undermine their tax-supported status ... Libraries should be part of exemptions for culture ... (CLA, 1999: 'Position', point 1)

Thus the CLA wants exemptions for libraries and cultural organisations and also wants to protect the public sector in general. (See also Chapter 6, section 6.4 for further information on the CLA.)

4.5.4 Steve Shrybman's report on GATS and public libraries, prepared for a variety of Canadian organisations

Steve Shrybman wrote an important report on the GATS and public libraries, commissioned by the Canadian Library Association (Shrybman, 2001). It was the first report of its kind and was updated by Ellen Gould in June 2004. As already stated, Canada has been very much at the forefront of raising awareness and undertaking research and writing on this important area, and so it is no surprise that the first such report came from Canada. Shrybman's report was published in 2001 and is entitled *An assessment of the impact of the General Agreement on Trade in Services on policy, programs and law concerning public sector libraries.*

The document was prepared for all the following bodies: the Canadian Library Association, the Canadian Association of University Teachers, the Canadian Association of Research Libraries, the Ontario Library Association, the Saskatchewan Library Association, the Manitoba Library Association, Industry Canada, the British Columbia Library Association, the Library Association of Alberta and the National Library of Canada. Thus it was prepared for a variety of Canadian organisations, which demonstrates the level of interest and concern about this subject in Canada. Shrybman stated in the Executive Summary of the document that in many ways the rationale for the delivery of public services is in conflict with the principles of trade liberalisation as embedded in the GATS. Furthermore, public libraries aim to correct the failure of free markets and to meet broader community goals. Thus he stated that:

> Given this inherent contradiction, it is not surprising that application of GATS disciplines to government measures concerning public sector libraries is consistently problematic. (Shrybman, 2001: 3)

Later in the document the likelihood of the private sector moving into the public library sector is considered. Shrybman said that while traditional services provided by libraries might not compete with other service suppliers, the situation with regard to online or digital services is likely to be different. So we need to be on our guard! (See also Chapter 6, section 6.5 for further information on Shrybman's report.)

4.5.5 Naomi Klein and Canadian libraries

Naomi Klein, the author of the best-selling book *No Logo* (2001), has given many talks seeking to raise awareness about the dangers inherent in globalisation and is very concerned about the direction in which it is going. She gave a speech at the joint American Library Association/ Canadian Library Association Conference in June 2003, and emphasised the importance of information and knowledge, saying that:

> Information – your stock and trade – ranks just below fuel as the most precious commodity coursing through the global economy. The U.S.'s single largest export is not manufactured goods or arms or food, it is copyright – patents on everything from books to drugs ... Water isn't the only thing that is fundamental to life. So is shelter. So, I would argue, is knowledge. (Klein, 2003: 8)

She noted that being a librarian meant that one was the 'guardian of knowledge' and in general she really recognised the importance and value of library and information work.

However, she then warned that the library and information profession needs to face up to certain realities, namely privatisation, outsourcing and the GATS.

Klein noted two main problems with the GATS. One is that full privatisation, as a result of the GATS, becomes irreversible. The other is that partial privatisation, such as outsourcing, helps to force through full privatisation. She concluded by emphasising that although Canadian libraries are not yet on the 'free trade table', Canada must not get complacent. She says:

> Even though Canada hasn't put libraries on the free trade table yet, last year the government sent out a questionnaire to public libraries asking them to identify areas where they might have 'export interests' – in other words, could Canadian libraries make money by offering research or cataloguing or binding services in New Zealand, or Uganda? (Klein, 2003: 11)

So, the question then is often not a moral one, about whether libraries should or should not be part of the GATS agreement, but instead, whether it is feasible to make money out of libraries. The philosophy behind the WTO agreements in general is about trade, trade, trade and the extension of global capitalism. Hence the question is whether effective trade can be undertaken through certain public services, and clearly libraries are one of the areas that lend themselves to this question. 'How can money be made out of libraries?', many people ask. Can money be made from online services, for example? On the other hand, to ask meaningful moral questions with regard to whether libraries should or should not be part of GATS can only be effectively achieved by looking outside this 'globalisation box' altogether. It is very heartening, though, that influential people such as Naomi Klein are taking up the GATS and libraries issue.

4.5.6 Canadian public libraries falling under the GATS under other sectors

There has been some consideration in general in Canada about whether Canadian libraries fall under the GATS within sectors in the GATS schedule of commitments other than Sector 10C.

The document *The GATS and Ontario Public Libraries*, published in 2002, considers whether Canadian libraries fall under the GATS under other sectors/categorisations. It says that, according to the UN classification system used to define GATS sectors, library services are:

> Services of libraries of all kinds. These include documentation services, i.e. collection, cataloguing, whether manually or computer-aided, and retrieval services of documents. The services may be provided to the general public or to a special clientele, such as students, scientists, employers, members, etc.

This is quite a broad definition of library services.

Although Canada has not, as yet, made commitments to library services in the GATS under Sector 10C, libraries in Canada could be affected in other GATS sectors, particularly in research and development (R&D) services. This is because Canada has made GATS commitments under library services within the R&D services sector. It says:

> In the case of R&D Services, Canada has made commitments under Library Services. In the case of R&D Services, Canada has made commitments and must provide market access and non-discriminatory treatment to foreign competitors. (GATS and Ontario Public Libraries, 2002: 3)

In other sectors related to library activities, such as education services, Canada has not made commitments. The document emphasises, though, how unclear the whole picture is. Where libraries are included within another service category, for example, it is not clear how they would be treated within a dispute process.

This, once again, demonstrates how important it is for the library and information profession to be aware of the fact that library and library-related services can fall under various sectors of the GATS schedule of commitments, and that the whole area is very complex. Furthermore, some areas of library and library-related services may fall under the GATS without library associations in nation states even being aware of it.

4.5.7 Multilateral Agreement on Investment

As already stated, before the GATS there was the Multilateral Agreement on Investment (MAI). Canada was also at the forefront of raising awareness about the MAI. In particular, Fiona Hunt considered how the MAI could have impacted on libraries in Canada, and endeavoured to warn the profession about the agreement. Fortunately, the MAI was never implemented, and Hunt has subsequently examined the implications of the GATS for libraries.

The MAI was a treaty that was negotiated by the OECD countries. It aimed to create a 'level playing field' for investors by establishing investment guidelines and standardising the way in which foreign investment was treated globally. It was similar to the North American Free Trade Agreement (NAFTA), but gave multinational corporations even more power. As Hunt indicated, under MAI:

> Public libraries could disappear altogether ... Libraries would be in competition with corporations and information would become a commodity in the marketplace. (Hunt, 1998b: 1–2)

She emphasised how under the MAI public libraries might have had to close through a lack of funds. Or they might have had to start their own fund-raising, such as fee-for-service schemes. The public may have found themselves paying the information services companies directly, or having to pay for services that were previously free.

Bakken (2002) also considered the MAI and the fact that, at first, it was a closed shop with secret processes. Furthermore, he notes the fact that it was meant to promote foreign investments all over the world, while decreasing the role of the nation state and increasing the power of transnational companies.

The MAI process collapsed in 1998. The IFLA MAI Working Group was then renamed the WTO Working Group, and it set out various recommendations, such as to actively encourage members:

> ... to lobby at national level to promote protections for libraries and culture in international trade agreements. (Bakken, 2000: 2)

Hence it is very commendable that IFLA has been taking up these issues, and very heartening that Canada initially brought all this to the attention of the library and information world.

4.5.8 Summary

The world should be very grateful to Canadian anti-MAI/GATS activists and analysts; Canada has been the leading light in raising international awareness and concerns about global trade rules and agreements for the service sector. Canada has also led the way in raising awareness about these agreements in the library and information profession. Fiona Hunt, for example, raised the issue of MAI and its likely impact on libraries in Canada, and later went on to consider the implications of GATS for libraries. The GATS issue was first raised by the British Columbia Library Association and then by the Canadian Library Association. Then IFLA took up the cause and this is considered further in Chapter 6, section 6.2.2. In particular, Paul Whitney from Canada was the IFLA representative at the WTO Ministerial in Seattle in 1999. Steve Shrybman wrote a report on the GATS and public libraries for various organisations in Canada (Shrybman, 2001), which was updated by Ellen Gould (June 2004). Influential Canadian individuals such as Naomi Klein have also addressed the GATS and libraries issue.

4.6 USA: libraries, cultural services and the GATS

4.6.1 Introduction

In general, as I have made clear throughout this book, the USA is very enthusiastic about global capitalism in general, and about the WTO and trade agenda in particular. Indeed, the USA is at the forefront of driving global capitalism forward. This is particularly highlighted in the TRIPS section of this book. The USA has played, and still plays, a very large part in the formulation of the TRIPS agreement. The US economy has much to gain from global capitalism in general, and from the GATS and TRIPS in particular. Therefore, these points will not be highlighted further in this section. Instead, the focus will be on the responses to the GATS, libraries and culture from the American Library Association (ALA) and the Writers' Guild of America, West (WGA).

The GATS and libraries agenda is making headway in the USA, as the USA has committed its library services to the GATS under Sector 10C. As Naomi Klein said:

> ... the U.S. Government has announced that it will accept bidding for library services under GATS. (Klein, 2003: 11)

4.6.2 American Library Association

The American Library Association endorsed the IFLA WTO position at its ALA mid-winter meeting 2000 (ALA, 2000) and is concerned about the likely implications of the GATS for libraries and information in the USA. IFLA is concerned about the possible effects of the GATS on the library and information profession internationally and it notes, for example, that:

> There is growing evidence that WTO decisions, directly or indirectly, may adversely affect the operations and future development of

library services, especially in the not-for-profit institutions. (IFLA, 2001b: 1, point 4)

This is considered further in Chapter 6, section 6.2.2. But what is important to realise here is that the ALA has endorsed the IFLA position. Furthermore, the USA has committed its library services to the GATS but the ALA was not consulted before this decision was taken, which is of concern (see Chapter 6, section 6.7, for further information).

4.6.3 Writers' Guild of America, West

Various creative and cultural organisations in America have also raised concerns about the GATS. The Writers' Guild of America, West (WGA), for example, is the largest professional association of performance writers in the world. It is a member of the Center for the Creative Community (CCC), which aims to 'Serve both America's Creative Community and the general public by working to safeguard and enrich the vitality and diversity of our nation's culture.'

Both the American and the Australian Writers' Guilds are of the opinion that culture cannot simply be commodified and operate purely according to economic principles. They argue that culture should be exempt from trade liberalisation and the GATS (see Australian Writers' Guild, 2003 and Writers Guild of America, West, undated). (See also Chapter 6, section 6.8 for further information on the WGA.)

4.6.4 Summary

In conclusion, the USA is enthusiastic about the liberalisation of trade in services in general and has committed its library service to the GATS. However, the American Library Association is concerned about the likely implications of the GATS for US libraries. Cultural organisations such as the Writers' Guild of America have also voiced concerns.

4.7 Japan: libraries, education services and the GATS

Japan has offered up its library services to the GATS under Sector 10C, and is very enthusiastic about the liberalisation of its trade in services in general, arguing that this will enhance Japan's prosperity. The service sector in Japan accounts for over 60 per cent of its gross domestic product and Japan wants to promote free trade agreements (FTAs) to supplement and strengthen the WTO (Ministry of Foreign Affairs of Japan, 2002a). The Ministry of Foreign Affairs of Japan stated:

> Japan takes the initiative in tabling its initial offer with a view to advancing the negotiation on trade in services, standing on the basic belief that liberalization of trade in services would benefit both the importing and exporting Members, by increasing the inflow of foreign direct investment and employment, facilitating transfer of technology, revitalizing market activities, multiplying consumers' choices and so forth. (Ministry of Foreign Affairs of Japan, 2003c: 1)

Furthermore, Japan is of the opinion that it has benefited from trade and has been able to enjoy economic growth from it in the past, through the GATT and the WTO system, and so it can continue do so in the future.

Japan is also enthusiastic about liberalising its education services. It has made GATS commitments on Market Access and National Treatment in higher education, adult education and other education services. In the past, it only made commitments for 'foreign language tuition services for adults'. However, it does want to do this within the framework of government policy and with appropriate regulations. The Ministry of Foreign Affairs of Japan emphasised these points in its paper *Negotiating Proposal on Education Services* and argues that to improve the quality of education in Japan, a certain level of liberalisation needs to be encouraged and promoted (Ministry of Foreign Affairs, of Japan, 2002b). However, as already stated, once WTO agreements come into effect in member states, this will largely override government legislation and policy in individual states, so this is clearly likely to cause potential problems.

There seems to be an assumption here that the WTO will operate in the best interests of its member states, but this is surely naive. The interests of one member state, for example, are bound to conflict with the interests of another at times. How then will this be resolved? It is highly likely that the interests of the rich, developed countries will take precedence over those from the poorer countries, as I have indicated on various occasions throughout this book.

Thus the approach that Japan is likely to take with regard to the liberalisation of its library services within the GATS agenda would seem to be fairly self-evident – it will be enthusiastic. Indeed, this is reflected in the fact that it has already committed its library services under Sector 10C.

China, on the other hand, has only recently joined the WTO, so China's approach to the GATS and libraries is likely to be under-developed, and will not be considered here. China has not, however, committed its library services to the GATS, as yet, under Sector 10C.

4.8 Australia: libraries, cultural services and the GATS

4.8.1 Introduction

Australia has not listed its library services in its GATS commitments under Sector 10C. This section will consider the Australian Library and Information Association's (ALIA) response to the GATS and libraries issue, and the Australian Writers' Guild (AWG) response to the GATS and cultural issue. It will also refer to some protests that have taken place in Australia in response to the contracting out of Australian library services and library closures, as well as to some of the views of Alex Byrne, the IFLA President-Elect, with regard to the role of libraries in the Australian community.

4.8.2 Australian Library and Information Association

The ALIA has made its concerns about the implications of the GATS for its publicly funded libraries very clear. Jennifer Nicholson on behalf of the ALIA said that the ALIA is concerned about:

> ... the potential for publicly funded libraries and information services to be subjected to unintended consequences from international trade agreements. (Nicholson, 2001: 1)

Furthermore, she noted the fact that the GATS appears to constrain government policy in favour of the market. The publicly funded library, on the other hand, she emphasised, seeks to correct some of the failures of the free market economy, and is concerned with broader community goals such as universal access to information and literacy.

The ALIA is also aware of and concerned about the fact that the GATS agenda of committing library services is gathering pace. Nicholson noted that 'two of the world's most influential economic powers', namely the USA and Japan, have committed their library services to the GATS, and that other nations are likely to follow suit. The ALIA emphasised the need to be able to promote Australian culture and the importance of libraries within this framework, and how international agreements on trade and investment could undermine this.

However, there is also an assumption that the 'right balance' can be found between the interests of individual member states and the interests of the WTO in general. But sometimes it will be impossible to get this balance right when different interests conflict. This lies within the heart of global capitalism itself, because it is a system that is based on contradictions. We spend much of our time trying to deal with and resolve these contradictions, but fundamentally they are irresolvable. Nicholson referred to this idealised notion of balance:

> Private rights and public interests need to be balanced and cultural expression should not be treated as a commodity. Placing publicly funded libraries within a commercially competitive environment and potentially undermining their tax-supported status would have a serious and detrimental impact on Australia's cultural heritage. (ALIA, 2001: 2)

Finally, the ALIA makes it clear that it is of the opinion that Australian libraries should be excluded from GATS disciplines:

> The provision of services for the benefit of our community and for the public good by publicly funded libraries should be recognised within the general exception ... (Nicholson, in ALIA, 2001: 2)

Yet another library association has issued a clear statement in regard to the GATS, and has requested that libraries are exempt from it. (See also Chapter 6, section 6.9 for further information on the ALIA.)

4.8.3 Australian Writers' Guild

There are also various cultural organisations in Australia that are concerned about the implications of the GATS. The Australian Writers' Guild (AWG), along with other professional associations in the cultural arena, is a member of the Australian Coalition for Cultural Diversity (ACCD). The AWG is a peak professional association for performance writers in TV, film, theatre, radio and multimedia. It was established in 1962 and has 2,000 members. The AWG has a clear position on the GATS saying that the government must not make any commitments within the cultural services sector or any other sector which would impact on the cultural services sector, now or in the future. Otherwise, the government will be compromised in its ability to adequately develop and implement cultural, economic and social policies (Australian Writers' Guild, 2003: 4). Thus the AWG argues that the Australian government should not, in general, commit cultural services in Australia to the GATS. Furthermore, this is important, otherwise the government will not be able to develop and implement cultural policies in the way in which it really wants to.

The AWG argues that cultural services must never bow under to trade, and that Australia must maintain its sovereignty over cultural issues and exclude culture from GATS negotiations. Also, the Australian government must retain current restrictions to Mode 4 supply, 'Presence of natural persons', and make no further commitments within Mode 4 at a horizontal level. Mode 4 – as explained in Chapter 3 (section 3.3.5) – covers cases where a foreign service supplier can travel in person to a country to supply a service. The horizontal level, as also explained in Chapter 3 (section 3.3.6), means that the WTO rules will apply 'horizontally' to all public services, whether or not the area has already been listed within the GATS. The AWG also argues that the Australian government must maintain current restrictions in the Most Favoured Nation Exemptions and that it should make no further commitments in this area. Furthermore, the Australian government must continue to have meaningful discussions with the cultural services industries throughout the GATS negotiations, as well as having any other meaningful discussions in multilateral or bilateral free trade negotiations which affect cultural services. Thus this all demonstrates the AWG's concern about the possibility of Australian culture losing some of its own identity as a result of the GATS.

The AWG emphasises how the cultural industry is different to other tradable goods and services. It is concerned about the culture of the nation and it emphasises the importance of not treating cultural goods and services as 'economic tradable commodities'. (Australian Writers' Guild, 2003: 7)

(See also Chapter 6, section 6.10 for further information on the AWG.)

4.8.4 Protests against contracting out Australian library services and library closures and defending Australian libraries

There have been various protests against contracting out library services and library closures in Australia. Obviously, once library services have been contracted out they can far more easily fall under the GATS disciplines. Beechey (1995) reported on the fact that the Australian Kennett government abolished local councils in the 1990s, for example, and replaced them with unelected commissioners, and these commissioners started contracting out various library services. Beechey said:

Commissioners will not guarantee that branch libraries will remain open beyond 12 months, and have refused to take part in meaningful consultations with library staff and users. Already the Armadale library has been closed. (Beechey, 1995: 1)

There was a campaign by residents and unions against all this. Various public meetings and protests were held, and some local library support groups were formed. The Australian Services Union (ASU), for example, did not collect fines as a form of protest. Richmond's Carringbush Library had a 'work-in' where staff kept the library open all night and provided refreshments and children's activities as well as normal services. Furthermore, the 'Defend our Public Libraries', an umbrella organisation representing local user groups and ASU members, took part in a 10,000-strong anti-privatisation rally held in June 1995. There was also a rally in July outside the State Library of Victoria, with a banner saying: 'Libraries for people, not profit' (Beechey, 1995). Many people expressed their protests. John Sawyer of Friends of Carringbush Library, for example, said that:

> Access to information and ideas is fundamental in a democratic society. It is dangerous to put the choice of what books we read in the hands of private suppliers whose sole aim is to make money.

Others have spoken about the need to support and defend Australian libraries. Alex Byrne, the IFLA President-Elect, considered, for example, whether libraries should be involved in any form of privatisation and what their role within the Australian community should be. He argued that we also need to ask the question 'who pays' and consider whether or not it continues to be appropriate for the community or government to pay for a country's library service (Byrne, 2000b: 11). However, the raising of such questions can easily invite in the GATS, so we must surely be very wary about going down this path. Byrne articulates his library vision, saying:

> Librarians should be known as the advocates and defenders of human rights. We should not strive simply to make better websites or implement better processes. We should be contributing to the creation of a better, fairer and more democratic society, in our own country and elsewhere. We should actively resist measures, however well intentioned, which will abrogate the rights of our fellow citizens and actively work to create a better informed and freer society – a society in which we can live in harmony and all will be able to know all we need to know. (Byrne, 2000b: 12)

This is very worthwhile: as far as I am concerned, libraries should be about trying to create a better, a fairer and a kinder world. However, libraries surely cannot fulfil this function and Byrne's vision if they fall under the jurisdiction of the GATS.

4.8.5 Summary

In conclusion, Australia has not committed its library services to the GATS under Sector 10C. The Australian Library and Information Association is concerned about the likely implications of the GATS for its publicly funded libraries. Other cultural organisations, such as the Australian Writers' Guild, are also concerned. Various other people and organisations, such as the Australian Services Union, have raised the issue and taken action with regard to the contracting out and privatisation of state-funded libraries in Australia.

4.9 New Zealand: libraries, education services and the GATS

New Zealand seems to be enthusiastically embracing the GATS, although it has not yet committed its library services under Sector 10C. However, about 40 countries have made commitments on education services, and New Zealand is one of them. It has made commitments on primary, secondary and tertiary education in private institutions, although there are no commitments on research and development, libraries or archives.

Many, such as Norman LaRocque, argue that the GATS is beneficial for New Zealand in general and brings the country prosperity. LaRocque said:

> ... GATS is important for New Zealand. We're a small trading nation whose economic well-being has always, and will in the future, depend on overseas trade; and good rules of the game are absolutely essential if firms are to invest, international trade is to flourish and economies are to grow – the surest way to achieve and maintain prosperity for rich and poor countries alike. (LaRocque, 2003: 1)

This is an argument that many people use – that trade helps a nation to prosper. Here, LaRocque is arguing that the trading that will take place through the GATS will help New Zealand to prosper, and indeed that such trade is very important for the country. He is also arguing that international trade helps both rich and poor countries. However, I have provided many examples throughout this book which shows this not to be true – instead, the developing world often suffers greatly as a direct result of international trade laws in general, and from the GATS in particular.

Trade in education services has been taking place for many years in New Zealand, and is not just something new that has arisen as a result of the GATS. Clearly, commercialisation and privatisation can and does take place in individual countries in abstraction from international rules and agreements such as the GATS. Furthermore, international trade can also take place in various ways without such agreements. However, international agreements help to cement these processes. Then, once they are in place, it makes them almost irreversible. The GATS is one way of cementing this. As Fritz and Fuchs say:

One of the characteristics of the GATS giving most cause for concern is the fact that once liberalization measures have been introduced, there is virtually no way of going back. (Fritz and Fuchs, 2003: 16)

Furthermore, the World Development Movement emphasised that:

... the irreversibility of GATS will ensure that once governments have opened up particular service sectors to WTO rules, there is no going back ... In future, citizens will no longer have the democratic right to decide whether or not services should be regulated. (World Development Movement, 2003b: 2)

Exporting education in New Zealand is also big business. In 2002 the Ministry of Foreign Affairs and Trade (MFAT) estimated that New Zealand earnings from education exports totalled about $900 million, which was up from $600 million in 2001 and $400 million in 1997. By 1999, the education sector was New Zealand's fourth largest service exporter.

New Zealand is a small trading nation and has always depended upon access to bigger markets for its prosperity and well-being. GATS will provide the certainty that our export education organisations need to protect their investments and will help formalise arrangements for access to good education opportunities. (GATS and the Globalisation of NZ Education, 2003: 8)

Hence the argument here is that the GATS is beneficial for exporting education in New Zealand. If this is its attitude to education, then it is very likely that New Zealand would have a similar attitude to libraries, given that it seems to be enthusiastic about the GATS in general and is of the opinion that it will bring the country greater prosperity. Thus in time libraries may well be thrown into the GATS arena in New Zealand under Sector 10C.

4.10 The developing world: libraries, the digital divide and the GATS

Several countries in the developing world have committed their library services to the GATS under Sector 10C: the Central African Republic,

Albania, Bolivia, Ecuador, Gambia and Sierre Leone. However, many developing countries do not have a good, robust, publicly funded library service anyway, so the issue probably seems quite irrelevant. I was not able to gather much information about the GATS and libraries in the developing world partly because of the absence of services. However, various developing countries, such as India and South Africa, are enthusiastic about liberalising their education services and are of the opinion that it will bring their countries growth and prosperity. Also, many countries in the developing world are concerned about the implications of the TRIPS, and this is considered further in Part 3, in Chapters 9 and 10.

However, much has been written about the 'digital divide' in general, the extent to which the developing world is suffering from this, and the part that libraries can help play to bridge this divide. The digital divide is the growing gap between those in the world that have easy access to computers and information technology, knowledge and information and those that do not. Christine Deschamps, in her article *Can Libraries Help Bridge the Digital Divide?*, says that:

> The digital divide is one of the biggest issues facing the world today ... Rapidly advancing information and telecommunications technologies (ICTs) potentially have the power to help improve living conditions in the countries of the South. But they also threaten to increase the gap in living standards. Can libraries help to bridge the growing digital divide? I believe they can, if we seize the opportunity. (Deschamps, 2002: 1)

She continues, saying that:

> Libraries can help bridge the digital divide. But we have much to do to persuade world leaders, international organizations and national governments that we are key players. (Deschamps, 2002: 6)

It is clear that this digital divide represents yet another inequality, another form of poverty, between the 'haves' and the 'have nots', although Deschamps is optimistic that libraries can play a valuable role here in helping to lessen this inequality. An editorial in the *Guardian* newspaper of 10 December 2003 noted that the digital divide within richer countries is narrowing. However, it also reported the fact that it is widening between the industrialised and developing worlds, because of the slow pace of change in the developing world. About 90 per cent of global

Internet users come from industrialised countries but they have less than 20 per cent of the world's population. Africa has 19 per cent of the world's population, but only has 1 per cent of Internet users. Thus, as the *Guardian* editorial says, the role of the United Nations could be very important here in helping to bridge the digital divide (Guardian Editorial, 2003: 103). However, the fact that many in the developing world have no access to computers at all is very disturbing in terms of increasing rather than decreasing inequalities.

The developing world, ideally, needs to be more vocal itself with regard to these matters, but when they have crushing problems such as whether people have enough to eat or drink, libraries and IT issues undoubtedly pale into insignificance. One of the big concerns has been about the GATS and water privatisation. The World Development Movement has undertaken a substantial amount of work in this area for the developing world. Bolivia, for example (one of the countries that has incidentally committed its library services to the GATS), has been heavily involved with fighting water privatisation, and did not commit its water system to the GATS (Zageman, undated). Poor people that are threatened with the possibility of having to pay high rates for their water as a result of the GATS face grave, life-threatening issues. In comparison, libraries must seem a real luxury. However, many third world countries do believe the rhetoric that globalisation and the WTO will bring them growth and prosperity. Also, a number of developing countries are enthusiastic about liberalising their education services. This makes these countries very vulnerable to the GATS agenda, and to global capitalism in general. To this extent, these developing countries are fooled by the capitalist propaganda and the 'TINA' philosophy – that capitalism can and ultimately will provide growth and benefit to all and that there is not a viable alternative to this system anyway. Therefore, rather than trying to sort out their own problems within their own nation states, many developing countries are looking towards organisations like the WTO. The WTO endeavours to convince these countries that it works for the benefit of all, when, in reality, it works for the benefit of rich countries and large corporations and not usually for the benefit of those in the developing world. With such views, it also seems that, in the long term, many of the countries in the developing world may well commit their library services (such as they are) to the GATS disciplines.

It should also be noted, though, that there are also many in the developing world that are very sceptical about the WTO agenda, but if and when they do not want to go along with the agenda they are often manipulated and cajoled into accepting it. Martin Khor, the Director of the Third World Network, refers to this (Khor, 2002b) and talks about the manipulation that took place by the developed countries of the developing countries at the WTO Doha Ministerial Conference on 9–14 November 2000, saying, for example, that:

> ... the Doha meeting was held in conditions of a pressure cooker, in which a set of elite countries, aided by the Secretariat, set upon the majority of developing countries and pressed them to accept major elements of a future work programme which this majority had been rejecting up to the scheduled final day. (Khor, 2002b: 1)

He finishes his paper by emphasising how undemocratic and deceptive the whole process was and how it relied on on 'power-based tactics'. The implications of manipulation on such a scale are clearly very disturbing.

4.11 India: libraries, education services and the GATS

India has not committed its library services to the GATS under Sector 10C. However, it also seems to be of the opinion that trading its educational services will benefit its economy, thus with this belief it could easily include libraries in its schedule of GATS commitments at a later date. Government expenditure on education in India is poor anyway, and there are already many private companies running various education services. Total government expenditure per capita on education for 1995 was less than $10 per year in India as against $1,400 in the USA (UNESCO, 1998). As Deodhar said with regard to this:

> ... the state of affairs in the government educational institutions is pathetic ... hence, private sector participation and trade in educational services seems imperative. (Deodhar, 2002: 2)

An awareness of the importance of education and knowledge in India is growing, particularly with regard to helping its economy to thrive. Ambani and Birla argued that:

> The education sector has been largely neglected in India. This neglect can turn out to be India's undoing and nemesis in the

information age where knowledge, research, creativity and innovation will be at a premium. Education oriented to foster a knowledge-based society can place India at the vanguard of nations. (Ambani and Birla, 2000: 17)

Deodhar argued that dealing with educational services in line with the GATS will benefit the Indian economy, saying:

> For the ensuing negotiations on trade in services, Indian authorities not only need to respond to the proposals and commitments made by others, but put forward India's own proposal and select commitments that are in the best interest of our country. (Deodhar, 2002: 4)

Deodhar is also of the opinion that there are many exemptions and safeguards in the GATS, and that by this means, Indian interests can be protected and its nationhood and its cultural ethos safeguarded.

Furthermore, Sharma (2002) has emphasised how India has taken steps forward with regard to the GATS and education services. In addition, the trading and marketisation of higher education has been gathering pace for some time now. In the beginning of the 1990s various foreign universities endeavoured to market their higher education programmes to India. Meanwhile, Murali Manohar Joshi, in the country paper presented at the United Nations Educational, Scientific and Cultural Organisation (UNESCO) Conference on Higher Education held at Paris in 1998, justified the privatisation of higher education, saying that:

> It is not only justifiable but desirable to raise money from private sources in order to ease pressure on public spending. (Referenced in Sharma, 2002: 16)

Two industrialists, Mukesh Ambani and Kumarmangalam Birla, wrote a report entitled *A policy framework for reforms in education* (2000), in which they emphasised how they regard education as a very profitable market in India. With the implementation of this report, only those that could afford to pay would be able to enter into higher education. Ambani and Birla see education as producing and shaping adaptable, competitive workers that can easily acquire new skills and who are also innovative. They are enthusiastic about an increase in the private financing of education, saying that:

> Private financing should be encouraged either to fund private institutions or to supplement the income of publicly funded institutions. (Ambani and Birla, 2000: 16)

Sharma's analysis with regard to the GATS and education is correct, though, as far as I am concerned. Sharma emphasised the importance of the privatisation of education for the furtherance of the WTO agenda in general, saying that:

> The world's trade representatives under WTO, who are leading the assault on education, are attempting to establish a 'New World Government' based on profit threatening and arm-twisting the national governments in order to make way for private profiteering. This would be a government of and for the corporate sector – an extremely undemocratic, authoritarian institution. In this assault, they have discovered the possibility of manufacturing the thinking and attitudes of their consumers, and creating an education system to reproduce standardized people. (Sharma, 2002: 20)

Thus Sharma argues that the WTO is driven by profit, that it threatens democracy in nation states, and that it is a government for the corporate sector. Furthermore, it is perverting the purpose of education towards a consumer-oriented mode of thinking.

Clearly, then, India is very enthusiastic about trading its educational services and this could easily lead to an enthusiasm for trading its library services at a future date, whereby library services could then be scheduled in India's GATS commitments under Sector 10C.

4.12 South Africa: libraries, education services and the GATS

South Africa has not committed its library services to the GATS under Sector 10C. However, the commercialisation of higher education is also gathering pace. Chris Hogwood reports on the South African Minister for Education's keynote address, saying:

> The commercialisation, marketisation and commodification of the sector are part of the increasing trans-nationalisation of HE.

> Higher education is a multi-billion dollar industry. (Hogwood, 2003: 1)

However, he then goes on to make the point that:

> As free trade is a 'quest for money rather than enlightenment', trade considerations cannot be allowed to erode the 'public good agenda for higher education', surrendering individual countries' national needs to liberal markets. (Hogwood, 2003: 1)

Thus there is an awareness that such an agenda might well not be for the 'public good'. He also says that GATS in education should be 'avoided at all costs'.

There have been anti-WTO protests in general in South Africa (South Africa Says No to WTO, 2001). On 9 November 2001, for example, people marched through central Johannesburg to protest about the Doha, Qatar ministerial meeting of the WTO, the South African government's participation in it and the continued effect of WTO-enforced neoliberalism on South Africa. Various grassroots organisations attended as well as individuals and they protested against the GATS and the TRIPS. They were protesting at:

> ... the WTO's proposals to promote privatization of basic services, under the GATS treaty, and prevent the sale and distibution of cheap medicines, under the TRIPS agreements – a genocidal measure in a country with a disastrous Aids epidemic. (South Africa Says No to WTO, 2001: 1)

At the same time the Congress of South African Trade Unions (COSATU) held a rally against the GATS. A statement of protest against the WTO was also formulated for Alec Erwin, the Minister of Trade and Industry.

The South African government seems to be very enthusiastic about the WTO agenda in general and the GATS in particular. There have been protests against it, but in general the neoliberal agenda appears to be gathering pace, as indeed does the commercialisation of education in particular. Thus the library community in South Africa cannot afford to be complacent, and indeed South Africa might well commit its library services to the GATS at a future date under Sector 10C.

4.13 Europe: libraries and the GATS

A number of European countries have committed their library services to the GATS under Sector 10C. These are Iceland, Austria, Lithuania, Georgia, Albania and Estonia. It is interesting to note, though, that most of these countries are relatively poor by European standards, and not all are members of the European Union.

The EU as a member of the WTO belongs to the WTO as a single entity (for legal reasons known as the European Communities (EC)). Individual members of the EC are also WTO members in their own right but they do not, on the whole, negotiate individually within the WTO. Instead, the European Commission speaks for all EU member states at nearly all WTO meetings (see *http://www.wto.org/english/thewto_e/ countries_e/european_communities_e.htm*). Thus, for the purpose of the GATS, the EC operates as a single entity and a single WTO member. Therefore no individual member of the EC will simply commit itself to the GATS, although individual members can argue within the EC whether the EC as a whole should sign up or not to particular service sectors (see also note 1 on p. 32).

The EC, as a member of the WTO, has not committed its library services to the GATS under Sector 10C. However, this is no cause for complacency. In 2002 there were about 224,000 library service points in Europe with about 140 million registered users. Library visits in 1998 were registered at 3.5 billion and loan transactions at over 3.5 billion each year (EBLIDA, 2002a). Therefore, state-funded libraries are a very important part of the European Communities and surely need to be rigorously defended.

The position of the European Bureau of Library, Information and Documentation Associations (EBLIDA) with regard to the GATS and libraries will be considered further in this section. EBLIDA is an independent, non-profit umbrella organisation of library, documentation and archive associations in Europe. Organisations such as the Norwegian Library Association, the Finnish Library Association and the Chartered Institute for Library and Information Professionals in the United Kingdom are all members. Other members include, for example, the Society of College, National and University Libraries (SCONUL), the Swedish National Council for Cultural Affairs and the Belgian Association for Documentation. EBLIDA represents the interests of its members to different European institutions, such as the European Commission, the European Parliament and the Council of Europe.

EBLIDA has various working groups, such as the Copyright Expert Group and the Working Group on Professional Education, and I personally am an observer on the EBLIDA WTO Working Group.

EBLIDA is very concerned about the possible implications of the GATS for libraries in Europe. It notes that the GATS could impact on libraries in a number of ways. It says:

> Libraries could face competition from foreign for-profit library services and suppliers. National treatment may have to be offered to these suppliers in competition with publicly funded services. Professional standards and qualification requirements may be challenged as a barrier to trade. (EBLIDA, 2000)

Thus EBLIDA is concerned that state-funded libraries in individual WTO member countries could be under threat from private foreign capital. Under the 'National Treatment' article in the GATS, any foreign company would have to be treated the same as any public-sector organisation in the member state running the library service, or a private company from within that country running the library service, or indeed any other possible supplier. Thus, if the government gave a subsidy to this particular service area, then a foreign company would also have to be offered this same level of subsidy. This, then, is reinforcing the point that was originally made by the British Columbia Library Association (BCLA).

Furthermore, professional standards could also be threatened if they are seen to be a barrier to trade, and I consider the qualification issue further in Chapter 5 under section 5.7.3. EBLIDA continues, saying that:

> It is essential that the library community is aware of these developments and can defend its interests. (EBLIDA, 2000)

EBLIDA, in responding to the European Commission public consultation on the GATS, urges the European Commission and other member states to continue its current policy, and not to make any commitments concerning libraries to the GATS (EBLIDA, 2003a). EBLIDA says:

> We strongly believe ... that libraries and archives should not be committed to the competition processes that result from GATS. (EBLIDA, 2003a: 3)

It notes that a small number of requests have been made to the European Commission to make commitments to library, archive and museum services, but urges the European Commission not to make commitments that call into question the funding and regulation of publicly funded library services. They also note that it is very important that subsidies and other forms of direct and indirect support continue to be excluded under Mode 3, Mode 3, as outlined in Chapter 3, being 'Commercial presence', whereby the service supplier establishes itself in a foreign market as a legal entity in the form of a subsidiary or a branch (EBLIDA, 2003a).

EBLIDA also recognises that libraries are an integral part of activities within educational services, and urges the European Commission to exclude educational services from any new commitments.

In continuing its desire to find out more information and to raise important questions about the GATS, EBLIDA and IFLA met representatives of the WTO and the European Commission in December 2002. Information about this meeting is provided in Chapter 6, section 6.15. Thus EBLIDA has raised awareness about the GATS and libraries issue in Europe. It has issued a statement against the GATS and it urges the EC not to make commitments to the GATS that could threaten publicly funded library services.

In conclusion, several relatively poor European countries have committed their library services to the GATS under Sector 10C, but the EC as a single WTO member has not so far committed itself. EBLIDA is concerned about the likely implications of the GATS for libraries and urges the European Commission to continue its current position of not committing EC library services. (See also Chapter 6, section 6.6 for further information on EBLIDA.)

4.14 The UK: libraries and the GATS

4.14.1 Introduction

In Chapter 5, I will consider how, in practical terms, the GATS is impacting on libraries in the United Kingdom and will provide many examples. However, in this section, I will consider the GATS and libraries in the UK in a more general way, and in particular focus on the level of awareness that there is – which has arisen from my own work in this area! I will also highlight the UK Chartered Institute of Library and Information Professionals (CILIP) position with regard to the GATS.

The UK, as an EC member, has not, as yet, committed its library services to the GATS under Sector 10C.

4.14.2 Information for Social Change

I started undertaking work on the GATS in the year 2001. This followed on from reading Glenn Rikowski's book, *The Battle in Seattle: Its Significance for Education* (2001b), about the WTO and its implications for education. I then found out about a group that 'challenged the dominant paradigms of library and information work' and met some people that had similar political views to myself. The group Information for Social Change (ISC) is one that is in liaison with the UK Chartered Institute of Library and Information Professionals (CILIP) and also produces its own journal (now an e-journal). After an initial discussion and having told the group about my interest in globalisation issues, John Pateman, who has edited most of the ISC issues although I am now co-editor with him, asked me if I would like to edit a special issue of ISC. The special issue would consider, in particular, the implications of the WTO and the GATS for libraries and information. I thought it sounded a very interesting and exciting idea, as well as being something that is very important, and so I agreed.

I contacted various people and asked them to write articles for the special issue. This included Clare Joy, the campaigns officer for the World Development Movement (WDM). Unbeknown to me, the WDM were involved with organising a British Broadcasting Corporation (BBC) Radio 4 programme on the GATS at the time. There was to be a 20-minute debate on the programme *You and Yours*. I was subsequently asked to participate in this programme, and I made the point that I feared that, in the future, because of the GATS, public libraries could be run by private companies. Also, the public could find themselves having to pay to go into their local library and this would be particularly likely to affect the poor and the disadvantaged (BBC, 2001a). I then wrote a long article myself for the issue, which was entitled *The Corporate Takeover of Libraries* (R. Rikowski, 2002a). This now forms Chapter 5 of this book, with various revisions and additions.

The special issue, *Globalisation and Information*, was published in Winter 2001/2. Shortly after its publication I was contacted by Anders Ericson, a freelance journalist and a librarian from Norway, who was very enthusiastic about my article in the issue. He subsequently came over to England and interviewed me about my work on the GATS and libraries, and wrote an article based on the interview which was published in the Norwegian library journal *Bok og bibliotek (BOB)* (Ericson, 2002). Many others, including Susan George, author of books such as *The Debt Boomerang: How Third World Debt Harms Us All*, were also interested in the special issue. I also discovered that I was not alone in the library world with regard to this topic. Instead, I found that some library associations and organisations had statements and resolutions against the GATS, such as the International Federation of Library Associations and Institutions, the European Bureau of Library, Information and Documentation Associations, the British Columbia Library Association and the Canadian Library Association. I felt very heartened.

4.14.3 Talks on the GATS and libraries in the UK

Following on from this, I spoke about the GATS, the WTO and libraries at a variety of events. This included talking at the UK CILIP Umbrella Conference in Manchester in 2003. I also spoke at the Library Association Headquarters in London, Sussex University and the London School of Economics, University of London, all in 2002. The first event was held at a library and information conference and the second event was held at the Library Association (as it was then called) Headquarters in London and was organised through the International Group of the Library Association. So, these events were specifically library-focused. The last two events examined the implications of the GATS across different service sectors, such as health, education and the police and security services, and my talk on libraries and the GATS was one talk among many others on the topic of the GATS. The event at the London School of Economics was organised through a non-governmental organisation called ATTAC – the Association for the Taxation of Financial Transactions. Thus I endeavoured, in various ways, to raise awareness.

I also won a First-Timers award from UK CILIP in order to attend the IFLA Conference in Glasgow in 2002, my application being based on my wish to raise awareness about the GATS. However, having obtained the award, I then found that I could not speak on the main programme, because this had already been planned and established well in advance. I felt disappointed, as my desire to go to the conference was specifically because I wanted to raise awareness about the GATS and libraries. Also, there was some urgency, as the GATS was due to be strengthened in 2005. So I decided to organise my own fringe meeting. I arranged all the speakers, booked the room and did all the publicity. It proved to be very time-consuming, but was a very successful event and some leading people in the library and information world attended. The meeting included two speakers from the library and information profession who had written and spoken about the GATS. These were Frode Bakken, the President of the Norwegian Library Association and Chief Librarian of Telemark's University Libraries in Norway, and Paul Whitney, City Librarian, Vancouver Public Library, British Columbia, Canada. I also spoke myself. Subsequent to this, Frode Bakken then spoke about libraries and the GATS at the 2nd Assembly of the European Regions (AER) Conference of European Regional Ministers for Culture and Education in Brixen, in October 2002 (Bakken, 2002).

4.14.4 Links between the UK and EBLIDA

I was invited by Frode Bakken (the then coordinator of the EBLIDA WTO Working Group) to become an observer on the EBLIDA WTO Working Group. The purpose of this group is to work on issues and raise awareness about the WTO agreements and how they impact on libraries and information. Its primary concern was with regard to the GATS, but more recently they have also included TRIPS in their remit. Toby Bainton, Secretary of SCONUL, is a UK member of the group. I went to my first EBLIDA meeting at the IFLA Conference in 2002. At this meeting, Teresa Hackett, the then director of EBLIDA, said that she was going to organise a meeting with the WTO and the European Commission so that we could ask them some pertinent questions. I contributed several questions, although I was not able to attend the meeting myself. It was, however, quite revealing and informative for those that attended, I understand, and further information about these meetings is given in Chapter 6, section 6.15. We also discussed the possibility of including the GATS on the main IFLA programme in the future.

I attended another EBLIDA meeting in December 2003. At this meeting another very important decision was made. This was that EBLIDA intends to hold a conference on the GATS and TRIPS in the UK, probably in the spring of 2005, the aim of the conference being to inform and raise awareness about these agreements among some of the most important and influential people in the library and information world, including various library associations and library schools. I have been invited to talk on TRIPS. Thus, through my work, the UK is now becoming a focal point for raising the issue of the GATS and TRIPS on the international stage, which is most encouraging.

4.14.5 Published material on the GATS and libraries in the UK

A variety of my articles on the GATS were also published during 2001–3 in a selection of different journals (some hard copy, some online and some both). These include *Managing Information, The Public Library Journal, The Commoner, Relay, Link-Up, Focus, BIS (Bibliotek i Samhaelle)* and more articles in *ISC (Information for Social Change)*. Thus I had publications featured across a wide range of different journals. *The Public Library Journal, Focus* and *Relay* are the journals for specific groups within the UK Chartered Institute of Library and Information Professionals – namely the Public Library Group, the International Library and Information Group and the University College and Research Group, respectively. *Managing Information* is the monthly Aslib (Association for Information Management) journal. *Link-Up* is a newsletter that is circulated to library workers in the developing world and *BIS* is a Swedish left library journal. Meanwhile, *The Commoner* is a left activist e-journal, so this reaches out beyond the library world to a wide range of people. An article of mine was also published on the subject for the House of Lords Select Committee on Economic Affairs, as part of its report on *Globalisation* (see references at the end of this book with regard to all these publications).

4.14.6 UK Chartered Institute of Library and Information Professionals

During this period, I also tried to persuade UK CILIP to pass a resolution against the GATS, or at least to write a statement showing its concern about it. At the time, they had no such resolution or statement. I wrote a short piece in the January/February 2003 issue of *Managing Information* about the agreements, and concluded by saying that:

> ... it would be very helpful if UK CILIP were to pass a resolution against the GATS, or at least have a formal statement showing concern, as various other library associations and bodies have done. (R. Rikowski, 2003d: 43)

I also contacted Bob McKee, the Chief Executive of CILIP, and Elspeth Hyams, the editor of *Library and Information Update* with regard to this – *Library and Information Update* being the monthly professional journal produced by CILIP that is distributed to its members. It replaced the previous *Library Association Record*. I should add here that during the compilation of the special ISC issue (2001/2), Matthew Mezey, the news editor of *Update*, gave me some useful contacts and was supportive in general. He also wrote three news items about the GATS and the special ISC issue in *Update* at the time. I would like to thank Matthew for this. However, no other official person at CILIP congratulated me for finding out about the issue and trying to raise awareness or informed me that they thought that it was an important topic that needed to be considered further. Jill Martin from CILIP did, though, support my application to attend the IFLA Conference in Glasgow in 2002, my application being based on my wish to raise awareness about the GATS, so I am grateful to CILIP for that. However, for a while, I became disillusioned and weary of the topic for a number of reasons. So I then decided to look at TRIPS as this is another very important area.

I only really returned to the topic of the GATS when I started undertaking some further research on the GATS for this book, in December 2003. I was then amazed and delighted to discover that UK CILIP *did* have a statement about the GATS! Furthermore, this statement had been issued in January 2003 – which was the same month that my piece appeared in *Managing Information*. So, obviously, they *must* surely have been influenced by my work. Furthermore, the statement is quite a strong one at that, which is most encouraging – but CILIP did not inform me about it and neither did they inform anyone at ISC.

In the UK CILIP statement it says that traditional library services, such as maintaining a reference service and the lending of fiction, might not be very attractive to commercial suppliers. However, through information and computer technology (ICT) libraries now provide many other services as well. These include online database retrieval services, electronic reference services, Internet access, the development of web portal/subject gateway services and electronic document delivery, and these may well be of interest to commercial suppliers seeking global opportunities. Therefore it notes that these services might fall under the remit of the GATS at some point.

Thus, while UK CILIP does not think that traditional library services are immediately 'attractive to commercial suppliers', CILIP can see that other information areas could be of interest to them. It considers how the GATS could impact on these services, saying:

Publicly funded libraries provide these services from the public purse, which are provided as part of a package, in order to serve the interests of the whole community. If authorities are obliged to provide the same level of subsidy, they would be faced with two choices: reduce subsidies to existing services or, less likely, extend the same level of subsidy to the competing private sector organization. (CILIP, 2003: 2)

From this it is clear that CILIP recognises the problem that the GATS poses for the state-funded sector of libraries. Under the GATS those competing from the private sector would have to be offered the same level of subsidy as those from the public sector. This, then, is in line with the thinking of other library associations, such as the BCLA and IFLA. CILIP then shows its concern clearly, saying that:

While the concept of allowing 'competition' appears benign, the eventual outcome of such challenges will be the undermining of the tax-supported status of public sector libraries at the national, regional and local levels. (CILIP, 2003: 2)

Without tax support, the library's role as a democratic institution will be undermined. CILIP then makes a very powerful statement, emphasising its concern about the possibility of profit margins taking priority over cultural and education services:

... CILIP is concerned at the potentially alarming consequences for the future operation and development of cultural and education services should the priority to preserve our cultural heritage, provide free access to information and the notion of a community-based library serving the needs of the local population cease to take priority over profit margins. (CILIP, 2003: 3)

It is interesting to note that Sue Brown, whose name appears at the bottom of the statement, was present at the talk on the GATS and libraries that I gave at the CILIP Umbrella Conference in Manchester in 2003, which was entitled 'Libraries: international tradable commodities or public services'. However, in the general discussion she made no reference to this statement at all, although there were plenty of opportunities for her to have done so. Also, the statement does not acknowledge or reference my work in this area. Neither does it make it clear that I informed CILIP about this whole subject. Thus, while I am delighted that CILIP now has such a clear statement about the GATS, I am deeply concerned about the way in which it was handled. Indeed, such an approach could seriously discourage others from raising important issues for the library and information community in the UK and working hard in these areas. This can surely only be detrimental to the library and information profession at large, in the long term. Let us hope that CILIP's approach to these matters will change in the future! (See also Chapter 6, section 6.11 for further information on CILIP.)

4.14.7 Concluding comments

In conclusion, through the work that I have undertaken, the topic of the GATS and libraries now has a much higher profile in the UK than it did. However, raising awareness is still very much an uphill struggle. There is still a lack of awareness about the GATS in general, let alone the implications of the GATS for libraries and information both in the UK and indeed internationally. This can be partly explained by a lack of media attention. It receives very little coverage even in newspapers such as the *Guardian* and the *Independent*, although some journalists, such as George Monbiot from the *Guardian*, have written powerfully on the topic. As I have already indicated, I *did* participate in a BBC Radio 4 programme on the GATS in 2001 (BBC, 2001a), which was most encouraging, but such programmes are very rare indeed. There was also an article about my work on the GATS and libraries written by the then news editor Jane Mackenzie in the *Big Issue* – a weekly magazine that is sold on the streets in the UK by and for homeless people. The *Big Issue* aims to help homeless people, as the homeless people that sell the magazine keep some of the revenue from the sales (MacKenzie, 2002). So, this was also encouraging. Yet, even in a journal like *Red Pepper* (a monthly red-green journal) it is not easy to make an impression. Hilary Wainwright, the editor of *Red Pepper*, asked me to write a piece about the GATS and libraries, for example, in 2002. I did this and she said she liked it and that it would probably be published, but it never saw the light of day. There was, though, a special issue on the GATS and education in *Red Pepper*, in November 2002. This book, though, will contribute to raising the profile.

Thus the issue of the GATS and libraries in the UK has largely arisen from the work that I have undertaken in this area. Within this context, this section has focused on Information for Social Change (ISC) and talks on the GATS and libraries as well as EBLIDA, my published material on the the GATS and libraries and the UK CILIP position with regard to the GATS.

4.15 Chile, the USA and Singapore: multilateral free trade agreements and cultural services

Chile has not committed its library service to the GATS under Sector 10C, but Singapore and the USA have. However, trade agreements other than the GATS are also taking place internationally. These include various bilateral and multilateral agreements, such as the multilateral free trade agreements that have been established between the USA, Chile and Singapore on cultural services (see Bernier, 2003). The agreements between the USA and Chile were concluded in December 2002 and with Singapore in February 2003. The USA is treating cultural goods and services in trade agreements in a somewhat different way to the way in which it treated them previously. Prior to this, cultural products were not seen as being any different to other products, and were not distinguished in trade agreements from other products. It seems that these agreements are now having a significant impact on the cultural sector in these countries.

These agreements have similar principles to those that are embedded in the GATS. This includes National Treatment, Most Favoured Nation and Market Access. However, one significant difference is that in the GATS obligations National Treatment and Market Access are only 'bottom up', whereas the obligations are 'top down' in these agreements. This means that once the agreements have been finalised and agreed, then there is no further choice regarding which parts of their services they might want to commit to the agreements (apart from any exceptions in the agreements). Under the Free Trade Agreements they have to be fully committed, whereas under the GATS partial commitments can be made.

What is interesting to note is that various Free Trade Agreements are also being established between different countries, outside of the GATS. Furthermore, these particular agreements actually go further than the GATS in their quest for liberalisation. This once again demonstrates that the GATS is merely a tool for aiding and abetting the furtherance of global capitalism. As is self-evident from these Free Trade Agreements, the liberalisation of trade in services would continue with or without the GATS. However, the GATS is a world-wide agreement that can embrace many countries. And this is its appeal, as far as those pushing forward the global capitalist agenda are concerned. One hundred and sixty members all agreeing to liberalise their trade in services will obviously help to push the global capitalist agenda forward in a highly significant way and at quite a pace. Two or three countries just making agreements among themselves (bilateral and multilateral agreements) will result in a much slower process, even if those agreements go beyond that of the GATS. However, it needs to be noted that such agreements are taking place, and we need to be aware of them. The main point to appreciate, though, is the general direction in which we are all being swept along, i.e. the liberalisation of trade in services and the transferring of more and more services into the marketplace, and how this is being undertaken by a variety of different mechanisms. The aim behind providing these services will not be for the public good, but to increase profit margins. This is what we need to remain crystal clear about.

4.16 Audio-visual industry and the GATS

The audio-visual (A-V) industry clearly also has links with libraries and information and is part of cultural services, so examining the impact of the GATS on the audio-visual industry is also useful. There have not, however, been many formal multilateral and bilateral trade talks in the A-V industry. Freedman in his paper 'Trade versus culture: an evaluation of the impact of current GATS negotiations on audio-visual industries' (2002) examines the current and potential impact of the GATS negotiations on the A-V sector. He says:

> While cultural policy is by no means at the forefront of multilateral trade agreements it is ... implicated in various GATS disciplines and connected to wider arguments about the direction and scope of free trade negotiations. (Freedman, 2002: 4)

Thus there is some awareness of the fact that the GATS could also have an impact on the A-V world. However, Freedman concludes that although the USA wants to secure commitments in the audio-visual sector, little has so far actually happened. This is the case for a number of reasons.

First, there is the issue of 'cultural distance', which includes factors such as language barriers and different viewing habits. This makes it more difficult for cultural products to flow freely between different nations. Therefore,

> ... it is not simply trade restrictions but also cultural barriers that impede the free flow of audio-visual materials. (Freedman, 2002: 10)

Secondly, defensive interests seem to operate more effectively than offensive ones with regard to multilateral agreements in the audio-visual industry – people want to safeguard their audio-visual industries in their own countries. Therefore:

> The GATS may be too blunt an instrument for 'freeing up' audio-visual trade given the growing determination of citizens to resist further encroachments of capital into important areas of their social and economic lives. (Freedman, 2002: 10)

However, Freedman also notes that even if the audio-visual industry as a whole is not opened up to GATS disciplines soon, the ideology of free trade is still being pursued daily in the media industry in other ways. Once again, this demonstrates the fact that the liberalisation of trade in services, as part of the global capitalist agenda, is being pursued in several different ways, and is not just restricted to the GATS. However, as I have already said, the GATS is a very effective tool enabling the escalation of such trade on a global basis.

4.17 Conclusion

The intention in this chapter has been to focus on some of the issues and concerns raised regarding the GATS, libraries and information in a variety of countries and by different organisations and some individuals, considering furthermore in some instances cultural and educational services as well, and showing some of the links between these and library services. This is an ambitious task, and it is a very new, unexplored area. The GATS is about the trading of services, and as such, the trading of libraries and information probably comes some way down the list. As many people have said, 'who can make money out of libraries?', the assumption being that no one thinks they can make much, so there is probably nothing to worry about anyway. But now there are also other related services, such as online database retrieval services, Internet access and electronic service delivery, and money could well be more easily made out of these areas.

However, the situation is more complex than on initial inspection. The philosophy behind the GATS is about the trading of all services, so libraries also fall within this remit and could be vulnerable under various categorisations or sectors within the GATS. As I have made clear, it is about the marketisation, commodification and privatisation of services for the enhancement of global capitalism.

In this chapter I have considered, specifically, which WTO member countries have committed their library services to the GATS under Sector 10C: Recreational, Cultural and Sporting Services of the GATS schedule of commitments, and there are 18 in all. However, as EBLIDA points out, library services also fall clearly under two other sectors in the schedules – Sector 2CJ: Telecommunication Services, and Sector 5: Educational Services. Various other sectors in the schedules also include library or library-related services, such as the sector on research and development. Any comprehensive analysis of the GATS and libraries would need to include an examination of all the sectors in the GATS that include library or library-related services, and then consider which WTO members have made commitments within these different sectors.

Furthermore, these sectors/categories are flexible entities, so that even though library or library-related services might not fall within a particular sector at the current time, they might well do so in the future. Sector 2B: Computer and Related Services is one such example here. At the meetings that representatives from EBLIDA and IFLA had with WTO representatives in December 2002, the WTO representatives said that it was possible that online services would go into this sector at a future date. In such a scenario, library-related services in Europe would fall under the GATS, even though the EC has not committed its library services under Sector 10C to the GATS.

Libraries and information can present us with hopes for an alternative world. The richness of fiction, facts about injustices and the free flow of information are all embedded within libraries, and they represent something that in many ways is far removed from the direction in which the GATS is pushing the world. As such, libraries could well pose a threat to the GATS agenda. Because of this there might be a particular keenness to push library services onto the GATS agenda in order to silence this potentially damaging force (as far as global capitalism is concerned).

When EBLIDA and IFLA met with the WTO and the European Commission, for example, it seemed that the WTO and European Commission representatives were rather surprised that the library community had been thinking about these issues in such depth. Furthermore, they seemed thankful that the delegation was only confining itself to addressing library issues. From this we can conclude that the library community is a force to be reckoned with, and one about which the WTO and European Commission representatives were somewhat concerned. But by the same token, in order for global capitalism to continue down its path effectively, the library community is also a force that needs to be 'dealt with' in some way. The free flow of information not embedded within intellectual property rights, however, can be dangerous. Many examples could be given here. One, though, will suffice: when it was discovered that the New Labour government in the UK was using information from a student's dissertation in 2003 to argue the case that we needed to go to war against Iraq. As was said in the *Kirkby Times* with regard to the Iraq War:

> Most of us with any sense know full well that Blair and New Labour fabricated the evidence ... the evidence amounted to little better than a second rate student's dissertation or thesis. We killed innocent people due to this evidence. (Kirkby Times, 2003: 3)

It is unlikely that the general public would have been informed about this without some notion of freedom of information (one of the library and information profession's key principles) and without the knowledge that this information can be obtained in libraries. Such free flow of information, information that can be made easily accessible in libraries, might well not be in the interests of global capitalism, although it sometimes can be (given that capitalism is based on a set of contradictions, although there is not the space to explore this further here).

Examining libraries and the GATS on an international basis is a largely unexplored area. I have started the process in this book, but much more needs to be done. Sometimes, I have examined cultural services and education in general rather than libraries in particular in order to obtain a broader perspective. Many countries put cultural and education services before library services, but there are many overlaps between all these areas. Furthermore, many WTO members are enthusiastically committing their educational services to the GATS. As Maude Barlow pointed out in 2001:

Already, over 40 countries, including all of Europe, have listed education within the realm of the GATS, opening up their public education sectors to foreign based corporate competition. (Barlow, 2001: 9)

A number of other important points have emerged in this chapter.

- It is important to consider the meaning of a 'public good' and how public goods differ from private goods.
- Some countries embrace trade liberalisation in general, such as Japan and New Zealand, while others, such as Canada, are far more sceptical about it.
- Some countries such as Japan and India are particularly enthusiastic about liberalising their trade in education services.
- Several library associations have noted the fact that, with the GATS, a government would have to give the same level of subsidy to other suppliers that might run the nation's library services, such as a foreign company, as that which it gives to its state-funded library services: other possible contenders for such funding would be trusts, charities and private companies.
- Some organisations, such as the British Columbia Library Association, have urged people to take action against the GATS.
- Various organisations have given clear statements against the GATS and want their library services to be exempt from it.
- Some important and influential people, such as Naomi Klein, have taken up the GATS and libraries issue.
- Organisations such as the Australian Writers' Guild and the Writers' Guild of America, West are concerned about the possible commodification of cultural services and culture being treated as an economic good.
- Various people such as Alex Byrne and various organisations have explored the notion of what a library service should ideally be about.
- There is not much information about GATS and libraries in the developing world. I think such information is limited, because many of these countries have more pressing and immediate concerns, such as water, food, shelter and disease (such as Aids).

However, I have not looked at the practical implications of the GATS in these different countries. Neither have I gathered clear, concise and comparable facts for the different countries. I have not examined all the sectors in the GATS schedules that include library or library-related services either and have not considered which WTO members have signed up to these sectors. Thus this is very much an overview, considering some of the thoughts and issues that are 'on the table' in some countries regarding the GATS and libraries and library-related issues at the current time. It is a very important topic and further research needs to be undertaken on it. This chapter has also sought to demonstrate the high level of concern that there is with regard to this subject. To put it succinctly: the library world is against libraries falling under the GATS.

Real-life examples of how the GATS is impacting on libraries in the UK

5.1 Introduction

Having considered the GATS agreement itself and the GATS, libraries, information and cultural services within an international perspective, I will now consider how the GATS is impacting on libraries in practical ways. I will focus on examples in the UK, particularly in public libraries, because of my detailed knowledge in this area. Thus, as I am from the UK, and have worked as an information professional/librarian in the UK for 25 years, I am well-placed to consider the practical implications of the GATS for libraries and information in the UK. In some areas, though, such as micropayments, my analysis will extend to the developed world in general and sometimes I will consider specific countries and areas, such as Australia and Europe.

My analysis will also provide a framework that others can use to consider the implications of the GATS and libraries in their own countries. This will be examined in this chapter. Indeed, the framework can be used to consider the implications of the GATS for the state-funded provision of services in general. In due course I hope to extend this analysis to other countries and other services.

5.2 The future role of public state-funded libraries in the UK

5.2.1 Introduction

First of all, though, I will consider the debate around the future role of state-funded libraries in the UK. It is important to examine this debate and to consider whether, and the extent to which, state-funded public libraries in the UK are valued today. Clearly such deliberations are very important within the wider context of the GATS, and the likely implications of the GATS on these state-funded libraries. Thus, does it seem that people in the UK want to see the state-funded provision of public libraries preserved?

5.2.2 Frank Webster's view of the future role of UK public libraries

Professor Frank Webster, then at the University of Birmingham and now at the City University, London, in his article *Public Libraries in the Information Age* (Webster, 1999b), poses this question – 'Do libraries have a future?' He then lists some facts, in an endeavour to show that they do. He says that there are over 4,000 library sites in the UK, for example, and over half the population are library members. Webster claimed that visiting the library is the fourth most popular pastime in the UK – more popular than going to the cinema or to a football game. However, he then referred to the move from public to private provision of many goods and services, which, of course, is very much tied up with the GATS agenda. He argued that there are many reasons for this, including Thatcherism, globalisation and the collapse of collectivism. Webster referred to the 'market model of information', and suggests the possibility that library services could become like Blockbuster video shops, arguing that:

> The market model of information dissemination is increasingly that of the Blockbuster video chain: let customers determine choice of stock, only supply the most popular as measured by issues, and let borrowers pay on the nail for what it is they want ... Growing commercialisation means that, more and more, what information is made available depends on what is saleable, and what people get hinges on what they are prepared (and able) to pay. (Webster, 1999b: 2)

He then emphasised the need for librarians to consider these issues more, and argues that:

> If librarians don't ask what it is they are about, then they meet the challenges of commercialisation unprepared and incapable

of doing more than adapting to a business agenda. (Webster, 1999b: 2)

Webster says that one of the main aims of the public library should be to strive towards promoting information as a *public good* and that this should not be related to the ability to pay. So, once again, we have the notion of the public good. He says that this is an ideal but it is 'at odds with recent history and continuing trends' (Webster, 1999b: 3). Instead, many librarians too readily focus on 'performance indicators' and a Blockbuster mentality, rather than playing a more active role with regard to deciding what to stock. As he points out, the better information from the Internet often comes from non-commercial sources, such as universities and charitable and government agencies. Meanwhile, commercial enterprises will use various devices to try to entice us into their web and:

> Like the drug dealers, internet providers realise the value of supplying free samples up front. Once hooked, then the price may well start to spiral. The fear is that, by then, libraries will be signed up into deals from which they cannot disentangle. (Webster, 1999b: 6)

He argued that librarians should be suspicious of the increased commercialisation of information, and hold tight to the notion of information being a public good. We must be cautious and vigilant and endeavour not to be fooled by the hype.

5.2.3 Charles Leadbeater's view of the future role of UK public libraries

More recently, Charles Leadbeater (2003) wrote a critical report for the Laser Foundation on the state of the UK public library service, arguing that it urgently needed to change to keep pace with the wider changes that are taking place in society. He said that fewer people were using libraries. Furthermore, he pointed out that figures from research undertaken by the Audit Commission in May 2002 reveal that visits to libraries have decreased by 17 per cent and book loans by a quarter since 1992; 23 per cent fewer people borrow books from public libraries than they did three years previously, while book sales have increased by 25 per cent during this period (1999–2002). He argued that public libraries used to be central to life in many communities, but now they are often marginalised. This decline is particularly serious because it takes about 5–10 years to turn a library service around; he is of the opinion that libraries in the UK lack leadership but need 'top quality' senior managers. Furthermore, Leadbeater argued that some inspirational goals for libraries are required and an imaginative marketing drive. He argues that there should be modern 'hub' libraries in shopping centres. The UK public library service is very valuable but it urgently needs to change. He concluded his report by saying that:

> Unless decisive action is taken now, the decline of the public library network could become terminal by the end of the decade. The revitalised public library network should be at the heart of a socially inclusive, knowledge-rich service economy. (Leadbeater, 2003: 35)

Meanwhile, John Pateman reviewed this report and said that it:

> ... is essential reading for all public library stakeholders ... [and] ... its final sentence – 'Libraries are sleepwalking to disaster: it's time they woke up' – should give us all food for thought. (Pateman, 2003: 2)

We have two rather different perspectives here from Webster and Leadbeater. However, both these commentators are clearly of the opinion that public libraries in the UK are important and need to be preserved in some way.

5.2.4 Research from the Audit Commission on the role of UK public libraries

Some of the findings from the Audit Commission report on libraries (2002) appeared in the daily press, and there was considerable interest in the findings of the report in general. Maev Kennedy writing in the *Guardian* (2002) reported on the fact that since 1992, 9 per cent fewer libraries were open for 30 hours or more a week, although the national library budget has remained stable at £770 million a year. Furthermore, over 50 per cent of library services are in poorly located buildings, or buildings that are in such a poor state of repair that library managers have recommended that they should be closed. However, Kennedy also listed some positive facts in the report. First, libraries still have a very important role in the community, and there were 290 million visits in 2001. There are now over 14,500 computer terminals for public use in libraries, which is 10,000 more than five years ago. Although in the past three years the numbers using libraries for borrowing has indeed fallen by 23 per cent, the numbers using libraries to study, use computers to access the Internet and for other community activities has risen. The Commission inspectors also found that good reader development work was being undertaken in two-thirds of the libraries that were visited.

However, the amount that libraries have been spending on books has also fallen by 33 per cent over the last ten years. The *Guardian* editorial of 17 May 2002 argued that:

> It is not that there isn't a demand. Last year there were 290 m library visits (more than for football matches or the cinema) and almost 30 per cent of the population said they had visited a library. The problem is that they are under-resourced, often don't open at the times people want to visit them and are not keeping up with the competition from bookshops and internet cafes. (Guardian Editorial, 2002c: 19)

Thus the *Guardian* editorial makes the same point that Webster (1999b) articulated – that visiting the library is still a very popular event. However, the problem is that libraries are often poorly resourced, and are not keeping up with competition from information sources in the private sector, it seems. But surely they should be operating outside of this competitive mentality, I would suggest.

Meanwhile, Cookson, writing in the *Socialist Worker* (2002), reported that, according to the Audit Commission report, there are also 8 per cent fewer mobile libraries and 7 per cent fewer libraries in total, compared with ten years ago. She expressed grave concern about the findings in the report in general, and emphasised that:

> Libraries are absolutely essential for working class people to have free access to information and culture. (Cookson, 2002: 11)

5.2.5 Tim Coates, the Libri Report and the future role of public libraries in the UK

The Libri Report, written by Tim Coates, a former managing director of the bookshop chain Waterstone's, and entitled *Who's in Charge* (2004) followed on from the Audit Commission report. Coates undertook research for the Audit Commission report. The Libri Report aimed to alert people to the urgency of the situation. Coates argues that libraries could be extinct within 15 years unless changes take place. He argues that libraries should be open from early in the morning until late at night and that spending on books and other reading material should be trebled so that readers have more chance of finding the bestseller that they want on the shelf rather than having to order it. Coates is critical of the way in which libraries are managed. However, Bob McKee, Chief Executive of the UK Chartered Institute of Library and Information Professionals (CILIP), said that:

> Libraries (unlike bookshops) don't just carry multiple copies of what's currently in print: they're required by law to be comprehensive, so they carry large numbers of out-of-print works as well. Managing them is a task that bookshops just don't have. Mr Coates also paints a picture of a public library service in terminal decline. It isn't. It certainly faces challenges – just like bookshops do from supermarkets selling cut-price books or the BBC does from cable and satellite. But the public library service is still a huge operation: nearly 60 per cent of the population are members, libraries lend 377 million books a year, and yet the whole service costs less than 2p in every pound councils spend. (McKee in Ezard, 2004: 5)

Thus Bob McKee seems to be arguing that Coates is viewing libraries too much through the eyes of a bookshop manager rather than through the eyes of a librarian/information professional. For McKee, Coates's outlook is unnecessarily depressing and does not paint a true picture of reality (Ezard, 2004). (See Coates, 2004 and Hutton, 2004 for further information about the Libri Report.)

5.2.6 Conclusion

Obviously, others have examined the issue of the importance of the role of state-funded libraries in the UK today in general, and the future role of public libraries in particular. There is not the space to examine this further here, but clearly such debates need to be taken seriously within the wider context of the GATS.

In conclusion, much debate and thought has been given to the current and future role of public libraries funded by the state in the UK. People such as Leadbeater, Webster and Coates have been very vocal in their opinions. Research has also been carried out on the subject, such as the Audit Commission research in 2002 which received considerable coverage in the daily press. However, while people might differ about the way in which they think state-funded public libraries should be preserved in the UK, most people would argue, I feel sure, that state-funded libraries are something that they value in the UK and that they want them to continue to thrive. I would argue that state-funded libraries are surely something worth preserving. Let us now consider some of the ways in which state-funded libraries in the UK have been and are being undermined, focusing in particular on public libraries, and demonstrate that they are, indeed, under threat from the GATS agenda.

5.3 Implications of the GATS for libraries and information: the development of a framework

5.3.1 Introduction

How, then, is the GATS making inroads into the state-funded provision of libraries? It is important to have a clear understanding of the big picture. There are two distinct aspects and both apply to state-funded provision in general. One is the GATS itself, and the other is the privatisation, commercialisation and capitalisation agenda for the state-funded provision of services. The privatisation and commercialisation of public services has been taking place and gathering pace for some considerable time, and can, on initial inspection, seem to have little if anything to do with the GATS. I have considered this in Chapter 3, section 3.4. Thus the essential point to demonstrate here is the link between these two areas.

To do this in an effective and systematic way, I have broken the 'corporate takeover of public services' down into three distinct areas – *commercialisation*, *privatisation* and *capitalisation*. This was developed in my article 'The Corporate Takeover of Libraries' (R. Rikowski, 2002a). Commercialisation involves making money from public services in various ways and private companies making money and promoting themselves through public services. Privatisation involves private capital actually moving into public services. Capitalisation involves the total extension of this 'businessification' on a global basis. I will give examples of how these three areas are developing in the UK with regard to state-funded libraries, focusing in particular on public libraries. I will also, on occasion, use examples that extend beyond the UK. The specific examples will focus more on privatisation and commercialisation than on capitalisation, as the latter is more of an all-pervading, general trend, although some examples of capitalisation will also be given.

Having considered these three areas in some depth, and having provided many examples demonstrating that the commercialisation, privatisation and capitalisation agenda is real, I will then seek to demonstrate how this agenda is linked to the GATS. I will do this by examining the mechanisms/facilitators that are enabling the GATS to come into effect in state-funded libraries, which G. Rikowski (2001a) has referred to as 'the national faces of the GATS'. Again, the examples will be taken from public libraries in the UK. The mechanisms that I will consider are Best Value, the Library Standards and the People's Network and the way in which they operate in the UK (see section 5.7). Even from this limited perspective, there will be many that will disagree with me, and will argue that Best Value, the Library Standards and the People's Network are intrinsically worthwhile and designed to benefit the ordinary people in the local community, and moreover that I am just scaremongering and/or exaggerating. However, if one reads the philosophy behind Best Value carefully, for example, it becomes apparent that its purpose is to create a market environment in the UK. The same philosophy lies behind the other examples of the mechanisms that I have given in this book. All this will be considered further in this chapter.

5.3.2 Commercialisation

Commercialisation involves finding different ways to make money out of libraries. There are various examples of commercialisation, and one of these is income generation. Many public libraries in the developed world have been seeking different ways of generating income for a number of years now. This includes selling items such as postcards, memorabilia, bookmarks, pens and other stationery items. Other materials are also hired out for a fee, such as videos, cassettes and CDs.

Another example is where private companies use libraries to promote themselves and their products. This is a subtle process. Companies cannot, at the moment, just blatantly advertise in libraries. However, companies are making inroads, and this will be considered later on in this chapter, in section 5.4.3.

5.3.3 Privatisation

I have broken *privatisation* down into three main areas – libraries being run directly for profit, private companies making a profit out of running libraries at a lower cost than the price they are contracted to run them, and the private sector running capital projects.

The first area is where *private companies are running libraries (or parts of libraries) directly, for profit*. There are some subscription libraries that fall under this category, but they are small in number. There are also company libraries that function to augment the capacity of the firm to make profits (e.g. libraries in law firms) and media libraries that generate revenue (e.g. newspaper libraries). However, what is of particular significance is where corporate capital is moving into public-sector libraries and electronic libraries are setting up in competition with mainstream public and academic libraries, operating on a for-profit basis. The second area is where *private companies are making a profit out of running libraries at a lower cost than the price they are contracted to run them*. Within this framework private companies then run and manage library services. The third area is where the *private sector takes over and runs capital projects*. The Private Finance Initiative (PFI) comes under this category and these areas will be considered further in this chapter.

It is, of course, a well-established fact that privatisation and outsourcing is increasing. As Edward Valauskas says, for example:

> Privatisation, outsourcing – these words have taken a weighty and almost frightening connotation for librarians around the world in the past twenty years. Both words have become part of the vocabularies of managers and staff as part of a language that stresses efficiency, profitability, and end results. (Valauskas, 1999: 1)

Valauskas also referred to outsourcing, saying that this involves the transfer of some functions or activities within an organisation to a third party, and that this is done with the aim of increasing efficiency and decreasing costs. He seemed to be rather enthusiastic about it all, saying that:

> Privatisation and outsourcing offer opportunities for libraries to prove their value to their communities in new and unexpected

ways. Creative and intelligent understanding of the role of the library within an organization, with plenty of quantitative evidence to support the key position of the library and its staff and collections, will prove the best tonic for survival. (Valauskas, 1999: 8)

We need to be aware of arguments such as the above that are put forward in support of privatisation and outsourcing when considering this within the context of the GATS.

Others have considered issues with regard to the privatisation of information-related topics. A book entitled *The Intelligent Corporation: The Privatisation of Intelligence*, edited by Jon Sigurdson and Yael Tagerud (1992), for example, explores the shift of information and intelligence functions away from state monopolies and towards the privatisation of these activities. It includes information about privatising intelligence, the emergence of corporate intelligence and intelligent management systems for intelligent corporations.

5.3.4 *Capitalisation*

The capitalisation of libraries and library services is a process that deepens over time with libraries becoming sites for capital accumulation and profit making. The other two processes – commercialisation and privatisation – feed off each other so that libraries and library services become increasingly *commodified* and then capitalised. This implies that library services are increasingly ruled by the goal of profit making. Notions of income generation, income streams, marketing, library products, the user as 'customer' or 'consumer' and the market, competition, cost-effectiveness and efficiency become the yardsticks for success. This implies a 'culture change' regarding the ways library staff are encouraged to view what they are about. The capitalisation of libraries implies their *businessification* – the library and library services as businesses, bathed in business values and outlooks. Fundamentally, it represents the all-pervading extension of global capitalism and the marketisation and commodification of all that surrounds us. This is the logic of capitalism. In a fundamental sense, though, this is an impossible goal. However, once again, this just highlights the inherent contradictions that reside within capitalism itself, and I will be examining this further in future works.

5.3.5 National faces of the GATS

The 'national faces of the GATS' are processes, mechanisms, agreements and directives, etc., that are introduced to enable the GATS to take effect – to help to bring it to fruition. They are hidden, to the extent that it will not be explicitly stated anywhere that these mechanisms will help to enable the GATS to come into effect. But the reality is that they will exist, as they help to pave the way for a commercialisation and privatisation agenda and eventually for a capitalisation agenda. However, these processes can also and indeed will operate in abstraction from the GATS. This is because, following the logic of capitalism, further commercialisation and privatisation is inevitable. It is the commercialisation, privatisation and capitalisation agenda that is an inherent part of capitalism.

The task then becomes one of identifying what the mechanisms are that will help to enable the GATS to take effect. In this chapter, I focus on three of these mechanisms that are effective in the UK in the public library sector. There will be others as well, but these three are very important and demonstrate the general trend. Other countries would need to identify what their own mechanisms are – it is not likely to be obvious. Some will argue that there are no such mechanisms at all. I hope, in this chapter, to demonstrate that they are real enough. However, this can only be effectively undertaken by knowing a country well, so others would be better placed to examine their own national mechanisms and, indeed, it is important that they should do so.

5.3.6 Conclusion

In this section I have designed a general framework to demonstrate the ways in which the GATS will impact on state-funded public services in general and the state-funded provision of libraries in particular. This framework can be used to examine the implications of the GATS for public service provision in other countries in general, for a wide variety of public service sectors and for the state-funded provision of libraries in particular. The following section will provide practical examples for all these areas within the UK – thereby demonstrating how the GATS is coming home to state-funded libraries in the UK.

5.4 Commercialisation of libraries in the UK

5.4.1 Income generation

Public libraries in the UK have been seeking ways to *generate income* for a considerable number of years now. Income generation was taken up enthusiastically when I was working in public libraries in the London Borough of Newham in the early 1990s. This included selling postcards, bookmarks and other memorabilia. Westminster libraries in London also forged ahead enthusiastically a few years ago with selling these types of items.

Greg Doehring's paper *Increasing Investment: Income Generation for Survival or Growth?* considers income generation in libraries in some detail. As he says:

> A survival strategy has been pursued by some libraries through the development and delivery of revenue generating products and services that are ancillary to their free library and information services. (Doehring, undated: 1)

Doehring acknowledged the fact that there is a growing trend for governments to shift service delivery from the public to the private sector, through outsourcing and privatisation. He also referred to fee-based services that are targeted at specific client groups and that are seen as supporting the free public library service. Various people have examined these different fee-paying services, such as Ward (1997), Berry (1997), Anderson (1997) and Webb and Winterton (2003). *Fee-Based Services in Library and Information Centres* by Sylvia Webb and Jules Winterton, for example, is the second edition of a book that was first published in 1994. In 1994, fee-based library services were a relatively new idea, but now they are far more established. The 2004 edition includes four case studies on fee-based library services, one of which was centred at the Institute of Advanced Legal Studies, University of London.

Meanwhile, the Library and Information Service of Western Australia (LISWA) decided that it could not deliver the level of service that it wanted to if it relied solely on money from the state government. So it developed an infrastructure that made it possible to generate income from customised information products and services which clients paid for, and hence it developed fee-based services. Doehring concluded by saying that all this:

> ... requires a shift in paradigms for the organisation and its staff – from delivery of free reference and public library and information services to include business activities that deliver a range of value added and customised fee based services and products. (Doehring, undated: 8)

Public Libraries Mobilising Advanced Networks (2003) points out the fact that the demands and expectations of the public are changing and new services that are provided, such as the Internet, have increased the cost of running public libraries. The increase in direct public funding of public libraries in Europe was only 16 per cent between 1991 and 1998 (see LibEcon newsletter). Meanwhile, in the same period, fees and charges increased by 134 per cent and income from 'special funds' by 133 per cent. In this situation, public libraries have sought other ways to find funding. The IFLA/UNESCO Public Library Manifesto states that 'the public library shall in principle be free of charge'. However, this idealised notion seems quite far removed from reality. In its 2002 survey report *The Public Library in the Electronic World*, the Danish National Library Authority (NAPLE), for example, says that there will probably be more budget reductions and a need for more alternative forms of financing and income generation in the future.

Thus income generation and fee-based library services are becoming increasingly established in state-funded libraries in the developed world in general, and in the public library sector in particular.

5.4.2 Market research approaches to library users and the creation of markets

The market research approach is concerned with creating or developing *markets or quasi-markets*. In this scenario, library users are transformed into 'consumers' or 'customers' and market research is undertaken to gather information on library and information consumers' current and potential wants and needs. Capitalism is also excellent at persuading people that they want things that they had never even thought about before!

Helen Weiss provided a powerful example here, when she discussed the development of strategies to obtain more information about borrowers' wants and needs in the *Library Association Record* (Weiss, 2000). She described how management information systems can help libraries adapt commercial marketing techniques to revolutionise their service. She spoke about supermarket loyalty cards which are used to analyse spending patterns and then suggested that, perhaps, borrowers' lending cards could be developed in the same way. Southwark Council used the TALIS library computer system to generate management information to help them to identify the characteristics of users and predict their future needs. Adrian Olsen, the Head of Southwark Council's Library Service, noted that:

> Having access to this sort of data gives us greater confidence that the products and services we are investing in will be fully utilised. With more and more libraries looking to broaden their appeal and offer Best Value the use of library management systems can be a major tool in measuring and improving effectiveness. (Cited in Weiss, 2000: 448)

Thus there could be information about the borrower inserted on their library card, outlining some facts and characteristics about the user that could provide indicators about their future product wants and needs. Users' library cards could contain information similar to that currently included on supermarket loyalty cards. Some library authorities in London are considering the use of smart cards, for example, and possibly linking these to Oyster cards, which are travel cards that can also be used on the London Underground and on London buses. With smart cards payments can be made for particular library services such as printing material (see section 5.4.4 for more information about smart cards). Of course, some may argue that these mechanisms are benign and just give librarians more useful information about user needs and desires to help them to provide a better library service that is more in tune with the needs of the local population. However, once this is in place its purpose can easily be shifted into a competitive market scenario, particularly if, in the future, the library supplier is a private company and not the local authority. In this situation, library users would then become 'consumers' (or customers), and could be treated in a similar way to supermarket customers. Information about business students in the local community could be obtained, for example, and the central library could then purchase business journals, textbooks and databases that are applicable to their particular needs. A separate business section could be established in the central library and business students could then be 'invited' into this section for a small fee. This form of commercialisation could also occur even if the library was still under local authority control. The model could be extended if the information was sold on to third parties, and they might then use it for mail shots and other marketing initiatives. Of course, the Data Protection Act curtails the passing on of this type of information. Yet once a private operator is running the library (or a chain of libraries) then the temptation to find ways around the data protection laws increases as the profit motive, rather than public good or public service values, becomes the dominant drive underpinning the service's operations. Once such a scenario is operational efforts could then be made to try to anticipate business students' future wants and needs and, indeed, to help to shape and create these wants and needs. They could be persuaded, for example, that belonging to a nearby law library for a small fee is crucial to their needs. This law library could happen to be run by the same organisation running the business library (whether this be a private company running the two libraries on its own, or a private company running them in conjunction with the local authority or with a voluntary organisation). The important point to realise, though, is that the private company starts to expand its business.

5.4.3 Companies 'benevolently' investing in libraries

On first consideration, it might appear that there are no examples of private enterprises *advertising and promoting* their products in libraries. Companies are not currently allowed to advertise blatantly in places such as libraries and schools. However, this *is* starting to happen in a subtle way. Bill Gates, for example, from the Bill and Melinda Gates Foundation gave £2.6 million to UK public libraries for the creation of information and computer technology (ICT) learning centres in deprived areas. It was used to expand the People's Network (Resource, 2001c). The People's Network involves installing a large number of computers in public libraries throughout the UK for the public to use. Bill Gates does not need to display big Microsoft posters in these ICT learning centres in order to promote Microsoft. Microsoft and Bill Gates are well known to much of the population already. This will place Bill Gates in a very favourable light – Bill Gates giving money to deprived areas, Bill Gates wanting to help the poor people, Bill Gates wanting to do something about the digital divide – the 'haves' and the 'have nots' in the IT world. Thus Microsoft, a large business corporation, is being promoted in our public libraries.

Secondly, in some public libraries in the UK, IT centres are being set up by private companies within libraries themselves, some of whom run training courses. They may even be allocated a small room within a large central library. There will be no big posters on the door advertising the company, but there will be a small sign outlining who is sponsoring the centre. In this way, the company is being advertised. Library users will probably find the centre very beneficial, thus providing the opportunity for the company to expand and develop this at a later date. This has taken place in the London Borough of Merton library service, for example.

Thirdly, private companies are now sometimes sponsoring events in libraries. In a public library in a London borough, for example, the Starbucks coffee shop sponsored an event for children in 2004. This trend is likely to escalate within other public libraries in the future.

5.4.4 Micropayments in the developed world

Definition of micropayments

Micropayments may become another form of library commercialisation, and this is in the form of extracting money from libraries. For some time now, various parties have been trying to think of ways in which money can be made from searching and undertaking transactions on the Internet. This has been taking place throughout the developed world. Introducing micropayments into the developing world will be far more problematic, as many in the developing world do not have access to computers and certainly do not have easy means for paying for transactions on the Internet – it is very difficult to obtain credit cards in Africa, for example.

Micropayments offer a solution to enable transactions on the Internet. Payments can be made in small amounts (as little as 0.1p). There are various definitions of micropayments. The W3C (undated), for example, refers to micropayments, noting that:

> Micropayments have to be suitable for the sale of non-tangible goods over the Internet. (W3C, undated: 3)

Problems with micropayments and how they are being overcome

However, there have been problems with bringing in micropayment systems (see, for example, Shirky, 2000 and Crocker, 1999 – Crocker was one of the founders of CyberCash which was a micropayment system that failed). Mechanisms for payments are complex, and there are problems relating to security and trust that have, so far, been prohibitive. However, the White Paper on Micropayments drafted by StorageTek (2001b) is a significant and revealing document. It says that most of the problems have now been overcome and that various options are now being set in place to make it easy for people to pay for undertaking searches on the Internet. David Slater, the Marketing Manager of StorageTek, spoke about the White Paper in 2001. He noted various problems with regard to making money from the Internet. In particular, there had been a lack of a trusted, cost-effective and convenient payments system, but that micropayments now provided a solution. The White Paper considers how companies and individuals can make money and generate revenue from micropayments, what some of the options and the problems are, and who is at the forefront with regard to this (David Slater, Marketing Manager, StorageTek, 2001a, Executive Summary: 1).

David Slater thought that micropayments could be implemented in the next 18 months. Note, in particular, the timescale here – the hope being that mechanisms for making money through transactions on the Internet would be in place within this period of time (by the end of 2002). In this way it would coincide with the GATS timetable, as it was set out at the time, although this timetable was not adhered to. This GATS timetable was laid out clearly by the World Development Movement, and adapted from Sinclair (2000). The date now being aimed at is 2005, although there has even been some slippage here. But the important points to note are the intentions behind and within this agenda.

Implications of micropayments for libraries and information

What implications, then, do micropayments yield for libraries and information? The concept of micropayments directly runs counter to the concept of the free flow of information, and will also exacerbate the digital divide. As stated by Oja Jay, in *Rethinking Micropayments*:

> The problem with micropayments, as traditionally conceived, is that they conflict with the free flow of information, which is essential if intellectual 'property' is to be noticed on the web. Other problems include lack of standards, and the creation of a whole new set of have-nots, e.g. are libraries going to pay for disadvantaged kids to surf the net? (Oja Jay, 2000: 1)

Another possibility is that people might use libraries less, because if they have to pay for their transactions on the Internet, wherever they are, then they might choose options other than libraries. Worden (1998) outlines this scenario, saying:

> With trusted systems in place one could envisage a pay-per-print system, which eliminates the risk that makes consumers wary about paying for information they may not be able to use ... as more and more users turn to the Web as their primary source of news information, one can expect a shift away from libraries and other traditional research venues to the convenience of a low cost alternative at home. (Worden, 1998: 6)

If people use libraries less in this way it could clearly have many repercussions. For example, it may lessen the availability of books and other sources of information for users. Library users would lose the benefit of the rich range of information sources that are available in the library but are not present at home. However, at this juncture I do not wish to go into the debate about whether people would be more likely to use the Internet at home rather than in their library in the future.

Significantly, what is implicit in Worden's quote is that libraries (those that do still exist) will be paying for transactions on the Internet and these payments will probably be made by the library service (be it private sector, voluntary sector or local authority) rather than individual users. Certainly, companies operating micropayments systems will not be happy with people paying to use the Internet at home, yet being exempt from such payments in libraries. If such exemptions could be introduced then the opposite scenario to the one envisaged by Worden might materialise. That is, people might use the library for their Internet transactions rather than stay at home and surf. In which case, all the hard work that has gone into trying to introduce micropayments would be undermined, with predictable complaints to various governmental departments from companies hit by this outcome. At a deeper level, it would seem that exemptions for libraries from micropayments constitutes a 'barrier to trade' under the WTO's GATS, and private corporations could seek to overturn such exemption rules as the GATS-inspired trade liberalisation regime takes increasing hold of the service sector. If library services are forced to engage with micropayments then they will need to recoup their money in some way, either through local authority subsidy for micropayments (which in theory also contravenes GATS rules) or by user subscription or user direct payment. In my radio interview (BBC, 2001a) I hinted at direct payments, but in reality this mechanism may well be too cumbersome, so the subscription option may be the preferred choice – with all the consequences for differential payments and exemptions for those on benefits or low incomes.

More generally, micropayments pose a significant threat to information flowing freely, one of the main components for an open and democratic society and one of the key principles embedded in the library and information profession. The free flow of information is considered further in Chapter 10 (section 10.2.1). Access to information and an informed public are vital checks on the operations and power of governments and corporations. The importance of public scrutiny regarding corporate and government policy cannot be overstated. Both require constant monitoring if the notions of public good and public interest are to have real and substantive meaning. Micropayments, viewed as opportunities for profit making, entail the limitation of access to information on condition of payment. As StorageTek (2001b) note:

> Online products such as data are becoming a commodity, so why not ... charge a small fee for them? (StorageTek, 2001b: 17)

Web content publishers and information providers are also driving the micropayments agenda forward. Content providers will offer more varied and innovative content, and then seek to charge a small fee for it, through micropayments, where possible. Many web publishers are now charging for content. These include *Encyclopedia Britannica*, *The Times*, the *Wall Street Journal* and *The Economist* (BBC, 2001b).

It is quite likely that, in the future, some vital information will only be available when accessed by micropayments. This sets up a new digital divide between those who can afford some of the more expensive items that can only be accessed by micropayments and those that cannot. This overlays the conventional definition of the digital divide between those who have access and know how to use information technology and can obtain information easily and those that do not. Hence, micropayments brings with it a *double* digital divide.

The four Cs in micropayments: collection, convergence, convenience and content

Amusingly, both micropayments and Best Value have four 'C's as under-pinning principles. In micropayments four key elements are identified as being essential to achieving net profits. These are:

- collection;
- convergence;
- convenience;
- content.

Collection is involved in particular with new innovations in e-payments and convenient online payment methods. Traditional online payment providers, such as banks and credit card networks, are losing their share of the market to person-to-person (P2P) payment providers. *Convergence* implies that payment service providers (PSPs) are becoming the next generation of banks. The traditional banking sector will become virtual telecommunications companies, and telecommunications companies will become banks. Thus:

> Everyone's main goal: to own the customer, the online experience and maximise profit. (StorageTek, 2001b: 3)

Convenience refers to considering and developing a range of convenient online payment methods. In particular, it focuses on new technologies and payment models that would change consumer spending habits. Credit cards are not seen as being very convenient. They cannot handle very small payments, for example, and are not available to those under 18. Therefore, alternative payment methods are being explored, such as smart cards and payment options through mobile devices (such as mobile phones). Sally Rumsey (1999) alerts us to some of the experiments and trials that are being undertaken in this field. She reports on the TOLIMAC – Total Library Management Concept – an electronic document delivery service that uses a smart card for enabling users to pay for secure access to specific articles on the Internet. Some public libraries in London are currently (as at 2004) considering using smart cards and also linking these to Oyster cards: travel cards that can be used on the Underground and on buses in London. In the micropayments world it is held that 'convenience will drive business' (StorageTek, 2001b: 3).

Content is significant to the extent that it enables and generates micropayment opportunities. Content that either cannot be charged for, or for which customers are unwilling to pay, is unacceptable in the world of micropayments. Furthermore, high quality content that generates payment encourages customers to click onto the next page – for which an additional charge can be made. Thus for StorageTek:

> The more clicks, the greater the number of transactions, the more revenue will be generated. (StorageTek, 2001a: 3)

The future of micropayments

Micropayments are likely to be introduced, first stealthily as proponents fear a public backlash to such payments, and then (if such a backlash is muted) with significantly greater speed and force. Currently, EU legislation is being standardised which will ease the process. Furthermore, the euro will probably address many of the tax and standardisation of payment issues generated by micropayments. Dealing with a large number of different currencies clearly complicates the matter and makes it more difficult to implement micropayments effectively. Efforts are being made to make micropayments user friendly and easier to deal with. Microsoft has been developing a smart card. As Worden writes:

> If Microsoft can successfully link its smart card business to its increasingly popular Windows suite of programs, then micropayments may be able to reach a critical enough mass for network effects to begin. (Worden, 1998: 4)

Worden notes that companies like British Telecom and Digital Equipment Corporation have invested millions in micropayment trials. However, many of these micropayment systems have not been very successful so far, but now the situation is starting to change, particularly as different technological forces converge, such as web TV, cheap network computers and smart cards holding digital cash.

There are many examples of where micropayments have been introduced and used. A number of these have been outlined by StorageTek in its White Paper. The *New York Times*, for example, implemented a micropayment solution to charge small fees to enable users to access past articles from the newspaper online. Also, *FT.com* (the online version of the *Financial Times*) changed its position with regard to free access to its content and Napster, the music service, was forced to introduce a micropayment system after a court ruling prevented the free distribution of copyrighted music on the Internet. Hyperion operated a micropayment system based on Barclay's BarclayCoin scheme and the CyberCoin scheme. This was a software-based scheme, and consumers were given a software 'wallet' on their PC. The wallet was charged up with a credit card that held digital money that could then be spent on the Web. The wallet was downloadable free from Barclays (Birch, 1998). Cybergold (Crocker, 1999) and MyPoints, interestingly, offer 'reverse' micropayments. With this scheme the customer is rewarded with points that can be exchanged for products and services for viewing content, responding to advertisements and reading articles.

On the evidence available, it appears that micropayments are likely to become a feature of Internet access in the not-too-distant future and this will have direct implications for Internet use in libraries. Our libraries could become profit-generating centres for Internet companies. The key issue would then become *how* libraries pay micropayments: whether users pay directly or by subscription to a library or whether libraries or local authorities become the payment provider with users paying indirectly through council taxes. Consideration of these options may well politicise the micropayments phenomenon, but the possibility of seeking micropayment-free zones for public libraries may offer the most equitable solution. This scenario potentially runs up against the GATS, though, as a 'barrier to trade'. The labyrinth that is developing before us may well function to cut off solutions that incorporate social justice.

5.4.5 Summary

This section has focused on examples of the commercialisation of public libraries in the UK and examined income generation, the market research approach to library users, companies commercially investing in libraries and micropayments. Various means for generating income have been considered. This included income generation in public libraries in the UK, and various fee-based library service schemes that have been, and are, in operation in Australia, the UK and Europe. The micropayment section is relevant to libraries throughout the developed world in general and is not just confined to the UK. I have argued that I think it is likely that micropayments will become a source of revenue for companies in the not too distant future. Furthermore, this is likely to have significant implications for libraries.

5.5 Privatisation of libraries in the UK

As already stated, *privatisation* can be broken down into three main areas – libraries being run directly for profit, private companies making a profit out of running libraries at a lower cost than the price they are contracted to run them, and the private sector running capital projects. These will all be considered in this section, giving practical examples of the privatisation of libraries in the UK for each of these three areas.

5.5.1 Private companies running libraries (or parts of libraries) directly for profit

Some subscription libraries fall under this category, but they are small in number. There are also company libraries that function to augment the capacity of the firm to make profits (e.g. libraries in law firms) and media libraries that generate revenue (e.g. newspaper libraries).

However, what is of particular significance is where corporate capital is moving into public sector libraries and electronic libraries are setting up in competition with mainstream public and academic libraries, operating on a for-profit basis. Examples of how this is starting to take place in the UK are given in this section.

There are now IT centres/Internet projects that are being set up in public libraries by private companies. Ormes (1996) described such projects in some detail. Cybercity was one such Internet project, which was situated at Bath Central Library. A separate area was created in the library, where the public could use the PCs and access the Internet. It proved to be very popular. The council could not afford to run such a project, so a local company called GlobalInternet ran it for profit instead. Ormes noted that:

> Cybercity is in fact not a library service at all, but a cybercafe (without the coffee!), which is run for profit by a local company called GlobalInternet. Cybercity, like all cybercafes, offers charged

> access to the Internet. How it differs from other cybercafes is that instead of being situated in a shop/café it is found in the public library. (Ormes, 1996: 1)

Ormes described another company that had been working with public libraries – Input/Output. She described how Input/Output set up ten centres in public libraries across the country. Marylebone Library was the first of these. It provided Internet access, but also provided access to software packages such as word processing and spreadsheets and ran computer-training courses. South Ayrshire Council started a South Ayrshire Cyber Project in 1996. The intention was to open a number of Cyber Centres in libraries across the county, providing the public with access to the Internet, software packages and CD-ROMs.

There are also various examples of electronic libraries now available, and these are certainly not just restricted to the UK. Instead, they are expanding throughout the developed world in general. Questia (Fox, 2001), netLibrary and ebrary (Crane, 2001) are all electronic libraries:

> ... with collections that include tens of thousands of books and they are growing fast; although modest by the standards of print collections, these commercial digital libraries already dwarf even the largest non-profit collections. (Crane, 2001: 1)

Questia is an Internet company aimed at serving students in an academic environment, providing online information from books, encyclopaedias and journals in the humanities and social sciences for fees (Fox, 2001). Questia:

> ... sells information online directly to consumers the way Amazon sells books online and the GAP sells clothes online. (Fox, 2001: 1)

Fox also refers to some other companies that have launched similar products aimed at both students and faculty staff. These are Proquest Academic Edition's Xanadu, and Jones's E-Global Library (ibid.). Many other examples could be given, but what they indicate is that the private sector is either moving into public sector and academic libraries or setting up alternative operations with the aim of making profits.

Many other examples of the privatisation of libraries and information could be given. See, for example, Bennahum (1995), Nehms (1997), Seetharama (1998), Private Libraries Association (1999) and Millward

(1998). See also Fiona Hunt's article, where she refers to companies launching 'information markets' on the Internet (Ott, 1999). This is a process that is still at an early stage of development, but it is expanding nevertheless.

5.5.2 Private companies making a profit out of running libraries at a lower cost than the price they are contracted to run them

This form of privatisation started to happen in the UK in the London Borough of Haringey, where a private company, Instant Library Ltd, ran the public library service in Haringey from 2001 to 2004. This was the first time that a private company had ever run a public library service in the UK. As the then managing director of Instant Library Ltd (now the Head of Haringey Library Service), Diana Edmonds, said:

> In February 2001, an Audit Commission inspection reported that Haringey libraries were 'poor' with 'no prospect of improvement'. In July 2001, the London Borough of Haringey took the innovative step of establishing a public-private partnership with Instant Library Ltd, and the company took over the management of the authority's Libraries, Archives and Museum Services. (Edmonds, 2003: 50)

Furthermore, the *Library Association Record* (September 2001) reported that:

> Consultants have been called in to run a local authority library service. This is a first – although the move is temporary. (*LA Record*, 2001f: 515)

Haringey received a very negative report by the Best Value Inspectors and this resulted in Instant Library Ltd being given the 'opportunity' to turn the Haringey library service round. However, Haringey was one of the first councils to undergo a Best Value review, and so were 'guinea pigs' in this respect.

Initially, Instant Library Ltd was on a six-month trial, and an assessment was made of the work undertaken after this period. It was seen to be making good 'progress' (in line with Best Value), so its contract was extended. As was reported in *Managing Information* (December 2003):

> The service's achievements have been justly recognised in the recent Best Value reinspection. Councillors, managers, library staff and Instant Library are all delighted with the result. (Managing Information, 2003: 10)

Furthermore, the Association of London Government said that:

> Instant Library's groundbreaking partnership with Haringey – the first time that a private company has taken on the direct management of a public library service – is now starting to turn things round. (Association of London Government, 2003: 2)

According to the bulletin the number of people visiting Haringey libraries had increased by 93 per cent and borrowing books had increased by 42 per cent during the period that Instant Library had been running the service, i.e. 2001–3.

So there we have it – the start of corporations moving into libraries. Am I being alarmist? Why then was the local authority in Haringey not given the chance to 'improve' under the Best Value imperative, rather than just allow Instant Library Ltd to move in? The *LA Record* (2001f) explains how Maria Stephenson, a middle manager in Haringey, said that they were not given guidelines on how to undertake Best Value and that they 'didn't have the skills'. They were one of the first authorities to undertake a Best Value review, so surely they should have been given more help and guidance. Yet we can speculate why that did not happen: it would not have provided the opportunity for the private sector to start to run our public library services. Furthermore, if no examples materialised from Best Value in this way – providing the opportunity for alternative suppliers – then the Best Value regime could be seen to be a waste of time in terms of its capacity for opening up libraries to corporate capital. Best Value would not be implemented as intended if all the Best Value Inspection Reports concluded that all local authorities were providing a good public library service, or at least a service that could be improved while remaining in the control of the local authority. Instead, Best Value had to be seen to be introducing alternative suppliers. The philosophy behind Best Value itself will be considered further in section 5.7.2. In 2004 Haringey Library Service did return to the council, although interestingly Diana Edmonds is now the Head of Haringey Public Library Service. This must not allow us to be complacent though. It could easily revert back to the private sector at a later date. As Lawson and Leighton suggest:

> Anything that has been decommodified will, if left unprotected, be remorselessly recommodified. (Lawson and Leighton, 2004: 32)

Furthermore, this is just the start of the private sector making inroads into state-funded libraries in the UK, I am sure. The 'Haringey experiment' was deemed to be successful, so there are almost sure to be more such projects in the future. If a private company can be seen to be 'turning a library service around' in this way, then clearly some will argue that other private companies should be given the opportunity to run other local authority-controlled public library services and 'turn them around'. Such projects clearly go hand in hand with the GATS agenda. We need to be fully aware of what is happening here.

5.5.3 Private sector taking over and running capital projects

The third form of privatisation is where the private sector takes over and runs capital projects, such as the building of a new central library or a service-wide ICT system. The Private Finance Initiative (PFI) comes under this category, and there are various examples of where PFI has been adopted in libraries. PFI is often portrayed as being an opportunity to get investment into our public services in general, although in his book *The Captive State*, George Monbiot (2000) has shown PFI to be an expensive, inefficient and undemocratic way of providing public services. Others such as Dexter Whitfield have also made this case (Whitfield, 2001). (See also Labour Left Briefing, 2000.)

Richard Sibthorpe (2001) describes the first PFI to incorporate construction and information technology solutions, which was undertaken in public libraries in Bournemouth in the UK. It provided Bournemouth with a new central library and information and computer technology (ICT) facilities across its whole branch network. A 30-year contract between the council and Information Resources (Bournemouth) Ltd was signed to build and facility-manage a new central library. This was a 'Pathfinder Agreement' and was one of 29 such agreements around the country. Pathfinder was an official UK government scheme and the UK

Department for the Environment, Transport and the Regions (DETR) gave nearly £15 million towards the new library. Linda Constable, ICT Development Officer and Bournemouth Council Library Officer, said:

> A great partnership has been developed between the council, Information Resources, Allied International and TALIS information, all working to deliver Best Value and service to both the other organisations involved in the deal and the library users in Bournemouth. (Constable, in Sibthorpe, 2001: 236)

The library needed to ensure that it remained technologically advanced throughout the 30-year period of the contract. It was difficult for them to know, or predict, what new technologies would develop, so the council obtained guidance from the DETR's newly published Treasury Task Force ICT Guidelines which introduced Technology Refreshed. Bournemouth council then went on to implement a series of change control agreements. Change control is an essential element of the PFI contract process, and is particularly important when implementing hardware and software information and computer technology projects as situations change so rapidly.

Shelagh Levett also referred to the *PFI solution for Bournemouth libraries* (Levett, undated). She noted how the project contributed to fulfilling the UK government's agenda with regard to encouraging partnerships with the private sector, and that the contract had to comply with the principles of Best Value and there were procedures for benchmarking. As a result of the project, she says that Bournemouth gained a 'stunning new town centre library' (p. 3), with approximately 3,800 square metres of internal space. Information technology was also input into 12 libraries. This included a library management system, Microsoft Office software, e-mail and the Internet, and community information. She argued that PFI is about defining the service(s) required, allocating the risk to a party that can bear it, giving value for money and relating payment to performance. She concluded by saying that for Bournemouth, PFI:

> ... has proved a successful process for both the public and private sectors. (Levett, undated: 4)

Meanwhile, Sibthorpe referred to PFI, saying that:

> The initiatives also provide private investors with valuable exposure to new markets. (Sibthorpe, 2001: 237)

Thus, PFI fits in closely with the GATS agenda. Sibthorpe concluded by saying that:

> Private Finance Initiatives enable the public sector to effectively purchase a service from the private sector ... PFIs look set to be the blueprint for the way in which this, and probably any government, will be aiming to do business with the private sector for the foreseeable future. (Sibthorpe, 2001: 237)

It is interesting how Sibthorpe notes the government's keenness to continue to do business with the private sector in the future and how PFI looks set to be the blueprint.

There are other examples of PFI in libraries. Hackney Technology Learning Centre, which includes a new central library and museum, has used the PFI initiative to build its new library (*LA Record*, 2001a). MPM Capita, the project management division of Capita Property Consultancy (CPC), announced the completion of the £19m redevelopment of the centre on 22 February 2002. MPM Capita were first appointed in March 2000 by the International Bank of Japan which provided the funding for the scheme (Capital Property Consultancy, 2002). Kent County Council is operating a PFI contract for the provision, financing and operation of the council's IT system. This includes the public library system and a public information network of over 1,000 terminals. Brighton has also developed a new central public library through PFI (*LA Record*, 2000e).

Others have considered the privatisation agenda for state-funded libraries in the UK. Suzanne Burge, for example, in her IFLA 1998 paper *Much Pain, Little Gain: Privatisation and UK Government Libraries*, considered privatisation and market testing in UK government libraries. She looked at a number of case studies, including the Department of Health, Ordnance Survey, the Export Market Intelligence Centre of the Department of Trade and Industry and the Department of Transport and considered how each of these illustrate different aspects of the process. She also examined government librarians' attitudes to privatisation, based on a research study carried out in 1993 and updated by a smaller study in 1996–7. Burge concludes by suggesting that there is 'much pain, little gain' to be achieved by the privatisation of government libraries.

5.5.4 Summary

The privatisation of libraries in the UK was considered in this section and this was broken down into three main aspects. Firstly, private companies may run libraries (or parts of libraries) directly for profit. Examples here included IT centres and projects such as Input/Output and Cybercity and electronic libraries such as Questia, netLibrary and ebrary. Secondly, private companies may make a profit out of running libraries at a lower cost than the price they are contracted to run them. Here the focus was on Instant Library Ltd when it ran the public library service in the London Borough of Haringey for a period. Thirdly, the private sector may take over and run capital projects. Here the emphasis was on the Private Finance Initiative and I focused, in particular, on Bournemouth libraries.

5.6 Capitalisation of libraries in the UK

Continual library reviews and reorganisation provide an example of the way in which the capitalisation process has been working in the UK. The public library service in the London Borough of Newham underwent two library reviews, for example, the first of which resulted in the loss of a large number of professional librarians. Another review was taking place in summer 2004. Similarly, in 2004 there was a reorganisation of senior library managers and librarians in another London borough and new posts of Assistant Librarian were created. All the successful applicants had neither library qualifications nor experience, despite unsuccessful applicants having both. Management and marketing skills were prioritised over library skills. Management also intended to move all library staff around the borough, to different libraries. However, most members of staff have acquired local experience and knowledge, and such changes are likely to be detrimental to the aim of providing a library service that meets the wants and needs of the people in the local community. However, the borough is strongly unionised with effective Unison shop stewards, so the aim behind this restructuring might well be to weaken this union stronghold. Library reviews and reorganisation inevitably question the fundamental principles of the profession. They throw the whole library service into the melting pot and usually make staff feel very insecure, weakening trade union activity. They provide a wealth of opportunities for further marketisation, commodification and privatisation of libraries – indeed, they help to pave the way for the eventual capitalisation of libraries.

The capitalisation of libraries and library services is a process, a process that deepens over time with libraries becoming sites for capital accumulation and profit making. There are three aspects to this.

First, the other two processes – commercialisation and privatisation – feed off each other such that libraries and library services become increasingly *commodified*. This implies that library services are increasingly ruled by the goal of profit making. Notions of income generation, income streams, marketing, library products, the user as 'customer' or 'consumer' and the market, competition, cost-effectiveness and efficiency become the yardsticks for success. This implies a 'culture change' regarding the ways library staff are encouraged to view what they are about. The capitalisation of libraries implies its *businessification* – the library and library services as businesses, bathed in business values and outlooks.

Second, as the commodification and business takeover of library services increases then library enterprises become traded, bought and sold. The companies running library services can start to figure in stock markets and international capital and this is aided and abetted by the GATS process. This process can be seen more readily in what is happening to schools in contemporary Britain. Some of the companies taking over the running of schools and local education authorities are traded on the stock market. Indeed, as Bernard Regan (2001) pointed out, the average share prices of these 'education businesses' have outperformed the overall level of share prices in the last few years. Thus it can be envisaged that the business takeover of library services may have similar outcomes and effects to what is happening in schools, with profits made from running services at a lower cost than contract price. It might not seem, at the current time, that much money can be made out of libraries. But I am describing the logic of capitalism – the path down which it must inevitably go.

Third, and most fundamentally at the heart of the capitalisation of libraries, is a particular form of *labour*: the value form. When workers work, or labourers labour (in this case library workers), they produce value. Workers have a social relation with this process (the value-creating process) and with value itself (value being the necessary substance for capitalism). However, labour in capitalism becomes exploited, alienated and objectified. This is because only labourers can produce value – value cannot be produced by any other means. For the capitalist, this seems like a 'gift from nature' and the aim is to extract as much value from the labourer as he/she is able to. As Marx said when referring to new or added value, this:

> ... is a gift of Nature ... which is very advantageous to the capitalist. (Marx, 1887: 200)

This value is essential for the perpetuation of capitalism. I am arguing that there are various forms and aspects of value, and this is considered further in Chapter 11 (section 11.7), but I will be exploring this all in more depth in my future works. In essence, the forms of value are *use value* and *exchange value*, and the aspects of value are *added value* and *surplus value*. There is also the concept of value itself. Value, the forms of value and the aspects of value all become embedded in the commodity in capitalism. I consider this in some depth in a dissertation that I have written on *Value theory and value creation through knowledge in the knowledge revolution* (R. Rikowski, 2003h).

What is important to note at this point is that when workers work they produce more value (added value and surplus value) than that represented by their wages (the value of their own labour-power, their capacity to labour). Thus surplus value arises when workers produce more value than that incorporated in their wages: *surplus value*. Profit is a part of this surplus value (other elements leaving the enterprise as tax, rents and so on), and it is this that drives on the managers of capitalised libraries to restructure services continually to maximise profits. It rests on the notions of value, price, profit and competition, and all this takes place within markets. The maximisation of such profits is dependent on the extraction of value from labour. Only labour can create value, so this can only be achieved by the alienation and exploitation of labour. This form of labour, the value form, is antithetical to outmoded and 'traditional' forms of labour resting on notions of public service or the public good. Under the public service ideology, the value that labour creates is not, and cannot be, embedded in the commodity in this way, because there are no such commodities. As I outline in Chapter 4 (section 4.2.6), public goods are not, in essence, commodities, whereas private goods are. Instead, public services provide public goods, and are run on a different set of principles, outside of the marketplace. This is very wasteful, as far as capitalism is concerned. We hear time and time again about public services being wasteful and inefficient. People do not generally understand this, but what they mean here, in essence, is that the value that is being created is not being embedded in the commodity for the enhancement of capitalism, so this value is being 'wasted', as is the labour that produces it. How far removed we are now from notions about caring for the community, fairness and any sense of a decent way of life for the many rather than just the few – principles that are all held to be important within the public service ethos. As Lawson and Leighton say:

> Tradition, community, establishment and vested interests are all swept away in the search for profit ... the struggle between markets and the public domain is ultimately a struggle for our souls, for our vision of what constitutes the 'good life'. (Lawson and Leighton, 2004: 32)

What I am arguing in this book (and this will be expanded on in Chapters 11 and 12) is that through the GATS and TRIPS public services and intellectual property rights are being transformed into international tradable commodities. Thus commodification is the driver, the value that is extracted from labour becomes embedded in the commodity and the surplus value that is created from this then sustains capitalism. Clearly, then, the continued capitalisation of libraries becomes essential while we live under global capitalism.

It should be emphasised that the capitalisation of library labour is typically a drawn-out process, certainly not something that is carried out overnight. This is because it is developed as the other two processes – commercialisation and privatisation – are being nurtured. All this has tremendous implications for restructuring library workers' labour, and the forces and motivations driving it. The labour of library workers changes its mode; it becomes a different form of labour, the value form. The concept of the capitalisation of libraries addresses these momentous changes that are currently taking place before our eyes.

The capitalisation of libraries and the imposition of the value form of labour imply a whole raft of 'softening up' processes. Library workers' labour is reconfigured so that it becomes more flexible, adaptable and adequate to the facilitation of libraries being turned into businesses. Reviews of library services, modernisation programmes and redefinitions of 'professional' duties become apparent necessities. Furthermore, professional values and jobs that appear to stand in the way of the capitalisation of libraries become at risk. This is because the process of turning labour into value-creating labour that is the source of surplus value out of which arises profit is antagonistic to professional principles and attitudes that place 'service' and the needs of library users above all other considerations – including commercial ones. Many library services have witnessed the decimation of their professional staff as the way is being cleared for further capitalisation of library services. In the London Borough of Newham Public Library Service where I worked up to 1995, a Library Review held in the early 1990s had the effect of clearing out swathes of professionally qualified staff (my own post as Training Officer being one of the posts that was eventually abolished). The Local Studies Librarian's post was also abolished and a few years later this man's body was found in the river Thames – though whether there was a link no one ever actually knew for sure, to my knowledge. Yet this is how devastating such reviews can potentially become and helps to illustrate how it is possible for them to impact on people's everyday lives in serious ways. Since then there have been two more reviews in Newham.

These continual reviews also have the effect of making staff feel more insecure so they may be less likely to join trade unions and take industrial action. After the review that I had been involved with, our workforce became fragmented and disjointed, with an increase in casual employment. In Newham, staff were either not replaced at all, or replaced with unqualified staff and/or casual staff or 'sessional workers', as they were called. Such staff are likely to have less loyalty and commitment and are less likely to join trade unions. This process was not unique; many other library services suffered and are suffering a similar fate. Thus, on data compiled by Loughborough University in 1996–7, for example, the number of professional librarians per 10,000 of the population was at 1.1, whereas in 1991–2 it had been 1.3 (British Council, 1999: 1). But the capitalisation of libraries does not just threaten professional posts; it undercuts the service ethos as it reconfigures the prevailing values and goals of library services in terms of value-creation, cost-effectiveness and profit. It changes the whole face of library work as it takes hold and seeps into the everyday operations of library services. Professional principles and the service ethos can act as barriers to the businessification and capitalisation of library services, and those pushing through the business reforms cannot tolerate that. Fundamentally, the profit ethos becomes far more important than the service ethos. The furtherance of global capitalism takes on a new significance, as the commodification and marketisation of all that surrounds us really starts to take a hold.

5.7 The national faces of the GATS in the UK

5.7.1 Introduction

In this section, I will outline some of the mechanisms that are in place that will help to enable the GATS to take effect in public libraries in the UK, i.e. the 'national faces of the GATS'. In this way, I aim to demonstrate the links between the GATS and the commercialisation, privatisation and capitalisation agenda.

As already indicated, I will focus on three main mechanisms that are having a profound effect on the public library service in the UK: Best Value, the Library Standards and the People's Network.

5.7.2 Best Value

Definition of Best Value

Best Value in the UK has been defined and described by Angela Watson in the *Best Returns* report in the following way:

> Best Value is part of a broad package of reforms that affect all aspects of local government. It aims to bring about continuous improvement in local authority services, and to give local people more say in the services they receive. Best Value forms part of the Government's agenda to modernise the way that public services are provided. (Watson, 2001, Section 3 – 'About Best Value': 3)

Thus Best Value is part of the UK government's agenda for public service provision in the UK in general, and is certainly not just confined to libraries. However, it is being implemented very effectively in libraries (as far as those driving the commercialisation and the privatisation agenda forward are concerned).

The 4Cs: Challenge, Compare, Consult and Competition

The four 'Best Value Principles', the '4Cs', are described in Section 5 of the report, 'Best Value Returns'. The 4Cs are:

- *Challenge* why, how and by whom a service is provided.
- *Compare* performance with others, including the private and the voluntary sectors.
- *Consult* with local taxpayers, service users, partners, the business community and the voluntary sector.
- *Competition* – use fair and open competition, wherever possible, to secure efficient and effective services.

The concept of 'Best Value' might sound promising in itself, but even just by glancing at the above definition and the '4Cs' it quickly becomes apparent that all is not as promising as it might initially appear to be. There is no clear reference to what the aims and goals of the public library service should actually be within the Best Value guidelines – not from a philosophical perspective. The International Federation of Library Associations and Institutions (IFLA), in contrast, has a clear view about this. It says that libraries are a public good and that they provide a broad range of information to different sectors of the public. Furthermore, they help to achieve the goals of intellectual freedom and equitable access to information (IFLA, 2001b).

Second, the reference in Best Value to continual improvement is tied up with capitalism. Why do we need to continually seek improvements – the latest brand of this, the latest brand of that? This is because 'innovation' is an essential drive within capitalism: accumulation of capital demands constant reorganisation of production and of social life. This is a dehumanising process. Libby Brooks referred to Paul Robinson's views about the capitalist system in the *Guardian*, emphasising that Robinson views capitalism as:

> ... a dehumanising system that occupies people with clawing back their humanity, leaving them with little time to query the powers that be. (Brooks, 2001: 17)

Referring to Robinson is illuminating because he was a library worker at the University College, London library who was involved in the anti-capitalist protests at Gothenberg, and was subsequently arrested and then imprisoned as a result of this.

Finally, all the '4Cs' expose clearly the main purpose behind Best Value, for example *compare* performance with other sectors, i.e. the private and voluntary sectors; use fair and open *competition* and *consult* with others, e.g. the business community. The 'hidden' – or not-so-hidden – message here with regard to libraries is clear: local authorities in the UK should no longer be free to organise and run their public library services as they see fit and in line with the needs of the people in the local community. Instead, there is a set of supposedly higher priorities – consulting, competing and opening up the service to other possible suppliers, which in the long term will mean consulting and then competing with the private sector. We are fed rhetoric, such as the idea that this is necessary to provide an 'efficient public library service'. However, from a social justice perspective 'efficiency' should not be the main aim within our public libraries: values such as creating a sense of community and belonging should surely override 'efficiency' considerations, as should the service ethos in general.

Best Value and public services

Best Value is one of the clearest and most transparent mechanisms for enabling the GATS to come to fruition in the public library sector in the UK. The Best Value process is being implemented in other public service sectors, but it seems to be particularly virulent in the public library sector. Many people working in public libraries seem to see 'Best Value' as worthwhile on the surface, and would probably be rather surprised that I make critical statements about where Best Value is leading. The concept of Best Value sounds appealing. Best Value sounds like a way of providing an efficient, effective and worthwhile public library service that fulfils the wants and needs of the local community. But this is not really what its purpose is. We must be wary of the use and misuse of words. We witness the UK Prime Minister, Tony Blair, talking about 'modernising' our public services, for example, and bringing about radical change in their delivery. Being 'radical', traditionally, has been associated with many socialist approaches to reorganising society. However, this is not what Tony Blair means when he talks about 'modernising' our public services and bringing about radical change. Far from it – what he means is introducing elements of competition and privatisation!

Best Value and public libraries

Introduction

So what is the main purpose behind Best Value for libraries? In essence, Best Value is a mechanism for enabling the public library service in the UK to be opened up to different suppliers, rather than library provision just residing within the orbit of local authorities, thereby creating a market environment. As Angela Watson noted in *Best Returns*:

> At present, there may be few or no serious alternative suppliers of library functions. Some authorities appear to see this as a reason for not addressing competition. But library authorities will need to demonstrate that they have seriously considered new approaches and alternative ways of delivering services. As one of the case study authorities remarked; 'you just can't say there isn't anybody else out there'. Under Best Value retaining library services in-house can only be justified where the authority demonstrates that there really are no other more efficient and effective ways of delivering the quality of service required. Library authorities should explore potential future providers and take steps to encourage them – to create a climate for competition that will enable the market to develop. (Watson, section 5, para. 5.1)

Thus here it appears that local authority library services are being instructed and guided to bring about their own demise. For Watson, local authorities should consider alternative suppliers 'in good spirit' and with a good will. The strategy for the marketisation and privatisation of public libraries and the role of Best Value in this enterprise is so clearly outlined by Watson that little further comment is required. The intention behind Best Value is to create competition and a market environment that will thereby facilitate the corporate takeover of public libraries in line with the GATS agenda. Obviously, the process will take time, and there could be backlashes – from either public library workers or library users, or both, that will slow or terminate the strategy. Furthermore, some library services may try to subvert Best Value for truly community centred and social justice goals, either intentionally or unintentionally. They might not play the Best Value game in the correct competitive spirit. I feel sure that many local authorities, when implementing Best Value for their library services, have been and will be implementing it in ways that they believe is to the ultimate benefit of the local population.

Furthermore, some will think that this is what Best Value is about any-way, rather than for creating a marketisation agenda. The main purpose of Best Value is not made very obvious. Locating the Watson quotes in the *Best Returns* document that clarified the main purpose behind Best Value was not easy – they were hidden within a weighty document. Thus such people are innocently assuming that the purpose of Best Value has admirable aims and objectives. They may drive, and some have driven, through progressive programmes and innovations that will indeed have such outcomes. This must be frustrating to those with a marketising agenda for public libraries. It slows down the process and strategy as outlined by Watson, costs money and 'wastes time'. As it was reported in the *Library Association Record* in October 2001:

> The essence of Best Value has not been grasped by many library authorities ... (*LA Record*, 2001g: 594)

Best Value and North East Lincolnshire Public Libraries

We only have to look at the North East Lincolnshire Best Value Inspection to find a clear example of a local authority trying to make the best of Best Value. At the very beginning of this document, in the *Summary and Recommendations* section (Audit Commission, 2000, Section 1, point 7: 5), it was noted that:

> ... we find that the Council recognises the need to move forward, but has yet to make key decisions on the future direction of the service. As a result, the Best Value Review is not driving fundamen-tal change. The absence of key corporate policies also hinders improvement. On this basis we judge that the service will not improve in the way required by Best Value unless action is taken along lines recommended in this report.

The real 'fundamental change' required of North East Lincolnshire was to move rapidly towards market solutions for its public library services. The Best Value Inspectors saw insufficient evidence of this. As was reported in the Library Association Record (2001c):

> N.E. Lincs gets just one star, for 'fairly'. Partly this is bad luck, as the council's BV review of libraries was the first it had done for any

service. It had much to learn. Also, lack of 'key corporate policies' and cross-sectoral thinking at council level makes it hard for libraries to plan well ... [the inspectors said] ... the service should be seeking 'step change', not incremental improvements. (*LA Record*, 2001c: 134)

If there is any doubt about the underlying purpose of Best Value in North East Lincolnshire we only need to look at the recommendations on the very next page (ibid.: 6). The recommendations do not focus primarily on providing a better service for the local community but highlight other issues (Audit Commission, 2000).

There are four main recommendations (covered in Point 9 of the *Recommendations* section). Point 9 does refer to improving the public library service, but within the context of providing better *value for money* – and this is the key, and most seductive point. To attain value for money, it is recommended that the council should promote joined-up working across departments and 'accelerate the development and implementation of key corporate policies' to deliver enhanced customer services. However, Point 9 also stresses that this must take place within the context of a revised Best Value Improvement Plan aimed at achieving 'greater value for money'. The speed of change should be greater and the Best Value Improvement Plan should include 'costed options for service points' – making for alternative scenarios in service delivery. From here, the recommendations in Point 9 go on to emphasise inter-agency and cross-departmental working to maximise use of premises, to improve locations (of libraries) and opening hours to increase service take-up, and to improve access to ICT (information and computer technology) and lifelong learning opportunities. On these issues, library professionals could readily concur. However, Point 9 ends with a recommendation that all of this must take place through the evaluation of each service using the 'principles of performance management' constituted by the Audit Commission. Thus we are driven back into the labyrinth of Best Value, value for money and the marketisation of public library services with the spectre of privatisation haunting the whole process. Those wishing to develop library services based on social justice, inclusion and social equality have to negotiate a Best Value process that incorporates another world for public library services. This is a world where value for money, costed options, competition and markets facilitating the corporate takeover of public libraries provide the centre of gravity. In North East Lincolnshire, the library service did not seem to be playing the Best Value tune with the requisite enthusiasm and vigour.

In response, Lincolnshire (as a whole) has wanted to reinvent itself as a modernising and innovative environment for libraries. In McInroy and Coult (2001), some of the problems Lincolnshire faces were highlighted. It is the fourth largest rural county in England, which has resulted in a poor transport infrastructure with pockets of rural deprivation and substantial numbers of people socially excluded. Furthermore, Lincolnshire as a whole lagged behind in the implementation of telecommunications technology. Rob McInroy, the then operations manager for library support services in Lincolnshire County Council, and now the Development Manager, expressed enthusiasm about improving the IT and telecommunications infrastructure. He said:

> Public libraries now have the highest profile that they have had during my professional life. It's great to see, and it's great that the Prime Minister is in a library giving a speech about the importance of libraries ... In Lincolnshire we are now seen by the Council as key to e-government, and giving access to our network of public access PCs. (McInroy, in McInroy and Coult, 2001: 47)

McInroy then refers in some detail to the implementation of the People's Network (p. 48) and some of the funding problems they have had. The point to emphasise here is that the People's Network is another mechanism for enabling the GATS to take effect within the context of the public library service in the UK. North East Lincolnshire has not been so successful to date in the implementation of Best Value as GATS facilitator. Perhaps, though, they can remedy this to some extent by focusing on the People's Network. Lincolnshire is in a very disadvantageous position regarding IT and telecommunications. If they could be seen to be surpassing other local authorities that do not have such disadvantages on the implementation of the People's Network and other IT strategies then this would be a considerable achievement for them in relation to official priorities.

In essence, it seems that Lincolnshire has been endeavouring to provide a public library service to meet the wants and needs of the people in the local community, and that it has been placing the public service ethos above efficiency and target considerations. Thus it has not really been adopting mechanisms such as Best Value in the right spirit as far as those seeking to drive capitalism forward are concerned.

Best Value and the London Borough of Hounslow Public Library Service

There are other local authorities where Best Value Inspectors praise public library services for developing according to marketisation and privatisation agendas with greater effectiveness, clarity and enthusiasm (e.g. in Hounslow – see Audit Commission, 2001). In the London Borough of Hounslow the management of the libraries was being undertaken by a trust, the Community Initiative Partnership (CIP), which was a not-for-profit distributory organisation that had been set up by the council for a ten-year period which started in May 1998. Hounslow was the first public library authority to transfer the management of its public library service to a trust in this way. The CIP was formed with the purpose of being a leisure and cultural regeneration agency, but the inclusion of 11 public libraries with their related services came as something of a surprise to many and added a new dimension to the CIP (Allen, 2001: 754).

The CIP was managing statutory services and a variety of services – not just libraries. These included museums, tourism, leisure centres and open spaces. Thus the local authority was starting to lose some control of its public libraries. Since the launch of the CIP the council in Hounslow was able to reduce its revenue budget support by over £2.5 million. There was also recognition in Hounslow of the need to further exploit different income generation opportunities and to improve the marketing of their services. It is also interesting to note that the CIP advertised posts in the *Library Association Appointments* supplement of 4 January 2002, using words such as 'business planning process' and 'performance targets' in the advertisements (*LA Record*, 2002).

There was particular interest in Hounslow, as it was something of a testing ground, to see how well a 'trust model' could perform under Best Value. As Allen said:

> What makes this assessment, and the report of the inspection, of such interest is that it represents the first full, independent examination of the trust management model for libraries, and of the impact that model has had on the service review and on the management of the service. Perhaps, most importantly, it also discusses why the service is expected to improve under that model. (Allen, 2001: 754)

Hounslow performed favourably under Best Value and as Allen noted:

> ... this inspection confirms that the trust works for Hounslow's libraries, and Best Value challenges every authority to evaluate this model as part of their review process. (Allen, 2001: 755)

Thus, in essence, authorities such as the London Borough of Hounslow are leaders and beacons in the movement towards a library environment dominated by markets and the law of money.

Concluding comments

It is important for those officials driving Best Value that the purposes and values informing the process are not made too explicit, otherwise professionals and other library workers in the public library services might question their engagement in instituting the Best Value regime. The willingness and cooperation of library workers is important (see Resource, 2001a – a consultation paper on Best Value). Official obfuscation about the aims and purposes of Best Value is necessary so that it can function effectively as one of the 'national faces of the GATS'. On the other hand, given that there is such a smokescreen regarding the real nature and purposes of Best Value many might be innocent of what the real game and real stakes are. The UK Library Association (as it was then called – now renamed the Chartered Institute of Library and Information Professionals), as a body, might itself be one such example of this. In *Best Returns* (Watson, 2001), under section 2 (Introduction: 1), Angela Watson writes:

> The Library Association has a role in supporting library authorities to prepare for Best Value and in clarifying how Best Value links with recent developments in the public library sector. (Watson, 2001)

Furthermore, as was noted in a news item in the *Library Association Record*, the then monthly professional journal of the UK Library Association, now renamed *Library and Information Update* (*LA Record*, 2000d), the LA itself has produced a 42-page guidance booklet for local authorities. This is entitled *Best Value Guidance for Library Authorities in England*, and in the document the LA notes that 'BV requires a fundamental cultural shift'. In the same news item (*LA*

Record, 2000d: 489) readers are alerted to a more critical perspective on Best Value. It refers to a booklet entitled *Best Value – a critical guide to Best Value, the government's new regime for local authority services* published by the Centre for Democratic Policy Making. In referring to Best Value, the booklet says:

> Its political importance is too often disguised. Too many authorities treat it as a technical issue to be left to officials to sort out ... the danger is that the prime purpose of BV – efficiency, economy and effectiveness – remains exactly the same as the commercially driven objectives set nearly 20 years ago under the Tories. (Cited in *LA Record*, 2000d: 489)

The overall implications of Best Value and its place in relation to the global trade agenda set by the WTO and the GATS need to be at the heart of an appreciation of its true significance. Because of the official requirement to mask these issues, it is quite easy to view Best Value as a technicist, neutral mechanism, or even as an innovation that can be a vehicle for addressing community needs. However, the undercover face of Best Value – as GATS facilitator and enabler in the public library sector – needs to be seen to ascertain its nature. Its purpose is to encourage alternative suppliers to move into our public libraries. The neoliberal project kick-started in the Thatcher/Reagan era has been pushed forward by the WTO/GATS in the international trade arena. This pinpoints the real significance of the intrusion of the Best Value regime into public library services in the UK. The UK New Labour government (less so the Labour Party) is an enthusiastic supporter of this project, but needs all the friends it can get to push this through with sufficient speed, depth and effectiveness for the interests of British capital.

5.7.3 *The Library Standards*

The Library Standards that have been established in the UK need to be approached with extreme caution. Who can argue, theoretically, with the idea of 'library standards'? It sounds very good – to ensure that our libraries are maintained to certain standards. However, if we examine the standards in more detail a different picture emerges, and it becomes clear, once again, that standards are being established that actually fall in line with the GATS. The UK CILIP itself says that Best Value and the mandatory standards for public libraries must have a 'clear' relationship and must 'both inform each other and complement each other' (*LA Record*, 2000a: 7) (even though this might be unbeknown to some of those that have written the Library Standards document – let us be charitable!). Similarly, in *the Library Association Record* (now renamed *Library and Information Update*) of June 2000 it was reported that:

> Best Value Performance Indicators must also be adhered to, and the Best Value inspectorate will 'draw on the standards'. (*LA Record*, 2000b: 303)

In the *LA Record*, August 2000, it describes how there are areas of standards in three sectors, and that one of these areas is Best Value, thereby illustrating how the two areas are intertwined (*LA Record*, 2000c).

The *LA Record* of March 2001 (2001b) reported the fact that the full standards were published in February 2001 (see also Lashmer and Oliver, 2000; and see Department for Culture, Media and Sport, 2000a for further information about the Library Standards). The *LA Record* (2001b) noted that there were 19 standards in the final document, although there had been 24 standards in the draft. The central aim expressed in the standards was that all libraries should try to match the performance of the top 25 per cent, and they had three years in which to achieve this. No reference was made to the inherent contradiction in this statement – that there can only ever be 25 per cent in the top 25 per cent! If two new authorities move up into the top 25 per cent, then logic dictates that two others must move out of the top 25 per cent. So be it. What is more concerning is what the standards include and, even more significantly, what they do *not* include. There was a standard for numbers of qualified staff in the draft (25 per cent or 29 per cent), but this was removed in the final document. Following on from this, services only had to show in their Annual Library Plans that they are employing 'appropriate' numbers of qualified staff. In this *LA Record* news item it says that:

> Some will also worry that 'information management' and ICT are the only qualifications specified. But at least the LA is to commission research to define 'appropriate'. (*LA Record*, 2001b: 131)

Hence it seems that we are left to play with the word 'appropriate', as we were left to play with the word 'interpretation' with regard to the meaning of 'services' when applied to the GATS (R. Rikowski, 2001, 2002a, 2002b). (The meaning of 'services' with regard to the GATS is considered in Chapter 3, section 3.4.3 of this book.) To any professional librarian this would surely seem bizarre: whatever reason can there be for removing professional standards from the document? The situation becomes clearer, though, when we refer back to the GATS document, where it becomes evident that professional standards can be seen to be a barrier to trade. This topic is addressed under Article 7 of the GATS on 'Recognition' under the 'General Obligations and Disciplines' section. In Article 7(V) it says:

> Wherever appropriate, recognition should be based on multilaterally agreed criteria. In appropriate cases Members shall work in co-operation with relevant inter-governmental and non-governmental organisations towards the establishment and adoption of common international standards and criteria for recognition and common international standards for the practice of relevant service trades and professions. (WTO, 1994)

Note that it refers to members of the WTO setting up 'standards', but does not indicate which members will be involved. Professional bodies are not mentioned here at all, but presumably large corporations will be heavily involved. Even assuming that professional library bodies are involved, though, they will not have the same amount of power and say over library qualifications and standards that they currently have, as they will have to be sharing this power with other WTO members and with other inter-governmental and non-governmental organisations. Where no such international standards exist then existing qualifications could be deemed to be a 'barrier to trade' if corporations are denied access to libraries on qualification grounds. Fiona Hunt (2001a) also made this point. If a foreign supplier took over one of our public library services, for example, and brought staff with them from their own country, these staff might not have the requisite British Library qualifications (or their equivalent). Not allowing such staff to work in this particular public library service could be interpreted as a 'barrier to trade'.

As was pointed out in the *LA Record*, even heads of libraries are concerned about this. It says:

> The word is that library chiefs are most concerned by the standard on numbers of professional staff. (*LA Record*, 2000c: 426)

Furthermore, the British Council (1999: 1) highlights the fact that the number of professional librarians is decreasing.

Other omissions in the standards (as explained in *LA Record*, 2001b) are also illuminating. There was no standard on *spending* for stock (although it did specify the number of items to be purchased). Defining the *quality* of stock was deferred pending further work (the Audit Commission was to come up with some 'quality measures'). There was no standard for *floor space* (although there had been one in the draft) and there were no ICT standards specifically, except for ICT qualifications for library staff.

However, the four points above can be linked to the drive towards the commercialisation, privatisation and capitalisation of libraries. There is likely to be a growing trend towards paying for information provision in libraries through micropayments, as I have already described. Hence there was probably no apparent need to be greatly concerned about the quantity or quality of stock, or floor space, as the aim is to get more people to use the Internet, and so there were no clear commitments to the traditional book stock or shelf space. The lack of commitment to floor space can be explained by the fact that there is uncertainty about how many people will want to use computers, and how much space this is likely to take up in comparison with book shelf space. Also, there is uncertainty about if and how gaining access to the Internet will be paid for. The government wants more people to use computers, but will people (or at least enough people) respond? It is an uncertain future in this respect. So, for the time being, these standards were removed.

It also needs to be emphasised that the standards issue is an ongoing and flexible one. In 2004 the Department for Culture, Media and Sport (DCMS) issued consultation papers to the English library authorities and other stakeholders on proposed new Public Library Standards. These standards were prepared with the Advisory Council on Libraries. The standards are similar to the original version, but with some modifications. The DCMS plans to supplement the proposed service standards with impact measures, showing the contribution that library authorities make to the community. So once again, we come back to the notion of yardsticks and measurements (Advisory Council on Libraries, 2004).

In conclusion, the standards no longer appear to be such worthwhile aims. We must approach all such schemes with a clear head. The 'bread and butter' of any worthwhile public library standards would surely be standards for stock and staff, and yet these areas have not been adequately considered at all. This is because many of the aims of the standards are not as we would be led to believe, I would suggest. Instead, 'standards' are another mechanism, another facilitator, to help enable the GATS to take effect – the standards are another 'national face of the GATS'. Or to put it more bluntly, the Library Standards are another means for extending and intensifying global capitalism. The Library Standards might be made to appear pleasant, inclusive and attractive in various ways, but this is because there is a need to keep library workers on board and working with them. But we must not fooled by the fact that the hidden (or perhaps not always so hidden) agenda is the extension of global capitalism. The Library Standards can aid and abet this process, and when this is coupled with the GATS as well, it starts to become a very powerful force indeed.

5.7.4 The People's Network

What is the People's Network?

The People's Network is a government initiative to install computers throughout public libraries in the UK for the public to use. However, the People's Network is also another mechanism to enable the GATS to take effect in these libraries. Many people may be shocked that I should make such claims here, as many think that the People's Network is wonderful, enabling the poor and disadvantaged to have access to computers the same as the rest of the population. We hear much talk about the digital divide. With the digital divide those who do not have a computer at home, or do not have access to a computer and the Internet in some other way, and so do not have access to the information that is available from the computer, will be disadvantaged (see, for example, Shimmon, 2001). So, does not the People's Network solve this problem? Sadly not. Even the term itself, the 'People's Network', sounds as though it is 'for the people', for the 'ordinary people'. It is very enticing, it is almost a rallying cry – in fact, it almost sounds radical. Yet this is really far from the case.

The People's Network is being driven forward at a tremendous pace. The aim was to ensure that PCs were put into most public libraries in the UK, and that most public libraries were online by the end of 2002 (which coincidentally was in line with the original GATS timetable, as previously explained). As Benjamin said in the *Guardian* in June 2001:

The government has stated an intention to ensure that at least 75% of public libraries are online by the end of 2002, when the National Grid for Learning and the University of Industry go live. Several government funding channels have been created to get libraries wired up, including a £200m programme under the National Lottery New Opportunities Fund. (Benjamin, 2001: 4)

The financing of the People's Network

How is the People's Network being financed? There are over 4,000 public libraries altogether in the UK, and the aim was to connect all of them to the 'information superhighway', through the People's Network. There were three funding programmes for the People's Network under the New Opportunities Fund: £20 million was to be allocated to the *training* of all library staff in the use of ICT, £50 million was being allocated for *content creation* which public libraries could bid for and £200 million was allocated for the creation of the *lifelong learning centres and grids* (People's Network, 2000). Furthermore, the UK DCMS gave a £9 million cash boost that was to be spread over three years (starting in December 2000) to get UK libraries online by 2002 (DCMS, 2000b). (See also NOF, 2001 for more information about the New Opportunities Fund.)

Funding has also come from various other sources. It is particularly interesting to note that Bill Gates himself gave some money to the People's Network. Resource announced on 20 July 2001 that both Resource (the Council for Museums, Archives and Libraries) and the Bill and Melinda Gates Foundation have given £2.6 million to UK public libraries for the creation of ICT learning centres in deprived areas. This meant that each library would be able to install an extra 2–12 terminals, thereby ensuring that there were ICT learning centres in all 4,300 public libraries. The People's Network project can be seen to be a partnership between Resource and the New Opportunities Fund, but the money given by Bill Gates was an additional bonus. As the then UK Libraries Minister, Tessa Blackstone, said about Bill Gates's contribution:

> I warmly welcome this generous award from the Foundation, which comes as a most useful addition to existing Lottery-funded support for ICT in libraries. This funding will ensure that Internet access is available through our libraries, to everyone, right across the country. (Blackstone, in Resource, 2001c)

Many rejoice at the apparently 'free' money that is being poured into the People's Network. Stephen Dunmore, the Chief Executive of the New Opportunities Fund, in 2001 praised the People's Network, saying how popular it was, how it gave so many different people the opportunity to use computers, and how '... it is an important part of the nation's lifelong learning strategy' (Resource, 2001e).

Similarly, Dunmore also said that:

> The transformation of local libraries nationwide into high-tech learning centres with suites of computers is one of the best kept secrets. Local communities need to know that lifelong learning will be free to users at local library branches being equipped with information and communications technology. (Resource, 2001e)

Meanwhile, Resource spoke about the joys of free Internet access and noted that:

> Free access to the Internet is fast becoming a key service at local libraries in the UK as the People's Network is set up. Overall, £100 million of National Lottery money from the New Opportunities Fund is equipping local libraries with state-of-the-art computer technology to enable everyone in the community to hook up to the Internet free. (Resource, 2001e)

Thus a considerable amount of finance has been poured into the People's Network in various ways.

The People's Network in libraries

The People's Network sounds like such a great opportunity. Not only does it offer help to the disadvantaged, but also it (apparently) provides libraries with a real opportunity to move forward into the twenty-first century and to be at the forefront of what is happening. Now this is tempting bait for libraries, as they are too often seen to be a backwater, the 'forgotten sector', the sector that gets 'left behind'. They are too often perceived as 'Cinderellas', while other departments and other experts seemingly take the glory and the credit. Chris Batt, the Chief Executive at Resource, had primary responsibility for implementing the People's Network. They had £120 million altogether, to connect all the UK public libraries to the Internet, to give them new technology and train the staff. Batt spoke enthusiastically about the need for the public library service to move forward and the great opportunity that the People's Network can provide in this regard. As he said in the *Library Association Record*, in October 2001:

> The successful roll-out of the People's Network is crucial to the future status and role of the UK public library service. But it is only part of a jigsaw and the picture is now only vaguely visible to us. One thing is certain: we will see the landscape more clearly, and sooner, if we explore it together rather than apart. So get networking! (Batt, 2001: 584)

Batt is very enthusiastic; yet there is a hidden message even here. The picture is only 'vaguely visible', notes Batt. But it is not a picture that many wish to see! Batt's enthusiasm is boundless. He says that it will give public libraries the opportunity to develop within the emerging Information Society (Batt, in Simmons, 2000: 328). He says that over the next three years the Network would be viewed as:

> ... a window on the world of information, bringing together a wide range of public service information. (Batt, in Simmons, 2000: 26)

In some authorities such as Leeds (*LA Record*, 2001e), the People's Network has been connected to schools and other learning organisations, as well as to the libraries themselves. Children are then able, for example, to log on to their school site in the library. Batt also sees a role for the People's Network in providing education and lifelong learning. He argues that:

> If we develop the access routes, the incentive will be in place for colleges and commercial organisations. Using public networks, they know that people can follow a course moderated through the library, with one of the country's largest captive audiences. Users will only exchange money (or have their learning account debited) when they actually start a course. (Batt, in Simmons, 2000: 27)

Batt also spoke to Simmons about the People's Network in the *Times Higher Education Supplement*. This demonstrates how important he thinks the impact of the People's Network will be on education, as well as on libraries, seeing it as a 'network of information, not a network of libraries' (Simmons, 1999: 15). However, we should exercise some caution, I would suggest, when considering how worthwhile the notion of the People's Network in itself is anyway. We must not be fooled into the idea that computers will solve everything. They still need to be used sensibly and discerningly. If they are not used in this way, then people might start to lose their ability to think critically and creatively. If they are used sensibly, though, they are obviously a great asset.

Meanwhile, Frank Webster also refers to the People's Network. He points out the fact that the UK New Labour government went ahead with the People's Network project, although the original report was commissioned by John Major, who was the UK Prime Minister for the Conservative government from 1990 to 1997. Furthermore, New Labour promised additional resources should libraries enter wholeheartedly into the network era. In this way, public libraries could be enticed to play a central role in lifelong learning, Webster suggests. He emphasised that:

> Not surprisingly, many a librarian has been tempted by this offering. After years of being attacked, it is understandable that the profession seizes the embrace of those who express some affection. (Webster, 1999b: 4)

And so, librarians have indeed been tempted. However, we must not be fooled by the rhetoric surrounding the People's Network. The hidden agenda (GATS implementation and the extension of global capitalism) cannot really be developed unless librarians happily take the People's Network project on board. The People's Network needs to be set in place and this can only be done by librarians and library workers in local authorities undertaking the work. The private sector will only want to move in when it can make money. Workers in the public sector need to work hard to make this happen – they need to work hard to help to bring about their own demise, as was also described under Best Value. Thus they are just pawns in a bigger game. The solution is not to take on someone else's agenda (by which we are dispensable), but to establish our own agenda for the future of our library service. As I have indicated in previous articles, library and information workers need to be more proactive (R. Rikowski, 2000a, 2000c).

However, it sounds so enticing. Many seem to be persuaded by the rhetoric. Take Rob McInroy, for example, the then Operations Manager for Library Support Services for Lincolnshire County Council. McInroy has spoken very enthusiastically about the implementation of the People's Network (although he also recognises that there are some problems). He said:

> Nationally, £200 million of capital resources has been committed to investment in the People's Network. However, we have to make sure that this funding continues. In a year's time, the NOF funding dries up. This will be a major challenge for libraries. That's why it is important that libraries play a central role in the egovernment debate. (McInroy, in McInroy and Coult, 2001: 48)

It is interesting to note McInroy's awareness that the funding will dry up and the concern he shows about what will happen then.

McInroy goes on to say that Lincolnshire had a lot of difficulty in attracting funding for the People's Network. This was due in part to the fact that Lincolnshire is a large rural area with a low-density population, and with no efficient transport infrastructure or modern telecommunications technology in place. However, once money was provided from both the New Opportunities Fund and Lincolnshire Council they were able to set up the Network. They have also started other initiatives such as a Rural Academy in South Lincolnshire, which is a way for schools to share resources, i.e. the Community Grid for Learning (CGFL) and Linnet, the Lincolnshire Community Information Network. In conclusion, McInroy says:

> We don't want to turn people away from the library. We give people access to computers, even just for chatting, otherwise they will go to EasyEverything. It is a way of getting people into the library, and once they are there, we can show them what else we do. In all, it's a very exciting time to be working in public libraries. It's a chance to be in the forefront. We won't get the opportunity again, so we must grasp it now. (McInroy, in McInroy and Coult, 2001: 51)

So there we have it: a wonderful opportunity, and a chance to be at the forefront. But at the forefront of what exactly?

The People's Network – another mechanism to help to bring in the GATS

Let us explore my basic argument further – that the People's Network will help to bring in the GATS. Why am I arguing this? There was a need for the People's Network to be set up by the end of year 2002, to fit in with the GATS timetable (although as I have already stated, this original timetable has now changed). This is one of the main reasons why there was such an apparent urgency to get all the libraries online by then, I would suggest. But once the money has run out, what then? It costs money to support, maintain and upgrade computer systems, and local authorities running public libraries are not likely to be able to afford to maintain and upgrade their networks. It is likely to be far more costly than buying books! So where will this money come from? It can be predicted that this will be achieved by opening up the public library service to other possible suppliers (such as private companies injecting money as an investment into the projects) as is outlined in Best Value. Indeed, Best Value stipulates that this *must* be done – it is not an option. As Angela Watson says in the *Best Returns* report, the government:

> ... is looking for variety in the ways services are delivered, and a mix of service providers from the public, private and voluntary sectors. (Watson, 2001: 8)

Furthermore:

> Library authorities should also explore potential future providers and take steps to encourage them to create a climate for competition that will enable the market to develop. (Watson, 2001: 9)

A news item in the *Library Association Record* also hinted that this is the direction in which the People's Network is likely to go. It said:

> One of this year's jobs is to 'plan the long-term sustainability of the People's Network after the NOF funding ends and extend the network to museums and archives'. In 2002 Resource will examine models for funding arrangements, including partnerships and sponsorship, and ensure that the sector is fully informed of the relative merits of different models ... (*LA Record*, 2001d: 389)

So, there we have it. It is almost an order – that the People's Network *must* be funded, in the future, by private companies in a variety of ways. Coupled with this will be the need to charge for information. This will fall neatly into place with micropayments. Libraries start to provide much of their information through the Internet (through the People's Network) rather than traditional books. Micropayments are then set up for transactions on the Internet. Libraries cannot be excluded from the implementation of micropayments (this could be seen to constitute a bar-rier to trade according to the GATS – as described above, in section 5.4.4 on micropayments). Thus libraries begin to charge for information. We have come full circle. The aims are to make money, create markets and privatise services.

It should also be noted here, though, that I am not suggesting that we should not have computers in libraries or that they are not worthwhile sources of information. Computers have opened up a whole new world of possibilities. But I am just emphasising the fact that we need to look at the bigger picture when we consider the way in which computers are being installed in public libraries in the UK through the People's Network.

It is quite possible that some of my predictions will not come to pass. I am probably making it all sound too neat and tidy and carefully planned, when I am, in fact, fully aware that the capitalist system is not actually planned in any neat and coherent way. However, this does not lessen the strength of my argument. In a sense, this shows that corporations may be wary about what critics like myself stand for and what we are saying, so they decide to back down (for a while) and take a softly-softly approach. However, the wishes of corporations will rear their ugly heads again if this happens, but in a different guise (witness the Multilateral Agreement on Investment that failed but is now in evidence again in WTO agreements). Also, there might be practical problems that prevent corporations from achieving their aims. There is also the need to retain the active cooperation of library workers in order for these plans to take full effect.

Furthermore, staff may not always be willing to go down this path. Witness the North East Lincolnshire Best Value report, for example, where many of the staff appeared to hold different aims and to be working towards a different agenda to those implicit in Best Value. Furthermore, I am not suggesting that all these scenarios will definitely come to pass; instead I am just describing and illustrating the trend and the way in which the situation is developing. The people at the forefront of these changes spell it out for us, loud and clear, as I have illustrated many times. There is little in the rhetoric about providing a public library service that fulfils the wants and needs of the local population, or about enabling and enhancing human expression, or about the public service ethos. Where such sentiments are expressed, they are clouded by and embraced within other terminology such as the need to be 'competitive' and 'efficient', thus the terminology is used as a means to keep certain people (the cynics, the critics, the 'do-gooders', etc.) on board or marginalised. But let us face up to the reality of the situation.

5.7.5 Summary

In summary, I have highlighted three mechanisms that are currently in place in the UK which can all be seen to be 'national faces of the GATS'. This is because they will pave the way to make it easier to implement the GATS in public libraries in the UK. These are Best Value, the Library Standards and the People's Network. With regard to Best Value, libraries have to demonstrate that they are providing 'Best Value' (in line with concepts such as efficiency and performance targets), while at the same time endeavouring to think of other possible suppliers that could move into libraries. Thus those running state-funded public libraries are, in essence, being asked to think about ways to bring about their own demise, and to encourage the private sector to move into and take over the running of state-funded libraries.

Second, the Library Standards are being put into place, but on a more careful inspection it becomes clear that the standards are not in the end being introduced as a means to help to provide a better library service for the wants and needs of the local community. Instead, they will help to pave the way for a commercialisation agenda, and for the GATS itself, particularly with regard to areas such as qualification standards.

Third, the People's Network has been introduced at a rapid pace, and seems to offer many benefits to ordinary people. While it is good that the public now have access to computers, the People's Network will help to bring in the GATS, as those running the Network in libraries seek alternative forms of funding to upgrade and maintain the Network. This will inevitably involve them turning to the private sector.

5.8 Conclusions

I hope that by now I have been able to convince the reader of the power and reality of the commercialisation, privatisation and capitalisation agenda that is taking place in state-funded libraries in the UK, particularly in the public library sector, and also how this process is being made much easier to implement by the mechanisms/facilitators that are in place, i.e. 'the national faces of the GATS'. This chapter has sought to demonstrate how the GATS is 'coming home' to state-funded libraries in the UK.

As Webster says, with regard to the general trend which has continued since Tony Blair became the UK prime minister:

> ... the neo-liberal consensus has remained firmly in place, cuts in book budgets have continued, and the wider informational domain – publishing, broadcasting, electronic services etc. – has gone on being marketised wherever possible and developed by private corporations firmly along commercial lines. (Webster, 1999a: 2)

Furthermore:

> ... the commercialisation of just about everything and the rhetoric that technology is the master key to change – leads me to be cautious and conservative when it comes to libraries. I worry that the 'information grid' may lead to libraries being by-passed, to librarians being displaced, and to information being charged at a metered rate as an individual rather than a public good. The result of that, I believe, will be an information-saturated and simultaneously ignorant public. (Webster, 1999a: 3)

We therefore need to be very aware of the neoliberal juggernaut that is gathering pace before our eyes.

In this chapter I have also provided a framework that other countries can use to explore and demonstrate how the GATS is 'coming home' to the state-funded libraries in their own countries. Indeed, it is a framework that can be used by all public services when considering the implications of the GATS. With such powerful material at our disposal it will make the task of those who want to implement these capitalist-led policies that much more difficult. Thus I suggest that others take this framework on board and explore the commercialisation, privatisation and capitalisation that is taking place in public services in their own countries, and the mechanisms that are in place that are helping all this to take effect. As a librarian/information professional I would obviously be particularly keen to see this happen within library services in other countries. However, it is also extremely important that this exercise is undertaken in a wide range of other public service sectors, such as education, health and social services within different countries, if meaningful progress is to be made with regard to slowing down the pace of the GATS juggernaut on a global basis. The following chapter will now consider a number of statements and positions which various library and library-related bodies have taken with regard to the GATS.

Note

This material was originally published in an article of mine entitled 'The corporate takeover of libraries', in *Information for Social Change* (2002a). Various revisions and additions have been included in this chapter.

Positions taken by various library and cultural bodies on the GATS

6.1 Introduction

This chapter will consider the statements and positions on the GATS from a variety of international library associations and library, information and cultural bodies. First, it will consider the position of the International Federation of Library Associations and Institutions. This represents the collective voice of various library associations and library interests internationally. It will then consider the position taken by other library associations and other library, information and cultural bodies internationally. It should be noted, though, that these very much represent the voice of organisations from the developed world, but the developing world is considered in some depth in Part 3 of the book covering the TRIPS (Trade-Related Aspects of Intellectual Property Rights) Agreement.

6.2 International Federation of Library Associations and Institutions

6.2.1 Overview

First of all, I will consider the position of the International Federation of Library Associations and Institutions (IFLA). This is because of the high regard, status and importance that IFLA holds within the international library and information community. There is, surely, no more powerful international library voice. IFLA is the body that represents library associations and library interests from many different countries on the international stage. It sees itself as being an 'active international alliance of library and information associations, libraries and information services, and concerned individuals' (IFLA, 2001a). IFLA is very concerned about the WTO and the GATS programme and the effect that it is likely to have on libraries and information, although, as already stated, it was actually the BCLA that first raised the issue.

6.2.2 IFLA's position on the WTO and the GATS

IFLA makes its position on the WTO very clear on its website. It also states what it regards as being the main purpose of libraries, emphasising that 'libraries are a public good'. Furthermore, it states that libraries provide a range of information to different sectors of the population, irrespective of age, religion, race and gender, and it says that:

> The well-being of libraries is essential in ensuring access to the full range of human expression and providing individuals with skills necessary to access and use this content. (IFLA, 2001b: 1, point 3)

The value of libraries is emphasised strongly here. This statement has many similarities to what most librarians consider the main purpose of libraries to be, I am sure. However, IFLA could be accused of being 'romantic', but it is surely better to have rather utopian hopes than no hope at all! IFLA speaks for various library workers and organisations throughout the world, and I feel sure that most library and information workers and professionals and library and information bodies would agree with these sentiments.

From this powerful statement, IFLA then voices its concern about the WTO agenda, saying that:

> There is growing evidence that WTO decisions, directly or indirectly, may adversely affect the operations and future development of library services, especially in not-for-profit institutions. (IFLA, 2001b: 1, point 4)

A little later in the document it refers to the GATS, noting that it could open up all aspects of a national economy to competition, and that this includes public services such as libraries. Furthermore, various corporations could compete against public services and claim National

Treatment, whereby they receive the same level of subsidy from the government as public sector agencies do. IFLA says that with an increase in profit-focused online content providers, the potential for GATS challenges to library services is increasing and that:

> While the concept of allowing 'competition' appears benign, the eventual outcome of such challenges will be the undermining of the tax-supported status of public sector libraries at the national, regional and local levels. Without tax support, the library's role as a democratic institution, making available the widest range of material reflecting the diversity of society, will be compromised. (IFLA, 2001b: point 7)

Many others, such as Fiona Hunt (2001a) and Anneliese Dodds (2001), have expressed fear that the subsidy or the tax support might be cut down or removed altogether. The British Columbia Library Association (BCLA) also raised this point.

IFLA says that it would like to see more of an open debate on these issues and that it will continue to build links with library and information, archive, museum, education and other organisations and continue to raise awareness about the implications of international trade treaties in the public sector. Thus this provides us with some very clear guidelines on how library workers should try to respond and deal with the WTO and the GATS agenda.

Some very important statements were also made in the position IFLA maintained in February 2001, which was displayed on its website at that time (IFLA, 2001a). It said:

> The future of libraries of all kinds could be jeopardized by a series of international trade treaties that are currently being negotiated. (IFLA, 2001a)

It described how IFLA was formally represented at the WTO Ministerial in Seattle in 1999 and voiced some of its concerns, including the observation that:

> Privatization of libraries may result from the proposals for expansion of the GATS agreement. (IFLA, 2001a)

It also spoke about the possible erosion of professional standards, as these could be seen to be an unnecessary barrier to trade in services, which is an issue that both Fiona Hunt (2001) and myself have addressed (see Chapter 5, section 5.7.3). As IFLA said:

> Professional standards could come under challenge as a trade barrier ... the Council for Trade in Services is empowered to set review panels to assess whether qualification requirements and procedures, technical standards and licensing requirements constitute unnecessary barriers to trade in services. (IFLA, 2001a)

IFLA then proceeded to make its position clear, emphasising that the WTO enriches corporations by forcing public services into the private sector through privatisation, decreasing budgets and international trade agreements (IFLA, 2001a). It also stated that publicly funded libraries are part of the cultural sector and so need to be protected. The paper concluded by adding that:

> IFLA is opposed to the expansion of the GATS agreement but should it go forward, it will concentrate on a separate agreement/exemption for libraries and cultural organizations while continuing to push for protection of the broadly defined public sector. (IFLA, 2001a)

Thus IFLA's fundamental opposition to the GATS agenda is clear. IFLA highlights many of the key issues surrounding the GATS and libraries and also illustrates the international library response to the WTO and to the GATS agenda.

6.2.3 Frode Bakken, Paul Whitney, Ross Shimmon and the GATS and libraries

Frode Bakken, who is on the EBLIDA WTO Working Group and was the coordinator of it at the time (Information Society, 2001), provides further background information about IFLA's role and position. He presented a paper at the 66th IFLA Council and General Conference in Jerusalem in August 2000 and described how IFLA came to have a representative at the WTO Ministerial in Seattle, and how this was quite an unusual departure from IFLA's previous activities (Bakken, 2000).

Paul Whitney, the then Chief Librarian at Burnaby Public Library and now the City Librarian for Vancouver Public Library, British Columbia and the Canadian appointee to the Copyright and Other Legal Matters Committee (CLM) of IFLA, became the official IFLA representative at the WTO Ministerial in Seattle in 1999. This was a significant break-through, and it meant that the international library community had a much clearer and deeper understanding about what the WTO was doing and planning, and it meant that information could be more effectively disseminated to the library and information profession on this important matter.

When I began editing the special ISC issue on *Globalisation and Information*, I did not know that an IFLA representative had been at the WTO meeting in Seattle, or that IFLA had a position on the WTO. As already stated, I was inspired by Glenn Rikowski's book *The Battle in Seattle: Its Significance for Education* (G. Rikowski, 2001b) where he focused on some of the likely implications arising from the WTO Ministerial in Seattle for education. Therefore we are in fact stronger than I could have hoped for. The international library community needs to work together now, to disseminate this important information, and to resist pressures from the WTO that would undermine many of the main purposes of our working lives in the library and information world and indeed could, in time, lead to a fundamental and catastrophic change to our whole way of life. Under the WTO agenda in general, and the GATS in particular, we could become completely subservient to the needs of corporate capital. As Bakken notes:

> The aim of the WTO is to enhance world trade through liberalisa-tion of world trade or as this is formulated by WTO itself: 'the main function is to ensure that trade flows as smoothly, predictably and freely as possible'. (Bakken, 2000: 1)

Paul Whitney has also emphasised how the WTO has a binding dispute mechanism and the threat that this could pose to national decision-making. He goes on to say that:

> What has to be of concern are the potential GATS *unintended consequences* for libraries and other public sector institutions. (Whitney, 2000: 2)

This illustrates the fact that libraries can sometimes be seen to be a 'backwater'. Libraries will be swept along in the tide of the global corporate agenda, but they are hardly deserving of a mention in their own right while this is taking place, it seems. Witness, in contrast, the coverage that is sometimes given to areas such as health and education in the media, although many other areas that are threatened by the GATS are also often excluded from the mainstream media. Whitney also speaks about the commodification of information. He emphasises the need for effective communication and access to information within the library community on these issues, so that we will be better placed to be able to do something about it.

Ross Shimmon, the then Secretary-General of IFLA, summarised some of the main issues with regard to the GATS and libraries quite succinctly in an article that he wrote entitled *Can we bridge the digital divide?* (Shimmon, 2001). In particular, he noted that it is probable that many more countries will be entering into GATS negotiations in the future that are likely to affect their library services, even if their library services themselves are not actually listed in their GATS commitments.

Thus some important and influential people in the library and information profession, working in and through IFLA, have raised the issue of the GATS and libraries and their concerns with regard to it.

6.2.4 Conclusion

This section has highlighted the crucial importance of IFLA's role in general in the library and information profession internationally. It then emphasised the clear position that IFLA has taken on the WTO and the GATS and considered some of IFLA's statements on the subject. It then also considered what Frode Bakken, Paul Whitney and Ross Shimmon, who are all highly influential people in the library and information profession in general, and within IFLA in particular, have said on the topic. It concludes by emphasising how IFLA has been a leading light on the topic. Many other library associations should now take the lead from IFLA, and issue statements against the GATS and, where possible, take action against it.

Thus this clear and powerful message coming from IFLA should provide the library and information profession with hope and a way forward with regard to taking on the GATS and libraries issue.

6.3 British Columbia Library Association

The position of the British Columbia Library Association (BCLA) is very clear (see also Chapter 4, section 4.5.2). As already stated, it was the BCLA who first developed a library approach to the GATS, informed the world library community and communicated with IFLA about it all. Canada is very much in the forefront on many of the GATS issues. On their website, the BCLA outlines a scenario that could easily occur under the National Treatment guidelines of GATS. This is that an 'informed services' company could enter Canada and offer a service similar to that currently being provided by the Canadian libraries. Under the National Treatment clause of the GATS, the company could claim the same level of government subsidy as those currently running the Canadian libraries, and the government would be forced to pay this subsidy. The government might then decide to discontinue paying the subsidy in general, so that it did not find itself in the position of having to deal with further such claims in the future. The BCLA say that:

> Discontinuing funds to libraries would be the surest way for governments to protect themselves, and libraries could be forced to generate income or close. If public libraries are forced to close, or to operate on a break-even basis, the public would have to buy their information from the 'information companies' or from fee-charging libraries. If a free flow of information is fundamental in a democratic society, the very basis of our democratic system would be threatened by this scenario. (BCLA, undated:a, in section 'A threatening scenario for libraries')

All this could force people down the route of having to pay for information that was previously available for free in libraries. The BCLA is therefore asking people to take action: to write to their MPs, ask for an explicit and permanent exemption for libraries in GATS negotiations, not be intimidated by the language used by government and trade officials, and keep informed. The BCLA has another short paper on the Web, entitled *GATS and the threat to libraries*. In this document it says that the activities of the WTO '... may result in the eventual elimination of the public sector ...' Furthermore, the GATS represents '... the first ever set of multilateral legally-enforceable rules covering international trade in services'. It also notes how the WTO will limit the powers of governments in nation states. It then encourages people to take some action (BCLA, undated:b: 1).

6.4 Canadian Library Association

The Canadian Library Association (CLA) voices similar sentiments to the BCLA and is concerned about the possible privatisation of libraries as a result of the GATS (see also Chapter 4, section 4.5.3). It emphasises how:

> Libraries are unique social organizations dedicated to providing the broadest range of information and ideas to the public regardless of age, religion, social status, race, gender and language. (CLA, 1999, in section 'Background')

The CLA aims to protect libraries and wants exemptions from the GATS for libraries and cultural organisations. It says that the:

> CLA will concentrate on a separate agreement/exemption for libraries and cultural organizations while continuing to push for protection of the public sector as broadly defined. (CLA, 1999, in section 'Positions', point 3)

The CLA has, in general, been very active with regard to the GATS and libraries issue. They supported Steve Shrybman's report, for example, and Ellen Gould's update of this report (see section 6.5 below and Chapter 4, section 4.5.4), and gave me support for the IFLA fringe meeting that I organised in 2002 (see Chapter 4, section 4.14.3).

6.5 Other Canadian library bodies

Steve Shrybman (2001) wrote a document on the GATS and public libraries entitled *An assessment of the impact of the General Agreement on Trade in Services on policy, programs and law concerning public sector libraries* (see also Chapter 4, section 4.5.4). This document was commissioned by the Canadian Library Association (CLA) and has recently been updated by Ellen Gould (Gould, 2004). Shrybman's document was prepared for the following Canadian bodies: the Canadian Library Association, the Canadian Association of University Teachers, the Canadian Association of Research Libraries, the Ontario Library Association, the Saskatchewan Library Association, the Manitoba Library Association, Industry Canada, the British Columbia

Library Association, the Library Association of Alberta and the National Library of Canada. Thus all these organisations are concerned about the likely impact of the GATS on libraries and think that it is an important topic. In the Executive Summary of the document Shrybman notes that the rationale for public sector service delivery is in conflict with the principles of the GATS:

> In simple terms, the GATS seeks to constrain government policy and regulatory options in favour of free market solutions. Public sector libraries on the other hand serve a public policy agenda that intends to correct the failure of free markets to meet broader community goals such as universal access to information and literacy. Given this inherent contradiction, it is not surprising that application of GATS disciplines to government measures concerning public sector libraries is consistently problematic. (Shrybman, 2001: 3)

Later in the document the likelihood of the private sector moving into the public library sector is considered, and Shrybman says that:

> The more difficult point to establish is that public sector library services are not supplied in competition with the private sector. While the more traditional services provided by public libraries may not compete with other service suppliers, this is not the case for on-line or digital services. In other words, the bricks and mortar or more traditional library services may be excluded as supplied in the exercise of government authority while on-line and digital information services are not. This coincides of course with the areas of competition with private sector suppliers of e-book and e-library services. (Shrybman, 2001: 7)

Thus while the more traditional library services might not be of interest to commercial suppliers, online and digital services might well be. This is a very interesting statement. As already indicated, the GATS, as part of the general global capitalist agenda, will be introduced gradually. The proposals under Best Value, for example, include the possibility of local authorities working with the voluntary sector, at least initially. Then, when the time is 'ripe', the voluntary sector could take over the public library service from the local authority, and then at a still later date, this voluntary organisation could change and become a private company (once enough money can be made out of the project). Thus it is a 'slippery slope', and in a sense the divide between public library provision and other types of library and information provision could become blurred. Thus in the early days, as indicated above, the bricks and mortar of the traditional public library could remain intact, but online and digital information could be opened up to the private sector. This also fits in closely with the micropayments scenario that I have outlined (see Chapter 5, section 5.4.4). The physical library building might (or might not!) remain with the local authority, but users have to pay (albeit indirectly) to undertake transactions on the Internet. It is difficult, indeed almost impossible, to predict precisely what outcome will emerge, but this is the general direction. So, access to information could be 'privatised' (as it were) and, at a later date, everything else could be privatised (library buildings, the books, etc.) when the time is ripe and sufficient profits can be made.

Steve Shrybman's report is an important document and has helped to raise awareness and understanding about the GATS and libraries issue.

6.6 European Bureau of Library, Information and Documentation Associations

The European Bureau of Library, Information and Documentation Associations (EBLIDA) has raised serious concerns about the possible implications of the GATS for libraries in Europe (see also Chapter 4, section 4.1.3). It says that libraries could face competition from profit-making foreign library services and suppliers. Furthermore, EBLIDA notes that professional standards could be challenged as they could be seen to be a barrier to trade (EBLIDA, 2000). It also states that:

> It is essential that the library community is aware of these developments and can defend its interests. (EBLIDA, 2000)

EBLIDA, in responding to the European Commission public consultation on the GATS, urges the European Commission and other member states to continue its current policy, and not to make any commitments concerning libraries to the GATS. It also recognises that libraries are an integral part of activities within educational services, and has urged the European Commission to exclude educational services from any new commitments.

6.7 American Library Association

The American Library Association (ALA) is concerned about the likely implications of the GATS for libraries and information in the US (see also Chapter 4, section 4.6.2). It endorsed the IFLA WTO position at its ALA mid-winter meeting 2000 (ALA, 2000). The ALA has also taken some action with regard to the issue. A selection of articles was published in the *American Libraries* journal, discussing the GATS (Hunt and the American Library Association, Washington Office, 2001) and Berry (2002).

In May 2002 the ALA President, John W. Berry, wrote to the US Trade Representative (USTR) to confirm its position that governmental support (local, state and federal) for core library services was not subject to the GATS. It sought assurance that the US did not intend to enter into any international obligations that might undermine the ability of governmental bodies to support core library services. It requested that the ALA and the library community be consulted before any action is taken that might impact on domestic policy supporting public libraries in a negative way (Berry, 2002). Furthermore, in May 2002 the ALA also submitted formal comments to the USTR, responding to its request for comments regarding the Doha Trade Negotiations and Agenda on services. It said that it was concerned that the USTR did not consult with the ALA in the past, before taking action that could impact on the domestic policy of US public libraries. In particular, the ALA was not consulted prior to the listing of libraries on the United States Schedule of Specific Commitments. Thus the USA has committed its library services to the GATS in the schedule of commitments, but the ALA was not consulted about this. If the professional association for librarians in America is not consulted on this important matter then this could also start to happen in other countries. Governments in other countries could commit their library services to the GATS without first consulting with the professional library associations in those countries. This represents another erosion of democracy, and must surely give us cause for concern.

The ALA then asked the Executive Branch of the USTR to make a public commitment to protect the ability of public libraries to provide their core services and to be sensitive to potential threats to public library services. Furthermore, it should work with the ALA to ensure that the USTR and other relevant sections of the US government are informed of the needs of the ALA and core library services, and also take action at the WTO as necessary to ensure that the GATS obligations do not restrict the ability of federal, state and local governmental bodies to support the provision of core library services. It said that the ALA will continue to consult with the Office of the US Trade Representative to ensure that it understands the importance of protecting public library services. Meanwhile, in September 2001, the ALA Washington Office said it is paying careful attention to the developments in various international negotiations, including the WTO, Free Trade Agreements of the Americas (FTAA), the Hague Conference on Private International Law and the World Intellectual Property Organisation (WIPO). Further, they:

> ... are in regular discussions with US officials in the Office of the US Trade Representative, the Department of Commerce, the State Department, the Federal Trade Commission, and the Patents and Trademark Office – all of whom are active in these important negotiations. (ALA Washington Office, 2001: 2)

Therefore the ALA is concerned about and has taken some action with regard to the GATS and libraries issue, although it is concerning that US library services have been listed in the GATS commitments, and that the ALA were not consulted about it and did not seem to have been able to do anything about it.

6.8 Writers' Guild of America, West

The Writers' Guild of America, West (WGA) is the largest professional association of performance writers in the world. It is a member of the Center for the Creative Community (CCC) and this aims to 'Serve both America's Creative Community and the general public by working to safeguard and enrich the vitality and diversity of our nation's culture' (Australian Writers' Guild, 2003).

The WGA is of the opinion that culture cannot simply be commodified and cannot operate simply according to economic principles. They argue that culture should be exempt from trade liberalisation and the GATS (see also Chapter 4, section 4.6.3).

6.9 Australian Library and Information Association

The Australian Library and Information Association (ALIA) has made its concerns about the implications of the GATS for its publicly funded libraries very clear (see also Chapter 4, section 4.8.2). Jennifer Nicholson, on behalf of the ALIA, said:

> ALIA has concerns about the potential for publicly funded libraries and information services to be subjected to unintended consequences from international trade agreements. In simple terms, the GATS appear to constrain government policy and regulatory options in favour of free market solutions. Publicly funded libraries on the other hand serve a public policy agenda that corrects the failure of free markets to meet broader community goals such as universal access to information and literacy. (Nicholson, in Australian Library and Information Association, 2001: 1)

The ALIA is also aware of and concerned about the fact that the committing of library services to the GATS agenda is gathering pace. As Nicholson says:

> Australia has declined to list library services in its schedule of commitments. However, several other countries have done so including Japan and the USA. The fact that two of the world's most influential economic powers have listed library services suggests that other nations are likely to be pressed to follow suit. (Nicholson, in Australian Library and Information Association, 2001: 2)

The ALIA emphasises the need to be able to promote Australian culture, the importance of libraries within this framework and how international agreements on trade and investment could undermine this. It also emphasises the importance of publicly funded libraries, saying that they provide access to a full range of human expression and enable individuals to acquire skills needed to use information effectively so that they can participate in a democratic society.

Finally, the ALIA makes it clear that it is of the opinion that Australian libraries should be excluded from GATS disciplines, saying:

Trade agreements should ensure that publicly funded libraries are protected and included in any possible separate treaty that allows special consideration for cultural goods and services in international trade. The provision of services for the benefit of our community and for the public good by publicly funded libraries should be recognised within the general exception without precluding such libraries from participating in trade in other services where there is a commercial imperative. (Nicholson, in 'Trade Negotiations in the WTO': 2)

This is another library association that has issued a clear statement with regard to the GATS and has requested that libraries be exempt from it.

6.10 Australian Writers' Guild

The Australian Writers' Guild (AWG), along with other professional associations in the cultural arena, is a member of the Australian Coalition for Cultural Diversity (ACCD) (see also Chapter 4, section 4.8.3). The AWG is a peak professional association for performance writers in TV, film, theatre, radio and multimedia. The AWG has a clear position on the GATS as follows:

The AWG believes that in terms of any bilateral or multilateral agreement, including GATS, the government must refrain from making any commitments within the cultural services sector or any other sector which would impact on the cultural services sector, now or in the future. The AWG contends that unless such a 'cultural carveout' is made, the government will compromise its ability to develop and implement cultural, economic, and social policy and thus be fettered in its achievements of cultural, social and economic objectives. (Australian Writers' Guild, 2003: 4)

Thus the AWG argues that the Australian government should not commit cultural services in Australia to the GATS. Furthermore, the AWG notes that this is important, otherwise the government will not be able to develop and implement cultural policies in the way in which it really wants to.

The AWG emphasises how the cultural industry is different to other tradable goods and services, stating that:

The AWG believes that the output of cultural industries is inherently different to that of other tradable goods and services because the culture of one nation is interchangeable with that of another. (Australian Writers' Guild, 2003: 7)

Furthermore, it emphasises the importance of not treating cultural goods and services as 'economic tradable commodities', saying that:

It is important to realise that within the global context, creative industries and their professional organisations of many nations share the position that cultural goods and services cannot be treated as economic tradable commodities alone. It is important to also realise that creative industries within the United States also state that it is inappropriate to treat cultural products and services as economic commodities as they have specific and unique cultural value. (Australian Writers' Guild, 2003: 8)

The AWG contends that cultural goods and services, the arts, and audio-visual and entertainment industries should be exempt from GATS negotiations. It emphasises the need to continue to 'sustain, develop and promote' Australian culture.

The AWG urges the Australian government to continue to insist upon comprehensive rights for Australian governments at all levels to sustain, develop and promote Australian culture and Australian cultural expressions. (Australian Writers' Guild, 2003: 22)

Thus the emphasis is on the need to sustain, develop and promote Australian culture through the Australian government, i.e. the nation state keeping control over its own cultural affairs and not losing this power to the WTO.

6.11 The UK's Chartered Institute of Library and Information Professionals

The UK Chartered Institute of Library and Information Professionals (CILIP) (previously known as the Library Association) wrote a statement outlining its position with regard to the GATS in January 2003 (after my work on the GATS and libraries, as I outlined in Chapter 4, section 4.14.6). This was undertaken as part of a consultation process with the Department of Trade and Industry. CILIP said that it wants to ensure that the UK government is '... aware of the diverse nature and full extent of the role of publicly funded library and information services in the UK' (CILIP, 2003: 1). It then emphasises the importance of the publicly funded library as a democratic institution and notes that although traditional library services, such as reference and lending services, might not be attractive options for commercial suppliers, nevertheless:

> ... the new opportunities offered by ICT mean that libraries now provide a wide range of expanding services, which are of increasing interest to commercial suppliers seeking new global opportunities in the information marketplace. These services include: online database retrieval services, electronic reference services, Internet access, the development of Web portal/subject gateway services, electronic document delivery. (CILIP, 2003: 2)

Thus ICT-based services that libraries supply might be of increasing interest to commercial suppliers on a global basis. These services include online database retrieval services, Internet access and electronic document delivery.

CILIP then shows its concern about the possibility of competition from the private sector with regard to the provision of these services, saying that:

> Without tax support, the library's role as a democratic institution, making available the widest range of material reflecting the diversity of society, will be compromised and threaten the objectives of Government Social Inclusion policies. (CILIP, 2003: 2–3)

CILIP makes its position very clear, saying:

> ... CILIP is concerned at the potentially alarming consequences for the future operation and development of cultural and education services should the priority to preserve our cultural heritage, provide free access to information and the notion of a community-based library serving the needs of the local population cease to take priority over profit margins. (CILIP, 2003: 3)

They voice their concern about the possibility of cultural and education services being compromised if these services have to be part of a competitive market environment. Furthermore, CILIP argues that commitments should not be made that call into question the current funding procedures for publicly funded library services in the UK, which is a statutory provision under the Public Libraries and Museums Act 1964 for English authorities. Also:

> CILIP strongly urges the Government to continue with its present policy not to agree to any requests to extend the coverage and/or to remove the existing restrictions in the sub-sector 'Libraries, archives, museums and other cultural services', and to make a commitment not to include this sub-sector in future negotiations. (CILIP, 2003: 3)

Thus, clearly, CILIP along with many other library associations and bodies is very concerned about the possible threat that the GATS could pose to the state-funded provision of libraries, particularly in areas such as Internet access and electronic document delivery. It also urges the UK government to argue the case against throwing the UK state-funded library service into the GATS arena. However, it needs to be remembered that the UK alone would not commit its library services to the GATS. Instead, it will do so within the context of the EU (or the legally correct term European Communities in WTO business). However, the UK could argue that the EU commits, or does not commit, its library services to the GATS, so to that extent the voice and opinion of CILIP is important, as is the voice of all the other library associations in the countries within the EU. This does, though, once again demonstrate some erosion of democracy, I would suggest, within nation states.

6.12 Library Association of Ireland

As a member of the EU Ireland has not committed its library service to the GATS but the Library Association of Ireland is also concerned about the possible consequences of the GATS for libraries and information services in Ireland. In the Library Association of Ireland Annual General Meeting of 2003 it said that it notes with:

> ... deep concern the potential implications of the General Agreement on Trade in Services (GATS) for libraries and information services ... (Library Association of Ireland, 2003)

It then urges the Irish government not to agree to any request to remove the restrictions that already exist in the sub-sector 'Libraries, archives, museums and other cultural services'. It asks the government not to make commitments that threaten national government funding procedures, and to ensure that subsidies and other forms of direct and indirect support continue to be excluded under Mode 3 of the agreement. It asks for the Irish government to pursue these objectives at the European level as well. The County and City Librarians' Group of the Library Association of Ireland proposed this request.

Clearly, then, the Library Association of Ireland wants to try to ensure that libraries in Ireland continue to be excluded from the GATS negotiations.

6.13 Professional Associations from the Cultural Milieu

Sometimes, groups of countries and/or organisations get together and make clear statements about the GATS. There is a final declaration from the first international meeting of the Professional Associations from the Cultural Milieu (2001), for example, which took place in Montreal. The declaration included representatives from Argentina, Australia, Brazil, Canada, Chile, Denmark, France, Korea, Mexico, Poland, Spain and the EU. These representatives were from professional associations of writers, composers, screenwriters, directors, performers, independent producers, distributors, publishers, broadcasters and distributors from the film, radio/television, book and music sectors in these countries. In their declaration the associations made a number of points. They emphasised, for example, that cultural goods and services were not commodities and cannot be reduced purely to economic terms. They emphasised their concern that:

> In applying the rules that usually govern international trade agreements to the cultural sector, there is a risk that many cultural policies would be dismantled. (Professional Associations from the Cultural Milieu, 2001: 1)

The document requests that the member states do not make commitments that limit the rights of states and governments to establish their own cultural policies, in terms of both the creation and distribution of artistic works. Thus, once again, the emphasis is on ensuring that individual governments maintain control over their own cultural services and are opposed to bringing these within a WTO setting.

The intention was to present this declaration to their respective governments and cultural agencies, as well as to other professional associations. Also there was a need to develop links with various associations to:

> ... defend their own cultural policies, and to promote cultural diversity. (Professional Associations from the Cultural Milieu, 2001: 2)

It is heartening to know that the GATS issue is also being taken seriously by organisations such as this.

6.14 Concluding comments: responses of library, information and cultural bodies to the GATS

In conclusion, this chapter so far has examined the responses of a variety of library associations and library, information and cultural bodies to the GATS. This has included the International Federation of Library Associations and Institutions, the British Columbia Library Association, the Canadian Library Association and the American Library Association, as well as the European Bureau of Library, Information and Documentation Associations, the Australian Library and Information Association, the Writers' Guild of America, West, the Australian Writers' Guild, the Chartered Institute of Library and Information Professionals in the UK, the Professional Associations from the Cultural Milieu and a variety of Canadian library organisations. All these organisations are very concerned about the likely implications of the GATS for libraries, information and cultural services and are openly articulating their concerns. Obviously this coverage is not comprehensive. In particular, it does not include any information from library associations from the developing world specifically, although IFLA does represent both the developing world and the developed world. But those from the developing world often have more immediate, pressing problems than libraries. However, the chapter has sought to provide a useful overview which can then be built on. It is also extremely heartening that all of these library associations are fundamentally opposed to library services falling under the GATS. We may be certain that none of them are celebrating the possibility.

6.15 EBLIDA/IFLA meeting the WTO/European Commission to discuss GATS and libraries

To raise the debate further and to find out more about the GATS and libraries, EBLIDA and IFLA representatives met representatives from the WTO and the European Commission in December 2002. They asked them a number of pertinent questions, focusing in particular on the GATS, although a few questions on TRIPS were also asked. I contributed some questions to this debate, although unfortunately I was unable to attend the meetings myself.

Kjell Nilsson, the coordinator of the EBLIDA WTO Working Group and the Director of BIBSAM, the Swedish Royal Library, Department for National Coordination and Development, wrote a report on the meeting (Nilsson, 2003). The people that represented EBLIDA and IFLA were: Frode Bakken, the President of the Norwegian Library Association and the then chairperson of the EBLIDA WTO Working Group, and Teresa Hackett, the then Director of EBLIDA. Also present were Ross Shimmon, the then Secretary General of IFLA, and Kjell Nilsson, member of the IFLA/CLM (Copyright and Other Legal Matters) Working Group on WTO-related matters and the current chair of the EBLIDA WTO Working Group. This delegation met with the following representatives from the WTO and the European Commission at the WTO headquarters: Dale Honeck, a Counsellor in the Trade in Services Division of the WTO; Pierre Latrille, GATS counsellor for Education; and Martin Roy, Economic Affairs Officer of the GATS secretariat. At the European Commission delegation it met with Ann Mary Redmond, one of the European Commission officials involved in the GATS negotiations.

The two most fundamental questions that they raised with the WTO representatives were:

- Are the services of publicly funded libraries included in the scope of GATS, or should they be regarded as 'Supplied in the exercise of governmental authority?' (Article I:3(c)) and therefore by definition be excluded from the treaty?

- Are there any sectors in the treaty, except Subsector 10C: 'Libraries, archives and museums' and Sector 5: 'Educational services', that involve library services? (For example, where do you place library services provided online?)

The meeting was much longer than the scheduled two hours. However, the IFLA and EBLIDA representatives were not given very clear answers in many ways and the counsellors often seemed to be uncertain about their interpretation of the treaty. Nilsson did conclude, though, after having attended the meeting, that the services of publicly funded libraries definitely are within the scope of the GATS. This in itself is extremely revealing and reinforces and substantiates my own thinking on this matter (see the section on the definition of services with regard to the GATS in Chapter 3, section 3.4.3). The WTO and European Commission representatives said that it is also possible that online library services will go into Sector 2B 'Computer and Related Services' and this sector has already been committed by the EC (see Chapter 4, section 4.3.2 for more information regarding this). This shows how library services can become committed to the GATS by the 'back door'. So, although a country's library service might not be committed under the main category, Sector 10C: Recreational, Cultural and Sporting Services, it may find that its library services fall under the GATS in other ways and under other sectors. Furthermore, this could even take place without library associations in nation states being aware that it has happened. Thus, as the EU is a member of the WTO as one entity (for legal reasons referred to as the EC), countries that are members of the EU might find that their online services (and these are part of 'library services') have been committed to the GATS. Nilsson concludes by saying that:

> A lasting impression from our talks in Geneva is that a complex international treaty like GATS gives room for different interpretations. Also, it is a live organism, the wording of which might be

> subject to many changes during its lifetime ... on the library side there are simply too few people who are knowledgeable on this subject. (Nilsson, 2003: 3–4)

It is interesting and important to note Nilsson's remarks about there being too few people in the library world that are knowledgeable on the subject – which is an issue that I am hoping to address, to some extent, by writing this book! Nilsson also makes clear that there is room for different interpretations – a real problem. This applies to many of the WTO agreements.

Nilsson notes a couple of issues that he thinks particularly need the attention of the library community. First is the fact that 'educational services' within the GATS often include a substantial part of the publicly funded libraries (including school, college and university libraries). Second is the importance of considering the issue of online library services further and the fact that the EC has a working group that is examining electronic services issues.

Since this, Anders Ericson, a freelance Norwegian journalist and a librarian, interviewed Frode Bakken, who attended the WTO and European Commission meetings, and asked him various questions. Frode Bakken made the point that he did not think that much money could be made from running libraries at the current time, but that this is no reason to be complacent. He said:

> ... you do not make much money from running libraries ... but at the same time there is no reason for librarians to put this issue aside. (Bakken, in Ericson and Bakken, 2003: 1)

Ericson then asked Bakken about his views on the interpretation of the meaning of 'services' and Bakken said:

> It is obvious after the thorough conversations with the WTO representatives that there is no such authoritative definition or interpretation and a lot of the problems about the WTO are how to make the countries agree on common interpretations of various questions in the agreements, not yet agreed upon. (Ericson and Bakken, 2003: 1–2)

Once again, we have this problem of different interpretations. There is a lack of clear definitions and interpretations with regard to many of the

WTO agreements in general, and I think this is a serious problem. However, I suggest that it is highly likely that this is a deliberate policy. The philosophy behind the WTO is about trade, trade and more trade. But obviously various parties will find certain aspects of this unpleasant and unacceptable, so there needs to be some sort of 'get-out' clause and, indeed, camouflage. Having such loose interpretations provides easy get-out clauses. So when certain parties are concerned that their service sectors might be threatened by the GATS, this issue of the meaning of 'services' can always be raised. In this way, WTO officials are not forced into the position of having to say whether particular, individual services will or will definitely not fall under the remit of the GATS. However, the more advanced that the GATS negotiations become, the more difficult it is likely to be to maintain this position.

6.16 Concluding comments

It is simply not the case that all library and information workers are happily swimming along with the tide, accepting all the supposed 'goodies' that global capitalism has to offer and embracing whatever is thrown their way as a result of capital's infinite drive to incorporate all areas of social life. Instead, there is a considerable number of library associations and library, information and cultural bodies that have expressed grave concerns. This should bolster our confidence. I hope this book will encourage others to think deeply about these subjects and to think further about how we might proceed on these questions together, to halt, or at least slow down, the relentless pace of library capitalisation, and then to try to turn the tide around.

Within this remit I hope that more library associations and cultural bodies will pass resolutions against the GATS or at least express their concern. It would be particularly helpful if some library associations from the developing world were to add their voice to the debate. We need to make the WTO sit up, take notice and listen. Let us scare them into taking notice of us! What an achievement it would be for the library world, if it was the library and information profession, in particular, that was able to get the WTO to take notice! Many think this would lie more in the hands of other service sectors, such as education and health, and not in the supposedly meek and mild library world. Let us give them all a shock and a surprise. Let our voice he heard. Let us challenge the principles embedded within the WTO and the GATS and the way in which these threaten the state-funded provision of libraries – indeed, will ultimately threaten the whole way of life for the library and information profession and for the library and information world at large.

Note

Part 2 of this book, the chapters on the GATS (Chapters 3–6), build on my published articles on the GATS and libraries which have appeared in *Information for Social Change, Managing Information, Link-up, Public Library Journal, Focus, Bibliotek i Samhaelle, The Commoner, House of Lords Report on Globalisation* and *Relay.*

Part 3
Agreement on Trade-Related Aspects of Intellectual Property Rights

An outline of the WTO's Agreement on TRIPS

7.1 Introduction

The other agreement that is being developed at the WTO that is likely to have significant implications for libraries and information is the Trade-Related Aspects of Intellectual Property Rights (TRIPS) Agreement. While the GATS impacts more directly on libraries, the TRIPS impacts more directly on information and knowledge, although both obviously affect libraries and, indeed, affect cultural and education services as well. In this book I am arguing that the TRIPS is about transforming information, knowledge and ideas into intellectual property rights which can then be traded on the global market in the form of internationally tradable commodities. Furthermore, TRIPS is concerned with the trading of these intellectual property rights, and is not concerned with moral, humane and public service ethos issues.

Once again, the power of large corporations and rich countries in the developed world and the lack of democracy at the WTO are also illustrated clearly through the TRIPS. The developed countries typically benefit at the expense of the developing countries. The Pharmaceutical Research and Manufacturers of America (PhRMA), for example, is probably the world's most powerful industrial lobby and in many ways it shapes the TRIPS agenda. It has about 300 full-time lobbyists in Washington alone. Watkins emphasises how the TRIPS has been pushed through by the USA, and by the pharmaceutical industry, saying that:

> Dictated by the US pharmaceutical industry, and driven through by threats of US trade sanctions, the agreement was opposed by virtually every developing country in the Uruguay Round. (Watkins, 2003: 32)

Furthermore, he says that '... TRIPS enshrines the US patent law in the multilateral trade system ...' It forces developing countries to adopt the standards of the rich countries in the West. Over 90 per cent of patents for new technologies are held by corporations in rich countries and the Agreement is likely to stifle innovation in poorer countries. Freedman has pointed out that:

> TRIPS has provided an effective means for the world's largest right holders to pursue disciplinary action against smaller states. (Freedman, 2002: 2)

Thus the pattern is repeating itself here and the TRIPS, in many ways, is being driven forward by large multinational companies, particularly those in the pharmaceutical industry and by the USA in general.

This chapter will provide an overview of the TRIPS Agreement itself and the meaning of intellectual property rights. It will then examine the different parts of the Agreement. It will consider Parts I and III–VII, including a consideration of articles such as 'National Treatment' and 'Most-Favoured-Nation Treatment'. These articles are also embedded in the GATS, as I explain in Chapter 3, section 3.3.3. Part II of the agreement will then be considered, which covers all the different types of intellectual property rights that are included in the agreement. These will all be examined, apart from copyright and patents which are examined separately in Chapters 8 and 9, respectively. It will also consider whether TRIPS is part of trade, and whether TRIPS belongs to the WTO. Chapter 8 focuses on TRIPS, copyright, libraries and information. It will first provide a historical perspective on copyright, followed by a consideration of moral and economic rights in copyright and the balancing act involved. It then examines the copyright section of TRIPS and moral rights and TRIPS.

Chapter 9 focuses on TRIPS, patents, traditional knowledge, information and libraries. It examines the patent section of TRIPS, followed by sections on TRIPS, patents and copyright and traditional, indigenous knowledge, and TRIPS in the developing world. Chapter 10 considers the implications of TRIPS for the library and information profession in general. It also considers further implications within an international perspective, where a number of different countries are examined. The implications of TRIPS for the library and information profession in general is broken down into three main areas: copyright, patents and the WTO. The copyright section explores the notion of balance, to which, it is argued, there are actually three parts. It looks in particular at the free flow of information (one side of the balance). It also considers the implications of copyright issues in TRIPS for libraries in the developing world, the complexity of copyright legislation and how TRIPS can override copyright legislation in individual WTO member states. In the international perspective, TRIPS, information and libraries in the following countries are examined: India and the developing world in general, Canada, the USA, Africa, Europe and the UK.

7.2 Overview of the TRIPS Agreement

The TRIPS Agreement was established at the WTO on 1 January 1995, along with many other WTO agreements. TRIPS materialised from the Uruguay Round (which lasted from 1986 to 1994), and which also created the WTO itself. The TRIPS Agreement was drawn up by a relatively small number of people. Drahos and Braithwaite (2002: 10) interviewed a senior US trade negotiator in 1994, who said that probably less than 50 people were responsible for TRIPS. TRIPS is concerned with the trading of intellectual property rights (IPRs), these being the rights that society awards to individuals or organisations for their creative works. IPRs give creators the right to be able to prevent others from unauthorised use of their works for a stated period. According to the WTO the main purpose of TRIPS is to:

> ... reduce distortions and impediments to international trade ... taking into account the need to promote effective and adequate protection of intellectual property rights, and to ensure that measures and procedures to enforce intellectual property rights do not themselves become barriers to legitimate trade. (WTO, 1995: 1)

The general goals of the TRIPS Agreement are outlined in the Preamble, which reproduces the basic Uruguay Round negotiating objectives established in the TRIPS arena by the 1986 Punta del Este Declaration and the Montreal Mid-Term Review of the Round in December 1988. From this the 'Trade Policy Review Mechanism' was set up, which became part of the WTO in 1995, when intellectual property was included. During the Uruguay Round of negotiations it was also decided that the Berne Convention for the Protection of Literary and Artistic Works, which was included in the Agreement, provided most of the basic standards needed for copyright protection.

There has not been such a binding international agreement on intellectual property rights on this scale before. As the WTO itself says:

> The TRIPS Agreement ... is to date the most comprehensive multilateral agreement on intellectual property. (WTO, undated:a: 1)

Furthermore, Drahos and Braithwaite say that:

> TRIPS is the most important agreement on intellectual property of the 20th century. (Drahos and Braithwaite, 2002: 10)

There are three particularly important features of the Agreement, as defined by the WTO. These are standards, enforcement and dispute settlement. With regard to standards, the WTO says:

> ... the Agreement sets out the minimum standards of protection to be provided by each Member. Each of the main elements of protection is defined, namely the subject-matter to be protected, the rights to be conferred and permissible exceptions to those rights, and the minimum duration of protection. (WTO, undated:a: 1)

The Agreement defines certain general principles for enforcement procedures and a procedure for the settlement of disputes between WTO members with regard to intellectual property rights issues.

7.3 Intellectual property rights

Clearly, it is important, first of all, to define intellectual property rights (IPRs). Hefter and Litowitz spoke about IPRs:

> The most noticeable difference between intellectual property and other forms of property ... is that intellectual property is intangible, that is, it cannot be defined or identified by its own physical parameters. It must be expressed in some discernible way to be protectable. (Hefter and Litowitz, undated)

While Drahos and Braithwaite argued that:

> Intellectual property rights are, in essence, government tools for regulating markets in information. (Drahos and Braithwaite, 2002: 3)

Meanwhile, Jennifer Davis emphasised that the World Intellectual Property Organisation (WIPO) refers to intellectual property as being the products of the mind, which includes inventions, literary and artistic works and designs. However, an encapsulation of the most basic products of the mind, namely ideas, cannot usually be protected as intellectual property, she argued. Fundamentally, a conceptualisation of the intangible nature of intellectual property is essential, but this intellectual property needs to be expressed in a discernible, distinguished way if it is to be protected, i.e. for it to become an intellectual property right.

The World Intellectual Property Organisation emphasises the fact that there are many different types of intellectual property rights and these fall into two main categories – industrial property and artistic and literary property. The former includes patents, industrial designs, trade marks and trade secrets, while the latter includes copyright, database protection and plant breeders' rights. However, in the past these categories were treated separately. In the 1880s, industrial property (patents, designs, trade marks, etc.) were treated separately from copyright (intellectual property). Industrial property came under the Paris Convention 1883 (as revised), while copyright came under the Berne Convention 1886 (as revised). However, the generic term is now used in both TRIPS and WIPO.

However, the British Council also emphasises the fact that while there are many similarities between the different types of intellectual property rights, there are also some differences, and so:

> ... any evaluations of patents or trade marks do not automatically or necessarily apply to copyright. (British Council, 2001: 1)

Intellectual property rights are the rights that society awards to individuals or to organisations for their creative works – in whatever shape this may take (writing, art, music, etc.). Many different types of intellectual property rights are covered in TRIPS, and these include copyright and related rights; trademarks, including service marks; geographical indications; industrial designs; patents and the layout designs of integrated circuits; and undisclosed information including trade secrets and test data.

7.4 Parts I and III–VII of the TRIPS Agreement

The TRIPS Agreement is divided up into seven sections (WTO, 1995). Topics covered include general principles, standards, enforcements, acquisition of IPRs, dispute settlement and final provisions.

- Part I: General Provisions and Basic Principles.
- Part II: [Different types of IPRs in TRIPS – this is considered in some detail in section 7.5 of this chapter].
- Part III: Enforcement of Intellectual Property Rights.
- Part IV: Acquisition and Maintenance of Intellectual Property Rights and Related *Inter-Partes* Procedures.
- Part V: Dispute Prevention and Settlement.
- Part VI: Transitional Arrangements.
- Part VII: Institutional Arrangements; Final Provisions.

This section will examine these different parts in some detail.

Part I: General Provisions and Basic Principles

Part I refers to the role of the legal system of member states, i.e. the part that nation states play with regard to introducing and enforcing legislation in connection with TRIPS and IPR issues in their own respective countries. In Article 1, 'Nature and Scope of Obligations', paragraph 1, it says:

> Members shall give effect to the provisions of this Agreement. Members may, but shall not be obliged to, implement in their law more extensive protection than is required by this Agreement, provided that such protection does not contravene the provisions of this Agreement. Members shall be free to determine the appropriate method of implementing the provisions of this Agreement within their own legal system and practice.

Thus, while members do not have to introduce legislation that is more extensive than the TRIPS (i.e. that extends the basic principles embedded in the TRIPS still further), neither must they introduce legislation that contravenes the basic provisions and principles in the Agreement. Within these confines, members can and, indeed, probably need to introduce legislation in their own countries to ensure that the provisions within TRIPS are adequately implemented. This, once again, also reinforces the power of the WTO in general.

In Article 3 on National Treatment, paragraph 1, it says:

> Each Member shall accord to the nationals of other Members treatment no less favourable than that it accords to its own nationals with regard to the protection of intellectual property, subject to the exceptions already provided in, respectively, the Paris Convention (1967), the Berne Convention (1971), the Rome Convention or the Treaty on Intellectual Property in Respect of Integrated Circuits.

So, every member must be treated the same with regard to intellectual property right issues, and members must not favour nationals in their own countries over nationals from other member states.

Furthermore, in Article 4, Most-Favoured-Nation Treatment, it states that:

> ... any advantage, favour, privilege or immunity granted by a Member to the nationals of any other country shall be accorded immediately and unconditionally to the nationals of all other Members.

This means that if a member gives any preferential treatment to another member (no matter what form this might be in), then that privilege must also be given to all other members. This could be in the form of a government subsidy, for example. National Treatment and Most-Favoured-Nation are both articles that are also embedded in the GATS (see Chapter 3, section 3.3.3 in this book). A range of exceptions to this are then listed, such as various international agreements that exist of a general nature and are not just confined to the protection of intellectual property. The objectives are outlined in Article 7, where it says that:

> The protection and enforcement of intellectual property rights should contribute to the promotion of technological innovation and to the transfer and dissemination of technology, to the mutual advantage of producers and users of technological knowledge and in a manner conducive to social and economic welfare ...

This emphasises the importance of promoting technical innovations through intellectual property rights in general, and through the TRIPS in particular.

In Article 8, paragraph 2, it emphasises that 'appropriate measures' might be needed to:

> ... prevent the abuse of intellectual property rights by rights holders or the resort to practices which unreasonably restrain trade or adversely affect the international transfer of technology.

Thus this article emphasises the underlying philosophy within TRIPS, which is the trading of intellectual property rights and that 'appropriate measures' might be taken if any factors seem to be hindering the achievement of this.

Part III: Enforcement of Intellectual Property Rights

Part III states that members need to ensure that enforcement procedures consistent with the TRIPS are implemented in their own countries under their laws and that:

> Procedures concerning the enforcement of intellectual property rights shall be fair and equitable. They shall not be unnecessarily complicated or costly, or entail unreasonable time-limits or unwarranted delays. (Article 41, paragraph 2)

There will be a judicial authority overseeing the process. Once administrative decisions have been made they can be reviewed by this judicial authority, if so requested by WTO members. Furthermore:

> The judicial authorities shall have the authority to order the infringer to pay the right holder damages adequate to compensate for the injury the right holder has suffered because of an infringement of that person's intellectual property right by an infringer who knowingly, or with reasonable grounds to know, engaged in infringing activity. (Article 45, paragraph 1)

Various other safeguards, remedies and periods of suspension of activities are all covered in this section in order to try to ensure that enforcement procedures operate effectively.

Part IV: Acquisition and Maintenance of Intellectual Property Rrights and Related *Inter-Partes* Procedures

Part IV states that when members acquire or maintain intellectual property rights, it is acceptable for members to introduce 'reasonable procedures and formalities' as and when necessary, provided that these are consistent with the provisions of the agreement (Article 62, paragraph 1). If this is through a grant or registration procedure, then this needs to be completed within a 'reasonable period of time'. Final administrative procedures in any of these procedures will be 'subject to review by a judicial or quasi-judicial authority' (Article 62, paragraph 5).

Part V: Dispute Prevention and Settlement

A Dispute Settlement Understanding will be used for the settlement of disputes in the Agreement, and this will be based on the provisions of Articles XXII and XXIII of GATT 1994. The Dispute Settlement Process is considered in more detail in Chapter 2, section 2.2.5.

'Transparency' is a term that is also frequently used in various WTO agreements. Transparency is referred to in this section in Article 63, paragraph 1. It states that laws and regulations, final judicial decisions and administrative rulings that are made effective by a WTO member on a subject that is relevant to the Agreement must be published, or, if it is not practically possible for these to be published, then they must be made publicly available in some other way, so that governments and rights holders can become familiar with the material. Agreements concerning the subject matter in TRIPS between the government or the government agency of one member state and that of another state must also be published. Thus those laws and agreements made in individual nation states that are members of the WTO and that are connected with the TRIPS Agreement must be made available to other members, i.e. they must be made transparent.

Members must also notify the Council for TRIPS about these laws and agreements. It does note though that members will not be required to:

> ... disclose confidential information which would impede law enforcement or otherwise be contrary to the public interest or would prejudice the legitimate commercial interests of particular enterprises, public or private. (Article 63, paragraph 4)

Part VI: Transitional Arrangements

Once WTO members from the developed world have signed up to the Agreement they have one year in which to implement the provisions. Thus Part VI states that no member:

> ... shall be obliged to apply the provisions of this Agreement before the expiry of a general period of one year following the date of entry into force of the WTO Agreement. (Article 65, paragraph 1)

Meanwhile, a developing country member is entitled to a delay of up to four years. It also makes it clear that TRIPS is part of the process of the creation of a world-based market, free-enterprise economy as it says in point 3 that:

> Any other Member which is in the process of transformation from a centrally-planned into a market, free-enterprise economy and which is undertaking structural reform of its intellectual property system and facing special problems in the preparation and implementation of intellectual property laws and regulations, may also benefit from a period of delay ...

Part VII: Institutional Arrangements; Final Provisions

The Council for TRIPS will:

> ... monitor the operation of this Agreement and in particular, Members' compliance with their obligations hereunder ... (Article 65)

The Council for TRIPS will review the implementation of the agreement after the transitional period has expired and at further defined periods after this. It will also undertake reviews as and when there are new developments that might need to be incorporated into the Agreement. Finally, there is nothing in the agreement that requires a member to disclose information that it considers to be contrary to its essential security interests.

In conclusion

Some of the main points covered in Parts I and III–VII are:

- IPR legislation in member states must comply with the TRIPS.
- Members must introduce laws and enforcements in their own countries, to ensure that TRIPS is implemented effectively in each member state.

- Appropriate measures will be taken to prevent any abuse with regard to IPRs and to prevent any practices which unreasonably restrict trade.

- No one member must be given additional favourable treatment over another member with regard to IPRs.

- Laws and agreements made in individual member states with regard to IPRs must be made publicly available, i.e. they must be made 'transparent'.

- There will be a judicial authority to ensure that enforcement of TRIPS is carried out effectively.

- The TRIPS agreement will be monitored and reviewed.

7.5 Part II of the TRIPS Agreement (excluding copyright and patents)

Part II of the Agreement covers the different types of intellectual property rights that are covered in TRIPS and is entitled Standards Concerning the Availability, Scope and Use of Intellectual Property Rights. These different intellectual property right areas that are covered within the TRIPS Agreement will be considered further in this chapter, apart from copyright and patents which will be examined separately in Chapters 8 and 9, respectively.

7.5.1 Trade marks

The TRIPS Agreement specifies what types of signs are eligible for protection as trade marks, and what the minimum rights for the owners of the trade marks are. Service marks must be protected in the same way as goods marks. Trade marks are covered under Section 2, within Part II of the TRIPS Agreement, and in Article 15, 'Protectable Subject Matter', paragraph 1 it says that:

> Any sign, or any combination of signs, capable of distinguishing the goods or services of one undertaking from those of other undertakings, shall be capable of constituting a trademark.

These signs include personal names, letters, numerals, figurative elements and combinations of colours. Where signs do not clearly distinguish the relevant goods or services, members can register signs on the grounds of distinctiveness acquired through use.

With regard to the 'rights conferred' in Article 16, it says:

> The owner of a registered trademark shall have the exclusive right to prevent all third parties not having the owner's consent from using in the course of trade identical or similar signs for goods or services which are identical or similar to those in respect of which the trademark is registered where such use would result in a likelihood of confusion. In case of the use of an identical sign for identical goods or services, a likelihood of confusion shall be presumed.

Thus, once a trade mark is registered, the owner of the trade mark will have the exclusive right to stop anyone else from using the trade mark without the owner's consent. The initial registration of a trade mark lasts for a period of no less than seven years. Registration of a trade mark can be renewed indefinitely.

7.5.2 Geographical indications

Sometimes, place names identify a product, such as 'Cheddar cheese', 'Stilton cheese' and 'Scotch whisky'. The place name usually identifies both the geographical origin of the product and its characteristics, i.e. it is a geographical indication, and this is another intellectual property right that is covered under TRIPS. The TRIPS Agreement seeks to prevent the misuse of place names, such as the use of a place name when the product was made elsewhere. Geographical indications are defined in the following way under Section 3, 'Geographical Indications', Article 22, paragraph 1:

> Geographical indications, are, for the purposes of this Agreement, indications which identify a good as originating in the territory of a Member, or a region or locality in that territory, where a given quality, reputation or other characteristic of the good is essentially attributable to its geographical origin.

Thus geographical indications in TRIPS are those indications that identify a good as originating in a particular member state, or in a particular territory within that state, where some distinguishing characteristic of the good is attributable to its geographical origin.

There are exceptions to this, such as 'cheddar', which now refers to a particular type of cheese that is not necessarily made in Cheddar. However, any country wanting to make such an exception must negotiate with the country that is seeking to protect the particular geographical indication in question.

7.5.3 Industrial designs

Industrial designs are covered under Section 4 in the TRIPS Agreement. In Article 25, paragraph 1, of this section, it says that WTO members will, under TRIPS, provide protection for independently created industrial designs that are new or original. Such protection will not extend to designs that are governed by technical or functional considerations.

The WTO, in its document *Trading into the Future*, refers to industrial designs, saying:

> Owners of protected designs must be able to prevent the manufacture, sale or importation of articles bearing or embodying a design which is a copy of the protected design. (WTO, *Trading into the Future*, undated)

Industrial designs have to be protected for at least ten years under TRIPS.

7.5.4 Integrated circuit designs

The protection of integrated circuit designs in TRIPS is based on the Washington Treaty on Intellectual Property in Respect of Integrated Circuits, which falls under WIPO. These IPRs fall under Section 6 of the TRIPS Agreement, which is entitled 'Layout-Designs (Topographies) of Integrated Circuits'. In Article 35 it says that:

> Members agree to provide protection to the layout-designs (topographies) of integrated circuits.

Furthermore, in Article 36 it states that certain acts are unlawful if performed without the authorisation of the right holder. These include importing, selling or distributing in some other manner a protected layout-design for commercial purposes, or an integrated circuit that incorporates a protected layout-design. Such protection must be available for at least ten years.

7.5.5 Trade secrets and undisclosed information

Trade secrets and 'undisclosed information' that have commercial value:

> ... must be protected against breach of confidence and other acts contrary to honest commercial practices. (WTO, *Trading into the Future*, undated)

This comes under Section 7, 'Protection of Undisclosed Information', and it says in Article 39.2 that this protection applies to information that is secret, that has commercial value because it is secret and where steps have been taken to keep it secret. Undisclosed information does not have to be treated as a form of property. However, a person that is lawfully in control of such information must be able to prevent it from being disclosed to, or acquired by, or used by others without his/her consent in a manner that is contrary to honest commercial practices.

Thus many different types of intellectual property rights are covered in the TRIPS Agreement. There are also many different exception clauses and further considerations, referred to in the Agreement itself with regard to these IPRs, some of which have been considered here. They all help to form an integral whole for the TRIPS Agreement.

7.6 Should TRIPS belong to the WTO – is it part of trade?

7.6.1 Introduction

The above, then, has considered the TRIPS Agreement within the overall WTO agenda. However, some have argued that TRIPS does not really belong to the WTO. They argue that whereas the WTO is about trade, TRIPS, in contrast, is about the *regulation* of trade, and is protectionist, so should not really be part of the WTO at all. Martin Khor, the Director of the Third World Network, is of this opinion. He says that:

It is an aberration that TRIPS is located in a trade organisation whose main functions are supposed to be the promotion of trade liberalisation and conditions of market competition, while TRIPS is protectionist and curbs competition. (Khor, 2002a: 10)

Furthermore, a non-governmental organisation (NGO) statement, which was signed by a wide variety of NGOs such as Oxfam International, Christian Aid UK, Public Services International and Grassroots Action, says in its paper *Re-thinking TRIPS in the WTO*:

For many hundreds of civil society groups and NGOs around the world, TRIPS represents one of the most damaging aspects of the WTO. The legitimacy of the WTO is closely linked to that of TRIPS. TRIPS has, in fact, given the multilateral trade system a bad name. (Non-Governmental Organisations, 2001: 1)

They say that TRIPS is being used as a 'protectionist instrument to promote corporate monopolies over technologies, seeds, genes and medicines' (p. 1). By the utilisation of intellectual property rights through TRIPS large corporations protect their markets. This shifts the balance 'away from the public interest, towards the monopolistic privileges of IPR holders' (p. 1). Furthermore, this undermines various sustainable development programmes, such as public health programmes, protecting the environment and the continued realisation of certain economic, social and cultural rights. They conclude by saying that:

We all share the common view that TRIPS represents a significant shift in the balance in intellectual property rights protection that is too heavily in favour of private right holders and against the public interest. (Non-Governmental Organisations, 2001: 5)

These NGOs also ask for the removal of TRIPS from the WTO.

7.6.2 TRIPS – protectionist or part of trade?

Thus some argue that while the WTO is about trade, TRIPS, in contrast, is about the regulation of trade and protectionism, so should not really be part of the WTO at all.

Martin Khor's basic position is that the TRIPS is not part of trade, but instead is primarily designed to help big business, as it engenders and encourages a protectionist environment through IPRs for the benefit of large corporations.

Many others have emphasised that TRIPS provides protection for big business in areas such as drugs, food and the patenting of life-forms. However, big business itself is necessarily part of trade: big business certainly does not operate outside of a trading environment, so to this extent, TRIPS *must* be part of trade, I would suggest. TRIPS is clearly protectionist in some ways, but its overarching aim is to encourage the trading of intellectual property rights. It is only protectionist, I would argue, while such protectionism encourages the trading of intellectual property rights in the long term.

7.6.3 *Trade language embedded in TRIPS*

Indeed, the language in the TRIPS Agreement makes it clear that it aims to create a competitive, market environment, and that it is enthusiastic about the trading of IPRs. It says that:

> Members agree that some licensing practices or conditions pertaining to intellectual property rights which restrain competition may have adverse effects on trade. (Article 40, paragraph 1)

This demonstrates that the TRIPS aims to engender a competitive environment and does not want particular aspects of IPRs to stifle or inhibit this. In Part I, Article 8, paragraph 2, it emphasises that 'appropriate measures' might be needed to:

> ... prevent the abuse of intellectual property rights by right holders or the resort to practices which unreasonably restrain trade ...

Furthermore, in Part I, Article 3 on National Treatment, paragraph 1, it says:

> Each Member shall accord to the nationals of other Members treatment no less favourable than that it accords to its own nationals with regard to the protection of intellectual property ...

Thus each member of the WTO must give nationals of other members the same protection of intellectual property as it does to the people and organisations in its own country. Furthermore, in Article 4 on Most-Favoured-Nation Treatment, it states that:

> ... any advantage, favour, privilege or immunity granted by a Member to the nationals of any other country shall be accorded immediately and unconditionally to the nationals of all other Members.

So, if any particular advantage is given to a member in their own country with regard to IPRs, then this advantage must also be given to all the other WTO members. Thus, if a French company in France, for example, was given certain privileges with regard to its intellectual property by the French government, then these same benefits would also have to be offered to a Belgian company operating in France. This is the same principle that is embedded in the GATS. The intention is clear: it is to create a supposedly 'fair' trading environment on a global basis, with no preferential treatment being given to specific companies operating in particular countries.

Martin Khor says simply that 'IPRs are not a trade issue'. However, the whole purpose of TRIPS is to develop an agreement about the trading of IPRs, so this means that IPRs can be, and indeed are, a trade issue in TRIPS. Once again, the language in the Agreement itself makes the philosophy behind TRIPS clear. In Part VI, Article 65, paragraph 3, for example, it says that:

> Any other Member which is in the process of transformation from a centrally-planned into a market, free-enterprise economy and which is undertaking structural reform of its intellectual property system and facing special problems in the preparation and implementation of intellectual property laws and regulations, may also benefit from a period of delay.

Implicit in this statement is joy within the WTO that countries are transforming from communist countries, embracing global capitalism and joining the WTO as 'one big happy global family'. Furthermore, moral rights have been excluded from the copyright section of the Agreement (this is considered further in Chapter 8, section 8.6), while economic rights have been included, which once again emphasises the focus on trade in TRIPS.

On initial consideration, the argument that TRIPS is not part of trade might sound rather appealing. However, upon closer examination, it became clear to me that the TRIPS Agreement definitely *is* part of trade. The language in the Agreement makes it transparently clear that it is about trade. As we enter the knowledge revolution (R. Rikowski, 2000b, 2000c), ideas, intellectual property rights, information, knowledge, intellectual capital and services, etc., will ensure the success of this latest phase of capitalism and all this will become increasingly more important than the production of manufactured goods. As Leadbeater says:

We are all in the thin-air business these days. (Leadbeater, 1999: 18)

Under this scenario, IPRs become tradable commodities with a price. So IPRs would be traded in the market, in the same spirit as any other goods or services.

In conclusion, the argument that TRIPS should not be part of the WTO might seem, at first, to be rather convincing. Clearly TRIPS is protectionist and encourages some anti-competitive practices. However, upon careful examination it is clear that the TRIPS Agreement definitely *is* part of trade, and indeed that this is its overriding aim. Within this, it has to be protectionist sometimes, otherwise it is unlikely that people would be motivated to create new ideas, and sometimes companies need to be given short-term protectionism with regard to their intellectual property rights to encourage more trading of them in the long term.

7.6.4 Concluding comment

Upon a careful reading of the TRIPS Agreement it is apparent that it is ultimately about trade, trade and more trade. Its primary aim is to trade intellectual property rights. Within this, it is sometimes necessary to be protectionist, but this is just so that more trade can be undertaken in the long term. In the next chapter, on copyright, I will illustrate how moral rights have been excluded from the copyright section of the TRIPS Agreement, which again emphasises the fact that it is about trade, pure and simple.

7.7 Summary

This chapter has considered the definition of intellectual property rights and has examined the TRIPS Agreement itself, and considered how

TRIPS deals with all the different types of intellectual property rights, apart from copyright and patents which are considered further in Chapters 8 and 9 respectively. It then highlights the fact that the language of the Agreement is very much the language of trade, and that the trading of intellectual property rights is its main, overriding objective. Furthermore, TRIPS therefore is very much part of the WTO. The following chapter will consider copyright in TRIPS and the connections with information and libraries.

TRIPS, copyright, libraries and information

8.1 Introduction

There are two types of intellectual property rights in the TRIPS Agreement that are of particular significance for libraries and information – copyright and patents. This chapter focuses on copyright and the following chapter will focus on patents. In the document *Tips for TRIPS*, which was written by the Committee on Copyright and Other Legal Matters (CLM), one of the committees of IFLA, it says:

> Of course, the most important type of intellectual property as far as libraries are concerned is copyright. (CLM, 2002b: 1)

Copyright is included in Part II of the TRIPS Agreement.

Copyright can be defined as the protection of the creators of works, but unlike patents, it protects the expression of ideas rather than the ideas themselves. Thus it is not the idea or the invention in itself that is protected but the form in which this idea is expressed. If it is not expressed in an external, tangible form, then it cannot be protected. Also, as Torremans says:

> Everything starts with the author who has to create works. If there are no works there is nothing to exploit for the entrepreneur. (Torremans, 2001: 220)

Thus everything starts with the creator, but it must be encapsulated in a tangible format.

Copyright protects the creators of, for example, literary, artistic and scientific works. It has also now been extended to protect computer software and databases. Usually, copyright owners have the ability to prevent the unauthorised reproduction, distribution (including rental), sale and adaptation of an original work. The length of protection has increased over time, and today it is usually the life of the author plus 50 years or 50 years or more for works that belong to corporate bodies or organisations.

While most librarians and information professionals are very familiar with copyright as a subject, they might not necessarily think of copyright as being one of the intellectual property rights that forms part of the TRIPS Agreement, particularly given the fact that awareness about GATS and TRIPS is still relatively low anyway. Furthermore, they are unlikely to see it as an important issue. Indeed, awareness is low about many of the agreements being established at the WTO in general.

However, before focusing on copyright in the TRIPS Agreement itself, I will firstly consider a number of key aspects with regard to copyright to provide some background information and to set the scene for the analysis of copyright in TRIPS. This will include a historical perspective on copyright and a focus on moral and economic rights in copyright for creators of works and copyright holders. The notion of balance in copyright and its importance within the library and information profession will also be considered. Following on from this, the chapter will examine the copyright section in TRIPS specifically, and copyright and moral rights with regard to TRIPS. All this will help to demonstrate the importance of copyright in general and the importance that is given to copyright as a subject within the library and information profession. It will become clear that copyright in TRIPS is a very one-sided affair, and it is not concerned with endeavouring to maintain some of the key principles embedded in copyright principles as laid out in the library and information profession. Quite the reverse. Its concern is purely with regard to trade issues pertaining to copyright.

8.2 Historical perspective on copyright

Historically, copyright has been linked to written literary works. Writing copies by hand was very time-consuming, so plagiarism was not really a problem and copyright was not much of an issue. However, with the invention of machinery that made it much easier to produce multiple copies of works, copyright then became an issue and plagiarism became much easier. The invention of the printing press led to the introduction of printing in Europe in the late fifteenth and early sixteenth centuries. Gutenberg, for example, invented the movable type and Caxton developed the printing press in the second half of the fifteenth century. After this, different countries started to introduce copyright legislation. There were two main strands to the copyright legislation. One was the exclusive right to make copies – the entrepreneurial side to copyright. The other was the need to protect the author once multiple copies were being made of their work.

8.2.1 Historical analysis of copyright in several different countries

The history of copyright goes back some 300 years. The first real copyright statute in the UK was the Statute of Anne in 1709, and copyright protection lasted for 14 years. The emphasis was very much on the commercial exploitation of books. Furthermore, as Torremans says:

> Especially in Britain copyright has always had an entrepreneurial, almost industrial, orientation. (Torremans, 2001: 12.)

While the entrepreneurial side dominated in the UK and US, Europe, in contrast, had, and largely still does have, more concern for the author and the creators of works. Towards the end of the eighteenth and the beginning of the nineteenth century the duration for the term of copyright protection gradually increased.

From the mid-1700s other countries developed their own copyright legislation. Denmark and Norway adopted an ordinance in 1741 and Spain introduced a copyright law in 1762. In Prussia, copyright for publishers was first recognised in the Prussian Code of 1794, although authors were not able to obtain rights of their own in Prussia until 1837. Privileges were not replaced by copyright in various Italian States until the early nineteenth century. A law on copyright in Italy was adopted in 1865. In France there were the revolutionary French Decrees of 1791 and 1793, which incorporated copyright and public interest issues. They recognised the rights of the authors, but also the rights of the public to have access to the works. During the next 150 years, the law relating to the rights of authors developed further.

In the USA, the British Colonies in America had no separate copyright statute. However, after the War of Independence (1775–83) Congress passed a resolution with regard to copyright issues and a copyright clause in the American Constitution was formulated in 1787. During the following two or three years, 12 of the 13 States passed Copyright Acts. The terms of protection for the different acts varied and the longest was for 21 years. Congress then passed the Copyright Act of 1790. Between 1789 and 1905 there were 25 laws dealing with copyright in the USA. The House Report on the Copyright Act of 1909 emphasised the importance of encouraging the growth of learning and culture. The Berne Convention Implementation Act of 1988 paved the way and enabled the US to adhere to the Berne Convention for the Protection of Literary and Artistic Works in 1989 (more details with regard to the Berne Convention are given below in section 8.2.2). This brought the USA into the major multilateral copyright convention. Furthermore, moral rights were finally starting to be provided in the USA.

Other UK major copyright legislation has included the 1911 Copyright Act, which increased the term of protection to the life of the author plus 50 years, and introduced reforms which brought UK law into line with the Berne Convention. The 1956 Copyright Act allowed the UK to ratify the Brussels Act of the Berne Convention and provided specific protection for films and TV recordings. Then there was the 1988 Copyright, Designs and Patents Act. This took account of the technological developments that had taken place over the 30 years since the 1956 Act. It also incorporated changes to international protection under the 1971 Paris Act. It dealt with industrial designs, patents and trade marks, as well as with copyright. Gillian Davies (2002: 49) made the point that the 1988 Act restated the law on a more logical and consistent basis, and in a clearer language than the 1956 Act had done. It also introduced protection for satellite broadcasting and cable programmes and the granting of the right to control rental to the authors of films and phonograms and computer programs. Furthermore, it included moral rights and the replacement of the Performing Right Tribunal with a Copyright Tribunal with extended powers over collecting societies. The 1988 Act has now been amended to implement the Information Society Directive, which allows for the ratification of the World Intellectual Property Organisation (WIPO) Copyright Treaty and WIPO Phonograms and Performance Treaty.

Thus copyright laws in individual countries have been extended and developed quite rapidly over the last 300 years. They have gradually included more and more aspects and have been introduced and revised in more and more countries. Today, over 150 countries now have copyright laws. However, what are particularly important to be aware of for this analysis of TRIPS are the international conventions and agreements that have been established for copyright.

8.2.2 International conventions on copyright

Berne Convention

The most important of these international conventions is the *Berne Convention for the Protection of Literary and Artistic Works*, often referred to as the Berne Convention, which was signed at Berne in 1886. It was the Berne Convention that first established the recognition of copyrights between sovereign nations. Before the Berne Convention nations would often not recognise the works of other countries as being copyrighted. Thus a work that had been published in Spain by a Spanish national, for example, would be protected by copyright in Spain, but could be reproduced in other countries without a need to be concerned about any ensuing copyright issues that originated from Spain. The Berne Convention overcame this problem and ensured that each contracting state would recognise the copyright status of works produced in each and every of the other contracting states. The term of copyright protection was for the author's life and 50 years, but parties could now provide longer terms of copyright protection if they wanted to.

The Berne Convention has been revised several times since 1886. It was revised in 1908, for example, as it was felt that there was a need to agree on further minimal rules. No registration was now required, no copyright notice was needed and neither was there a need for any other formality – it just rested on the act of creation of a work. During the 1960s, developing countries asked for major changes to be made to Berne. The result was the Stockholm 1967 and Paris 1971 Revisions of the Berne Convention, but only minimum concessions were granted in the end. The most recent revision was in 1979.

The Berne Convention endeavours to maintain the so-called 'balance in copyright', giving rights to authors while also wanting people to be able to access these works. As Pedley (2003a) emphasised, the Berne Convention is based on three principles:

- 'reciprocal protection' – each state must protect the works of others to the same level as in their own countries;

- minimum standards for the duration and scope of rights – the author's life plus 50 years, or for anonymous works 50 years after first making it available to the public;

- automatic protection, whereby no registration is required.

The Berne Convention now has many members – 150 member states as of 30 June 2002.

Rome Convention

Meanwhile, the *Convention on the Protection of Performers, Producers of Phonograms and Broadcasting Organisations* was signed in Rome in 1961 – generally known as the Rome Convention. The necessity for this emerged with the arrival of sound recording and film industries, when an artist's performance could then be recorded, and there were concerns raised about the way in which such recordings could be used or misused. As Okpaluba says with regard to these performers:

> This led performers to fear that with the spread of new recording techniques they would soon be made redundant and furthermore, secondary uses of performances yielded profits in which the performer wished to share. Consequently, performers wishing to preserve 'live' performances as a means of their employment began to seek protection to control the use of their performances. (Okpaluba, undated: 1)

Proposals to address this issue were put forward at the 1928 Revision Conference for the Berne Convention in Rome, but the French delegation said that performers were not authors, and that performances were not 'works' as defined by the Berne Convention. This delayed the implementation, but at the Rome Convention in 1961 an international convention was drawn up for the protection of the rights of performers, producers of phonograms and broadcasting organisations. This convention provided a minimum standard of protection. In essence, it incorporated three separate conventions for the three areas. However, the Rome Convention never reached the same level of adherence between nations as did the Berne Convention.

Universal Copyright Convention

The Universal Copyright Convention (UCC) was agreed at a UNESCO conference in Geneva in 1952. To begin with, the US would not be part of the Berne Convention (but this has now changed), as it would have required large changes to US copyright law, particularly with regard to moral rights and the registration of copyright works. Thus the Universal Copyright Convention was mainly adopted to cater for the needs of the US. There are several important features of this convention. First, works of a particular country must include a copyright notice to ensure protection in other UCC countries. This was the copyright symbol ©. Second, there is the national treatment principle, whereby foreign works must be treated as though they are national works. There is some similarity here with the principles embedded in both GATS and TRIPS. Third, there is a minimum protection of life plus 50 years. Fourth, the author's translation rights may be subjected to compulsory licensing.

World Intellectual Property Organisation

The World Intellectual Property Organisation (WIPO) is responsible for administering 23 different international treaties that deal with different aspects of intellectual property protection. Its headquarters are in Geneva, Switzerland, and it is one of 16 specialised agencies of the United Nations. There is also a variety of European legislation and a number of directives, such as the European Copyright Directive of 2002. The European Commission aims to harmonise copyright laws in EU member states.

Note

Information for this section was obtained from the following sources of reference – Berne Convention, Davies (2002), Davis (2003), Okpaluba (undated), Pedley (2003a), Torremans (2001).

8.2.3 *Summary*

Copyright has a long history and is a complex issue, with a plethora of legislation, directives, agreements and conventions. Many of the international agreements emphasise the desire to try to obtain harmonisation between countries on copyright issues and to persuade countries to work together on these matters. The Berne Convention, in particular, has played a highly significant part in the formulation of the TRIPS Agreement and this will be considered further in this chapter in sections 8.5 and 8.6.

8.3 Moral and economic rights in copyright for creators of works and copyright holders

8.3.1 Introduction

In terms of analysing copyright within TRIPS, what it is particularly important to consider are the two main rights in copyright for creators of works and copyright holders – these are moral and economic rights. WIPO has emphasised these two main rights, noting that:

> The *economic rights* are the rights of reproduction, broadcasting, public performance, adaptation, translation, public recitation, public display, distribution and so on. The *moral rights* include the author's right to object to any distortion, mutilation or other modification of his work that might be prejudicial to his honor or reputation. (World Intellectual Property Organisation, 2001: 4)

Thus both these sets of rights belong to the creator and/or to the copyright owner and he or she can use them as and when appropriate, if they are included in the appropriate copyright legislation and they have not been waived. However, moral rights have often been excluded from copyright legislation. Even if they are included they are often waived for various reasons and/or they benefit copyright owners more than creators of works, if and when their interests conflict. This will be considered further in this chapter, in section 8.3.2.

The need for a balance is also recognised between the rights of the creator and the entrepreneur. The entrepreneur takes the work, makes it commercially viable, exploits it, and is then able to make a profit out of it. As Torremans says:

What is needed in a perfect copyright system is a sound balance between the rights of the author-creator and those of the entrepreneur who exploits the work. (Torremans, 2001: 220)

Historically, more consideration has been given to the entrepreneur in copyright legislation in the UK and the USA than has been given to the creator. The entrepreneur is sometimes the copyright owner. The entrepreneur could be one and the same person as the creator of the work if the creator then decides to sell and distribute their own work, but usually the creator of the work will offload this risk onto a third party. In the case of authors this will tend to be with an established publisher. Economic rights are likely to benefit the entrepreneur and the copyright owner more than the creator of works. Even moral rights often operate more to the advantage of the entrepreneur in practice.

At the international level, the economic and moral rights are conferred by the Berne Convention. Moral rights are in the middle of the articles that deal with the substance of copyright in the Berne Convention, which illustrates the fact that they are seen to be an important part of the Convention.

8.3.2 Historical perspective on moral rights and problems with regard to enforcing moral rights

It has taken a long time for moral rights to be included in much of national copyright legislation. Europe has been far more enlightened and ahead of the UK and the USA in this regard. Moral rights were only incorporated in Britain for the first time in the 1988 Copyright, Designs and Patents Act (CDPA). As Torremans said:

The introduction of moral rights in the Act was clearly a step in the right direction ... It becomes clear that the concept of moral rights is not yet fully integrated in the UK's entrepreneurial style copyright system. (Torremans, 2001: 233)

Moral rights in the US were also introduced at around this time. Bently emphasised the fact that the problem with UK copyright law is that it treats copyright like any other property and allows it to be sold.

Furthermore, even in the 1988 Act there is a waiver facility, whereby moral rights can be, and in fact usually are, surrendered. As Bently said:

> In practice, the effect of the waiver facility is that 'moral rights' do in fact tend to be waived by authors, composers, photographers and directors, when they assign their rights. The 1988 Act may have given creators moral rights, but the waiver provision means that in nearly all cases the creator is forced to give them up. (Bently, 2002: 9)

The picture in Europe is different: more consideration has been given to the creators of works and to their moral rights. In France, for example, moral rights were given a prominent place in the 1957 legislation. Gillian Davies emphasises that:

> The moral rights of the author were given pride of place so as to protect the personality of the author through the work. (Davies, 2002: 171)

In Germany, moral rights were included in the German Copyright Act of 9 September 1965 and Dutch copyright law was largely founded in the Copyright Act of 1912, which conferred both moral and economic rights on authors. Italian copyright law is mainly contained in the Law no. 633 of 22 April 1941 and this also gave authors both moral and economic rights (Bently, 2002: 63–74).

Meanwhile, the British Copyright Council considers moral rights particularly with regard to the digital age, saying:

> Today, in our digital society, the opportunities to interfere with and distort the works of authors and performers are greater than ever before (as implicitly acknowledged by Art. 5 of the WIPO Performances and Phonograms Treaty, 1996). It is increasingly important to ensure that moral rights are effectively protected and to limit the opportunities for those using the works of creators to unreasonably avoid their application. (British Copyright Council, 2001: 3)

There is a recognition here with regard to the difficulty of enforcing moral rights, and that there are many opportunities to exploit, lessen or even nullify the moral rights of creators. Furthermore, this has certainly not been lessened by the digital age, and the problems might well increase. The British Copyright Council also makes the point that the rights of creators in general, as recognised by Article 27(2) of the Universal Declaration of Human Rights, still need full legislative recognition, practical application and enforcement in many jurisdictions. Many creators believe their moral rights in their creative works to be as important, if not more so, than their economic rights, which emphasises the importance of moral rights. However, some countries still do not express the moral rights, or even if there is provision for expression, the rights are sometimes inadequately expressed or are limited in the scope that they cover, or as already indicated, they can be, and are, waived in various ways. It can also be costly to enforce moral rights.

8.3.3 Moral rights

What exactly are these *moral rights*? Four distinct moral rights can be identified.

- paternity right – the right to be identified as the author or director of a work;
- integrity right – the right of the author or director of a work to object to derogatory treatment of their work;
- the right for everyone not to have a work falsely attributed to them;
- the commissioner's right of privacy in respect of a photograph or film made for private and domestic purposes.

Only the first two of these are full moral rights as the last two do not confer special rights on the actual creator of the work.

The aim with regard to *paternity right* is to give rights to the creator of the work. This right is restricted to literary, dramatic, musical or artistic works and films. Every commercial publication and every public performance requires the identification of the author and identification is not just restricted to the first publication or performance. The identification must be very clear. The paternity right is not granted automatically. Instead, the author, director, creator or composer that wants to benefit from it has to assert it. There has to be a written document, which must be signed by or on behalf of the author or creator. The paternity right can be asserted at any time during the life of the author and or creator, but it is not retrospective.

The *integrity* right, the right to object to derogatory treatment of a work, applies to the authors or creators of literary, dramatic, musical and artistic works and directors of films (the same as with paternity rights). It only applies to works that are and remain in copyright. Derogatory treatment involves additions, deletions, alterations or adaptations that cause distortion or mutilation of the work. But this does not include criticism of a work. However, when does an act amount to distortion or mutilation? This is a difficult and complex decision. This decision obviously cannot be left to the creator. Instead, it has to be proven:

> ... that the distortion or other mutilation of [the] work really prejudices [the author's] lawful intellectual or personal interests in the work. (Dietz, 1994)

With regard to 'false attribution of the work', this is where the authors or directors have the right to be identified. They should only have a right to be so identified if they really are the creators of the work. This applies to literary, dramatic, musical and artistic works and films. This right applies, for example, to adaptations that are falsely presented as adaptations of the work of a person. Thus it helps to ensure that the person who has created the work is clearly identified and that no one else can falsely pretend that they are the creator.

Finally, with regard to the 'right to privacy in relation to commissioned photos', this concerns the role of the commissioner of photographs. When someone commissions a photograph, the photographers gain ownership of the copyright, as they are the creators of the work. But sometimes those commissioning photographs might not be happy for the photographs to be distributed just according to the wishes of the photographers. Someone commissioning their wedding photographs might not want these distributed freely by the photographer, for example. Hence, this right seeks to offer some protection to the commissioner, and the commissioner has the right not to have copies of the photograph issued to the public, for example, and not to have the photograph included in a broadcast or a cable programme service.

In general, moral rights recognise the importance of treating the works of creators with respect. However, as Jennifer Davis (2003: 140) said, in reality moral rights often favour the copyright owner over the creator, if and when their interests conflict. Furthermore, many authors and creators of works are ignorant of their moral rights, or do not have much bargaining strength if the copyright owner asks for them to be waived (i.e. where copyright owners and creators are not one and the same person and where their interests conflict). Moral rights can also be expensive to enforce. Furthermore, some copyright legislation, such as the UK CDPA 1988, sets out important exceptions and waivers where moral rights do not apply. Also, paternity rights and integrity rights do not apply where works are made for the reporting of current events or for publication in newspapers, magazines or periodicals. Thus this places limitations on the moral rights that creators can claim. All these factors can make it very difficult for creators to claim their full moral rights.

8.3.4 Economic rights

In contrast, what are *economic rights*? Paul Pedley in his book *Essential Law for Information Professionals* (2003a: 19) explains clearly what these rights are. Economic rights cover the following areas: the right to copy the work (which includes storing it electronically), the right to issue copies of the work to the public and the right to rent or lend the work, as well as the right to perform, show or play the work in public, the right to communicate the work to the public (this was introduced by the WIPO treaty and then by the European Directive) and the right to make an adaptation or translation of the work. As Pedley emphasises, if anyone other than the copyright owner performs any of these activities without permission or licence, unless it falls under a statutory exception, then that would constitute an infringement of the copyright. Various other acts constitute secondary infringements. These include importing an infringing copy, possessing or dealing with an infringing copy, providing the means for making infringing copies, permitting the use of premises for infringing performance and providing apparatus for infringing performance. Economic rights particularly benefit the entrepreneurial side.

8.3.5 Summary

In summary, creators of works and copyright owners have two rights – moral and economic. Moral rights have to be claimed, but it can sometimes be difficult to claim one's moral rights and they can also be expensive to enforce. Also, there are various waivers to moral rights and at times there is no or inadequate expression of one's moral rights. Furthermore, where the rights of the creator(s) of the work and the copyright owner conflict, the copyright owner is more likely to gain the moral rights and to come out on the winning side. Thus the interests of the person or organisation that is commercially exploiting the work often take precedence over those of the creator of the work – the person(s) who had the ideas and inspiration behind and in the creation of the work. This, once again, illustrates the power and logic of capitalism. Commercial exploitation, profit-making, trading and markets are viewed as being more important and take precedence over people and their ideas. Meanwhile, economic rights are more part of the entrepre-neurial side, where money can be made from creative works. This could be by the creators themselves if they decide to market, sell and distribute their own work, but more often than not it is by a third party, such as a publisher. Economic rights include, for example, the right to copy the work and the right to rent or lend the work.

The significance of these rights in TRIPS is considered later in this chapter, in section 8.6. However, an understanding and appreciation of the importance of moral and economic rights in copyright is important. Moral rights should be included in all copyright agreements, legislation, directives and conventions, I would suggest, but they have often not been. This applies to the TRIPS, in particular, from which moral rights have been excluded.

Note

Information for this section was obtained from the following sources of reference – Bently (2002), Davies (2002), Davis (2003), Pedley (2003a), Torremans (2001).

8.4 The 'balancing act' in copyright and the library and information profession

8.4.1 Introduction

However, the most important principle with regard to copyright, as far as the library and information profession is concerned, is the aim to achieve a balance in copyright. This concerns trying to achieve a balance between the creators of works and copyright holders (both their moral and their economic rights) with the free flow of information, which enables the public to have easy access to these works. The moral and economic rights, as described above, represent one half of this balance. As Gillian Davies said with regard to this overall balance:

> The copyright system as it has developed over the past nearly 300 years has created, in the public interest, a balance between the rights of the authors, on the one hand, and the interest of the public in access to protected works, on the other. (Davies, 2002: 7)

The balance in copyright has been expressed in Article 27 of the Universal Declaration of Human Rights.

8.4.2 Statute of Anne

The balance in copyright was first introduced in the UK Statute of Anne of 1709 and four principles with regard to the balance were defined. These were natural law, just reward for labour, stimulus to creativity and social requirements. The principle of the natural law of property first came from Locke (1690). This natural law originated from the premise that people had a natural right of property with regard to their own bodies, and so therefore people also had a natural right to own the labour of their bodies. With regard to copyright, this would usually mean the right to own the fruits of their intellectual labour. (Interesting parallels could be drawn here between this and Marx's concept of labour and labour power, but this will not be developed here.) The 'just reward for labour' is about giving authors economic rewards. 'Just reward for labour' provided a stimulus to creativity. So, the third principle is about encouraging creators to create. The 'social requirement' concerned the wider interests of society with regard to these issues. Thus it is in the public interest that authors and other right owners should be encouraged to publish their works (G. Davies, 2002: 13–17).

8.4.3 The balance in copyright and the principles of balance embedded within the library and information profession in general and in IFLA in particular

It is clear that both people and organisations that come up with new ideas need to be able to have those ideas protected, otherwise they will not feel inclined to share their ideas with others in the future. People could be open to exploitation if they were not protected in this way and often they want some form of monetary compensation, i.e. they ideally need to receive both their moral and economic rights. Rules on copyright therefore try to overcome this problem. However, there is obviously a dilemma, because too much protection can go against the free flow of ideas and might not be for the good of society as a whole. The library and information profession is very aware of the importance of all this. As IFLA states librarians and information professionals are committed to giving access to copyright works, and to the free flow of information, while also recognising the importance of the rights of authors, creators of works and copyright owners. Indeed:

> IFLA supports balanced copyright law that promotes the advancement of society as a whole by giving support and effective protection for the interests of rightsholders as well as reasonable access in order to encourage creativity, innovation, research, education and learning. (IFLA, 2000, revised 2001: 1)

In a paper that he presented at the IFLA Conference in Jerusalem in August 2000 Nick Smith emphasised that copyright provides an incentive for authors to create their own works. He said that there is little to be gained by having freedom of access to information if there is no information to access, and copyright provides this incentive. Without this, only the rich or those that are willing to tolerate poverty are likely to be prepared to share their ideas. If you are not hungry then you will be better equipped to enjoy freedom of expression. So, copyright provides an incentive for creators, but also means that restrictions are placed on who can have access to these works of creation.

Furthermore, Pedley refers to the role that library and information professionals find themselves playing on copyright matters, noting that:

> Library and information service professionals find themselves in a difficult situation playing the role of 'piggy in the middle', acting as guardians of intellectual property whilst at the same time being committed to supporting their users' needs to gain access to copyright works and the ideas that they contain. (Pedley, 2003a: 47)

Thus library and information professionals find themselves playing a 'piggy in the middle' role, trying to obtain some overall, idealised balance.

The IFLA Committee on Copyright and Other Legal Matters (CLM, 2001) is particularly concerned about copyright and control issues, and is keen to try to ensure that copyright law does not inhibit the free flow of information. The CLM says that copyright protection should encourage rather than inhibit use and creativity. Furthermore, it argues that access to information, rather than the control of information, increases use. The CLM argues that copyright law should not give power to enable copyright rightsholders to override exceptions.

There are also problems of inequality and copyright, which the CLM considers in its paper 'Limitations and exceptions to copyright' (CLM, 2002a). It emphasises the need to make information available in libraries and information centres to lessen inequalities in the provision of information (between the haves and the have-nots in the information world), but also emphasises the need to protect the rights of authors and the creators of original works. They say:

> IFLA maintains that unless libraries and citizens are granted exceptions which allow reasonable and fair use for purposes which do not harm the interests of right owners, and which are in the public interest and in line with fair practice such as education and research, there is a danger that only those who can afford information will be able to take advantage of the benefits of the Information Society. (CLM, 2002a: 13)

The CLM refers to the dangers which large corporate conglomerates can pose, particularly now that we live in a digital age. They say that some copyright owners can wield enormous power by setting their own rules, and that this does not take into account the need for balance. The CLM does not want to witness a situation where control of information lies within the power of a small number of large international corporations, and it says that:

> If all uses of information are controlled, only the affluent will be able to receive the benefit of access to the world's creative output. IFLA is concerned that, unless this control is limited, it will interfere with the greater good of society. (CLM, 2002a: 16)

The CLM says that it is the role of governments to put the interests of society first on these matters. Once again, this highlights the problem with regard to the large amount of power that large corporations can wield in relation to copyright, and the importance of government intervention. Clearly, micropayments could also play a significant part here. Large corporations could control information on the Internet through copyright rules and then gradually micropayment mechanisms could be introduced, whereby people have to pay for this information through the Net. All this could have serious implications when endeavouring to maintain the balance in copyright.

Nick Smith (2000) also refers to the *digital age* and copyright and how this could become an even greater barrier to the freedom of access to information:

> Copyright in the digital environment frequently allows a level of control over information that a totalitarian state would find attractive ... in the digital environment, there are no copyright free zones as far as libraries are concerned. To provide services digitally that are anything like services that are provided in cyberspace, libraries either need licences or they need to be operating under a copyright exception of some kind. There is no digital equivalent of just buying a book and putting it on a shelf without having to worry about copyright. (Smith, 2000: 4–6)

Smith finds it ironic that we now live in a digital age, where access to information should be easier, when in reality it is often made more difficult because of copyright. Now, to provide information digitally, libraries either need licences or need to be operating under a copyright exception.

Thus the balance in copyright is an important principle in the library and information profession, and it covers many different areas and concerns. The balance in copyright and its place within TRIPS is considered further in this chapter in the following section (section 8.4.4) and in section 8.7. I also return to the topic in Chapter 10, section 10.2.1.

8.4.4 The balance in copyright: three parts to the balance – not just one

The previous section emphasised how important the balance of copyright issue is to the library and information profession, and focused on some of the many different areas that the profession has considered. However, there is an important omission from the literature. This concerns the way in which the balance is expressed and analysed. It is often presented as though there is just one balance – this being the free flow of information versus the rights of creators of works and copyright holders. Yet, although there is only one main balance, there also needs to be a balance within each half of the balance. Thus, for clarity, there is a need to clearly articulate the fact that there are actually three parts to the balance, rather than just one. This is not expressed explicitly in the copyright literature in general, or in the copyright literature in the library and information profession in particular. This can lead to confusion and a lack of understanding in relation to the main issues that are involved, and can make it more difficult for people to conceptualise this notion of balance.

Thus there is the main balance – endeavouring to maintain a balance between the rights of creators of works and copyright holders versus the free flow of information. But then there is the need to try to obtain a balance for each half of the balance. For the rights of creators of works and copyright holders this involves endeavouring to obtain a balance between economic rights and moral rights, although, as I have already outlined, this balance is seldom really aimed at or achieved.

Meanwhile, the free flow of information encompasses a number of different aspects, including free access to information, intellectual freedom, freedom of expression and freedom of information. However, to obtain a balance between all these different aspects is not easy, even on initial inspection. But if one investigates this at a deeper level, the situation becomes even more problematic. I am suggesting in this book that there are four main aspects with regard to the free flow of information which need to be balanced, but others might well disagree with me – it is not as clearly laid out as the rights for creators of works and copyright holders are. There are two types of rights, moral (of which there are four) and economic (six). But the free flow of information? It is not clearly laid down, stipulating what the different aspects are, how many there are, and how they are categorised. So, while I am arguing that there are four main aspects, others might disagree with me, and say there are more or less or different aspects, or that I have broken down the categories incorrectly. Byrne (2000a), for example, argues that intellectual freedom encompasses freedom of thought, freedom of inquiry and freedom of expression. For him, freedom of expression is a sub-category within intellectual freedom, whereas I am giving them equal weighting.

Even if agreement can be established about what the aspects are, the next question then becomes – how much weighting should they be given? If there are four main aspects, as I am suggesting, then should they all be given equal weighting – 25 per cent each? Or should freedom of information be considered to be more important than freedom of expression, for example? So, should freedom of information be given a weighting of, say, 30 per cent and freedom of expression be given a weighting of, say, 20 per cent? Then, how does one go about measuring the weighting? The task starts to become enormous. The weighting problem also applies to the rights for creators of works and copyright holders, but this task is not quite as big as the free flow of information task, as we have definite categories and points that we can work with. However, the more one starts to think about all these issues, then the more complex it all starts to become. Indeed, it essentially becomes impossible. Although I have highlighted these problems, it is not fundamentally my task to try to solve them. That is the responsibility for those arguing that there is a need for a balance in copyright, and that it is ultimately possible to achieve this balance in global capitalism.

However, there is definitely a need for more clarity in the way this balance is expressed and analysed. Only once we have this clarity can we then move on to a more theoretical level. Then, the inadequacies in relation to this notion of balance would be more clearly exposed. Thus I hope that in the future, in the light of my work, the issue will be addressed, particularly within the library and information profession itself.

It is impossible to achieve this balance in any idealised sense while we live under global capitalism, as far as I am concerned. More specifically, we are asking the wrong set of questions altogether. Rather than focusing so closely on the notion of balance and other ethical issues, we need to address and work with Marx's concepts, as these concepts expose the intrinsic workings of the capitalist system. Notions of free access to information in particular, and the balance in copyright in general, just tamper with it and try to make it more palatable. It is better to have these idealised notions, rather than just swim happily along in the capitalist tide. To this extent the activities of the library and information profession should be commended. But if we try to work with them, and endeavour to find real, meaningful and lasting solutions to these issues, we will be continually frustrated and find ourselves going round in circles. We are asking the wrong set of questions, and in an ultimate sense, not getting anywhere! This brings us back to the need for and importance of Marxism.

8.4.5 Conclusion

In conclusion, the main balance in copyright is about trying to obtain a balance between rights for the creators of works and copyright holders and the free flow of information. However, these two aims are fundamentally contradictory. We try to obtain a balance, but no ideal balance can ever really be found, I would suggest, while we live under global capitalism. Endeavouring to obtain this balance certainly holds no real place in the TRIPS Agreement, and TRIPS represents part of the sharp edge of capitalism. The language of balance does not form any real part of the TRIPS Agreement.

Thus there is an idealistic desire to try to obtain this so-called 'balance'. The assumption seems to be that all that is required is some sort of 'balancing act' and that solutions can be found which will suit all the various parties. But it is an idealised notion. It is commendable that the library and information profession has these worthwhile aims (it is certainly better than not having them), and better than being totally sucked into the aims of the capitalist web, but their utopian nature needs to be fully appreciated.

However, I would contend that global capitalism does not enable ultimate solutions to be found and that, instead, it is a system upon which only various compromises can ever be made and that within any given situation some people will suffer more than others. Global capitalism is a system based on irresolvable contradictions and is not founded on any moral base, and this is considered further in Chapter 12, section 12.3. We all live in this global capitalist world and we attempt to make sense of it, but in an ultimate sense it is impossible to do this. So, this idealised balance can never be arrived at in an ultimate way. The workings of capitalism are such that it cannot be concerned with trying to obtain this balance. Instead, its aim is to increase trade and competition. This is demonstrated clearly through TRIPS, and this fact is highlighted in this book. Thus there is no significant reference to the balance in copyright in the TRIPS Agreement because this is not its ultimate concern. Indeed, it cannot be its ultimate concern, which is the trading of intellectual property rights.

To the extent that considering the notion of balance can help such trade, then the balance will be taken seriously and efforts will be made to try to ensure that some balance is obtained. With regard to the rights of creators of works and copyright holders, for example, creators need to receive some rights otherwise many will not be motivated enough to create, and this would be seriously damaging for capitalism (to say the least). Therefore, creators are given some rights, but these rights must not, indeed cannot, override trade considerations. So, economic rights are given more importance, are included in more of the copyright legislation than moral rights and are easier to claim than moral rights – which is one useful way of trying to deal with this issue.

Similarly, to some extent, various elements of the free flow of information are necessary to enable global capitalism to thrive. Companies need to be able to obtain some information easily, for example, and creators need some easy access to information and, indeed, this also extends to the public at large. It is impossible to predict where the next pocket of success for capitalism might lie – it seeks new markets, new ideas and new means for obtaining value from everywhere. It must be looked at within this context. Thus only the free access to information that is beneficial to global capitalism is celebrated. But obviously, it can be difficult to decipher where this actually resides. So, we have many anomalies in capitalism, and many contradictions arise within its never-ending quest for new markets, new commodities and new forms for establishing and perpetuating trade.

However, the important point always to bear in mind is that trade considerations will, and indeed must, always override other considerations. This is exemplified and highlighted in TRIPS, from which moral rights, for example, have been excluded (this is considered further in section 8.6). This means that, ultimately, the notion of the free flow of information is subservient to the trade agenda. Thus principles embedded in the library and information profession, including the notion of balance in copyright, must always take second place to trade and to the needs of capitalism itself.

8.5 Copyright in TRIPS (in Part II of the Agreement)

'Copyright and Related Rights' is in Section 1 of Part II of the TRIPS Agreement, which is entitled 'Standards Concerning the Availability, Scope and Use of Intellectual Property Rights'. In Article 9 in this section it says in relation to copyright that:

> Members shall comply with Articles 1 through 21 of the Berne Convention (1971) and the Appendix thereto.

During the Uruguay Round negotiations, it was recognised that the Berne Convention already largely provided adequate basic standards for copyright protection. However, members also have to comply with the provisions of the Paris Act of 1971 of the Berne Convention, i.e. Articles 1–21 of the the Berne Convention (1971) and the Appendix (but moral rights are excluded from this – see section 8.6 below). Thus, as the WTO says:

> The provisions of the Berne Convention referred to deal with questions such as subject-matter to be protected, minimum term of protection, and rights to be conferred and permissible limitations to those rights. The Appendix allows developing countries, under certain conditions, to make some limitations to the right of translation and the right of reproduction. (WTO, undated:a)

Thus most of the Berne Convention is incorporated in TRIPS. This also illustrates the importance of examining the international conventions and agreements that have been established, as I outlined in section 8.2.2. The pattern starts to fit together. It also makes it clear in the TRIPS Agreement that copyright in TRIPS covers the expression of ideas and not the ideas themselves.

Other areas that fall within the copyright section of the TRIPS Agreement includes computer programs and compilations of data and other material, either in machine readable form or other form:

> ... which by reasons of the selection or arrangement of their contents constitute intellectual creations. (Article 10)

It also includes rental rights, where authors can authorise or prohibit the commercial rental to the public of their copyright works (Article 11).

The 'Term of Protection' is laid out in Article 12. For authors, protection is for the life of the author plus 50 years. Whenever the term of protection of a work, other than a photographic work or a work of applied art, is calculated on a basis that is not the life of the natural person, then that term will not be less than 50 years.

Meanwhile, Article 14 is about the 'Protection of Performers, Producers of Phonograms (Sound Recordings) and Broadcasting Organizations'. This article enables performers and broadcasting organisations to prevent acts from being performed, without their authorisation, for a certain period of time. The term of protection for performers and phonograms lasts for at least 50 years from the end of the calendar year in which the fixation was made or the performance took place.

The final section in Part II of the TRIPS Agreement is Section 8 and is entitled 'Control of Anti-competitive Practices in Contractual Licences' and it notes in paragraph 1 of Article 40 that:

> Members agree that some licensing practices or conditions pertaining to intellectual property rights which restrain competition may have adverse effects on trade and may impede the transfer and dissemination of technology.

Thus it notes that some licensing practices or other conditions in relation to intellectual property rights inhibit competition and may have a detrimental effect on trade.

In paragraph 2 of Article 40 it notes that:

> Nothing in this Agreement shall prevent Members from specifying in their legislation licensing practices or conditions that may in particular cases constitute an abuse of intellectual property rights having an adverse effect on competition in the relevant market.

Thus, in essence, this article is emphasising its enthusiasm with regard to (or, at least, it certainly does not want to be a barrier to) WTO member countries including conditions in their intellectual property rights legislation that will aid in creating a competitive environment for intellectual property rights. That is, if members should wish to do so.

Members can also adopt measures to prevent or control practices, such as grantback conditions. Thus this section emphasises the need to maintain a competitive environment and introduces measures to try to prevent abuses of intellectual property rights.

The copyright section of TRIPS is quite short, but remains a very important section as far as the library and information profession is concerned.

8.6 Moral rights and the copyright section of TRIPS

As I have already outlined in section 8.3, there are two rights in copyright – moral and economic rights. Ideally, both of these should be included in all copyright legislation, agreements, directives and conventions, although in reality moral rights are often excluded. This, as I have suggested, is because of the drive embedded within capitalism itself, where entrepreneurial motives and trade are bound to take precedence over moral and humane considerations.

Moral rights have been excluded from the copyright section of the TRIPS Agreement. The WTO says that most of the Berne Convention is to be included in TRIPS but that this does not include the moral rights in the Berne Convention. It says:

> With the exception of the provisions of the Berne convention on moral rights, all the main substantive provisions ... are incorporated by reference and thus become obligations under the TRIPS Agreement between TRIPS Member countries. (WTO, undated:a: 1)

Later on in this same document it elaborates on this point further, saying that:

> However, Members do not have rights or obligations under the TRIPS Agreement in respect of the rights conferred under Article 6 bis of that Convention, i.e. the moral rights (the right to claim authorship and to object to any derogatory action in relation to a work, which would be prejudicial to the author's honour or reputation), or of the rights derived therefrom. (WTO, undated:a: 4)

Thus a very important part of the Berne Convention that was established over 100 years ago has been excluded from the TRIPS Agreement.

As I have already indicated, even where moral rights are included in copyright legislation, they can sometimes be difficult to enforce, there are often waiver facilities, and it can be difficult for creators to obtain their appropriate moral rights. But if they are not there at all, then creators really are at a serious disadvantage!

Meanwhile, the IFLA CLM notes that:

> The only provisions of the Berne Convention which have not been incorporated into TRIPS concern moral rights. Moral rights are the right of the author to control certain uses of their works to protect their reputation as artists, and for their authorship to be recognized. Moral rights are distinct from what are sometimes known as

> economic rights (such as the right to make copies or the right to broadcast). (CLM, 2002b: 1)

Note, in particular, that moral rights are the only part of the Berne Convention that have been excluded. The European Commission has some appreciation of the fact that 'moral rights' are not always taken seriously and, indeed, Europe has placed far more importance on moral rights than either the USA or the UK has done historically (see section 8.3.2). The European Commission exposes the fact that the US is not meeting its obligations with regard to 'moral rights' for authors, saying:

> Despite the unequivocal obligation contained in Article 6 bis of the Berne Convention, to which the US acceded in 1989, to make 'moral rights' available for authors, the US has never introduced such rights and has repeatedly announced that it has no intention to do so in the future. It is clear that while US authors benefit fully from moral rights in the EU, the converse is not true, which leads to an imbalance of benefits from Berne Convention membership to the detriment of the European side. It is noted that the US has ratified and implemented the World Intellectual Property Organisation (WIPO) Copyright Treaty and the WIPO Performances and Phonograms Treaty. Adherence to these Treaties by the US requires legislation on moral rights at least for performers. (European Commission, 2003: 63.)

Thus the USA benefits from moral rights in the European Union, but does not reciprocate. However, in signing up to the WIPO Treaty and the WIPO Performances and Phonograms Treaty the USA does, at least, have to meet its obligations with regard to moral rights for performers. However, all this demonstrates that the USA is not 'playing fair' with Europe, let alone with the developing world, with regard to IPR issues. The report notes that several parts of US intellectual property legislation are not consistent with various US international commitments, and that, in this regard, there is a lack of recognition of the moral rights of authors. Furthermore, Drahos and Braithwaite are particularly critical of the USA with regard to TRIPS, saying that:

> The US has also been successful in excluding from TRIPS the recognition of authors' rights, based on European philosophical traditions that recognise an indissoluble link between creators and their

works, the key ones being the right to paternity – which gives, for example, the composer of a song the right to be identified as such, and the right to integrity – the right of the author of any type of work and film to object to any addition to, deletion from or change to his or her work if this is detrimental to the work or to the reputation of the author. (Drahos and Braithwaite, 2003: 16–17)

This could all be interpreted simply as the USA being 'the bad guys' but this would be over-simplifying the issue and indeed would surely be missing the fundamental point. This is that the USA represents the sharp edge of capitalism – capitalism will always be particularly strident in certain areas and sectors, and it is virulent in the USA. But it is the global capitalist agenda itself that is pushing this forward. Thus economic considerations and trade will and must always override moral considerations in global capitalism, and this agenda is being driven forward particularly powerfully in the US, the powerhouse of capitalism, through TRIPS.

8.7 The balance in copyright and TRIPS

As already indicated, the most important principle regarding copyright as far as the library and information profession is concerned, is the aim to achieve a balance in copyright. The notion of a balance between the rights of creators of works and copyright holders and the free flow of information goes back some 300 years. However, while it is commendable that the profession has this idealised notion, rather than accepting global capitalism at face value, it needs to be recognised that it is a utopian aim. Furthermore, it is not actually possible to achieve it under this political system. TRIPS is at the forefront of driving global capitalism forward. Notions of balance can hinder the progress of capitalism, although not necessarily so, at least in the short term. But this explains why there is no significant reference to this notion of balance in TRIPS. Further analysis of the balance in copyright will be examined in Chapter 10, section 10.2.1. However, in this chapter I have focused on moral rights in copyright, and the fact that they have been excluded from TRIPS. In this way I have illustrated the fact that TRIPS is not concerned with endeavouring to achieve a balance, and that trade considerations must override moral ones.

8.8 Conclusion

This chapter has considered copyright issues in general, including a historical analysis of copyright, moral and economic rights in copyright for creators of works and copyright holders, the balancing act in copyright, the copyright section in TRIPS specifically and copyright and moral rights issues in TRIPS. Given the importance that the TRIPS Agreement is likely to have on a global basis in the long term, an analysis of how copyright in TRIPS is likely to impact on the library and information profession is clearly very important. This will be examined further in Chapter 10, section 10.2.1, building on the work in this chapter. As Dr David Gervais said:

> The TRIPS Agreement, together with the 1968 Stockholm Conference that adopted the revised Berne and Paris Conventions and created the World Intellectual Property Organization (WIPO), is undoubtedly the most significant milestone in the development of intellectual property in the twentieth century. (Gervais, 2003: 3)

Thus this significant milestone must not and cannot be easily ignored! The following chapter will examine patents in TRIPS and traditional knowledge, focusing in particular on the developing world.

TRIPS, patents, traditional knowledge, information and libraries in the developing world

9.1 Introduction

This chapter will examine the patent section of TRIPS and its relationship to traditional knowledge, information and libraries in the developing world. First the patent section of TRIPS, in Part II of the Agreement, will be examined. Then I will consider TRIPS, patents, copyright and traditional knowledge. Finally, TRIPS in the developing world in general will be explored. The role of the librarian/information professional in all these areas will be considered. The patent section of TRIPS and its implications for libraries and information in the developed world will not be explored. The situation with regard to these matters in the developing world seems to be of far more concern and immediate than for those in the developed world.

9.2 Patents in TRIPS (in Part II of the Agreement)

Patents are another intellectual property right that is included in TRIPS and are in Part II of the Agreement. Patent law has been developed, in general, to provide an incentive for inventors, so that their inventions can then be made accessible to the public. Patent invention must be available for different inventions for at least 20 years in TRIPS and this includes patents for both products and processes. Patents are in Section 5, and in Article 27 it says that:

> ... patents shall be available for any inventions, whether products or processes, in all fields of technology, provided that they are new, involve an inventive step and are capable of industrial application.

Plant varieties, also, must be protected by patents or by a special system, such as breeder's rights. Included in the agreement are the minimum rights that a patent owner has. The agreement also seeks to ensure that the patent owner does not abuse these rights, which he/she could do by, for example, not supplying the product on the market. To overcome this, governments can issue 'compulsory licences' that allow competitors to produce the product or use the process under licence. Thus this also reflects the enthusiasm for trade that is embedded in the agreement.

There are also various exclusions. If governments decide that the commercial exploitation of a particular invention could have undesirable consequences for public order and morality, then that government can refuse to issue a patent. Other types of patents can also be excluded, such as diagnostic and surgical methods and plants and animals.

9.3 TRIPS, patents, copyright and traditional, indigenous knowledge

The patent section of TRIPS impacts on the library and information profession, albeit somewhat more indirectly than the copyright section. Certainly, patents are not considered to be such an important topic for the library and information profession as copyright, yet it still plays a significant part. In this section, I will examine traditional, indigenous knowledge in the developing world and the patenting of this knowledge. Copyright issues will also be considered in relation to this, where they are applicable.

9.3.1 The TRIPS Agreement and traditional knowledge

The TRIPS Agreement does not refer to traditional knowledge (TK) directly. However, it is clear that the TRIPS agreement is likely to impact on TK. Drahos and Braithwaite refer to patent law and TRIPS, for example, saying that:

> Patent law ... has become one of the main mechanisms by which public knowledge assets have been privatized. TRIPS itself is an outcome of this process of privatization of the intellectual commons. (Drahos and Braithwaite, 2002: 150)

Here, Drahos and Braithwaite are drawing attention to the fact that the 'intellectual commons', which includes TK, is being patented and privatised, and then traded through TRIPS.

It should be noted that most people and organisations such as NGOs that look at and are concerned about patents in TRIPS examine areas other than libraries and information. They focus, in particular, on areas such as drugs, genes and the patenting of life-forms. Thus I am exploring a very new, undeveloped area here.

The TRIPS Agreement, as I have already made clear, is fundamentally about the trading of intellectual property rights. So, the aim is to encapsulate knowledge, information, ideas, creative works, brain-power, inventions, etc., into intellectual property rights that are then commodified and can be traded in the marketplace. The interest in TRIPS is in relation to the trading of these intellectual property rights, rather than moral and humane issues. The TRIPS Agreement, I am arguing, is about transforming intellectual property rights into international tradable commodities. Within this general scenario, traditional knowledge for the benefit of the local, indigenous population is under threat, and it is this which will be considered further in this chapter.

9.3.2 Definition of traditional knowledge

First of all, what exactly is meant by 'traditional knowledge', or 'folklore' or 'indigenous knowledge'? Traditional knowledge is usually associated with knowledge that has been gathered over a long period among local, indigenous communities in the developing world, although it does not necessarily only apply to these communities. Weeraworawit provides a fairly general definition, while also emphasising that there is no internationally accepted definition, saying:

> ... TK is knowledge that has been developed based on the traditions of a certain community or nation. (Weeraworawit, 2003: 159)

Meanwhile, Pushpangadan described TK in the following way:

> A Traditional Knowledge System (TKS) is a community-based system of knowledge that has been developed, preserved and maintained over many generations by the local and indigenous communities through their continuous interactions, observations and experimentations with their surrounding environment. It is unique to a given culture or society and is developed as a result of the co-evolution and co-existence of both the indigenous cultures and their traditional practices of resource use and ecosystem management. (Pushpangadan, 2002: 1)

Martin Khor, the director of the Third World Network, makes the point that traditional knowledge sometimes has a place in modern societies, emphasising that:

> Traditional knowledge is now widely recognised as having played and as still playing crucial roles in economic, social and cultural life and development, not only in traditional societies, but also in modern societies. (Khor, 2002c: 15)

Often this traditional knowledge has been accumulated over hundreds of years. It has existed for centuries in India, for example, and has been the mainstay of India's existence in many ways, especially with regard to food and health. According to RAFI (1997: 4, referenced in Khor, 2002c: 17), 80 per cent of the population in the world relies on food provided through the indigenous knowledge of plants, animals, insects, microbes and farming systems.

9.3.3 Traditional knowledge, patents and copyright in the developing world

Traditional knowledge and intellectual property rights issues

Traditional knowledge and folklore cannot be encapsulated in copyright, which would provide copyright protection, unless it is in a tangible form. This is the big problem. This means that local indigenous communities in the developing world are very vulnerable. Many have been gathering their knowledge for hundreds of years. However, most of these people would not have the skills and capabilities to be able to write down what they know, and to transform it into a tangible form, and indeed many are illiterate. This makes it easy for large companies to come along and appropriate this knowledge, to patent it, turn it into an intellectual property right and make money out of it, but without giving due recompense to the indigenous population. This is the problem that the developing world is up against and how these people in the local communities are often being exploited. As Utkarsh says, with globalisation:

> ... knowledge and other public goods are rapidly being appropriated, transformed and marketed by commercial concerns, without any benefit being shared with the original producers. (Utkarsh, 2003: 190)

Furthermore, Pushpangadan argued that:

> Many traditional communities ... fear that they are losing control of their knowledge systems and that outsiders are appropriating their knowledge and resources without their consent and approval. (Pushpangadan, 2002: 2)

Denise Nicholson (2002) also emphasised how rural people are often at the mercy of large international corporations with regard to their TK, as these large corporations recognise the potential to be gained from traditional remedies, craftwork and other cultural traditions.

On the other hand, if the knowledge were to be transferred into a tangible format it could then be protected by copyright and the creators of TK could then be recompensed. This is gradually starting to happen more. As Weeraworawit said:

> In the world of information technology, satellite broadcasting and the internet, expressions of folklore have gained more economic value due to their very own creativity preserved and refined by the indigenous or local communities. (Weeraworawit, 2003: 162)

Furthermore, as Sahai said:

> Copyright can be used to protect the artistic manifestations of the holders of indigenous knowledge, especially artists who belong to

indigenous and native communities, against unauthorised reproduction and exploitation of those manifestations. (Sahai, 2003: 169)

Weeraworawit argued that more continuous and balanced consultation and negotiation in general with regard to intellectual property rights and traditional knowledge is needed to improve the IPR situation for the developing world.

Apart from the fact that the developed world, particularly large corporations, often appropriates this knowledge, transforms it and captures it in patents without compensating the original creators, western law also often treats TK as part of the public domain and thus freely available to everyone. So, this is another problem. This may be exacerbated by the cultural make-up of the indigenous community itself, many of which have an emphasis on sharing and community spirit. Many people in the developing world see indigenous knowledge as being part of Nature itself, and there are also many strong affinities with religion. Thus many would be against any notion of people owning, or seeming to own, any of this knowledge, or turning it into any form of intellectual property right. In July 1999, 114 indigenous peoples' organisations from various countries around the world and 68 indigenous peoples' support groups issued a joint indigenous peoples' statement on TRIPS (Tebtebba Foundation, 1999). One of their statements said, for example, that nobody:

> ... can own what exists in nature except nature herself ... Humankind is part of Mother Nature, we have created nothing and so we can in no way claim to be owners of what does not belong to us ... Western legal property regimes have been imposed on us, contradicting our own cosmologies and values. (Referenced in Khor, 2002c: 29)

Thus people in general start to regard traditional knowledge as simply being in the public domain. But once again, this means that those in the developing world can and do suffer. Some argue that no protection should be considered for knowledge that has become part of the public domain. Nevertheless knowledge originally comes from a source, and as Aguilar (2003) said, just because it is in the public domain that does not necessarily mean that the source has disappeared. Hence there is no justification for saying that this knowledge should then be handed over, free of charge, particularly if it turns out it is largely for the benefit of the rich at the expense of the poor.

There has been considerable debate and thought given to the systems of protection that can be adopted to provide legal protection for the intellectual property of indigenous populations. Most of this has revolved around patents and copyright. However, as Sahai says, the problem is that there is a mismatch between the protection of finite, inanimate objects and '... flowing, mutable and variable properties of ... IK' (Sahai, 2003: 173). Thus, it can be difficult to encapsulate some of this indigenous knowledge.

Meanwhile, Aguilar argued that patents and other intellectual property rights are not really suitable for protecting traditional knowledge for both practical and cultural reasons. Aguilar said that there is a need to look for viable alternatives, otherwise those in the indigenous communities will become the 'victims of knowledge piracy' (Aguilar, 2003: 181). He argued that a *sui generis* system tied to the framework that is provided by the Convention on Biological Diversity (CBD) and in Article 27, paragraph 3(b) of TRIPS is needed urgently. Pushpangadan (2002) argued that developing countries should strive to develop policies and legislation that reflect the values and rights of the indigenous communities over their knowledge.

Recording traditional knowledge

However, traditional knowledge is now starting to be recorded and made available in various ways. The CBD, for example, makes genetic resources and knowledge available. But there has to be 'prior informed consent' (PIC) and mutually agreed terms of benefit sharing. Also, as Utkarsh (2003) has pointed out, corporations can often easily access the material, as happened with products such as neem, turmeric and basmati. Therefore benefit sharing through PIC is often confined to untapped traditional knowledge or folk innovations that are in remote villages. The CBD has been ratified by over 180 countries and has been implemented through national legislation or biodiversity action plans. A number of different mechanisms have been proposed to ensure that the acquisition of various intellectual property rights fits in with the principles and objectives of the CBD. Thus the CBD is doing some useful work in endeavouring to capture TK. However, although its aims are to ensure that the various parties benefit, in reality large corporations still often benefit more, as they can often access the material more easily. This, once again, emphasises the value of the library, where such TK could be made available for much of the local population in general. But the knowledge still has to be captured first.

Different projects have been undertaken to consider ways in which indigenous knowledge can be protected and recorded. Ana Salgar (2003), for example, described a pilot project launched in Colombia by the Sustainable Biotrade Programme of the Alexander von Humboldt Institute. The project aimed to devise some mechanisms for protecting knowledge, innovations and traditional practices related to the use of medicinal plants.

Furthermore, a substantial amount of work is being undertaken in India to document indigenous knowledge. Once the material is documented, it can then be protected by copyright. One example is the People's Biodiversity Registers (PBRs). To prevent biopiracy, the Indian government is developing a digital database of traditional knowledge in the public domain related to medicinal plants. The plan is to make the database available to patent offices on a global basis. PBRs are village-level documents of people's knowledge of biodiversity, which encompasses conservation and sustainable utilisation. The People's Biodiversity Registers are often developed by local teachers, students and NGO researchers. They are also developed by villagers, although the villagers are not usually educated. PBRs have been recognised by the Indian Biological Diversity Bill as a means to help to ensure equitable access and benefit sharing.

Utkarsh (2003) says that the development of the concept of the People's Biodiversity Registers provides a number of important lessons for South Asian and other countries. Traditional knowledge can be better protected from erosion and biopiracy, for example. PBRs can also help to sustain local trade. Registration can be followed up with social incentives to preserve and share knowledge, and knowledgeable individuals can be given recognition. Finally, computerised databases can assist in the decision-making process in an endeavour to allocate financial and other benefits in a fair way and this can be generated by using information that is in the People's Biodiversity Registers. Thus there are many mechanisms being set in place to capture, record, distribute and make TK available.

The role of the librarian/information professional in patents, copyright, traditional knowledge and TRIPS issues in the developing world

Traditional knowledge is an area that librarians and information professionals should be taking a lively interest in and contributing to, I would suggest. They could, for example, help to play a lively role in endeavouring to overcome the illiteracy problem. Holding literacy classes and reading classes in the library can be very beneficial as can undertaking more outreach work. Outreach work can include, for example, liaising with medicine men in the local community. The librarian could endeavour to explain to these medicine men that it is to the advantage of the local community to have their TK protected, and why this is the case. Librarians/information professionals could even assist with the documentation process itself. Again, this could be undertaken in the library.

The benefits that can accrue to the local population by having their TK in a tangible format can also be emphasised by the librarian. They could explain how the knowledge could then be made available in the local library for the benefit of all the local population, as opposed to the benefits being transferred to rich corporations in the developed world. They could also seek to educate the local population and help them to overcome their fears about recording their traditional knowledge. Discussion groups about whether or not it is morally acceptable for TK to be transferred into intellectual property rights might also be useful and the profession could and should also listen to the views of the indigenous population themselves in this regard. Furthermore, the librarian/information professional could also explain what moral and economic rights in copyright are to the local indigenous population and help to make them more aware about these rights, once their TK is recorded and transformed into a tangible format. Leaflets could be produced providing clear information. Given that it can be difficult for creators of works and copyright holders to claim their moral rights, this could also be explained and advice given on how to try to claim their moral rights. The profession could also liaise with the governments of the different developing countries, and endeavour to obtain more resources for libraries, for example, to help tackle some of these issues. The profession should be exploring these and other ways to help these indigenous communities to overcome these serious problems.

However, while I think it is and would be very worthwhile for the library and information profession to engage with all these activities, we also have to be fully aware of what we are up against here. This brings us back to relating TK, copyright and patents to TRIPS. Thus the TRIPS Agreement could hamper any progress that is made in any of these endeavours. The librarian could persuade the local population that they should record their traditional knowledge, for example, and then have this TK encapsulated in an intellectual property right, such as a copyright. However, the indigenous population might then find that they are not actually gaining any reward. In this way, they might even conclude that the librarian misled them and took them down a 'blind alley', if the librarian tried to convince them that they would gain from such an enterprise. This is because of the enthusiasm for trade that is embedded in TRIPS. So the TK might be recorded by the indigenous population and then copyrighted. Then, the indigenous population might decide that they want to try to obtain some economic rewards for it, but that they cannot afford to take the entrepreneurial risk. So this is given to a third party, who obviously seeks to gain from it. So, it could be that the indigenous population ends up 'doing a deal' with a large corporation in the developed world anyway and then they find that, through TRIPS, the entrepreneur gains all the economic rights from this transaction, but that the indigenous population gains very little from it. The local community could become very disillusioned, to say the least. Obviously, they might not make any such decisions, but we need to be fully aware of the fact that the TRIPS Agreement does not have the needs of the developing world uppermost in its mind – quite the reverse!

Furthermore, once again, librarians and information professionals might be able to negotiate and persuade the indigenous populations in the developing world of the importance of recording their TK and encapsulating it into an intellectual property right. The governments of these countries might then decide to assist with the process by making resources available, for example, and even by passing intellectual property rights legislation to benefit the indigenous population, to help ensure that they can reap the benefits from their own TK. However, as I have already indicated, if such legislation is not compliant with TRIPS, then it might well have to be changed and revised so that it does fit in, and once again, this is likely to be disadvantageous for indigenous populations in the developing world. This could also lead to a sense of disillusionment for these indigenous populations.

All this emphasises the fact that we are up against so much. Librarians and information professionals seeking to try to improve the situation and make an impact could also try to explain some of these potential problems to the indigenous population. However, the problem with such an approach is that the indigenous population might then not want to record their TK at all! Thus I think we should try, in various ways, to improve the situation while we live under global capitalism, yet also be aware of the fact that no real solution can ever be found within this system. It is better to take this approach than to fool people, especially when one is working with poor people in the developing world. This certainly applies to any work one might undertake that is connected with the TRIPS Agreement.

Concluding comments

In conclusion, the TRIPS Agreement does not refer to traditional knowledge specifically, but clearly the TRIPS is going to have a significant impact on TK in the developing world. As it stands, large corporations in the developed world can easily appropriate traditional knowledge, transform it into an intellectual property right, patent it and make money out of it, without having to compensate the original creators of this knowledge. This is likely to lead to those in the developing world being still further impoverished. One very good example here is how herbs and local remedies have been patented and sold as drugs by large corporations. The patent section of TRIPS aids with this process, as its overriding concern is with the trading of patents. TRIPS will make it easier for large corporations to patent all this TK and make money out of it. Meanwhile, the indigenous populations will be further impoverished because they may, through the over-collecting or harvesting of natural resources, no longer have the herbs so easily and readily available to them and might well find themselves having to pay for herbs that used to be freely available. This should be an area of concern for the library and information profession.

Part of the problem is that TK is often not preserved in any tangible format, so those in the indigenous communities and the creators of the traditional knowledge are not protected by copyright. Neither are they able to protect their traditional knowledge by encapsulating it into any other intellectual property, such as a patent. This is the case for a number of reasons. Traditionally, this has not been the way in which these cultures and communities operate, and these cultures and practices have been in existence for hundreds of years so it would involve a great change in their ways of thinking and operating. We could also, perhaps, question whether we should actually be doing this – trying to impose western values on these communities.

Second, many of these indigenous people are illiterate, so would not be able to transform their traditional knowledge into a tangible format of use to them.

Third, TK is often seen as just being part of the public domain, so it is not seen as necessary to document it in this way. Also, there is the assumption by many (including those in the West) that the knowledge is just there for everyone, no one owns it, and there were no original creators. But obviously there must have been some original creators at some point.

Fourth, encapsulating TK into intellectual property rights goes against some of the ethical and religious principles of these indigenous populations, who do not think that their traditional knowledge really belongs to them (even if they created it) but rather that it belongs to God and/or Mother Nature.

Fifth, some argue that there need to be methods other than copyright or patents for protecting TK. However, some in the developing world are starting to document their traditional knowledge. One good example here is the People's Biodiversity Register that is being developed in India. In general, this is an area that the library and information profession should be taking a lively interest in, I suggest, and endeavouring to improve the situation. Also, the profession needs to think further about all this in relation to TRIPS and needs to be highly aware of the dangers that TRIPS poses to the way of life for these indigenous populations.

9.4 TRIPS and the developing world

9.4.1 Introduction

The implications of TRIPS for libraries and information in the developing world are considered in Chapter 10, section 10.3.5. First, though, we need to consider what the implications of TRIPS are for the developing world in general. From this position we can then meaningfully consider the implications for libraries and information specifically. Many are very sceptical about this, particularly various NGOs, arguing that TRIPS is largely disadvantageous for the developing world. As Martin Khor, the Director of the Third World Network, says: '... the developing countries are in general sceptical about the claimed benefits for them of IPRs and TRIPS' (Khor, 2002a: 10).

Developing countries have raised a number of concerns.

First, the strong IPR systems and practices that are being established in WTO member countries through TRIPS will give monopoly rights to many privately-run research organisations and to various powerful private corporations.

Second, the TRIPS makes it mandatory for WTO member countries to patent some categories of life forms and other living processes. This has raised various ethical, religious and environmental questions.

Third, it is of concern that TRIPS favours large private companies and modern technology.

Fourth, much traditional knowledge is being misappropriated and there is a lack of concern about the rights of local communities, indigenous populations and farmers, and the important role that they have played in developing this traditional knowledge.

9.4.2 UK Commission on Intellectual Property Rights and issues pertaining to intellectual property rights in the developing world

Various organisations and individuals have endeavoured to address some of these issues. The United Kingdom Commission on Intellectual Property Rights, which is an organisation that was established by Clare Short, the then Secretary of State for International Development for the UK government, for example, has sought ways in which IPRs and TRIPS can benefit the developing world. In its report *Integrating Intellectual Property Rights and Development Policy* (2002) it notes that there often seem to be two completely different views about intellectual property rights, one arguing that IPRs are intrinsically good and the other that they are bad. In the developed world there is a powerful lobby which argues that IPRs are good for business, benefit the public in general and assist with technical progress. On the other hand, many would argue that IPRs cripple the development of local industry and technology, and harm the developing world in general. The TRIPS Agreement itself has helped to keep this debate very much in the limelight.

It is largely those in the developed world, particularly those in big business, who argue that IPRs in general and TRIPS specifically are all for the good. However, they do not just argue that it is good for big business but that it is good for everyone; as big businesses thrive, the economy prospers and everyone will enjoy the fruits of this prosperity. Hence, just as the WTO is often seen to be a force for good and prevents anarchy (see Chapter 2), so here the argument is that TRIPS specifically is also a force for good for all. However, I would argue that the reality is very different from this, and TRIPS will largely increase inequality.

The aims of the UK Commission on Intellectual Property Rights, though, was to investigate how IPRs could help to lessen poverty, particularly the poverty of those in the developing world. As it says in its report:

> The international community has set itself the target of reducing the proportion of people in poverty by half by 2015 ... it is our task

to consider whether and how intellectual property rights (IPRs) could play a role in helping the world meet these targets ... (Commission on Intellectual Property Rights, 2002: 1)

However, shortly after this statement it refers to some of the practical difficulties that the developing world has, and will continue to have, in relation to IPRs. They note that most developing countries have weak scientific and technical infrastructures, for example, and so are likely to be placed at a disadvantage and face costs through IPRs given to technologies that are established in the West. This cost is likely to outweigh any potential benefits that could be gained from IPRs for their own scientific and technical inventions. However, the Commission notes that the developing world does have:

... genetic resources and traditional knowledge, which have value both to them and to the world at large. These are not necessarily IP resources in the sense that they are understood in developed countries, but they are certainly resources on the basis of which protected intellectual property can, and has been, created. (Commission on Intellectual Property Rights, 2002: 7)

The Commission says that further consideration needs to be given to see how these resources in the developing world can interact with 'modern' IP systems. It also acknowledges, though, that the developing world is placed in an unfavourable position and that the interests of the 'producer' often dominate in IP policy. So, policy is often determined more by commercial interests than by notions of the 'greater public good'. Within this framework, once again, the developing world often suffers. In the developed world, producers' interests often drive forward IP policy to protect their export markets, while those in the developing countries are not so well equipped and are not so able to put forward their own interests. So:

Developing countries – and in particular poor consumers of products which may be protected by IP rights – negotiate from a position of relative weakness. (Commission on Intellectual Property Rights, 2002: 7)

The Commission says that developing countries need to be given more attention with regard to international intellectual property (IP) policy.

Furthermore, developing countries need to be able to create their own IP systems, systems that are relevant to their particular needs and to their economic and social circumstances. As I have already discussed, though, some people in the developing world are opposed to any IP system at all, saying that all knowledge comes from God/Nature and that therefore humans cannot own it in this way.

The Commission, however, notes the difficulties in achieving this anyway, within the complex set of international, multilateral, regional and bilateral IP rules and standards that currently exists, and that these rules limit the ability of individual countries and governments to operate as they see fit with regard to IP. Now, TRIPS will add another layer of complexity.

It seems clear that, despite the rhetoric of 'prosperity for all', it is highly likely that TRIPS will particularly benefit large corporations in the industrialised world. As Oxfam says:

> WTO intellectual property rules reward innovation at the expense of broader social objectives. They also place a higher value on corporate profits than on individual lives. (Oxfam, 2001)

Once again, profit considerations override people.

9.4.3 Intellectual property rights and TRIPS in the developing world

Meanwhile, Martin Khor (2002a) referred to the 'one-size-fits-all' approach of TRIPS, where similar standards are set for countries that have different levels of development, and how this does not operate in the interest of the developing world. He argued that TRIPS has resulted in a shift in the balance in IPRs away from the public interest and towards the monopolistic privileges of IPR holders. This will obviously particularly benefit large corporations in the developed world.

Furthermore, as discussed in the previous section, many developing countries do not have much intellectual property of their own to protect, as TK is often not transferred into an intellectual property. Therefore they are often not keen to support and to be involved with international standards of protection that will result in them paying large sums of money to use technology they need, or even deny them access to this technology. Furthermore, Shiva says that the TRIPS is:

... weighted against citizens in general, and Third World peasants and forest dwellers in particular. People everywhere innovate and create. In fact, the poorest have to be most innovative, since they have to work for survival, which is under daily threat. Further, TRIPS is weighted against basic needs and survival and in favour of trade. (Shiva, 2001: 95)

Thus Shiva is arguing that poor people have to be more innovative and creative to survive, while at the same time, TRIPS is far more concerned about trade than basic needs, so poor people are likely to suffer doubly!

Shiva emphasised how the TRIPS Agreement was not negotiated by GATT members, but was imposed by multinational companies who used the US government to force it onto other members. Shiva says that the TRIPS:

... is the most blatant example of the undemocratic, non-transparent nature of the WTO. (Shiva, 2001: 95)

9.4.4 Patents and TRIPS in the developing world

As already stated, it is the patent part of TRIPS that is of particular concern to many in the developing world. The TRIPS patent system was established in the joint statement presented to the GATT Secretariat in June 1988 by the Intellectual Property Committee (IPC) of the USA and industry associations of Japan and Europe. The IPC is a coalition of 13 major US corporations which aims to ensure that TRIPS works to its advantage. The members of IPC include corporations like Hewlett Packard, General Motors, IBM, Rockwell and Warner.

Patent laws have existed in various developing countries for over 100 years – which reflects the importance of patents for many developing countries. Patent laws were first introduced in India in the 1850s, for example, and were part of the colonial rule. In 1911 there was the first Patent Act and in 1970 there was a new Patent Act. The 1970 Act prevented monopolies in health and nutrition by excluding food and medicine from product patents. This helped to protect the public interest. Thus embedded in these patent laws was some desire to help the indigenous populations. But this is now all threatened by TRIPS because of the lack of a democratic process. As Shiva said:

The Indian experience on the implementation of the TRIPS Agreement has made it evident that the IPR regimes embodied in TRIPS necessitate the bypassing of the democratic process. The debate is growing between those who support the democratic choice of nationally suited and independently evolved patent regimes and those who opt for the authoritarian imposition of a universalized patent system evolved by MNCs, and pushed by the governments of industrialized countries in the Uruguay Round of GATT. (Shiva, 2001: 111–12)

So Shiva referred to various patent systems that have been evolved by multinational corporations and have been pushed by governments in the developed world through TRIPS, and how this can damage the democratic process of nation states.

Thus the question remains – can TRIPS in general, and the patent section of TRIPS in particular, be implemented in a way that will benefit the developing world? It is interesting to see that it is not only people like Martin Khor and various NGOs that are sceptical of TRIPS. In addition, some governments and other bodies in the West are also concerned. As I have already indicated, the UK government through the Commission on Intellectual Property Rights is one example here, and it is concerned that TRIPS and IPRs have not really benefited developing countries in a significant way so far. Furthermore, it is concerned about the extent to which it will be able to do so in the future – even though the Commission remains optimistic in tone.

9.4.5 Role of the librarian/information professional with regard to TRIPS in the developing world

What role, then, can librarians/information professionals play in relation to all of this? I suggest that they should be proactive. They could, for example, engage in political action and try to change the situation. I know that some would argue that librarians should not be taking political action in this way, and that they should be 'neutral'. However, I believe that there is no such thing as neutrality, so this does not pose any real problem as far as I am concerned. Objectivity is another issue in itself, but there is not the space to consider this further here. However, we do need to be aware of the fact that we do not use Marxist terminology in our everyday language although, in my opinion, it is only Marxist concepts and terminology that can really explain the intrinsic workings and nature of the capitalist system. Instead, we are largely immersed in terminology that supports capitalism, or at least does not expose and critique its intrinsic workings. This alone demonstrates that it is nonsensical to claim that any real sense of objectivity is possible.

Librarians/information professionals could also, for example, consider other ways in which developing countries could develop their own intellectual property systems. Given that, as Shiva says, poor people often have to be more innovative rather than less, information professionals could offer some assistance and provide them with rich material to help them. Then, once again, literacy classes and reading classes could be provided and outreach work undertaken. They could also assist with the documentation process itself, for knowledge that has not been recorded. They can try to engage and understand the local culture and the hopes and fears that people have. Furthermore, they could provide more information about the TRIPS Agreement itself, as well as information about intellectual property rights, copyright and patents in general. Such information could be provided in an easily digestible format such as leaflets and posters. They could also provide information about the dangers that large corporations can pose to the indigenous population if action is not taken. Finally, they could endeavour to obtain more resources for library and information centres.

9.4.6 Concluding comments

It is clear that TRIPS can, and indeed is, seriously affecting the developing world, and that it is likely to impoverish the people in the developing world more rather than less in the future. There is certainly nothing to indicate that TRIPS is likely to benefit us all, as many suggest. This comes back to the issue that I raised at the beginning of the book – the notion that somehow globalisation in general, or rather global capitalism to be more precise, can benefit all. I hope that by now I have demonstrated the impossibility of all this. Instead, those in the rich countries and large corporations stand to gain the most from TRIPS. In some cases, rich organisations and research departments will be given monopoly rights over certain areas as a result of TRIPS, for example. Furthermore, many countries in the developing world have weak technical, scientific and IT structures. Therefore they are likely to incur large costs rather than benefits as a result of TRIPS. They will probably find themselves having to pay more for some technology than they did previously, as knowledge around these areas becomes more encapsulated in intellectual property rights. Or perhaps they will not even be able to access the technology at all. Instead perhaps developing countries should be developing their own, alternative intellectual property rights systems, although this will undoubtedly pose a different set of problems for them. This would include the difficulty involved in carrying out this process and the cost and the problems of implementing such systems even when they have been formulated. But at least, in this way, the developing world would have a voice. Those in the developing world could think about the best way to get intellectual property to work for them, whereas those pushing through TRIPS have been, and are, thinking about how it will benefit them. The USA and the pharmaceutical industry, in particular, have been instrumental in bringing TRIPS to fruition, and they have been keen to ensure that TRIPS works to their advantage. We are up against so much! In particular, it is highly apparent that traditional, indigenous knowledge in the developing countries is increasingly being transformed into patents by large corporations. This is having a serious and detrimental effect on the people in these communities. While this might not always directly impact on the library and information profession, it is clear to see that it impacts indirectly. As a profession we are supposedly concerned about preserving knowledge and information for the local community and making it easily available, where possible. If this knowledge is just appropriated by large corporations it may never see light in a library and the local population might never reap the benefits from it.

However, fundamentally, my position is clear – it will be impossible to implement TRIPS in a way that will significantly be of benefit to the developing world because of the inherent inequalities and contradictions that are built into the very fabric of global capitalism itself. Furthermore, the drives of capital are infinite; it will never be satisfied. So there will never come a point where it will be decided that the inequalities need to be lessened in any fundamental way. Instead, TRIPS, as a tool which aids the furtherance of global capitalism, is likely to increase inequality. Furthermore, inequality and poverty will only ever be lessened (and then largely on a temporary basis) when pressure is placed on those in positions of power. In relation to TRIPS this rests on putting pressure on the WTO through organisations such as the Third World Network and various NGOs to soften some of the most worrying of the implications of TRIPS for the poor and those in the developing world.

IFLA could play a valuable role in this regard. Just as it had a represent-ative (Paul Whitney) at the WTO Ministerial in Seattle, it could also have a representative at other WTO Ministerial meetings, for example. This would provide the library and information community with a voice on the global stage while also ensuring that it is kept well informed. Also, IFLA could have further meetings with the WTO and build on the meet-ing that IFLA and EBLIDA had with the WTO in December 2002. It would also be highly beneficial if library associations from the develop-ing world had a clear voice in these activities.

However, capitalism is a battlefield upon which various compromises are and can only ever be made, but it can never ultimately be for the ben-efit of the labourer and the poor. To change the situation on a permanent basis, we need to terminate capitalism and replace it with socialism and eventually with communism. I am convinced of this. Meanwhile, we can try to lessen some of the horrors and take some action. Raising such awareness can significantly change the map in various ways.

9.5 Conclusion

This chapter has considered the patent section of TRIPS and its likely implications for libraries and information, focusing in particular on traditional, indigenous knowledge in the developing world, and the likely impact of the patent section of TRIPS on this knowledge. It also consid-ered relevant copyright issues within this framework. Furthermore, it examined TRIPS in the developing world in general. The role and poten-tial role of the librarian/information professional within these settings was also explored. The following chapter will consider the implications of TRIPS for the library and information profession both in general and within an international perspective by looking at a number of different countries.

Implications of TRIPS for information and libraries internationally

10.1 Introduction

This chapter will first consider some of the general implications of TRIPS for the library and information profession. It will examine copyright in TRIPS, patents in TRIPS and the World Trade Organisation itself, and the implications of these three areas for the library and information world. It will then examine some of the implications of the TRIPS Agreement for libraries and information in a number of different regions and countries. The countries and regions that will be examined are: India, Canada, the USA, Africa, the developing world in general, Europe and the UK.

10.2 Implications of the TRIPS Agreement for the library and information profession

Unravelling the likely implications of TRIPS for the library and information profession is complex. Having given this some considerable thought I have concluded that there are a number of key issues that need to be addressed, and these will be considered in this section. These will be broken down into three main areas – copyright, patents and the WTO in general.

10.2.1 Copyright in TRIPS and its implications for the library and information profession

Introduction

This section will examine various aspects of copyright in relation to TRIPS and the library and information profession. First, it will consider the balance in copyright, and will argue that as far as TRIPS is concerned, notions of balance are largely irrelevant. Overall, none of the three parts of the balance hold any importance for TRIPS – not the main balance, or the two halves of the balance. It will also consider the two halves of the balance individually, and will examine the free flow of information in particular in some detail, as this has not yet been examined in this book, and the position of the library and information profession in regard to this. The section will also consider the implications of copyright issues in TRIPS for libraries in the developing world, the complexity of copyright legislation in general and how TRIPS overrides other copyright legislation.

The irrelevance of 'balance in copyright' in the TRIPS agreement – the free flow of information versus the giving of rights to creators of works and copyright holders

With regard to copyright, what is particularly important as far the library and information profession is concerned, as I have already indicated, is the aim for 'balance in copyright'. The profession is very enthusiastic about trying to maintain a balance between the free flow of information and the giving of rewards to authors of creative works and to copyright holders. Indeed, it is one of its key principles. Hence, the Committee on Copyright and Other Legal Matters (CLM) of IFLA says that:

> The greater public interest is served in two ways: firstly, by giving authors an incentive to create; and secondly, by encouraging the dissemination of new knowledge. (CLM, 2002a: 2)

However, as I have already indicated, TRIPS is not concerned about endeavouring to obtain this balance at all. The language of balance itself does not form any real part of the agreement. Notions such as free access to information, freedom of information and intellectual freedom, for example, are not referred to in any meaningful way. Neither is any importance attached to the giving of rights to creators and copyright holders from any humane perspective. Economic rights form part of the agreement, but this is because such rights will help to exacerbate trade. Economic rights largely represent the entrepreneurial side of copyright issues, whether this be through commercial exploitation by others, such as publishers, or whether it is through creators selling and distributing their own works. Moral rights have no such clear connection with trade, so they have been excluded. The TRIPS Agreement is simply concerned with the successful trading of intellectual property rights, as this will enhance capitalism. If obtaining some sort of balance aids this process, then all well and good. But if not, then from the global capitalist perspective notions of balance can be, indeed probably should be and are abandoned.

Thus the overriding aim in TRIPS is to encourage and exacerbate the trading of intellectual property rights, as I have already indicated, and it is not concerned with trying to achieve the main balance in copyright, i.e. the balance between the free flow of information and the giving of rights to creators of works and copyright holders. Neither is it concerned with trying to obtain a balance for each half of the main balance, i.e. a balance between moral and economic rights and between different aspects of the free flow of information.

There is nothing in the language of the TRIPS agreement to indicate that it has any real concern or interest in overall balance. Obviously, implicitly the fact that it includes copyright in its remit means that some aspects of the balance must inevitably fall within its parameters. So the economic rights of creators are included but moral rights are not. Sometimes TRIPS functions as a vehicle to protect intellectual property (as Martin Khor has emphasised, and this is explored further in Chapter 7, section 7.6), thereby implicitly limiting the free flow of information. At other times it does appear to operate to encourage some free flow of information, at least to the extent that it encourages a competitive environment for intellectual property, which in some ways can encourage a greater sharing of knowledge.

To phrase this another way – capitalism needs new ideas and creations in order to sustain itself. To this extent it will encourage a free flow of information. However, these ideas ideally then need to be commodified, and they can be commodified through TRIPS. So this supposedly 'free flow of information' needs to be contained. Too much free flow of information might lead to people thinking at a deeper level, for example, critiquing capitalism and then thinking about possible alternatives, such as socialism. Once again, it can all become quite complex.

However, the important point to bear in mind is that the main aim of TRIPS is *not* to endeavour to maintain this balance, in contrast to the aims of the library and information profession. As I have outlined in Chapter 8, section 8.4.3, the profession also focuses on a wide range of different areas in relation to this, such as the inequality in the provision of information and copyright issues in the digital age. Furthermore, TRIPS is not concerned about obtaining a balance for each half of the balance. The former includes balancing free access to information, freedom of information, intellectual freedom and freedom of expression, the latter balancing economic and moral rights for the creators of works and copyright holders. None of this is of any real interest or concern for TRIPS. No aspect of the notion of balance is referred to in the agreement at all in any significant or meaningful way.

Thus sometimes TRIPS is protectionist for some copyright holders and creators of works, but this is only because companies need some protection if they are to succeed and trade effectively in the long term. So companies are offered some protection through intellectual property rights, by giving copyright holders certain rights. Furthermore, creators of works need to be given some rights in order to be given some incentive to continue to be creative and thus benefit capitalism. But this protectionist angle is a short-term measure to enable the exacerbation of the trading of intellectual property rights in the long term.

Fundamentally, TRIPS is not concerned with and does not 'fit in' with the library and information profession's agenda, with its concern for balance and with its basic professional ethics. It must surely give us concern that an international agreement on intellectual property rights that could so profoundly affect our lives gives no credence to and sees no need to consider issues that are of paramount importance to the library and information profession.

The giving of rights to creators of works and copyright holders – economic and moral rights: the unequal balance in TRIPS

Thus, as I have already indicated, creators of works and copyright holders have two types of rights – economic and moral – but moral rights have been excluded from the copyright section of TRIPS. Moral rights have been excluded from much other copyright legislation as well, but as a profession we should surely be endeavouring to ensure that more copyright legislation and agreements include moral rights. Therefore, not enough consideration is being given to the creators of works and to copyright owners in the agreement. This is because this is not what TRIPS is ultimately concerned about – it is not its ultimate aim. If moral rights have been included in copyright legislation, trying to obtain some sort of balance does, at least, seem to be theoretically possible. However, if one starts to think about this in a little more depth, another layer of complications arises, such as how to weight the balance between moral and economic rights, but there is not the space to consider that here! Suffice it to say that moral rights have been excluded from TRIPS, so TRIPS is obviously not trying to maintain any kind of balance for creators of works and copyright holders – this being one-half of the balance.

Free flow of information – the other half of the balance in copyright – and related TRIPS issues

Given the philosophy behind the TRIPS Agreement, it is not concerned about providing easy access to information and helping to ensure that information flows freely either, i.e. the other half of the balance. Given that its overriding concern is to encapsulate ideas and creations of works into intellectual property rights, and then to trade these, it cannot really be concerned about providing a free flow of information. This section will consider the free flow of and easy access to information in some detail and its different aspects, and the library and information profession's position in relation to it. It will focus on four aspects in particular, namely free access to information, intellectual freedom, freedom of expression and freedom of information. This will all help to illustrate how concerning it is that such an important issue for the profession is given no real consideration within TRIPS.

Others might argue that more or different aspects should be included. Or that the categorisations should be changed in some way, and/or that sub-categories within these main aspects need to be considered further. As I have already explained (in Chapter 8, section 8.4.4) this is a watery area that needs to be thought through at a deeper level. However, I will focus on these areas, as it seems to me that these are particularly significant.

Many in the library and information profession have emphasised the importance of having free access to information. Alex Byrne, the IFLA President-Elect, for example, says that:

> Through their preservation of recorded information, libraries are the bastions of freedom, essential elements of a civilized community

> ... librarians must stand for the principle that every individual and all the peoples of the world have the right to access the information needed to live and prosper and the inseparable right to express their ideas and opinions. This intellectual freedom encompasses the essential principles of freedom of thought, freedom of inquiry and freedom of expression. (Byrne, 2000a: 256–7)

Thus Byrne emphasises how librarians must stand by the principle that everyone has the right to access information easily, thereby enabling them to prosper and live full lives. Also, everyone has the right to be able to express both their ideas and their opinions. In relation to Byrne's analysis of intellectual freedom, though, it is interesting to note that he argues that intellectual freedom should be broken down into three main sub-categories – freedom of thought, freedom of enquiry and freedom of expression – whereas I am suggesting that freedom of expression should be considered as a distinct category from intellectual freedom. It seems to me that freedom of expression is somewhat different to intellectual freedom – one can want to be able to express oneself freely without necessarily wanting to obtain intellectual freedom – i.e. without aiming to be an intellectual. This is all cause for a good debate anyway, and illustrates the complexity of the topic and how further thought needs to be given to it all.

However, to return to the main point with regard to the free flow of information, on another occasion Byrne (1999) says that the human right to freedom of expression and free access to information provides a foundation of autonomy, both for the individual and for society. Furthermore, librarians must defend this right rigorously. Meanwhile, Yushkiavitshus, writing in the *IFLA Journal*, said:

> Information needs to be universally applicable to all to empower people to enjoy intellectual freedom and to take charge of their future. (Yushkiavitshus, 2000: 288)

Inoue also noted that:

> Libraries have the responsibility and duty to ensure an environment where each person recognizes fundamental human rights. (Inoue, 2000: 293)

Admittedly, the phraseology in relation to the free flow of information in the library and information profession can seem rather romantic, but the intentions are good and it illustrates some of its worthwhile aims.

IFLA and FAIFE (the Committee on Free Access to Information and Freedom of Expression) have both made their positions very clear in relation to these subject areas, those positions being drawn from Article 19 of the United Nations Universal Declaration of Human Rights. This states that:

> Everyone has the right to freedom of expression; this right includes freedom to hold opinions without interference and to seek, receive and impart information and ideas through any media and regardless of frontiers. (Referenced in Seidelin, 2002)

The United Nations Educational, Scientific and Cultural Organisation (UNESCO) also has similar aims and principles. It wants to promote easy access to information for all and is enthusiastic about intellectual freedom. It also wants to see cooperation between different countries around the world in relation to this. As Yushkiavitshus said:

> UNESCO action is strongly committed to the formulation of principles that will promote widespread, affordable and equitable access to information for all, including the Eastern European countries in transition, so that the emerging information society be more sharing, just and respectful of each other and a cradle for intellectual freedom. (Yushkiavitshus, 2000: 288)

The IFLA Governing Board has defined its objectives in the light of this statement.

FAIFE is an initiative within IFLA itself, which seeks to defend and promote basic human rights as defined in Article 19 of the United Nations Universal Declaration of Human Rights. Also, FAIFE aims to further freedom of access to information and expression in all aspects, directly or indirectly, related to libraries and information services. It monitors the state of intellectual freedom within the library and information community on a worldwide basis. Finally, FAIFE supports the IFLA policy with regard to the development of and cooperation with other international human rights organisations and responds to violations of freedom of access to information and freedom of expression.

The principles of both IFLA and FAIFE in relation to these areas have been broken down in various ways. Byrne (2000a) outlines the principles of the FAIFE Committee and Office. Firstly, there is the promotion of freedom of access to information and freedom of expression as fundamental human rights. This is essential if libraries are to be the gateways to the knowledge which supports human rights principles and democracy, Byrne argued. Second, it is to be the leading organisation for responding to attacks and limitations on libraries. Third, it is to support other organisations that are dealing with relevant issues which may indirectly influence libraries.

Meanwhile, the IFLA Statement on Libraries and Intellectual Freedom, which was approved by the Executive Board in 1999, says that intellectual freedom is a fundamental human right. It says that there are two aspects to this right – the right to know and freedom of expression, and that the library and information profession needs to promote and defend both of these rights (IFLA, 1999).

Also, at the IFLA Conference in Boston 2001, the IFLA/FAIFE Committee identified seven priorities for its strategy for 2001–3. Included in these seven priorities was the need to safeguard free access to information for all individuals, to make IFLA/FAIFE the authoritative source on libraries and intellectual freedom through the *IFLA/FAIFE World Report* and other forms of communication and to provide free and equal access to digital information (Seidelin, 2002).

IFLA has been active in various other ways as well in relation to free access to information. It ran a series of workshops in Germany on *Intellectual Freedom and Libraries: International Aspects*, for example. One of the aims of the workshop was to make librarians more conscious about their own beliefs and attitudes with regard to intellectual freedom and censorship. Furthermore, there was an emphasis on the fact that the right to freedom of opinion and information is not boundless. Instead, limits are set by the law (Schleihagen, 2002).

Other writers have emphasised codes of ethics and professional values which include topics such as free access to information. Froehlich (2000), for example, focuses on three main values in his article 'Intellectual freedom, ethical deliberation and codes of ethics'. First, there is intellectual freedom, which is the freedom to read and access a wide variety of materials and the freedom to challenge forms of censorship. Second, there is freedom of expression. This is the ability to express one's ideas without fear of reprisal, such as intimidation or imprisonment. Third, there is free access to information, which Froehlich describes as being access to information that is essential to the issues of one's daily life. These values are often expressed through the codes of ethics of various library associations, such as the American Library Association's Library Bill of Rights. These values, then, are all very important to the library and information profession.

Froehlich also outlines some professional values, based on the work of Michael Bayles. One of these categories is 'minimal well-being' and he argues that free access to information can fall under this category. However, there is also an emphasis on the fact that:

> ... information is not an homogeneous good: different kinds of information are needed by different people at different times for various kinds of purposes and a good portion of available information regardless of its quality, is not useful to most people. (Froehlich, 2000: 265)

So, we have to endeavour to use the free access to information principle wisely. Freedom of expression can fall under the category of 'recognition of one's work' (this was not included in Bayles's set). Freedom of expression can include a need for validation for the expresser, either in economic or honorific terms, the right to paternity and the right to prevent the distortion of one's work.

Finally, free flow of information and freedom of expression are now becoming globalised. But we must not be fooled into thinking that globalisation will necessarily enhance the free flow of information, for as Hamilton said:

> ... globalisation has also interfered with the flow of data on the Internet by taking some of the control of this flow away from nation states and placing it in the hands of the corporations. (Hamilton, 2002: 191)

Hamilton emphasised how, according to the theorist Herbert Schiller, information is being turned into goods that are sold. Furthermore, this will develop into an 'advanced capitalist model'. Therefore, globalisation in general, and the Internet in particular, could result in the commodification of information, which will increase class inequalities and give priorities to large corporations. Hamilton argued that this 'increasing commodification of the Internet' and the effect that this will have on information access should be of concern to librarians. Hamilton is undertaking some research to consider what barriers exist around the world to prevent access to information on the Internet. He is a PhD student at the Royal School of Library and Information Science in Copenhagen, Denmark and his project is co-sponsored by IFLA and FAIFE.

Freedom of information is another of the aspects of the free flow of information. As Pedley says with regard to freedom of information:

> Library and information professionals are uniquely placed and skilled to defend and deliver freedom of information ... Freedom of information is a fundamental human right and is the touchstone of all the freedoms to which the United Nations is consecrated ... (Pedley, 2003a: 95)

Various library associations and bodies have made their position clear with regard to freedom of information. The UK Chartered Institute of Library and Information Professionals (CILIP), for example, has a policy on information access, which states that:

> ... the right of access to information is essential for a civilized society. If citizens are to exercise their democratic rights, and to make information choices, they must have access to political, social, scientific and economic information. If our culture is to thrive and to grow, people need access to the widest range of ideas, information and images. (CILIP, 1998: 'Introduction', Point 1.2)

There have been various pieces of freedom of information legislation. In the UK the present New Labour government has always maintained its commitment to and enthusiasm for the notion of freedom of information and put through a Freedom of Information Act (FOIA), which came into force in 2000. On 1 January 2005 the Freedom of Information Act will be extended. As Pedley (2003a) emphasised, this will include the individual right of access to information across all public authorities. Furthermore, the person will not have to live in the UK in order to be able to request the information. Neither will they have to be a British citizen or say why they want the information. There are no limits on the type of information that can be requested, although the authority does not have to provide it all. All this sounds most promising indeed.

It is interesting to note, however, that David Hencke reported in the *Guardian*, in May 2004, that charges of between £50 and £575 were being proposed and that this represents an increase in fees that are between 666 per cent and 958 per cent higher than ministers indicated when the bill first passed through Parliament four years ago. This would mean, once again, as with the WTO, that large corporations would benefit at the expense of ordinary people, given that only large corporations are likely to be able to afford such an astronomical increase in fees. Lord Filkin, Parliamentary under Secretary of State at the Department for Constitutional Affairs, said (in June 2004) that the report was inaccurate and that no final decision had yet been made with regard to the actual fee that would be charged. Instead, he said that the original draft fees regulations only proposed a charge of up to 10 per cent of the costs of dealing with a request plus the full cost of any disbursements. However, he also said that a draft report has been compiled by an Advisory Group and that this report outlines possible alternative charging regimes (Filkin, 2004). Thus surely the fact that charging for information is being raised and discussed in this way goes against the spirit of freedom of information. This is the type of reality and problems that we face as we live in and through capitalism. However, the intentions behind the principle with regard to freedom of information are obviously very worthwhile.

There has also been legislation on Open Government in the UK, whereby the general public are given more information about how the government operates and some of the main decisions that are made. A UK White Paper on Open Government was published in 1993, for example. Following on from this, there was the 1994 Open Government Code, which went into its second edition in 1997. It included five commitments. Pedley (2003a) outlined these as being: to supply facts and analysis on major policy decisions; to open up internal guidelines about departments' dealings with the public; to give reasons for the administrative decisions that are made; to provide information under the Citizen's Charter about public services, what they cost, targets, performance, complaints and redress; and to respond to requests for information.

Thus much important legislation is being put into place in order to enhance freedom of information in the UK and similar legislation is in place in other countries. However, in reality, much of the legislation could be made redundant as a result of TRIPS, I would suggest. With TRIPS, the enthusiasm is to encapsulate information into intellectual property rights which are then traded. Clearly, then, the TRIPS could hinder and damage any notion of freedom of information. Also, TRIPS overrides legislation in nation states, as the other WTO agreements also do.

Therefore TRIPS could seriously damage the aims within pieces of freedom of information legislation in nation states if it seemed to be in its interest to do so.

In conclusion, this section has considered the balance in copyright – the free flow of information versus the giving of rights to creators of works and copyright holders – and has focused with some detail on the library and information profession's position with regard to the free flow of information. Within this, it has considered freedom of information, free access to information, intellectual freedom and freedom of expression, although other aspects could also have been included, such as freedom of opinion, and some might argue that it should have been defined within different categorisations. I have not, however, defined and analysed each of these categories individually in great detail, such as the meaning of intellectual freedom. This would add another layer of philosophical complexity and there is not the space to consider this here. Furthermore, as a Marxist, I do not readily see the need to do this. Instead, this would, once again, be the task for those that are arguing that achieving a balance in copyright is actually possible, and that these notions, such as intellectual freedom, are not utopian but are actually achievable under capitalism.

The section has emphasised how important the library and information profession considers the balance in copyright topic to be in general, as well as how important IFLA and FAIFE consider this topic to be, and that their positions are drawn from the United Nations Universal Declaration of Human Rights. It also highlights some of the work that IFLA and FAIFE have undertaken in this area, such as running workshops and undertaking research. Furthermore, Alex Byrne, the IFLA President-Elect, has emphasised the importance of these principles.

While all these aims are clearly rather utopian, they are very worthwhile. However, TRIPS poses a very serious threat to them. This is because, as already stated, TRIPS is not concerned with trying to ensure that information flows freely but with the trading of intellectual property rights. At times this process might be aided by having some information flow freely, but at other times the free flow of information will hamper this main aim. The important point to bear in mind is that it is the trading of IPRs that is the aim in TRIPS, and not the achievement of any kind of balance in copyright. Parallels can be drawn here between private companies and the GATS. The main aim of a private company must be to make a profit and this must come before the wants and needs of the people in the local community – this is its *raison d'être*. Given the importance of the TRIPS Agreement, and the highly significant part that it is likely to play with regard to intellectual property right decisions on the global stage in the future, then this is very concerning indeed, if not alarming! TRIPS is not concerned with obtaining this balance in any significant way – either for the main balance or for the two halves of the balance. Its overriding concern is with trade, trade, trade and more trade in intellectual property rights!

Implications of copyright issues in TRIPS for libraries in the developing world

It is likely that copyright issues in TRIPS will be particularly disadvantageous for those in the developing world, as these people tend to have less knowledge and understanding about copyright legislation and their rights. The problem is exacerbated by the level of illiteracy that there is in the developing world, and the fact that many would not want to convert their traditional knowledge into a tangible format that can be copyright protected anyway, as this would be seen to go against their religious beliefs. Denise Nicholson, from the University of South Africa and a member of the IFLA CLM Committee, said, for example, that:

> As a result of ignorance of their intellectual property and other rights, rural people are often at the mercy of large international corporations and individuals who recognize the potential in their traditional remedies, music, folklore, craftwork and other cultural traditions. These people are not aware of the legal requirements of having to put their oral expressions or traditional methods into a tangible format, before they can claim copyright ownership ... In some instances, however, the communities are becoming aware of their rights and are involving themselves in projects to exploit their intellectual property. They are receiving some monetary benefits as compensation, mainly through development trusts. (Nicholson, 2002: 261)

This will impact on libraries and information in the developing world. If large corporations in the West simply take the local knowledge and encapsulate it into IPRs there might not even be the opportunity to codify and classify that local knowledge and information. As I have already outlined, large corporations often appropriate local herbs, medicines and local knowledge, and then obtain patents for this knowledge.

In this way, local indigenous knowledge is transformed into intellectual property rights. But this only benefits the large corporations – not the people who had these ideas or the local population in general. Thus creators in the indigenous population would not then obtain their rights in relation to copyright, because they have not been able to put their creative ideas into a tangible format that can be copyright protected. The knowledge would not be stored in a local library, resource or community centre either, for the benefit of the local, indigenous population – traditional knowledge cannot go into a library if it is not in a tangible format. Also, if the knowledge is patented by large corporations, they will probably not be interested in making this information available to local libraries. Instead, they would probably want to keep the TK secret (or most of it anyway), so that they can make money out of it.

Furthermore, where knowledge is recorded and copyright protected it does not necessarily mean that this will be for the good of the local community anyway, under TRIPS. This is because TRIPS is concerned with trading issues in relation to copyright and the entrepreneurial side and not with moral and humane issues and certainly not with the needs of the indigenous populations in the developing world.

The complexity of copyright legislation and TRIPS overriding other copyright legislation

Finally, copyright legislation, agreements and directives are becoming more and more complex and many people in the developed world, let alone those in the developing world, are often not fully aware of the facts and their rights. Indeed, librarians and information professionals themselves can experience difficulties in understanding and implementing copyright legislation because it is now so complex. This problem has increased still further now that we are in the digital age with the ensuing copyright issues that accompany it. All this is reflected in many of the different library and information professional journals, as they strive to keep abreast with many of the changes. The Aslib monthly journal *Managing Information*, for example, devotes many of its pages to copyright issues. In the December 2003 issue, for example, Paul Pedley (Pedley, 2003b) provided an overview of the new copyright licensing agency licences, and intellectual property was the issue theme for the November 2003 issue. Meanwhile, the September 2003 issue included an article by Professor Charles Oppenheim entitled 'The New Copyright Legislation'. Large corporations are likely to be better placed to keep abreast of these many changes, as they are likely to have more resources available than many individuals to help them become aware of and understand the changes. Thus, for this reason alone, it is more likely that they will be able to reap greater benefits from TRIPS than individual creators. They can consider how TRIPS can be utilised to their benefit more effectively. This is in addition to the fact that TRIPS favours big business anyway and some large corporations have even assisted with its formulation.

The TRIPS Agreement in itself is a very complex document. It does not make for easy reading for anyone, let alone for someone who can only just read and write, whereas large corporations might well be able to afford to pay lawyers to decipher it if they thought that was necessary. So, once again, large corporations will be placed at an advantage, and are likely to be able to benefit more effectively from the TRIPS Agreement than those who have fewer resources at their disposal. Such a situation cannot be healthy for the library and information profession. The information professional, in trying to provide a service for all, might find that factors outside of their control mean that they are favouring large corporations over others.

Meanwhile, Christine Deschamps in her article 'Can libraries help bridge the digital divide?' emphasised how TRIPS could override other hard-won legal copyright battles in nation states:

> The danger in the TRIPS agreement is that it could negate hard-won achievements in recent negotiations on copyright law. A WTO dispute panel has, for example, recently found that a permitted use in a national copyright law was in violation of international trade treaty commitments. So we are alerting our National Association Members, and urging them to work to ensure that the interests of libraries and library users are not marginalized through the application of the WTO regime to domestic copyright legislation. (Deschamps, 2002: 5)

This illustrates, once again, what I have discussed elsewhere in this book – that WTO agreements can override legislation in nation states. Thus copyright legislation in individual WTO member states could become superfluous, or at least have to be seriously revised, if it was found to be incompatible with the TRIPS. This would make it even more difficult for those in the library and information profession to have any significant impact on copyright legislation. Furthermore, librarians and information professionals might spend some time endeavouring to understand and implement copyright legislation for the benefit of library users, only to find that this has been a waste of time if the legislation was then found to be in violation of the TRIPS and so became invalid.

In conclusion, there are a number of issues here, as far as the librarian/information professional is concerned. First is the increasing complexity of copyright legislation itself and the need for the profession to keep abreast of the changes, to understand them and to implement them, together with the fact that the TRIPS Agreement itself is a complex document. Second, it is likely to become more and more difficult for the profession to influence copyright legislation. Third, large corporations are likely to be better placed to be able to understand all this legislation in general and the TRIPS Agreement in particular. Librarians/information professionals might well find themselves unwittingly providing a better service to large corporations (as they are more likely to know what questions to ask, as well as how to get the copyright legislation to work to their advantage), than to other groups of library users. Fourth, copyright legislation in nation states has to fall in line with TRIPS and there are implications here for democracy.

Conclusion

In conclusion, there are a number of issues to consider in relation to copyright in TRIPS and its implications for the library and information profession. First of all, there is the notion of balance in copyright, which the library and information profession aims to achieve. This is concerned with maintaining a balance between the free flow of information and the giving of rights to creators of works and copyright holders. The profession spends a considerable amount of time seeking to achieve this balance. However, the TRIPS Agreement is not concerned with it; indeed, it is not referred to in any meaningful way. Nor does it address the balance between economic and moral rights for creators of works and copyright holders – quite the reverse, as moral rights are excluded from TRIPS. It is also not engaged in balancing free access to information, intellectual freedom, freedom of expression and freedom of information. These terms are not even referred to in the Agreement in any real sense.

In this section, I consider in particular, the efforts that the library and information profession makes in trying to ensure that information flows freely, that there are adequate provisions for freedom of information, that there is intellectual freedom, that there is freedom of expression, etc., but these are not issues that concern TRIPS in any real sense.

Second, countries in the developing world are likely to be at a particular disadvantage with regard to TRIPS and copyright issues. Much traditional knowledge is not captured, so cannot be copyright protected. Instead, TK is often just passed down from one generation to another by word of mouth. Furthermore, many are unfamiliar with many of the copyright laws and this includes TRIPS. Yet, even if TK was copyrighted, this would not generally be good news for the developing world with regard to TRIPS because TRIPS is concerned with trading issues in relation to copyright and with economic rights, but not with moral rights. Fundamentally, it is not concerned with the needs of the indigenous populations in the developing world.

Third, copyright legislation is becoming very complex and the TRIPS agreement itself is one example of this. This could have serious implications for the library and information profession as we try to grapple with something that we do not fully understand. Indeed, knowledge about TRIPS itself in the library and information profession is very low. Such a lack of understanding will make it easier for those leading the WTO agreements, particularly the large corporations, to achieve what they want to from TRIPS. Also, some of these corporations have been involved with writing and amending TRIPS itself anyway, so are obviously placed at an advantage when it comes to understanding it and making it work in their favour. Meanwhile, the voice of the library and information profession might not be heard at all, or at least only very slightly. We have examples already about the lack of consultation with the library and information profession in relation to WTO-focused decisions. The American Library Association was not consulted before US libraries were committed to the GATS, for example (see Chapter 6, section 6.7). Thus it could be easy to override issues that the profession is concerned about and seeking to defend. So, we need to be on our guard! Finally, TRIPS overrides copyright legislation in member states, and in this way poses a threat to democracy.

10.2.2 Patents in TRIPS and its implications for the library and information community

In this book, I have focused on local, traditional knowledge and patents in the developing world in Chapter 9, and some of the implications of this for the library and information world will now be considered.

When traditional knowledge is taken by large corporations and transformed into intellectual property rights, as happens so frequently today in the developing world, this is clearly going to have significant implications for the library and information profession. As Denise Nicholson says in relation to indigenous populations:

> Without access to information, they are unaware that their intellectual property is often misappropriated and used for commercial exploitation abroad. As a result, the rural community or individuals do not receive any compensation. (Nicholson, 2002: 261)

The local indigenous population often does not have the knowledge or understanding to be able to transfer their knowledge and ideas into a tangible format, and therefore it cannot be protected by copyright, as I have already indicated. However, it also means that it offers ripe opportunities for large corporations to appropriate this knowledge, patent it, and thus transform it into an intellectual property right.

The problem with this though is that it clearly benefits large corporations, but offers few if any benefits to the indigenous population, as they will then have to pay for the information in the patent, such as paying for drugs – information that was previously available for free. This goes against some of the basic principles of the library and information profession, with its enthusiasm for providing free access to information for all. It will also mean that it will be more difficult to store this knowledge in the local library and make it freely available. So, in a sense, information and knowledge that should be part of the community and made available through libraries and information resource centres is being denied. Part of the problem here is that the notion of the library and information profession in the developing world is probably quite weak in comparison with the developed world. A library and information service is something of a luxury for those that are poor and starving. However, the patenting of this local indigenous knowledge exacerbates the problem, and will make it even more difficult for library professional standards and ethics to make a real impact on the developing world. Instead, the power and influence will reside even more with large corporations; they will be deciding what, if any, traditional knowledge to make available easily, how much of it to make available and where to make it available. This is likely to increase rather than lessen poverty in the developing world. So, these are very serious issues indeed for the library and information profession.

This also raises issues about how relevant and important the library and information profession actually is, on a global basis, which must surely also give the profession cause for concern. I suggest that the profession, through organisations such as IFLA, should be making statements, giving talks, organising campaigns, holding conferences, etc., on this important subject. While copyright can easily be seen to be an important topic for the profession, and the IFLA CLM Committee is very active on copyright issues, little is being undertaken, in comparison, on patent issues. This is probably a subject that needs to be addressed quite urgently by the profession.

10.2.3 Implications of the WTO in general for the library and information profession

Large corporations and rich countries wield a very considerable amount of power and influence at the WTO. The UK House of Lords Select Committee on Economic Affairs, in its report on *Globalisation*, spoke about the influence that rich countries wield at the WTO, saying:

> We recognise that member countries of the WTO vary in size and economic power. They vary, therefore, in their capacity to influence decisions in the WTO and, more fundamentally, to maintain a presence at the WTO. It would be naïve to believe that an organisation like the WTO would not be dominated by a small number of rich countries. (House of Lords: 10, 2002)

It is highly significant that an institution like the UK House of Lords recognises the imbalance at the WTO, and how rich countries have more influence and more decision-making powers. Thus, clearly, there are many implications here for libraries and information. If more knowledge and information is encapsulated in IPRs that are owned by large corporations in rich countries, for example, whether this be in the developed world or in the developing world, then it is less likely that this information will be made freely available. Instead the IPRs will be traded, as in the spirit of TRIPS. Therefore, libraries may find themselves having to pay for this information, in which case they will probably have to pass this cost on to library users. The marketisation of information is already happening, and there are many information products on the market, such as ebrary and Questia, as I outline in Chapter 5, section 5.5.1. This is likely to have a particularly severe effect on the poor and disadvantaged and will increase the digital divide. There are many other such implications possible and further consideration should be given to this.

A further concern is the fact that many important decisions as a result of these different agreements will reside within the WTO itself, rather than within individual nation states. This involves an erosion of the power of nation states, which I have referred to elsewhere in this book. In this respect, it is likely that more IPR legislation in WTO member states will have to fall in line with TRIPS. Thus the power and influence of the library and information profession over IPR legislation and directives is likely to be even more minimal. There was an IFLA representative at the WTO Ministerial at Seattle (Paul Whitney), but IFLA was not able to send a representative to the WTO Ministerial meetings at Doha and Cancun. Even if there had been a representative at those meetings it is unlikely that they would have been able to change very much or made any important decisions, although it would have meant that there was at least *some* possibility and useful information could also have been obtained. In any event, it should be easier to lobby the government in one's own nation state and try to make an impact in that way than it is to get through to WTO officials – even though the former is also very difficult. So, this lessens the voice of the library and information profession in general. This is particularly concerning given the fact that the WTO has a very large representation from big corporations. Furthermore, once the WTO agreements are in place, it will be very difficult to reverse them. In Part VII of the Agreement it says that the Council for TRIPS will:

> ... monitor the operation of this Agreement and in particular, Members' compliance with their obligation hereunder ... (Article 65)

10.2.4 Conclusion

The subject of the implications of TRIPS for the library and information profession is a very new and unexplored area. In this section I have considered some of the issues, but much more thought and research needs to be given to this whole, complex topic. Most of the research on TRIPS that has been undertaken has focused on other areas, particularly areas such as genetic engineering and the patenting of life-forms, and the patenting of drugs and the pharmaceutical industry. Various NGOs are very concerned about these areas. Yet libraries and information centres also play a very important part in society, therefore the implications of the TRIPS for the profession needs to be given more consideration. Furthermore, libraries as information resources can house information that impacts on these areas, such as the provision of information for the pharmaceutical industry. The implications of TRIPS for the library and information profession are many and varied.

In this section I first examined TRIPS in copyright and considered the balance in copyright, which involves the giving of rights to creators of works and copyright holders versus the free flow of information. I also emphasised that, for clarity, this balance actually needs to be analysed from three different angles, but that this whole notion of balance was of no real concern in TRIPS. I then focused on the complexity of copyright legislation, TRIPS and copyright overriding other copyright legislation and the implications of copyright issues for libraries in the developing world. Second, I considered patents in TRIPS, focusing in particular on TK in developing countries. Third, I considered the implications of the WTO in general for the library and information profession. The implications of other general parts of the TRIPS agreement for the profession also ideally need to be considered further, such as the dispute settlement procedures and the implications of important articles such as 'National Treatment' and 'Most-Favoured-Nation Treatment'.

Research on TRIPS and libraries is currently being undertaken in Canada, but research on the implications of TRIPS for libraries and information also needs to be undertaken in many other countries and regions, such as in Europe, Australia, the UK, China, the USA and India, and in the developing world in general. There also needs to be further investigation about how decisions made at the EU level in relation to IPRs, copyright and patents relates to decisions made at the WTO and the wider international level, as well as how copyright in the TRIPS Agreement differs from other copyright legislation, such as the European Copyright Directive.

10.3 TRIPS: information and libraries internationally

10.3.1 Introduction

Having considered the implications of TRIPS for the library and information profession in general, I will now consider the implications of TRIPS for libraries and information internationally, focusing on a select number of countries and regions from the developing and developed world. This section considers some of the issues and concerns, but as this is very much a new, unexplored area, much more research needs to be undertaken and more countries need to be examined. The section will highlight some of the important facts and some of the debates that are taking place.

10.3.2 Canada

As I have already indicated Canada is very much at the forefront of the TRIPS, libraries and information issue. Research on the implications of the TRIPS for libraries and information is being undertaken in Canada. This is the first such research to be undertaken. It was due to start about 18 months ago, but was delayed through lack of funding. The funding has now been secured, including money that was given by organisations such as EBLIDA and the Norwegian Library Association. The research is being undertaken by Professor Myra J. Tawfik of the University of Windsor, Canada. Professor Tawfik was selected by the Canadian Library Association (CLA) Trade Treaties Committee, and the project has been driven forward by the CLA. The study builds on the pioneering report *An assessment of the impact of the General Agreement on Trade in Services on policy, programs and law concerning public sector libraries* by Steve Shrybman, which the Canadian Library Association commissioned in 2001. (See Chapter 4, section 4.5.4 and Chapter 6, section 6.5 in this book for further information about Shrybman's study.)

The study will examine the role that TRIPS is playing in shaping domestic copyright policy, and so the intention is that it will play a role in influencing the ability of libraries to provide fair and easy access to information. The study will be of interest to various international organisations that are involved with public access to information. It will provide information on the TRIPS and its implications, including the necessary information to be able to engage with trade officials. In this way it hopes to influence the formulation of national positions on intellectual property with regard to international trade treaties.

In relation to the specifics of the research, the intention is to, firstly, consult with the Canadian Library Association and review the relevant literature, then to undertake the research and analyse the findings. The project will probably be completed in 2005. Thus this is a very exciting, worthwhile and important project.

10.3.3 Europe

EBLIDA represents many of the library voices in Europe (see Chapter 4, section 4.13 of this book for more information about EBLIDA), so the focus in this brief section will be on EBLIDA. Canada has been at the forefront of GATS and TRIPS, as I have already indicated, but this has been followed by Europe, especially Norway and Sweden. In particular, Frode Bakken from Norway and Kjell Nilsson from Sweden have both given talks and written papers on the GATS. They are both on the EBLIDA WTO Working Group, Kjell Nilsson being the current coordinator of the working group and Frode Bakken the coordinator before Nilsson. So, the Scandinavian countries have been particularly active. As already stated, EBLIDA had a meeting with representatives of the WTO and the European Commission in December 2002 (see Chapter 6, section 6.15 for further information). Although the primary focus was on the GATS, some questions around TRIPS were also raised and discussed.

We also discuss TRIPS at our EBLIDA WTO meetings, even though the focus, up until now, has been more on the GATS than on TRIPS. At the EBLIDA conference we plan to hold in the UK in 2005 both the GATS and TRIPS will be on the agenda and I have been invited to speak on TRIPS and libraries. So, hopefully, this will be the start of EBLIDA raising awareness about TRIPS and its likely implications for libraries and information throughout Europe.

10.3.4 The USA

The USA has been very much at the forefront in many of the decision-making processes with regard to intellectual property rights in general, and TRIPS in particular. As I have already indicated, Drahos and

Braithwaite emphasised how the US has been leading the globalisation of intellectual property issues in order to further its own agenda and for its own economic success:

> The US is globalising domestic intellectual property standards that meet its own economic needs and fit with its cultural and philosophical traditions. (Drahos and Braithwaite, 2003: 16)

They also say that the USA 'fashions and globalises intellectual property standards' in order to extend its own sovereignty and in the process largely ignores wider moral issues:

> Today's global intellectual property paradigm is about protecting the knowledge and skills of the leaders of the pack. In the US, state and multinationals remain committed partners in the institutional project of information feudalism: acquiring and maintaining global power based on the ownership of knowledge assets. Meanwhile the inequalities and problems of this global redistribution of property rights information are only slowly coming to be understood. (Drahos and Braithwaite, 2003: 17)

I have already emphasised how the developed world has far more power and influence in relation to the WTO in general, and how this extends to TRIPS. However, the USA, in particular, has more power and influence than other countries in the developed world with regard to TRIPS.

Alan Larson, the Under Secretary of State for Economic, Business and Agricultural Affairs in the USA, has emphasised how important intellectual property is to the success of the American economy, saying that:

> The United States is a knowledge-based, innovation-driven economy. The protection of intellectual property rights is critically important to our prosperity and economic leadership. (Larson, 2002: 1)

The copyright industries account for about 5 per cent of the US Gross Domestic Product and this sector has grown twice as fast as the rest of the US economy (Larson, 2002: 1). Clearly, then, this is an important and a growing industry in the USA. Larson also emphasises the drive forward in the knowledge revolution, and I consider the knowledge revolution further in Chapters 11 and 12. The Department of State has chaired an

Intellectual Property Rights Training Coordination Group, for example, which emphasises the government's commitment to training in this area. This group has worked with other US agencies and with the private sector in order to prioritise proposals for training programmes and to ensure that training resources are used effectively (Larson, 2002: 5).

The American Library Association (ALA) has taken some interest and action with regard to the WTO agreements that are likely to impact on the library and information profession, as I have emphasised in the section on GATS in this book (Chapter 6, section 6.7). In relation to TRIPS specifically, the ALA meets with and writes to the US government agencies, including the Office of the US Trade Representative, the US Departments of State and Commerce and the US Copyright Office, on matters relating to TRIPS. Furthermore, the ALA Committee on Legislation (COL) takes an active interest in this area (ALA Committee on Legislation, 2004). Thus the USA is very much at the forefront of the TRIPS agenda in general and is driving it forward, although the library and information profession in America is also taking an interest in it all.

10.3.5 India and the developing world in general

Several people in India have raised concerns about the likely implications of TRIPS for the Indian way of life. This section will consider this in relation to libraries and information, and also examine the developing world in general in this context.

In Indian culture life cannot be patented because it cannot be owned and is not manufactured. All this raises serious ethical issues and questions for the library and information profession and questions the philosophy behind the TRIPS Agreement in general. Shiva says that:

> TRIPS forces us to give up such moral values, economic priorities and sovereignty. (Shiva, 2001: 114)

Shiva says that the real problem for India is the 'piracy of centuries of innovation'. Furthermore, the patent laws will 'promote biopiracy and intellectual piracy' and encourage 'intellectual slavery' (Shiva, 2001: 132). Clearly, this is an issue that the library and information profession needs to be considering further. It certainly does not encourage easy access to information.

Shiva continues, saying that TRIPS has 'globalised US-style patent laws' (2001: 7). Furthermore, the indigenous knowledge which India has used for centuries for everyday needs is likely to be patented by the West for commercial gain. These include, for example, neem, haldi, karela, jamun, kali mirch, bhu amla and hundreds of other plants used in food and medicine. Shiva says that:

> Through intellectual property rights and patents, the minds and bodies of indigenous people are being pirated; life itself is being colonized. (Shiva, 2001: 9)

Another problem with regard to the library and information profession, though, is that I think that their voice is rather weak in the developing world compared to that in the developed world. From all the reading and research that I have been undertaking, I have found no evidence that the developing world is deeply considering the implications of the GATS and TRIPS for the library and information profession, for example. Nor have they undertaken any real work on the topic to my knowledge. As already indicated, it is Canada that has been at the forefront and is driving the debate forward, and it is Canada that has just started to undertake some research on TRIPS. Yet TRIPS is going to affect libraries and information in the developing world particularly hard, as I have made clear through-out this book. At the fringe meeting that I organised at the IFLA Conference in Glasgow it became very apparent, once again, that the developed world had a greater concern with regard to these issues, and were more proactive. Those that had both written on the subject and were vocal all came from the developed world. Furthermore, the people that attended the meeting were largely from the West. This can probably all be explained by a number of factors.

- High levels of illiteracy are found in the developing world. Also, libraries in the developing world cannot be institutions that are valued in the same way as libraries in the West are if people cannot read and write. There are more fundamental problems that need to be addressed first.

- English is a dominant language and people in the developing world are encouraged to learn it – indeed, some probably feel compelled to learn it. Those of us from the English-speaking world feel no such compulsion to reciprocate. Thus this presents those in the developing world with another potential barrier, as ideally those in the developing world have to learn to read and write in their own language as well as in English.

- While there are those in the developing world who are questioning and exploring issues around TRIPS and GATS they might not then be transforming these issues into a tangible format. So this in itself could become another form of local knowledge, which could be misused and even exploited.

- The WTO has been largely established by the developed world, as I have already discussed, which means that the West really has a head start anyway. The people that set something up are likely to have a better knowledge and understanding of the subject in hand, whereas those in the developing world have to become aware of the TRIPS topic. Then they have to understand it and finally critique it if they want to be able to make any valuable contribution.

- Developing countries often have limited financial and other resources.

- People in the developing world often have a completely different culture and way of life to those in the developed world. Yet they are being forced to think about western culture and the western view of the world. They also have to think about the developing world's interest with regard to commercialisation in general, which is exemplified in the GATS and TRIPS. Thus the West, because of its power base, could seriously damage and change the whole way of life of those in the developing world.

Meanwhile, the importance of knowledge in both the developed world and in the developing world is becoming more and more apparent. Kaushik argued that:

> The contribution of knowledge – both traditional and modern – as a factor of production has acquired a dominant role in trade, investment and technological change. (Kaushik, 2003: 255)

This means that it is more and more important to safeguard traditional knowledge, and it also means that it is an area that the library and information profession should be engaging with. Also, such knowledge should be made more accessible in libraries. Yet, so far, this has not really been happening. As Kaushik says, if the holders of traditional knowledge are not able to find a way to protect their intellectual property then this '... may result in the disappearance of the traditional systems of knowledge and the associated resources' (Kaushik, 2003: 255). Once again, as librarians this should concern us. It could mean the disappearance of some history, tradition, culture and ways of life for these indigenous populations as the information would not be recorded. So the value of the library as an institution really needs to be recognised. It is a place where history can be recorded and preserved for people to access today, as well as in future generations to come. It can also help to keep local cultures alive and thriving, by providing facilities for people to meet and discuss issues. Librarians and information professionals can also go out into the communities and try to locate other traditional knowledge that it might well be important to record and preserve for the future.

Traditionally knowledge in India has been preserved through 'smriti' and 'shruti'. This means through the word of the teacher so the knowledge is not documented. As already explained, though, this is starting to change now, and some TK is being documented. One good example of this is the People's Biodiversity Registers (PBR) in India. This is a digital database of traditional knowledge in the public domain related to medicinal plants and the intention is to make this available globally. This is worthwhile, and will mean that more traditional knowledge can be copyright protected, but it does not, on its own, ensure the sharing of benefits which can arise from the use of such knowledge. The librarian could also assist with the process of trying to ensure that the benefits are shared.

Thus some of the most important issues with regard to traditional knowledge in India – and in the developing world in general – include the prevention of misappropriation of TK, the development of effective systems for its protection and the development of a mechanism for the fair and equitable sharing of benefits arising out of its utilisation. The library and information profession could examine some of the ways in which TK is currently being documented in India and in the developing world in general. Then it could perhaps educate other indigenous communities and encourage them to document their own TK. The profession also needs to be thinking of other effective ways for preserving and protecting TK, as well as effective and fair means for sharing it. Clearly, the role of the library and information centre can play a crucial role here. Some of the big problems, though, that the developing world faces in relation to TRIPS are the domination of the USA and biopiracy, as well as the fundamental point that TRIPS has not been designed to benefit the developing world.

10.3.6 Africa

It is, perhaps, rather surprising to realise that 40 of the 140 members of the WTO are from African countries. Thus, clearly, the TRIPS is likely to have a significant impact on libraries and information in Africa.

It is interesting to note that developing countries, in general, are being given somewhat more time to implement TRIPS than the developed countries, because of the disadvantaged position that many of them find themselves in. The TRIPS was largely written by those in the West, especially the USA, so there is a recognition here that developing countries need more time to understand it and to implement it. As Mangeni says:

> The TRIPS Agreement was in essence written by developed country industry lobbies. (Mangeni, 2003: 230)

Also, the developing countries make up three-quarters of humankind, so to this extent, they cannot be easily ignored. So the WTO *is* listening to the developing world, but it is somewhat half-hearted, I would say, and only when it is seen to be to the advantage of the developed world.

In regard to South Africa specifically, Denise Nicholson has taken a very active interest in copyright issues and TRIPS in South Africa and has written various articles on the subject and given talks. Denise Nicholson works at the University of the Witwatersrand Library, Johannesburg, South Africa. Since 1996 she has been the Copyright Services Librarian. She is responsible for running the Copyright Services Office, administering the Central Copyright Fund and providing an advisory service for both staff and students, as well as for those outside the university. In 1997 she started a Copyquest Listserv in order to raise awareness about copyright in the library and educational sector. She liaises with FAIFE and government departments with regard to copyright matters. She is also a member of the IFLA CLM Committee and the Intellectual Property Sub-Committee of the University Research Committee, University of Witwatersrand. Therefore she represents a very powerful and authoritative voice on the situation in South Africa, with regard to copyright in general and TRIPS in particular.

Denise Nicholson (2002) refers to the illiteracy and dire poverty that exists in South Africa and how South Africa has endeavoured to address the literacy problem since apartheid ended in 1994. There are approximately 140 million people in sub-Saharan Africa, for example, who cannot read or write. In total, at least a quarter of the population of South Africa is illiterate. Many of these people live in rural areas, with no water or electricity services. So information is shared orally, in one of the 11 South African languages. Nicholson says:

> Very often these communities do not have any library services and depend on basic information spread verbally or information provided at local community resource centres. The lack of access to printed material, as well as multimedia and digital technology are severely hampering the illiterate in their educational pursuits. (Nicholson, 2002: 261)

So, there are very few libraries in these communities. Where there are libraries in rural areas, they are often far away from schools and homes, in poor buildings with a very limited budget and inadequate stock. Because of the problems, many move to the urban areas, but they encounter problems there as well, although public libraries are often the main source of information.

Denise Nicholson emphasised the fact that indigenous knowledge can easily be appropriated by large international corporations in South Africa. The people are ignorant and unaware of their intellectual property rights, and often are not able to put their ideas into a tangible format. So they do not receive any financial reward. Therefore these people need to be more aware of copyright and patent issues in general, as well as having an awareness and understanding about TRIPS in particular. She ends her article by emphasising the need to eradicate illiteracy.

People in South Africa have many pressing, life-threatening issues to deal with on a daily basis. Therefore libraries, information and TRIPS might seem to be relatively unimportant issues. However, if some of these issues are not tackled sooner rather than later, then many far more serious problems could ensue.

10.3.7 The UK

As with the GATS, the only work that has been undertaken specifically on TRIPS, libraries and information in the UK is the work that I have undertaken myself. First of all, I examined the GATS, and then I proceeded to examine TRIPS. This way I felt that I would have a grasp on the crucial main trade agreements that were taking place at the WTO that are likely to have significant implications for libraries and information. I read most of the whole of the TRIPS Agreement, in order to understand what was the main philosophy behind the TRIPS and what it was fundamentally about. I undertook some further background reading and then wrote three articles about TRIPS, libraries and information. The first was quite short, highlighting some of the main points. This was published in *Managing Information* (R. Rikowski, 2003c). The second was long and detailed and was published in the *IFLA Journal* (R. Rikowski, 2003b). The third focused on the moral, trade and information issues, and was published in *Business Information Review* (R. Rikowski, 2003a). I also gave two talks on TRIPS, one at the Library and Information Show at the Excel Exhibition in Docklands, East London and the other at Kingston University to a group of MSc students, both in 2003.

My interest in TRIPS specifically (in abstraction from the GATS) first started when I attended a conference that was organised by the UK Commission on Intellectual Property Rights in 2002. A report was then written following on from the Commission's investigation (Commission on Intellectual Property Rights, 2002). The two-day conference considered many issues around TRIPS and it also included a section on copyright and traditional knowledge specifically. Its aim was to consider how to make intellectual property rights work for the developing world. Denise Nicholson from the University of South Africa spoke about copyright issues in South Africa and Martin Khor, the Director of the Third World Network, spoke about TRIPS and whether it should really be part of the WTO. (See also Chapter 9, section 9.4.2.)

Also, from all the knowledge management (KM) research that I have undertaken (R. Rikowski, 2003h) I have concluded that there are clear links between the GATS, TRIPS and the knowledge economy/knowledge revolution – and these are all areas that are of concern to the library and information profession. As Davies says:

> The rationale for copyright and related rights in the United Kingdom continues to be that such rights play a vital role in protecting and promoting creativity and that 'the knowledge economy depends on strong intellectual property rights.' (Davies, 2002: 73)

Furthermore, as Drahos and Braithwaite say:

> ... the corporate actors responsible for TRIPS at the end of the 20th century were merely laying the foundations for the knowledge economies of the 21st. (Drahos and Braithwaite, 2003: 16)

This will all be considered in Chapters 11 and 12 in this book, although the development of my thinking in this regard will be explored further and in more depth in my future works.

10.3.8 Summary

This section has considered TRIPS in relation to libraries and information in a number of different countries. It is by no means exhaustive or comprehensive, but it provides an introductory examination and an overview. It emphasises, again, that the USA is driving TRIPS forward in general, and that the developing world is suffering and will continue to suffer in particular as a result of TRIPS.

Following on from this, a number of issues now need to be addressed. Further research needs to be undertaken on the implications of the TRIPS for libraries and information in a number of different countries. At the current time, only Canada is undertaking this research. The library and information profession needs to raise awareness further about these important issues. There have been talks on the topic at the IFLA conferences, but there need to be more talks, more conferences, more discussions and more articles written. However, there is also a need for lobbying and political action. Perhaps the WTO should be approached directly in this regard. Representatives from IFLA and EBLIDA could have further meetings with the WTO, for example, continuing on from the meeting they had with them in December 2002. A representative from IFLA should, ideally, be at all the WTO Ministerial meetings. Furthermore, the profession needs to be highly aware of the problems and issues that face the developing world in particular and try to make sure that they do not feel too marginalised. In this regard, it would be really helpful if more library associations from the developing world were to become more involved with the topic, particularly as it is likely to affect them so profoundly.

10.4 Conclusion

The chapters on TRIPS in this book have examined a wide range of different issues. Chapter 7 provided an overview of the agreement itself. Chapter 8 focused on copyright. First, it provided some background to copyright issues, focusing on the historical perspective on copyright, moral and economic rights in copyright and the balancing act in copyright. It then examined the copyright section of TRIPS specifically, followed by a section on moral rights and the copyright section of TRIPS. Chapter 9 considered patents and traditional knowledge and the significance of TRIPS for the developing world. Chapter 10 considered the implications of the TRIPS for the library and information profession specifically, focusing on copyright, patents and the WTO in general. Furthermore, it looked, in some depth, at the notion of the free flow of information in particular. It also included an international perspective, and considered TRIPS, libraries and information in a number of different countries.

It should now be clearly apparent that the GATS and TRIPS together represent powerful, far-reaching agreements that could, and I am sure will, have serious implications for the library and information profession. As a profession we surely need to take urgent action on these matters.

Note

The chapters in this book on TRIPS (Part 3, Chapters 7, 8, 9 and 10) build on my three published articles on TRIPS, libraries and information, which were published in the *IFLA Journal, Managing Information* and *Business Information Review*.

Part 4

An Open Marxist theoretical perspective on global capitalism and the World Trade Organisation

Implications of GATS and TRIPS: an Open Marxist approach

11.1 Introduction

Having now provided an overview of globalisation and the WTO, and a detailed analysis of the GATS and TRIPS and the implications of these agreements for the library and information profession, the last part of this book will place all this within a wider, theoretical framework.

This chapter begins by considering why we seem to accept so readily the 'TINA' (There Is No Alternative) philosophy with regard to global capitalism. It will examine various possible explanations for this and will suggest that what we need to be focusing on, in particular, is the evolutionary nature of social systems. If we were to accept the evolutionary nature of social systems as an established theory and an established fact, in the same way as we accept Darwin's theory of the origin of species through natural selection, we could then consider how to break free from this evolutionary process. We could then seek to be proactive (rather than just letting evolutionary processes take their course) and work towards creating a better social, economic and political system.

Global capitalism can only be effectively analysed and critiqued by developing relevant and credible social scientific theory. From such a position we can then seek to change it. The question then becomes one of deciding which social scientific theory analyses and critiques global capitalism most effectively, whether this is functionalism, critical realism, postmodernism, interactionism or whatever. For me, it is Marxism. Thus my task becomes one of relating Marxist theory to global capitalism today and this will be considered at a preliminary level in these final chapters.

This chapter will highlight the fact that I am developing a Marxist theoretical analysis of the GATS, TRIPS and knowledge management in the knowledge revolution, and why I think it is important to do this. In particular, I am developing an Open Marxist theoretical analysis of value and within this context I examine value and the commodity in particular. An overview of this will be provided in this chapter.

Chapter 12 will examine the furtherance of global capitalism through the WTO, and within this it will, first of all, reconsider the knowledge revolution, intellectual labour, value and the WTO. This is followed by a section outlining that global capitalism is sustained by value and not by morals. Within this framework it examines moral dilemmas, value creation and intellectual property rights in particular. I am arguing that capitalism is not founded on any moral base, and indeed, it can never be. Instead, it is sustained by value and this value is, and can only ever be, created from labour. It then briefly considers how the importance of creating value from knowledge has been referenced in the business and information literature. The final chapter, Chapter 13, provides some overall conclusions.

These last three chapters should be viewed very much as an introduction to my Open Marxist theoretical perspective on globalisation. In these last three chapters I have covered many areas in a short space in order to provide the reader with some basic understanding on the topic and hopefully to arouse the reader's interest. For these reasons, along with a lack of space and the complexity of the subject, these last chapters are not as heavily referenced as the rest of the book, and should be read very much in this context. Well-referenced and detailed arguments will be presented in my future works on this highly important topic.

Thus my intention in these last chapters is to convince the reader of the importance of bringing theory and practice together, and moreover to present the argument that Marxism provides a more adequate theoretical understanding and analysis of society and the economy and its intrinsic workings than any other theory. Therefore we need to be developing a Marxist theoretical analysis in order to understand and explain what is happening in global capitalism today in general, and within the context of the GATS and TRIPS in particular. Postone points out the fact that Marxism calls for a re-examination of social theory itself, and demands that other social theories become more rigorous. As Postone said, Marxism:

... raises more general questions regarding the nature of social theory. Marx's critical theory, which grasps capitalist society by means of a theory of the constitution of labor of a directionally dynamic, totalizing mediation that is historically specific, is a brilliant analysis of this society; and, it is, at the same time, a powerful argument regarding the nature of an adequate social theory. (Postone, 1996: 399)

Through Marxism we can understand why the GATS and TRIPS are being introduced, why it is so difficult to stop the process, why the WTO in general is so important and so powerful, and why it largely represents the interests of rich countries and large corporations. Furthermore, Marxism prevents us from going round in circles, which can happen if one tries to analyse all this within an overall moral framework, or indeed from any other perspective, theoretical or otherwise.

Thus these final chapters can be seen to be very much building a bridge between two very important subject areas in the library and information profession: namely globalisation and knowledge management. It then aims to place these subjects within an Open Marxist theoretical perspective (Open Marxism will be considered briefly and how it differs from traditional Marxism in section 11.4), the purpose of this being to endeavour to understand, analyse, explain, theorise, critique and then, finally, terminate capitalism.

The ethos and principles embedded in the library and information profession lie outside of the capitalist system in many ways. The possible privatisation of state-funded library provision and the perpetuation of the trading of intellectual property rights is no laughing, frivolous matter. However, having exposed these issues, positive action then needs to be taken. This can include activities such as lobbying, the holding of meetings (professional as well as other meetings), political demonstrations, various forms of writing, picketing, petitions, etc. These are all worthwhile activities, and I would very much urge the reader to engage in them. However, we also need to develop theory in order to understand, explain and critique all this at a deeper level, so that we can increase our chances that something can then be done about it all on a permanent basis. As far as I am concerned, not enough time has been or is being given to developing good social scientific theory.

11.2 Various possible explanations for the acceptance of the 'TINA' view of global capitalism

11.2.1 Introduction

We seem to celebrate capitalism, and yet it causes such death, misery and injustice. So, why do we think it is such a wonderful system? Why do we seem to accept capitalism so readily? – the 'There Is No Alternative' (TINA) philosophy (which I discuss in Chapters 1 and 2)? There are various possible explanations for this and some of these will be considered in this section. The explanations that will be considered are – religion, evolution, human nature, the death of communism and a lack of resources. The importance of viewing the evolutionary process of social systems as an established fact/theory will be emphasised.

11.2.2 Religion

Many seem to see capitalism as a gift from God today: we have capitalism, here it is and how wonderful it is. We know that capitalism is not perfect, but it is the best that we can hope for – 'There Is No Alternative'. This belief is particularly rife now that communism, apparently, largely appears to be dead – or at least that is how many see it with the collapse of communism in Soviet Russia, the collapse of the Berlin Wall and the decline in communist beliefs in China, etc., particularly now that China has joined the WTO. So TINA rears its head once again! This seems to be our underlying belief – or certainly, it is within the western world anyway (people such as Muslim fundamentalists might, perhaps, take a different position), although, of course, there are still a few communist countries such as Cuba and North Korea. But why do we believe in such a simple, naive notion? Perhaps it is partly because many still yearn for some religious framework in some way – witness our desire for 'goodies' and 'baddies' in films, for example. We still seem to want to divide the world into simply 'good' and 'bad' in many ways. A quote by Drahos and Braithwaite illustrates this point when they say that:

> If intellectual property rights are contingently a force for good or ill, how do we secure the good? (Drahos and Braithwaite, 2002: 189)

If only it were that simple! Obviously, many in the developing world are still very religious, but many in the developed world are no longer so blatantly religious, yet they still hanker after religion in some way.

Also, while we need to understand and endeavour to help those in the developing world, I do not think we should glorify them, and think that they have a better way of life than those in the developed world – even from an ethical point of view. People in the developing world suffer tremendous hardships – the answer is not for the West to endeavour to adopt a 'third world culture', as some green romantics might argue. No, we have been and are evolving through different social systems, and to this extent, the West is further forward than the developing world in many ways, in my view.

However, just because the developed world is more advanced in terms of medicine, information technology, education, etc., it does not mean that the developed world has all the answers. So, to suggest that capitalism is a perfect system and that nothing better is possible is surely very naive and unfortunate. It seems to me that although we might have rejected formal religion, we still often think in a religious way. Therefore, the assumption frequently seems to be that we do not have to worry too much about getting a really good, fair, social, economic and political system in our lifetime. Instead, it can all be obtained and sorted out in the next, i.e. all will be wonderful when we get to heaven! So, if capitalism causes death and misery, as it undoubtedly does, then this is just something that has to be tolerated. In the end, though, God will sort it all out and make it alright, and be fair and just and decide who will go to heaven and who will go to hell. We have the intellect to develop complex computer systems, we have the intellect to travel in space, etc., but we cannot seem to find it within ourselves to use our intellect to create a better social, economic and political system. It is interesting to note that Darwinism had, and sometimes still has, to battle against religious fundamentalists. I would suggest that arguing that social systems go through evolutionary processes presents us with the same type of battle – having to fight against religious notions, even if it is not religion itself.

11.2.3 *Human nature*

Another argument as to why we accept the 'TINA' notion is that it is just 'human nature'. This argument claims that some people will always be greedy and selfish, and want to get all they can out of life for themselves. Therefore, if they are doing well in capitalism, then they are happy, and they care nothing about the death, starvation, inequality and misery that is also being caused to others by it (such as in sweat shops in the developing world). Furthermore, it is these types of people that are driving capitalism forward. There will always be some who are greedy and selfish and in positions of power, so these people will always ensure the success of capitalism – so the argument goes. However, this is surely a naive and simplistic approach to take. Some might well relate this to religious notions – greedy people are 'bad' and so one day, presumably, will go to hell and justice will be done. But what makes a person greedy and selfish? Is it that they have simply been swayed by the devil? Is it in their genes or can it be attributed to environmental and social factors? If it is the latter, then once again this is because of the social system that we live in, which needs to be changed. Many sociological studies have found that children who are bought up in a very poor, working-class, deprived area, for example, are more likely to turn to crime (see, for example, Haralambos and Holborn, 2004) – and so could become more selfish and greedy. So, even to suggest that nothing can be done about it, that we will always have a social, economic and political system that causes death and misery because some people will always be greedy, is surely a very simplistic and flawed notion. Fundamentally, there are many inadequacies in this argument, but there is not the space to explore them here.

11.2.4 The death of communism

Another argument is that alternatives to capitalism, such as communism, have been tried and failed, and so these alternatives must be abandoned, and all that we have left is capitalism – so we must work with that and try to make the best of it – that indeed 'There Is No Alternative' (TINA). There is not the space to explore this in any depth, but I will just make a few points here.

First, some countries have had what has been called a communist state, but these have not encapsulated the core principles of communism.

Second, there are some countries where communism has been practised quite successfully.

Third, I suggest that communism within individual countries can never be truly successful while we still have capitalism. Indeed, we must not forget how powerful capitalism is – how it can tempt us with its offers of exciting products, the supposed 'good life', etc. This can give false illusions and temptations to people living in communist countries, and can lead them to think that all the 'good life' resides in capitalist countries, which is far from the truth for the majority of people. Capitalist countries largely do not want communist countries to succeed, so will try to hamper them. The US blockade of communist Cuba is one good example here. Furthermore, we must not forget that the logic of capitalism is the commodification and marketisation of all that surrounds us. So, just as public services offer ripe opportunities for capitalism (hence the reason for bringing in the GATS), so whole communist countries offer *really* ripe opportunities – so many areas to commodify! Therefore, communism really needs to be the accepted world order – it will never be able to operate effectively while it only resides in a few countries. However, this will take a long time, and involves raising people's levels of consciousness, and people engaging and thinking about all these issues at a much deeper level. Basically, the majority of the world population needs to be of the opinion that communism would be a much better way of life than capitalism, in my view.

Finally, we need to exercise some patience. Just because communism might not have been practised in the way that we would ideally like it to have been so far is no reason to abandon it. It is a small seed that needs to be nurtured, not killed at birth. If we are not of this persuasion, then it seems we are, indeed, left with global capitalism, with all the death, misery, injustice and suffering that it causes. I have endeavoured to demonstrate throughout this book (by examining notions such as the balance in copyright) that reforming capitalism is not an option – it simply does not work.

11.2.5 Lack of resources

A more important and powerful argument is that there is, and has been, a lack of resources available to spend on thinking and researching about how to create a better, a kinder and a fairer social system. It is certainly very true that far more money and resources have been devoted to developing scientific research and scientific theory than has been spent on developing social scientific research and social scientific theory in general. Capitalists spending money in order to help to bring about the demise of capitalism itself? Obviously, this does not make a lot of sense, from the capitalist's point of view! One might say, why then is any such critical social scientific research conducted at all? This is because some such research is needed in order for capitalism to thrive in the long term, in the same way that companies need to be offered some protectionism through intellectual property rights in order for them to trade more effectively in the long term. There needs to be some research and some thought and explanations given as to why there are particular social problems in capitalism and blatant examples of unfairness, such as the fact that very few children from a working-class background get to Oxbridge (Oxford and Cambridge universities in the UK). This is necessary in order to ensure the continued success of capitalism in the long term: otherwise some people will more readily critique and analyse its intrinsic workings, and want to bring about its demise. All this, then, helps to ensure the continued success of global capitalism. It is the same reason that TRIPS is protectionist, to some extent. Therefore, the 'lack of resources' argument is a very important one.

11.2.6 The evolutionary nature of social systems

Finally, there is the argument that social systems are an evolving process. As animals, our bodies have evolved in order to survive and cope with our changing environment – this is generally now accepted today. But just as we have changed as animals we have also had to operate and survive in a different social, economic and political system. Humans need to use their brains and their intellect much more now, and most of us do not need to be able to climb trees! So, out of all this, capitalism has evolved. Capitalism is a social system that has emerged/evolved from other social systems, such as feudalism and ancient slave-based societies. It is not a system that has developed as a result of a carefully thought-through process, using our intellect to think about what would be the best social, economic and political system to have. It is anarchic.

However, until the evolutionary nature of social systems is established as a theory and recognised as a fact, in the same way that Darwin's theory of natural selection is generally accepted for the evolution of species, it will be difficult to move forward. There have been social science discourses on the subject, but it has not been accepted as an established theory, in the same way that Darwinism has. Once it is accepted, we can then consider whether we want to continue to live in a social system that evolves (with the chances and mishaps that this can entail) or whether we want to actively seek to bring about a better social, economic and political system for ourselves, i.e. to be proactive.

Then, within this context, a Marxist analysis of capitalism would become invaluable, I am sure. Because natural selection is now largely recognised, people can move on and indeed now are moving on. The transhuman movement considers how to change and transform our bodies, to make them more suitable for the future, rather than just waiting for our bodies to evolve. With the extensive use of computers today, for example, we may well want and need to develop better eyesight and to do this quite soon, i.e. be proactive and endeavour to find ways to improve our eyesight, given how quickly computer technology is changing and developing. Therefore, if and when the evolutionary nature of social systems is accepted in the same way as the evolutionary nature of the species, then we can more easily and actively start to think about creating a better world for ourselves. Furthermore, we can do this by bringing theory and practice together and for me this involves adopting and developing an Open Marxist theoretical analysis.

11.2.7 Breaking free from the 'TINA' mentality and moving forward to socialism and ultimately to communism

There are many arguments that one could consider in an endeavour to explain why we have not used our intellect more to try to achieve a better social, economic and political system for ourselves and why we seem to have so readily accepted the 'TINA' philosophy. In this chapter, I have outlined five such arguments, although there are obviously others as well. There is not the space to examine this in any more depth in this book, but I want to emphasise here that some of these arguments would be found wanting on closer inspection, while others can complement each other rather than presenting either/or scenarios.

However, although I am very critical of capitalism, this does not mean to say that I am not also aware of its qualities. Capitalism is a better social system than previous systems, but just because it is better than previous social, political and economic systems does not mean that we cannot aim to create something even better for the future. Furthermore, it does not mean that it is the best possible system that we could ever have. Therefore, what we need to do is to take the good parts of capitalism (such as the level of health and education that it strives to maintain) but then move beyond it. This can only be done by using our intellect, I feel sure, and raising people's level of consciousness. However, it cannot be done by having a bloody revolution. That has been tried before and has failed – that, in itself, leaves far too much death and misery behind. No, the answer is to write, become educated, think 'outside the box', be critical, raise awareness, raise people's level of consciousness, develop theory, create new ideas and new ways of thinking – in essence, to try in many different ways to conceive of a better, a kinder and a fairer social, economic and political system, i.e. to conceive and work towards a socialist and ultimately towards a communist society.

I know that we have had so-called communist countries in the past, and still have some communist countries today, but more thought needs to be given in order for communism to become the respected and accepted world order over capitalism. Just because communism has not worked in the way that we might ideally want it to have done so far in various ways is no reason to say that we must abandon it altogether as far as I am concerned (see also my comments about this in section 11.2.4). Capitalism has not really existed for very long from a historical perspective. We need to exercise some patience in our work towards a better world, and not just cry 'TINA' when things start to seem a little tough.

One could argue that my socialist/communist dreams have religious connotations in themselves, i.e. socialism/communism = heaven, where everything will then be perfect. Maybe, in one sense, it can appear to be this way, but surely we need to try to find an optimistic/positive way forward. The alternative is just intolerable, as far as I am concerned. How can we continue to tolerate a system that causes so much death, destruction, starvation, misery, poverty, injustice and cruelty, and then say that this is acceptable? Although some people obviously benefit from capitalism, there is never any guarantee that these people will always fare well under capitalism anyway, because it has no moral base (this is considered further in Chapter 12, section 12.3). Someone could be a millionaire one day, and be bankrupt the next. This is because capitalism is a mad system that is based on contradictions. So we all struggle to live in this crazy world, but some will always come up against problems, such as the threat and reality of redundancy, and for some people these problems will prove insurmountable. But obviously, for those in the developing world, these struggles are far more acute and damaging. Therefore we need to think about and work towards creating a better social, economic and political system, one that is not essentially based on the exploitation, alienation and objectification of labour, and look to a system that does not cause such death, injustice and misery!

11.3 Developing social scientific theory

Developing sound social scientific theory is very important, as far as I am concerned. As I have already indicated, there are various social scientific theoretical positions that one can adopt, and indeed I emphasise this on the Research Methods courses that I teach to masters students. I urge students to posit their dissertations within a theoretical framework wherever possible, whether this is functionalism, postmodernism, critical realism, Marxism or whatever. Only when we start from the ground, in this way, can we ever hope to make real progress with regard to our theoretical thinking, our explanations and our analysis. Many students do not see the necessity for this, which means that they spend their time going round in circles and not really making progress. Then they produce inferior pieces of work. Some students seem to find it hard to conceptualise what I really mean – is it not that they simply want to look at marketing in the tourist industry in China, for example, and how a company in the tourist industry might improve its marketing technique? What has this got to do with underlying theoretical frameworks and concepts? But without this, the students could easily end up just being business consultants and little more – yet they are engaging in an academic discipline. Furthermore, they will not develop their thinking as fully in this way. But fundamentally it means that it will make it all the more difficult to use our intellect, to develop good social scientific theory and to critique capitalism. Students represent our hopes for the next generation of thinkers – if we are not achieving this, as educators, then something is seriously wrong. Thus more attention needs to be given to the need to develop relevant social scientific theory in general.

For me, personally, however, it is important to develop good Marxist theory and this is what I outline in these final chapters. However, I have not included an analysis of other social scientific theoretical positions. This is for a number of reasons. First, developing social scientific theories has not been a central focus within the library and information profession. Library schools and business schools do not actually devote a great deal of time to considering and developing social scientific theories in any real depth (I currently teach in university business schools). This is in contrast to academic subjects such as Sociology and Economics. Therefore, to this extent at least, I am breaking new ground. However, I would not readily see the need to investigate other social scientific theoretical perspectives anyway. It is not my task to investigate whether or not other social scientific theories can provide an adequate explanation and understanding of capitalism within the context of the WTO. That task can be left to those theoreticians themselves. My background reading on different social scientific theories over many years has led me to conclude that Marxism provides a far more adequate understanding and explanation of capitalism than any other social scientific theory. So then my task becomes one of developing Marxism, particularly given the limitations of time and the fact that the horrors in capitalism are so severe, are intensifying and urgently need to be exposed and addressed. Marx wrote 150 years ago, and yet the horrors continue. We need to devote more of our energies to exposing the intrinsic workings of capitalism and then look towards an alternative. Therefore the need to develop Marxist theory becomes quite urgent.

11.4 A Marxist theoretical analysis of the GATS, TRIPS and knowledge management in the knowledge revolution

My position is very clear. I am a Marxist. I approach the social sciences from a Marxist theoretical perspective, and this has been my position since I studied for my Social Studies degree, way back when I was 18 years old. For me, Marxism seeks to explain the social universe that we find ourselves in, critiques it and then aims to change it. Marx does not just create boxes for the sake of it, as functionalists can often appear to do. Marx had an acute awareness of the plight of the working class, and the poverty and misery that capitalism causes. He then sought to analyse and explain the reasons for this by placing these realities into a theoretical framework, thereby bringing theory and practice together. There is no better social scientific theory for understanding and explaining the intrinsic workings of capitalism than Marxism as far as I am concerned. If and when a better explanation is put forward, then, and only then, will I change my thinking! Marxism seeks to understand the world, to analyse it, to explain it and then to change it.

Some argue that Marxism is deterministic and box-like, but I would fundamentally challenge this. There is a school of thought known as 'Open Marxism' to which I adhere. An Open Marxist approach focuses on the dynamics and interrelationships of Marxist concepts – those needed to explain and unravel the intrinsic workings of the capitalist system – rather than adopting a more sterile box-like approach. Postone is an

Open Marxist and he wrote a very important book in 1996 entitled *Time, Labour and Social Domination*. I will be examining Postone, as well as Marx, in my future works, in the context of examining an Open Marxist theory of value and then considering this value theory in detail within the context of the GATS and TRIPS in the knowledge revolution. This will be considered at a preliminary level in the final chapters of this book.

Yet how can I demonstrate all these links? In a 'flash of inspiration', all became clear to me – services and intellectual property rights were being transformed into internationally tradable *commodities*, and *value* from labour was then being embedded in these commodities. The logic of capitalism is the commodification of all that surrounds us. Thus now we are seeing this process starting to take effect in areas that were unheard of before, libraries being one such area. They have generally been thought to be something beyond commercialisation and trading, a place where people can enjoy and share knowledge, information and ideas, as well as being a place for recreation and the community spirit. But through the WTO we are now witnessing a dramatic change. Much information is being turned into a commodity and being sold online – through electronic libraries like Questia, NetLibrary and ebrary. Furthermore, public library services themselves under local authority control are starting to be taken over by private companies – witness how Instant Library Ltd moved into the Haringey Public Library Service in the UK for a period. The logic of this at a future date will be that the public will probably have to pay for library services in the same way that they pay for other goods in shops and services provided by other private companies, such as a taxis. Alternatively, or in addition perhaps, libraries will not exist as physical spaces in the same way as they do today, or there will be some but fewer physical libraries. As more and more people are able to access information online there will probably no longer be such a need to access information in a physical library. But losing these areas for critical space and thinking is another deeply worrying possible scenario.

A careful reading of the TRIPS Agreement shows that the fundamental philosophy behind TRIPS is the trading of intellectual property rights, in the same way as the fundamental philosophy behind the GATS is the liberalisation of trade in services. So the aim in TRIPS is to transform knowledge, information and ideas into intellectual property rights that can then be traded in the marketplace. Fundamentally, the GATS and TRIPS assist with the process of commodifying more and more areas of social life.

It is fairly obvious that the continued creation and expansion of international tradable *commodities* (through the GATS and TRIPS) will help to enhance global capitalism, but how is this done specifically? It is being achieved by the creation and extraction of *value*, I would suggest. But then we need to consider exactly what value is. This is a question that many people would rather not explore in any depth – it all seems too complex. But we can only make real progress in our thinking by tackling these difficult questions. My theoretical position, which I explored and developed in a dissertation on value creation through knowledge (R. Rikowski, 2003h), is that capitalism is sustained by value. Capitalism goes through different stages, such as the agricultural revolution and the industrial revolution, and now we are moving into the knowledge revolution (see also R. Rikowski, 2000b, 2000c, 2003g). Throughout all these periods, capitalism is sustained by value, and this value can only ever be created by labour (see, for example, Caffentzis, 1997). In the industrial revolution, value was largely extracted from manual labour, but in the knowledge revolution value is being increasingly extracted from intellectual labour. Value is being created from intellectual labour in different ways, such as through the labourers' knowledge, ideas, creative thinking, information, brainpower, etc. Thus, within this framework, knowledge management (KM) also becomes very important. KM can be seen to be a process that enables knowledge, information and ideas to be more easily extracted from intellectual labour.

The essential point to realise, though, is that value is created by the exploitation of labour. However, I am now of the opinion that it is the way in which all Marx's concepts interact and relate to each other in capitalism, such as labour, value, markets, the commodity, profit, etc., that is specific to capitalism. But the important point to bear in mind here is that the GATS and TRIPS extend and perpetuate global capitalism by transforming public services and intellectual property rights into international tradable commodities. By this process, humans become exploited and alienated, yet they do not even realise that they are in chains. Today, as we enter the knowledge revolution, value is being created and extracted more from intellectual labour and less from manual labour (although both types of labour will always be needed) and this value is then embedded in the commodity. GATS and TRIPS assist with the process of creating more and more of these value-added commodities, which are then sold in the marketplace.

11.5 TRIPS revisited

There are many questions that can be asked in relation to TRIPS specifically. Indeed, when I first started examining TRIPS, I asked myself many of these questions, as TRIPS seemed to be a particularly complex subject. But when I posited it within an Open Marxist theoretical analysis of value all became much clearer. Listed below are some of the issues that it raises.

There is a high level of debate about many different intellectual property areas within the TRIPS agreement, particularly in areas such as the pharmaceutical and food industries and with regard to the patenting of life-forms. In particular, there is considerable concern about whether TRIPS unduly favours large corporations in the industrialised world.

TRIPS is a complex agreement, as indeed are so many of the other agreements that are being developed at the WTO. This, however, should not prevent us from trying to decipher it and understand it. On initial consideration, the TRIPS might appear to be attractive to many people, as it can perhaps be seen to be a vehicle that offers to protect intellectual property rights and the creators of ideas, while at the same time it also encourages trade. This applies to those countries that view trade as being something worthwhile, arguing that it will enhance their growth and prosperity. However, many criticisms have been levied against it. These include criticisms that it favours large corporations and that it is harmful to the developing world, particularly in areas such as medicine and local indigenous knowledge. Also, developing countries often have weak scientific and technical infrastructures and so are likely to be placed at a disadvantage, and the cost involved in implementing TRIPS is likely to outweigh any possible benefits. Furthermore, there will be a lessening in the control that national governments will have in being able to make and enforce IPR laws in their own countries. Developing countries are largely having to operate IP systems that have usually been created in the USA, other countries in the developed world and/or large corporations.

There are many questions that one could pose in relation to TRIPS. Is TRIPS fundamentally about encouraging trade or about placing limitations on the unsavoury aspects of trade, for example, or is it about just trying to benefit big business even more? Will it be particularly disadvantageous for the developing world? Or is it about establishing international rules for intellectual property rights that will ultimately benefit everyone in the globalised economy – the 'one big happy family' syndrome?

It might seem to be difficult, if not impossible, to answer these questions. However, if one places TRIPS within an Open Marxist theoretical framework, then it becomes easier. Thus I would contend that, ultimately, TRIPS is about turning knowledge, information, creative works and ideas (which are all created by intellectual labour) into international tradable commodities through IPRs. The value created from intellectual labour then becomes embedded in these commodities. These IPRs can then be traded, and from this value profits can be made, which are needed in order to ensure the success of the knowledge revolution, this being the latest phase of capitalism, and thus ensure the continued perpetuation and success of global capitalism.

11.6 GATS revisited

The GATS does not pose so many heart-rending questions as TRIPS. It is about the liberalisation of trade in services. Clearly, it is designed to encourage the trading of these services and, as such, threatens state-funded services and the philosophy behind public services and the public service ethos, i.e. it threatens the notion of putting the wants and needs of the local population above profit margins. The only real question that has to be asked is in regard to what services fall under the GATS. Do public services fall under the GATS? I have sought to demonstrate in this book that I am sure that the various public services do and will so fall. If we are all agreed on these points, the question then becomes – is this a good or a bad thing? Some argue that privatising public services will make them more efficient. However, we need to look somewhat deeper. Private companies, by definition, must make a profit – this is their *raison d'être*. Thus, with the best will in the world, they cannot put the wants and needs of the people in the local community above profit. This does not mean to say that state-funded services, in this case library services, will necessarily have the wants and needs of the local population uppermost in their minds. But it is *possible* for them to adopt such a stance, whereas for a private company there is no such possibility. We need to be fully aware of this basic fact. Furthermore, the logic of capitalism is the commodification of all that surrounds us. So there is no resting place. The privatisation of public services in general will go on and on (until we decide to do something about it), as will the privatisation of the state-funded provision of libraries in particular. So we witness the continued transformation of services into internationally tradable commodities.

11.7 An Open Marxist theoretical analysis of value and the commodity

The commodity and the different forms and aspects of value that are embedded in the commodity will be examined further in my future works. However, a brief summary is included here in order to emphasise why I am arguing that the GATS and TRIPS are such important mechanisms for driving global capitalism forward, and why we need to take them so seriously. I am arguing that the GATS and TRIPS are transforming services and intellectual property rights into *internationally tradable commodities*. Various other writers have referred to the extension of the commodification process. Stuart Hamilton, a PhD student sponsored by IFLA and FAIFE, who is undertaking a project investigating libraries, censorship and barriers to accessing information on the Internet, for example, talks about information becoming a commodity and how this is being exacerbated by globalisation. He says that:

> ... globalization has also interfered with the flow of data on the Internet by taking some of the control of this flow away from nation states and placing it in the hands of the corporations. (Hamilton, 2002: 191)

Furthermore:

> ... it is possible to suggest that the Internet, and the flow of information on it, will eventually revert to an 'advanced capitalist' model – that a combination of information as a commodity, class inequalities in the distribution and access of information, and the priorities of the large corporations will transform the Internet from a tool of democracy and a voice of the disenfranchised into an extension of the High Street, where all information costs money. (Hamilton, 2002: 192)

Thus Hamilton argued that information could become increasingly commodified on the Internet, which will lead to an increase in class inequalities and where priorities are given more and more to large corporations.

But why am I arguing that an examination of this commodification process, this creation of international tradable commodities, is so important, one might ask. This can only be explained by examining the concepts of value and the commodity in themselves, and fully understanding that value is created, and can only ever be created, from labour. This means that we need to return to Marx's analysis of the commodity and value.

Following on from Marx, any meaningful analysis of capitalism must begin with the *commodity* and he began Volume 1 of *Das Capital* by examining that concept:

> The wealth of those societies in which the capitalist mode of production prevails, presents itself as an 'immense accumulation of commodities', its unit being a single commodity. Our investigation must therefore begin with the analysis of a commodity. (Marx, 1887: 43)

Commodities have a physical natural form and a value form, and it is the latter that interests us here, i.e. the focus is on *value*. In capitalism, commodities are useful but they are also traded in the marketplace, i.e. they have two value-forms: use value and exchange value. *Value*, which Glenn Rikowski describes as *social energy*, is embedded in the commodity. Glenn Rikowski says that:

> ... value, within the social universe of capital, constitutes a social force field analogous to gravity as a force within the known physical universe ... value is a social energy whose effects as a social force are mediated by the movements of capital (in its various forms) and the social relations between labour and capital. (G. Rikowski, 2002a: 183)

Also, Mike Neary and Glenn Rikowski argued that:

> Value can be viewed as being social energy that undergoes transformations ... Value is a multi-dimensional field of social energy – a social substance with a directional dynamic but not social identity. It is the matter and anti-matter of Marx's social universe. (Neary and Rikowski, 2002: 60)

One of the most important types of social energy is *human labour*, i.e. humans, when they work, produce value. This value takes on different forms in the commodity (*forms of value*) – namely, the forms of *use value* and *exchange value*. Use value expresses the usefulness of a commodity. As Marx said:

> The utility of a thing makes it a use-value ... a commodity, such as iron, coal or a diamond, is therefore, so far as it is a material thing, a use-value, something useful ... Use-values become a reality only by use or consumption. (Marx, 1887: 44)

With regard to bread, for example, it is useful as a commodity because we can eat it. With regard to knowledge, some knowledge can be useful, while other forms of knowledge might not be so useful. Meanwhile, exchange value expresses the value that the commodity is exchanged for in the marketplace, which in capitalism is usually expressed in terms of the price of a commodity/good. Exchange value represents the objective way in which commodities can be exchanged, and is a more convenient means of expression/measurement than the quantity of labour, even though labour is the real measure. As Adam Smith said:

> The value of any commodity ... to the person who possesses it, and who means not to use it or consume it himself, but to exchange it for other commodities, is equal to the quantity of labour which it enables him to purchase or command. Labour, therefore, is the real measure of the exchangeable value of all commodities. (Smith, 1776: 133)

Meanwhile, there are also different *aspects of value*. These include *surplus value* and *added value*. Marx said that labourers, by virtue of their labour being of a specialised kind, create additional or new value, i.e. *added value*. Each time labourers work, they create new or added value, while also preserving the old value. This happens through the labour process itself, and can seem to be a 'gift from nature':

> While the labourer, by virtue of his labour being of a specialised kind that has a special object, preserves and transfers to the product the value of the means of production, he at the same time, by the mere act of working, creates each instant an *additional* or *new value*. (Marx, 1887: 201 – my emphasis)

This added value is then transformed into surplus value. Surplus value is created when labourers work for longer than is necessary to create the value of their own labour power. As Postone said:

> Surplus value is created when the workers labor for more time than is required to create the value of their labour power. That is when the value of labor power is less than the value this labor power valorizes in the production process. (Postone, 1996: 281)

Surplus value needs to be constantly expanded, and it becomes self-valorising. This is intensified by the *valorisation process*. As Postone further explained:

> ... Marx analyzes the valorization process – the process of creating surplus value – in terms of the process of creating value; his analysis is concerned not only with the source of the surplus but also with the form of the surplus wealth produced. Value ... is a category of a dynamic totality ... capital is 'self-valorizing value', according to Marx; it is characterized by the need to expand constantly. When value is the form of wealth, the goal of production necessarily is surplus value. That is, the goal of capitalist production is not simply value but the constant expansion of surplus value. (Postone, 1996: 308)

Value itself, the different aspects of value (surplus value and added value) and the different forms of value (use value and exchange value) are all embedded in the commodity. The commodity and the way in which value is realised in the commodity is the key for the continued success of capitalism. Furthermore, what also ensures its continued success is the way in which value and the different forms and aspects of value interact and operate together – a unique process is undergone which is specific to the capitalist mode of production. Its success is also ensured by the way in which value interacts with other Marxist concepts in capitalism, such as price, profit, rent, markets, etc.

Only labour can create value. Yet, although labour creates value, it has no value in itself. As Marx said:

> ... human labour creates value, but is not itself value. It becomes value only in its congealed state, when embodied in the form of some object. (Marx, 1887: 57)

The value is only realised once a labourer's work becomes objectified and embedded in the commodity. The labourer sells her/his *labour-power* as a commodity. Labour-power is the capacity to labour rather than the actual process of labouring itself (which is 'labour'), and labour-power is a commodity which the labourer has to sell in the marketplace. As Marx said:

> The labourer is the owner of his labour-power until he has done bargaining for its sale with the capitalist; and he can sell no more than what he has, i.e. his individual, isolated labour-power. (Marx, 1887: 315)

Once the labourer has sold their labour-power to the capitalist, they labour by using their labour-power, and this process creates value which is then embedded in the commodity. Labour-power has to be continually *nurtured* and *nourished*. This includes the bare necessities of life, such as enough to eat and drink and an adequate amount of sleep. As Marx said:

> Labour-power exists only as a capacity, or power of the living individual. Its production consequently pre-supposes his existence. Given the individual, the production of labour-power consists in his reproduction of himself or his maintenance. For his maintenance he requires a given quantity of the means of subsistence ... (Marx, 1887: 168)

But in the knowledge revolution that we find ourselves in today, it also includes a certain level of education and skills. Meanwhile, the length of the working day is arrived at by a process of compromise – the labourer cannot work for 24 hours. The length of the working day needs to be limited, so that labour-power, the capacity to labour, can be replenished. Therefore:

> The creation of a normal working-day is ... the product of a protracted civil war, more or less dissembled, between the capitalist class and the working-class. (Marx, 1887: 283)

Thus capitalism is sustained by value; its very existence depends on the creation of value, and this value is extracted from labour and can only ever be created from labour. This value is then embedded in the commodity in different forms and aspects and from this profits are derived, which ensures the continued success of companies and of global capitalism itself. Yet by this process labour is exploited, alienated and objectified, because labourers have to sell their labour-power in the marketplace in order to survive. Hence, if more and more services and intellectual property rights become commodified, then the exploitation and alienation of labour will be intensified – there will gradually be no resting place outside of the marketplace. In a more basic sense this means that ultimately the rich will get richer (the capitalists) while the poor will get poorer (the labourers).

This is very much a brief overview, and I will be exploring all this much further in my future works. However, this essentially is what is so disturbing about the GATS and TRIPS and why awareness about these agreements needs to be urgently raised. The human soul itself, it seems, is 'up for grabs', particularly where TRIPS is concerned, where the aim even extends to commodifying people's unconscious knowledge – knowledge that they did not even know that they had! I am arguing then that the GATS and TRIPS are transforming services and intellectual property rights into international tradable commodities. Labourers labour and create value. In terms of the GATS and TRIPS this is largely by the exertion of intellectual labour rather than manual labour. The value created from this intellectual labour becomes embedded in international tradable commodities that have been created by the GATS and TRIPS. These commodities can then be exchanged and sold in the marketplace, and profits can be made (which are derived from value). Thus labour is exploited but capitalism is sustained.

11.8 Conclusion

In conclusion, this chapter has examined different possible explanations for the 'TINA' (There Is No Alternative) philosophy. The arguments that it has considered involve religion, human nature, the death of communism, a lack of resources and the evolutionary nature of social systems, although there are obviously others as well. There has not been the space to consider these in depth, but while some of the arguments may complement each other rather than represent either/or scenarios, other arguments (such as 'human nature') would be found wanting on closer inspection, I feel sure.

However, I have argued, in particular, that we need to accept the evolutionary nature of social systems as a definite fact/theory, in the same way as we accept Darwin's theory of the origin of the species. From such a position we would then be able to understand that if we want to change our social, economic and political system, then the power lies within ourselves – rather than simply waiting for evolution to take its course. We need to be proactive. We can do this by developing good and rigorous social scientific theory. For me, this involves developing an Open Marxist theoretical perspective/framework. Then we can effectively explain, analyse and critique global capitalism, and from this position seek to change it.

In this chapter I then placed the GATS and TRIPS within an Open Marxist theoretical analysis of value and the commodity. I have emphasised how the GATS and TRIPS are transforming services and intellectual property rights into *commodities*, and how *value* from labour (particularly from intellectual labour) becomes embedded in these commodities, and how all this helps to perpetuate global capitalism.

In the following chapter I will consider the furtherance of global capitalism through the WTO.

The furtherance of global capitalism through the WTO

12.1 Introduction

This chapter will further consider how global capitalism is being extended through the WTO. It will do this by focusing on a number of areas. First, it will reconsider the knowledge revolution, intellectual labour, value and the WTO. Second, it will present the argument that global capitalism is sustained by value and not by morals. Within this framework it will consider moral dilemmas, value creation and intellectual property rights. The purpose of this section, in particular, is to demonstrate that while capitalism might pay lip-service to moral issues, it is not a system that is founded on any moral basis – indeed, it cannot be founded on any such base. Instead, it is sustained by value, and this value is, and can only ever be, derived from labour. Third, there is a section demonstrating the fact that many business people today realise the significance of value, and the importance of creating value from knowledge and information specifically. Indeed, this is referred to time and time again in the business literature. There is then a section on the extension of the commodification process through GATS and TRIPS, followed by a section on how intellectual property rights aid with the process of transforming labour into capital, i.e. transforming intellectual labour into intellectual capital.

12.2 Global capitalism, the knowledge revolution, intellectual labour, value and the WTO revisited

To recap – today as we enter the knowledge revolution, this being the latest phase of capitalism, value is increasingly being created and extracted from intellectual labour, from people's knowledge and understanding and the intellect that they use. The value that is created from this intellectual labour is then embedded in intangible goods/commodities, such as services and intellectual property rights. This is in contrast to the period of the industrial revolution, when there was a greater expenditure of manual labour, and this was embedded in tangible commodities/goods.

Human labour obviously comprises both manual and intellectual labour, and the value created from labour becomes embedded in both tangible and intangible goods/commodities, but the emphasis has changed. Thus in the knowledge revolution there is a greater expenditure (in terms of the amount of human energy that is utilised) of intellectual labour, and less expenditure of manual labour. An example here can illustrate this point. A computer programmer exerts both manual and intellectual labour. She/he exerts manual labour by typing into a keyboard, but exerts intellectual labour by thinking about and designing computer code and programs. However, she/he puts more energy into the intellectual labouring process than the manual labouring process, i.e. it is the exertion of intellectual labour that exhausts her/him. All this ensures the continued success of global capitalism.

Within this, the agreements that are being developed at the WTO play a highly significant role. This is because services and intellectual property rights are being transformed into international tradable commodities. Humans labour, they create value (and value can only ever be created from human labour), and this value becomes embedded in the commodity. From this value, profits can be generated, thus enabling companies to prosper and global capitalism to succeed in general. In this way, humans are exploited. Therefore more and more forms of life become commodified and the level of exploitation rises. With the GATS, more and more services are being liberalised and placed in the marketplace thereby becoming commodified, and with TRIPS ideas and creative works are being transformed into intellectual property rights which are commodified and can then be traded in the marketplace. Thus the two WTO agreements that are likely to have particularly significant implications for libraries and information are very much at the forefront in terms of pushing the global capitalist agenda forward and ensuring the continuance of global capitalism. This is my theory then – the Open Marxist theoretical position that I am developing.

However, the GATS and TRIPS agreements only form a part of the whole WTO agenda. As already stated, there are also many other trade agreements, and together they all represent a very powerful force for intensifying, extending and glorifying global capitalism. The WTO is at the sharp end of global capitalism and driving it forward. However, there are also many other important aspects to globalisation, such as the World Bank and the International Monetary Fund, the significance of global cultural issues and many other issues that were covered in Chapter 2 of this book. These all form part of the overall global capitalist agenda. Also, global capitalism does not simply rely on the WTO for its continued success; if the WTO was abolished tomorrow, this would not mean that global capitalism in general would collapse. Capitalism is far more powerful and insidious than that. The WTO is just a useful tool for capitalism. Abolish it and something else can take its place. Thus, as I have already stated, to that extent this book is timeless and cannot be made irrelevant or redundant as a result of any particular decisions that might take place at the WTO. The only way in which it would be made redundant would be if capitalism were to be terminated. However, even then it would be useful as a historical piece, and in terms of understanding and analysing capitalism.

In this process of struggling to use our intellects more wisely, to raise awareness and to generally rethink what we are all about, libraries and information can play an absolutely crucial part, I would suggest. But it will be far more difficult for them to do this if they themselves are privatised. Or perhaps libraries might not even exist as physical entities in the future, in the way that they do today, with the proliferation of IT-based information systems and the opportunities that will exist for people to be able to access information in places other than libraries. A large amount of book-shelf space will no longer be required. Physical spaces for critical thought would then be lost. Libraries will start to lose whatever neutrality they currently have (not that neutrality in an ultimate sense is possible). But they will no longer be part of the 'intellectual commons' – a common resource, with open access. So, once again, there is an urgent need to raise awareness about the implications of the GATS and TRIPS for the library and information community. If we are ultimately to avoid the commodification of human beings themselves then the situation is indeed becoming urgent. Meanwhile, we witness the continued furtherance of global capitalism through the WTO.

12.3 Global capitalism sustained by value, not morals

12.3.1 Introduction

This section will present the argument that global capitalism is sustained by value (and that value can only be created by labour) and not by morals. It will seek to demonstrate that moral dilemmas cannot be solved in capitalism, because capitalism is not and cannot be based on any set of moral principles. In order to appreciate the horrors of capitalism we need to be fully aware of the fact that capitalism is not, and cannot be, founded on any moral base. This is important in order to overcome any fanciful, romantic notions that we can sort various problems out, once and for all, within capitalism itself.

The library and information profession itself has these romantic, utopian notions – hence the particular importance of addressing this topic. It is commendable that the profession has ethical principles, rather than just totally accepting the trade and capitalist agenda. It is also worthwhile to have some utopian notions and some hope, but we need to develop an understanding and awareness that we cannot get an ideal system within capitalism. Basically, capitalism cannot be reformed and made to work for the benefit of the majority of the world population. Thus achieving the balance in copyright, for example, will ultimately be impossible while we live under capitalism. We are asking the wrong set of questions and using the wrong terminology.

Some might argue that I am being romantic in arguing for socialism/communism. But, in essence, it is even more romantic and naive to argue that we can get a perfect system *within* capitalism. Trying to 'sort out' the balance in copyright issue, for example, would be ultimately impossible. But the process of trying to find solutions and not being able to could leave one feeling depressed, particularly as one begins to realise the enormity and then the impossibility of the task. It is not pleasant to think that one cannot find a solution! Marxism, on the other hand, although it is very difficult (and this is partly because we do not speak and write using Marxist terminology on a daily basis – that would certainly not suit the needs of capital!), does provide us with some lasting hope that real solutions can be found. It prevents us from going round in circles.

There are various moral dilemmas and issues in relation to TRIPS and IPRs, some of which I have outlined in this book and many of which are clearly contradictory and seemingly irresolvable. Many realise that these are serious problems and may try to find solutions. However, my argument is that this just wastes vast amounts of time because it is impossible to find solutions to what are basically irresolvable problems. This is because global capitalism itself is established on a contradictory base, with in-built irresolvable issues. In order to uncover and understand the seemingly mysterious nature of capitalism itself, we need to return to Marx and Marx's concepts and to use these concepts in order to analyse capitalism and its intrinsic workings and in particular to further develop an Open Marxist theoretical analysis of value.

12.3.2 Moral dilemmas and value creation

Many do not want to acknowledge that capitalism has no moral base – it is too unpleasant. However, it is necessary that we do this, if we are to avoid going round in circles and getting nowhere. Capitalism is not based on moral principles and is certainly not sustained by them. As Marx said:

> Capital cares nothing for the length of life of labour-power. (Marx, 1887: 253)

If it cares nothing for the life of the labourer, then it certainly cares nothing about whether that labourer is given sufficient regard and monetary recompense for his/her own ideas and creativity. Whether or not one's ideas are recognised is a small matter compared with life and death itself. Thus, if capitalism has no moral concern, no moral set of codes in relation to whether a human lives or dies, then how can it possibly have a moral code in relation to IPR issues and humans?

This also explains why moral rights have been left out of the copyright section of the TRIPS Agreement. The WTO is at the cutting edge for the development of global capitalism, and the agreements established at the WTO are obviously intended to extend and expand global capitalism as far as possible. Moral rights can hamper and slow down this process. Therefore the moral rights that were established at the Berne Convention have been excluded from the TRIPS Agreement.

Capitalism is sustained and nourished by *value*. It is for this reason that I have chosen to focus on value rather than other Marxist concepts, although all the concepts are crucial for a full analysis of capitalism. But value is the key. In my article 'Value – the life-blood of capitalism:

knowledge is the current key' (R. Rikowski, 2003g), I illustrated how value is the essential ingredient for the continuation and perpetuation of capitalism and this is expanded on further in my dissertation on value creation through knowledge (R. Rikowski, 2003h). It is value that ensures the survival and success of capitalism. This value is created by labour. As Marx said:

> Human labour-power in motion, or human labour, creates value, but is not itself value. (Marx, 1887: 57–8)

Thus human labour creates value, and it is *only* human labour that can create value, even though human labour has no value in itself. This value becomes embedded in the commodity and this process exacerbates global capitalism. More and more forms of life will become commodified, and less and less will be outside of this capitalist web. Public services, for example, are outside of this capitalist web (to the extent that they are not commodities), as are ideas that are not captured into intellectual property rights. So the GATS and TRIPS seek to address this problem, as far as global capitalism is concerned. They seek to commodify intellectual property rights and public services. Thus the GATS and TRIPS will make the process of creating and extracting value from intellectual labour and embedding it in the commodity easier.

12.3.3 Intellectual property rights and moral issues

Allow me to return to moral issues in relation to IPRs, and to view this in abstraction from value and the commodity for the time being. In terms of intellectual property rights in general, clearly the rights of the creators of works should be given due consideration. However, protecting the ideas of *individuals* through intellectual property rights also needs to be considered separately from *organisations*. It is clear to see that, from an ethical perspective, the ideas, creativity and labour of individuals should be protected through copyright, for example, but the issues with regard to organisations and large corporations in particular is far more complex. A company might have developed something that could become an intellectual property right (a trade mark, a patent or whatever). However, this might have been largely the idea of one or two individuals rather than the idea of the company as a whole. In this case, should the intellectual property right not belong to the individual rather than to the company? The company might well answer 'no', as the individual works for the company and is paid a salary. This raises wide ethical issues.

The power and influence of many corporations with regard to intellectual property rights, once again, needs to be fully appreciated. As Drahos and Braithwaite say:

> The bulk of intellectual property rights are not owned by their initial creators but by corporations that acquire intellectual property portfolios through a process of buying and selling, merger and acquisition. (Drahos and Braithwaite, 2002: 15)

Thus, as Drahos and Braithwaite emphasise, many intellectual property rights are owned by large corporations rather than individuals, and these IPRs are then traded.

Furthermore, while on the one hand companies need to have intellectual property rights in order to protect their business and gain a competitive edge, intellectual property rights can also militate against some notions of the globalised economy, where the free flow of knowledge and information needs to be encouraged. So it seems that the success of global capitalism depends on companies both safeguarding their ideas and knowledge through intellectual property rights, while at the same time sharing those ideas between different companies, organisations and environments. This illustrates one of the irresolvable contradictions of capitalism.

There is yet another contradiction. In the knowledge-based economy, knowledge and information flows, so knowledge management and information management become increasingly important. Businesses and organisations often try to transform human capital into structural capital, which basically means that they try to capture the ideas, knowledge and information that employees have before they leave the company. Some refer to this as the 'leveraging' of ideas. As one of the participants in my knowledge management research said with regard to 'leverage':

> You have these wonderful phrases like leverage ... it's like, when you go back, when you were at school if you copied someone else's work that was called plagiarism, a really bad thing ... and when you get into business they call it leverage and that's a really good thing ... leverage is where you take someone else's knowledge and experience and use it for your client. You're leveraging their

> capabilities ... it's what is called plagiarism – you are copying them
> ... (R. Rikowski, 2003h)

The aim is to 'leverage' these ideas without having to pay a price for
them if possible – either as a one-off price or in terms of intellectual
property rights.

The assumption here is that the employees' salary is sufficient monetary recompense, but why should one employee give their ideas and
inspiration to the company while another employee does not, if the
former receives no additional monetary recompense? Some companies
recognise this fact and introduce various monetary incentives, bonus
schemes, etc., but this cannot easily form part of an overall company
position with regard to rights holders and IPRs. This whole area can be
seen, in effect, to be a battlefield. Monetary recompense will tend to be
given when it seems to be really 'necessary'. One step up from this, such
ideas could form part of an IPR if the employee fought hard enough for
it, or if the company decided that it was in its interest to encapsulate the
idea within an IPR. This could be done either by making the IPR the
property of the company, or by making it the property of the individual.
The battle for the employee with regard to IPRs can be compared to the
labourer fighting with the employer over the length of the working day,
as Marx described. Marx said that:

> The establishment of a normal working-day is the result of centu-
> ries of struggle between capitalist and labourer. (Marx, 1887: 257)

There is also the related problem of how to know whether the original
idea belonged to one person or a group of people. Furthermore, ideas do
not materialise out of thin air – the ideas may well partly have been
formed from within the company itself and by working with other
people within the company. So, would it be morally right for one
individual in a company to obtain an IPR for ideas that they have partly
formulated from working within the company itself? This can be
overcome by having 'joint IPR' schemes to some extent – but then, what
percentage of the IPR goes to one individual, and what percentage to
another? Another point is that someone might steal another person's
idea and claim it as their own. How could one respond to such a moral
dilemma? There are many different areas to consider.

Thus it seems that there are many complex ethical issues with regard
to intellectual property rights. Although none of these are addressed

within the TRIPS Agreement itself they will still need to be considered during the process of implementing TRIPS. These are also issues that must and do concern the library and information profession. Yet how do we find a way forward through all this? One cannot be found by approaching all this from within a moral framework at all, I would suggest – this is the important point to grasp. Instead, we need to move out of this mode of thinking completely, and develop a clearer theoretical position, which for me is an Open Marxist theoretical analysis of value. Otherwise, we will just go round in circles and never find adequate answers. Thus what is important to consider here is the fact that value that is extracted from intellectual labour goes into these commodities, rather any supposed rights of labourers, such as moral and economic rights.

12.3.4 Concluding comments

This section has sought to demonstrate that capitalism is not based on any set of moral principles, but instead is sustained by value, and this value is derived, and can only ever be derived, from labour (see Chapter 11, section 11.7 for further analysis on value). Within this context, it considered, in particular, moral issues with regard to intellectual property rights.

The purpose of this section has been to demonstrate that while capitalism might pay lip-service to moral issues, it is not a system that is founded on any moral basis – indeed, it cannot be founded on any such base. Instead, it is based on value, and this value is derived from labour. Furthermore, capitalism cannot be reformed and transformed into a system that can benefit the majority of the population – it is impossible for it to operate within a moral framework in that way. Therefore, if we consider moral issues in depth as part of our analysis of capitalism, such as moral issues in relation to intellectual property rights and moral and humane issues in relation to the balance in copyright, we will just find ourselves going round in circles. Also, at some point we will be unable to move forward from such a position productively. This is because capitalism is based on and is sustained by value, not morals. Once we are clear about this, we will be in a much more powerful position and will be able to analyse capitalism from a clearer perspective.

Given the fact that the library and information profession devotes a considerable amount of time to these moral and humane issues, and seems to be of the opinion that ultimate solutions can, in fact, be found, it has been particularly important to consider this moral dimension. While it is commendable that the profession has these worthwhile principles (far better than just whole-heartedly embracing capitalism), their utopian nature needs to be fully appreciated. This will prevent us from becoming disillusioned and under the misapprehension that capitalism can be reformed and made to work to the advantage of everyone from within a moral framework, as well as to counteract the argument that socialist/communist ideals are fanciful and unachievable, while reforming capitalism is not so. Quite the reverse – reforming capitalism is more fanciful, because it is unachievable. Analysing capitalism from a Marxist perspective, exposing its intrinsic workings (with all the inherent injustices that reside within it), and then seeking alternatives is far more demanding than making moral statements. However, with such an analysis we can make real and lasting progress, whereas working within a moral framework we will just find ourselves going round in circles. So, although the former option (analysing capitalism from a Marxist perspective) on initial inspection is more demanding, in the long term it will be less so, and it is far more productive.

12.4 References in the business and information literature with regard to the extraction of value from knowledge and information

Thus it is value, not morals, that sustains capitalism and this value is created by labour, and only by labour. In the knowledge revolution this value is being extracted more and more from intellectual labour. This short section will demonstrate how the business and information literature today recognises how important value is. This emphasises the fact that 'value' as a concept needs to be taken seriously. Business people are forever talking about value today, but usually do not place the concept within a historical perspective and certainly not within a theoretical perspective. Furthermore, most do not acknowledge that the concept was first formulated a long time ago, and that, indeed, value was a key aspect to Marx's work. Yet it is fascinating to witness how important those in business consider value to be.

There are many quotes in the business and information literature today that emphasise both how important the creation of value is for the success of the economy, and also that this value today is increasingly being created from knowledge, information, ideas, brainpower, etc.; a few of these quotes are highlighted here. As Tapscott said, for example:

> Innovation drives everything and competitive advantage is ephemeral. Firms must constantly seek new ways to *create value*. (Tapscott, 2000: 220, my emphasis)

Similarly, Welch argued that:

> The organisation has to recognise that its prime objective (perhaps its only objective) is to *add value*: not to cut costs. Making more profit, increasing the share price, increasing the *value* of intellectual assets (including brands) is what makes a company fit to survive. (Welch, 2000: 10, my emphases)

Others emphasise how this value today is in intangible assets/commodities. Meyer, for example, simply says that:

> *Value* is in the intangibles like knowledge, information, services, software and entertainment. (Meyer, 2000: 193, my emphasis)

Furthermore, Potter noted that:

> ... *value* and wealth derives from the process of creating, not making things. (Potter, 1999: 2, my emphasis)

Meanwhile, Byers, the then UK Secretary of State for the Department for Trade and Industry, speaking at the Mansion House in February 2000 said that:

> The main source of *value* and competitive advantage in the modern economy is human and intellectual capital. (Byers, 2000: 1, my emphasis)

Finally, Mougayar said that:

> The goal: create a business that relentlessly manipulates information to extract higher *value* from it, by reselling it, reusing it,

> repackaging it, or giving it away; either directly to end-users or indirectly via third parties. (Mougayar, 2000: 253, my emphasis.)

Furthermore, in referring to the Internet, Mougayar says that:

> *Value is digital value.* Digital value is 100 percent information-based. It surrounds, envelops, and sometimes makes obsolete current (or old) value ... Just as a factory is in charge of production, the infomediary is in charge of creating digital *value*. (Mougayar, 2000: 253–354, my emphasis)

Thus the need to create value from knowledge and information in today's knowledge economy cannot be overemphasised and businesses are very aware of this fact. This also, once again, demonstrates the importance of the role of the WTO in this whole process. It is necessary for value to be created from knowledge and information in this knowledge economy (or the knowledge revolution), but this value needs to be captured if it is to benefit capitalism. Thus we return to the need to commodify various aspects of social life, so that the value created from this knowledge and information (which ultimately can only ever be created by intellectual labour) can be captured and embedded in these commodities. The WTO through trade agreements such as the GATS and TRIPS assists with this process.

12.5 The extension of the commodification process: state-funded library services (through the GATS) and intellectual property rights (through TRIPS) being transformed into internationally tradable commodities

Given that value is extracted more from intellectual labour than manual labour in the knowledge revolution today in the form of ideas and knowledge, etc., then the successful implementation of international agreements such as TRIPS and the GATS, which are focused around these areas, becomes incredibly important in our global capitalist world. In terms of the GATS, as I have already indicated, this means that more services are commodified and placed in the marketplace, and the value that is extracted from intellectual labour is embedded in these commodities for the perpetuation of capitalism. This includes selling information through products such as NetLibrary, Questia and ebrary and privatising library services. In terms of TRIPS it means that the more that these intangible areas can be commodified and traded, the better. So, intellectual property rights, such as patents, trade marks and geographical indications, become tradable commodities, with a price on them (in some form or other). Intellectual property rights, which are created from intellectual labour, become commodities. Then the value that is created and extracted from intellectual labour becomes embedded in these commodities.

Once these IPRs have been concretised, then it will become much easier to extract value from them. Ideas in the abstract can get lost, under-utilised, etc., so any value that could be created from them would be lost. A concrete example can be provided here – the employee who leaves work at the end of the day and takes their knowledge with them. When this happens, the employee's company cannot use their knowledge to its advantage, it cannot encapsulate the value that is created from intellectual labour and embed it in a commodity. In order to overcome such problems, companies often seek to transform this human capital into structural capital, so that it becomes part of the company assets. One way to achieve this would be for the company to encapsulate such assets within an IPR and for the company to own this IPR – such as the company patenting this knowledge. Thus IPRs can make a valuable contribution to the extension of the commodification process and for the successful perpetuation of the knowledge revolution – and, indeed, for capitalism itself. Seen in these terms, capitalist enthusiasm for the adoption of TRIPS then becomes far clearer. It also cuts through many of the moral dilemmas that exist in relation to IPRs. So GATS and TRIPS help to extend the commodification process.

12.6 Intellectual property rights – transforming intellectual labour into intellectual capital

Intellectual property rights can become part of capital. IPRs can only ever originate from labour. Labour sustains capitalism in all its guises; it is the only thing that can sustain it, as value can only be created from labour. IPRs help to transform this labour into *capital* – often referred to in terms such as 'intellectual capital'. Thus IPRs can be seen to be mechanisms for enabling ideas and creativity to be transformed into capital and this is being aided and abetted by TRIPS. Or, to phrase this another way, IPRs in general and TRIPS in particular can aid with the process of transforming *intellectual labour* into *intellectual capital*. From this analysis, it becomes apparent that IPRs have not really been ultimately designed for the benefit of the individual artist, author or creator at all, even though IPRs can be clearly beneficial for individual creators. However, if creators were not given some rewards (such as money through copyright royalties), then many would not be inclined to develop their ideas and make them publicly available anyway. So capitalism has to try to reward them in some way, although if it could 'get away with not doing this' (such as through extracting ideas from employees in a company as described above), then so much the better. As said earlier, it is a battlefield upon which compromises are made, such as the battle over the length of the working day, a phenomenon that is relevant to recent events in France and Germany (see Johnson, 2004, and Culp, 2004).

12.7 Conclusion

In conclusion, this chapter has focused on a number of key aspects with regard to the furtherance of global capitalism through the WTO.

- It reconsidered the knowledge revolution, intellectual labour, value and the WTO.
- It outlined the fact that global capitalism is sustained by value and not by morals, and within this framework it focused, in particular, on moral dilemmas, value creation and intellectual property rights.
- It briefly considered some of the references in relation to the creation of value from knowledge and information that there are in the business and information literature.
- It examined the extension of the commodification process, and how state-funded services, through the GATS, and intellectual property rights, through TRIPS, are being transformed into internationally tradable commodities, and how intellectual property rights are aiding with the process of transforming intellectual labour into intellectual capital. Furthermore, as Marx emphasised in *Capital*, Vol. 1, our analysis of the capitalist mode of production must begin with the commodity.

In essence, global capitalism is being perpetuated and furthered through the WTO. This is because the trade agreements that are being developed at the WTO, such as the GATS and TRIPS, are helping to ensure that more and more areas of social life are being commodified. Capitalism is sustained by value, and not by any set of moral principles, and this includes any possible moral issues in relation to intellectual property rights. This value is, and can only be, created and extracted from labour. However, in the knowledge revolution, this being the latest phase of capitalism, it is being extracted more from intellectual labour and less from manual labour, through areas such as knowledge, information, ideas and brainpower. Those writing in the business literature are very aware of the importance of these knowledge areas for the success of the knowledge economy/knowledge revolution. Through the commodification process that is taking place at the WTO, this value is then being embedded in these commodities, these commodities are traded and sold in the market-place, profits are made (and profits can only ever ultimately be derived from value) and so global capitalism is perpetuated. Thus global capitalism is furthered through the WTO.

We need to try to grasp the complexities of the global capitalist world that we find ourselves in today, so that we can then try to find a way to break free from it all in order to create a better, kinder and fairer world. If one took a different position, and argued that global capitalism was a very good system and that we just need to work through the various issues and dilemmas, one would quickly come up against an insurmountable number of problems (as indeed people do) with regard to issues such as intellectual property rights, moral and humane issues, the public service ethos and the balance in copyright. A Marxist analysis is complex, but it seeks to explain and solve many of these real problems and contradictions, while also enabling us to face up to these contradictions. We need a theoretical analysis that helps us to understand and explain the system that we find ourselves in – global capitalism, with all its injustice, inequality, cruelty, suffering and death, and an Open Marxist theoretical analysis provides us with this. Once we have this understanding, we can then endeavour to create a better, kinder and fairer social, economic and political system that is based on human wants and needs and one that will enable humans to find self-expression and fulfilment, rather than a system that is based on the exploitation, alienation and objectification of labour, value-creation and the never-ending drive to increase profit margins.

13

Conclusions

I first started examining the WTO in 2000 and then considered the implications of the WTO GATS and TRIPS agreements for libraries and information. I could see how important this was as these world trade talks and agreements could and indeed are highly likely to change the whole way in which the library and information profession can and will operate. I had no idea whether any work had been undertaken on this area at all, nor indeed whether there was any awareness about this in the library community. My main motivation for writing was, and is, to understand, explain and critique global capitalism and then seek to change it, as well as to expose its intrinsic workings and to demonstrate that the world will always be an unfair and unjust place while we live in capitalism. In order to achieve this we need to bring theory and practice together.

In my research on the GATS, TRIPS, libraries and information I then discovered that there was a little awareness and that some work had been undertaken. However, it was limited, and if more work was not undertaken as soon as possible then the agreements would probably be implemented with little opposition or even awareness from the library community, which would probably lead to serious if not dire consequences. Awareness, such as it was, resided in organisations such as the International Federation of Library Associations and Institutions, the European Bureau of Library, Information and Documentation Associations, the British Columbia Library Association and the Canadian Library Association. As far as I could see there was little awareness of these agreements in the developing world, although there was considerable awareness about TRIPS in general.

During the process of the work that I then undertook I was struck by a number of salient points.

- There were quite a few people in the international library and information community that were interested in the topic, and thought it was important. This was reflected in the fact that quite a few people (including some very influential people in the library and information community) came to the fringe meeting that I organised at the IFLA Conference in Glasgow on the GATS in 2002, for example.

- The United Kingdom Chartered Institute of Library and Information Professionals (CILIP) seemed reluctant to take up the issue. I found out more recently that they did, in fact, issue a statement showing concern about the GATS, but only after I alerted them to it, and they did not inform me about the statement that they subsequently made. Neither did they refer to me.

- Although some people recognised its importance they did not really seem to see the urgency and the gravity of the situation, i.e. they did not really want to make the leap into thinking about it all on a more sophisticated, global, social, economic, political and theoretical level. It should be added here that, although in one sense it is urgent, in another sense it is not. We should not be panicked. Global capitalism will continue – something else will come along until we tackle the root problem. So, we need to develop theory and not just react to situations. But even so, the more that we become aware of the gravity of the situation and endeavour to do something about it the better.

- Many librarians in the developing world were not really engaging with the subject. Some people from the developing world did attend the IFLA fringe meeting that I organised, though, and we discussed the fact that it would be very helpful if their library associations were able to pass resolutions and raise awareness about the GATS.

- Considering the implications of the GATS proved to be considerably easier than considering the implications of TRIPS. This was because the only real issue to consider was whether state-funded library provision came under the GATS remit and the need to consider the definition of 'services' in the GATS. As I have shown in this book, it clearly does. So then it was just a matter of giving examples of how this could and will happen in reality (and the extent to which it is already happening), as well as to consider the level of awareness and concern that there is in the international library community about it all. This was still a difficult task, but it was easier to grasp than TRIPS. However, upon a careful reading of the TRIPS Agreement, I came to realise that TRIPS is very much purely and simply about the trading of intellectual property rights. It was certainly not concerned about moral issues such as trying to obtain the balance in copyright.

- Reading and understanding the agreements in general is difficult. I came to suspect that the agreements had been written partly this way on purpose, so that ordinary people feel that they are not fully equipped to understand them and make comments on them, and are certainly not likely to feel able to criticise them. Some people have said, for example, that I should seek the assistance of a legal expert when examining and writing about the agreements, i.e. in case I am not understanding and interpreting the agreements correctly. However, I was not happy about this for a number of reasons. For one thing, it is insulting my intelligence! For another, it assumes that I have the time, money and inclination to share my work and ideas with a legal expert. Also, I am approaching all this from a particular, clear, political angle, and it is this that motivates me. Lawyers, on the other hand, will aim to have a dispassionate, supposedly objective approach to it all, even though in reality they have to work in and through capitalism, the same as everyone else. Interestingly, Markus Krajewski (Krajewski, 2002a, 2002b) who at the time of writing was a lecturer in law at King's College, London, and now works at the University of Potsdam, Germany, analysed the GATS in great detail from a legal perspective and arrived at similar conclusions to myself with regard to the definition of services in the GATS. This was after exploring legal terms and a detailed consideration of the definitions of some terms, such as commercialisation and services. Krajewski's work is very important and valuable and lawyers analysing the agreements in this way can certainly help to give more weight to the argument. However, it might also sometimes suit the WTO that lawyers get involved in this way – it is not a straightforward situation! It takes up time and can sometimes take the passion out of the subject. Lawyers might spend a long time considering the meaning and implications of particular wording in the agreement. Having done all that, the WTO could then simply change the wording if it decided that after the lawyers' analysis they will not be able to easily progress with the agreement(s) in the way that they want to, as they currently stand. The wording is often deliberately unclear, I feel sure – it is no accident. So, people consider the meaning of 'services' in great depth, which once again can waste time. Also, it means that those trying to defend the agreement can argue with those that are worried about it that it will not affect them. Lord Newby, for example, on the *You and Yours* programme on Radio 4 in which I participated, took this position (BBC, 2001a). This is very convenient. Managers in support of global capitalism often argue that we need to make things clear and simple (implying that theoreticians like Marx and Adam Smith are over-complicating matters) and yet here we have these agreements which represent the sharp edge of capitalism – and they are incredibly complex. What does this tell us? Surely, it tells us that global capitalism is, indeed, very complex and cannot be reduced to ten bullet points on one A4 side of paper!

- Demonstrating the links between the GATS and the commercialisation, privatisation and capitalisation agenda that is taking place in individual member states is difficult. This is partly because many people cannot or do not want to see the links. Many want to think that Best Value, for example, is intrinsically worthwhile, whereas I have demonstrated the falseness of such thinking in this book. Instead, its underlying philosophy is clearly to pave the way for a privatisation agenda, and in this regard it helps to bring in the GATS.

- Having examined these agreements in some considerable depth, they then needed to be placed within a broader theoretical framework. Social systems evolve, and capitalism itself has evolved from previous systems. This needs to be accepted as a recognised theory and an established fact, just as Darwinism is, I would suggest. From this position we can then decide that if we want to create a better world, then we need to be proactive, rather than just wait for evolutionary processes to take their course. This can be achieved by understanding, explaining and critiquing capitalism at a deeper level, and within a wider theoretical framework. Marxism provides a far more adequate explanation of capitalism than any other theory does, as far as I am concerned. Therefore the task became one of explaining why these WTO agreements are being developed, by analysing them within a Marxist theoretical framework – or more precisely, within an Open Marxist theoretical framework, as Open Marxism appreciates and emphasises the dynamic, constantly changing nature of capitalism and does not analyse capitalism from a box-like, deterministic perspective. This did not prove to be easy! Then, it suddenly came to me in a 'flash of inspiration'.

These agreements will assist with the process of commodifying more and more areas of social life and will help with the process of extracting more value from labour, which then becomes embedded in these commodities. Capitalism is sustained by value, and not by any set of moral principles – and this is an issue that the library and information profession needs to become aware of and appreciate. Capitalism goes through various stages – it must do this in order to survive. It must always be seeking new markets, developing new commodities, creating new value, etc., everywhere. It does this by changing itself, and going through various phases. So, now, we are entering into the knowledge revolution. The success of the knowledge revolution will be and is being driven forward by factors such as knowledge, information, ideas and brainpower. These agreements will play an invaluable part in helping to drive all this forward. How? With regard to the GATS, the aim is to place more and more services into the marketplace, and to commodify them. The value that is created from intellectual labour will then be embedded in these commodities. Similarly, with regard to TRIPS. Through TRIPS, creative ideas will be turned into intellectual property rights, commodified and then traded in the marketplace. These ideas are created by intellectual labour. Through these agreements, services and creative ideas will be turned more and more into internationally tradable commodities. The emphasis changes – there are more intangible and less tangible assets/commodities.

Through manual and intellectual labour human labour creates value, but in the knowledge revolution there is a greater expenditure of intellectual than manual labour. If the labour is in public services then the value that is created can seem to be wasted, in capitalism's terms – it only goes towards the good of the people in the local community! But if that value is embedded in the commodity then the commodity can be sold in the marketplace for a price, profits can be made (profits and value ultimately being derived from labour), and this then enhances capitalism. So, GATS and TRIPS assist with the process of commodifying more and more forms of social life, thereby enabling value that has been created and which can only ever be created from labour to be embedded in these commodities.

The final message that I want to leave in this book is to demonstrate the links between all these different aspects and how important and pervasive the WTO agreements are within the grander picture. The WTO agreements are at the forefront in pushing the global capitalist agenda forward. Many factors hold back the furtherance of global capitalism, and professional concepts and ideas around library and information work can clearly be seen to be one of them. So, there is a need to encapsulate library and information work within WTO agreements (do not be fooled by the idea that libraries and information are unimportant – this is far from the case in reality, I am sure). To put it another way – human intellect must be commodified. Capitalism knows no resting place. We must demonstrate these links. It is not true to say that these

WTO agreements are taking place far from home and therefore do not affect our daily lives. They are affecting us all, and they will affect us more and more if we do not do something about it. But even if the WTO were to be abolished tomorrow something else would replace it, because this is the logic of global capitalism. There is only one real solution – to terminate global capitalism, and to replace it with a better, kinder, fairer social, economic and political system – to replace it with socialism, and eventually with communism. As Postone says:

> In socialism ... labor would emerge openly as the regulatory principle of social life, which would provide the basis for the realization of a rational and just society, based on general principles. (Postone, 1996: 64)

Furthermore, we need to abolish alienated labour:

> ... for Marx, overcoming the value form of social relations would mean overcoming alienated social necessity ... in Marx's view, then, the abolition of alienated labor would entail overcoming historical necessity, the historically specific social necessity constituted in the capitalist sphere of production; it would allow for historical freedom. (Postone, 1996: 382)

Let humans rejoice, then, in the world that they have developed with their labour – do not let them be dominated by it. Let us look towards a better future and a brighter world.

Bibliography

Advisory Council on Libraries (2004) *Proposed Revision of the Public Library Standards. Report on the Service Public Libraries Standards. Consultation Report on Options, Issues and Supporting Research*, Department for Culture, Media and Sport (DCMS), Consultation Papers. Available at: *http://www.libplans.ws/consultation_draft.pdf* (accessed on 19/07/04).

Aguilar, Grethel (2003) Access to genetic resources and protection of traditional knowledge in indigenous territories. In: *Trading in Knowledge: Development Perspectives on TRIPS, Trade and Sustainability* (eds Christophe Bellman, Graham Dutfield and Ricardo Meléndez-Ortiz), pp. 175–83. London: Earthscan.

Allen, Geoff (2001) Can you trust this model? How has the trust model worked for Hounslow, the first to adopt this approach to manage its public library service? The Best Value inspection report is just out and it answers some key questions, *Library Association Record*, 103 (12), 745–55.

Ambani, Mukesh and Birla, Kumarmangalam (2000) *A policy framework for reforms in education: special subject group on policy framework for private investment in education, health and rural development Prime Minister's Council on Trade and Industry Government of India*. Report on a Policy Framework for Reforms in Education. Submitted to the Prime Minister's Council on Trade and Industry in April 2000. Available at: *http://indiaimage.nic.in/pmcouncils/reports/education* (accessed on 19/07/04).

American Library Association (ALA) (2000) *American Library Association on the WTO and libraries, passed at the ALA and mid-winter meeting 2000 – resolution on the World Trade Organization policies affecting libraries*. Available at: *http://www.vcn.bc.ca/bcla-ip/globalization/alareswto.html* (accessed on 20/07/04).

American Library Association (ALA) (2001) Letter to the Editor of American Libraries, from the ALA Washington Office, re: Why the World Trade Organization is a threat to libraries, *American Libraries*.

Available at: http://libr.og/GATS/Hunt-Sheketoff.html (accessed on 20/07/04).

American Library Association (ALA) (2002) *WTO/GATS summary of issues and chronology, July.* Available at: *http://www.libr.org/GATS/alawash-GATS-issues-chronology.doc* (accessed on 20/07/04).

American Library Association (ALA) (2004) *ALA Committee on Legislation, Report to Council, Midwinter Meeting, San Diego, California, 2004 ALA midwinter meeting.* Available at: *http://www.ala .org/ala/washoff/ogr/councilrese/mw04cd20.pdf.* See also Councillor's Report for ALA's midwinter meeting, San Diego (2004). Available at: *http://www.nd.edu~jarcher/ifrtreport/no54/2.html* (accessed on 21/07/04).

Amin, Samir (1997) *Capitalism in the Age of Globalization.* London: Zed Books.

Anderson, A. J. (1997) How do you manage?, *Library Journal*, 122 (16): 58–60.

Anonymous (2001) Think locally to survive globally: Internet traders are finding that globalisation works very differently online than it does in the 'real world'. Cultural domination is not the way into new net markets, *Marketing Week*, 31 May: 67–70.

Anonymous (2002) *The GATS and Ontario public libraries.* Available at: *http://www.culture.gov.on.ca/english/culdiv/library/gats-faq.html* (accessed on 19/7/04).

Anonymous (undated) *Trade-related intellectual property rights: a new regime.* Available at: *http://southcentre.org/publications/trips/tripsmaintexttrans-01.htm* (accessed on 19/7/04).

Association of London Government (2003) *London bulletin: more than just books*, 24, July/August. Available at: *http://www.alg.gov.uk/doc.asp?doc=9444&cat=1228* (accessed on 19/07/04).

Atkinson, Mark and Elliott, Larry (2000) Short outline measures to reduce world poverty, *Guardian*, 12 December: 13.

Atuti, Richard M. et al. (2003) *Income Generation: Experiences from Public Library Systems in Eastern, Central and Southern Africa.* Oxford: International Network for the Availability of Scientific Publications (INASP).

Audit Commission (2000) *North East Lincolnshire Public Library Service: Best Value Inspection Report (Final).* Inspected by Café McDonald and Marilyn Lister, November. London: Audit Commission Best Value Inspection Service.

Audit Commission (2001) *London Borough of Hounslow Public Library Service: Best Value Inspection Report (Final)*. Inspected by Neill Foss and Jacquie Campbell, September. London: Audit Commission Best Value Inspection Service.

Audit Commission (2002) *Building better library services*. Available at: *http://www.audit-commission.gov.uk/index.asp* (accessed on 19/7/04).

Australian Coalition for Cultural Diversity (ACCD) (2003) Australia and GATS: submission to the Department of Foreign Affairs and Trade, 24 February. Available at: *http://www.mca.org.au/pdf/accdGATS26Feb03.pdf* (accessed on 21/07/04).

Australian Library and Information Association (ALIA), written by Jennifer Nicholson, Executive Director (2001) *Trade negotiations in the World Trade Organisation*. Available at: *http://www.alia.org.au/advocacy/submissions/trade.html* (accessed on 19/07/04).

Australian Writers' Guild (AWG) (2003) *General Agreement on Trade in Services (GATS) and Australia*, Submission to the Department of Foreign Affairs and Trade, February. Available at: *http://www.awg.com.au/artman/uploads/awggatssubfeb03.pdf* (accessed on 19/7/04).

Background document on the GATS (2000) Available at: *http://www.europa.eu.int/comm/avpolicy/extern/gats2000/conbg_en.htm* (accessed on 19/07/04).

Bakken, Frode (2000) WTO *and libraries – an introduction, Library of Bus Kerud, Norway*, a paper presented at the 66th IFLA Council and General Conference, Jerusalem, Israel, 13–18 August. Available at: *http://www.ifla.org/IV/fla66/papers/171-140e.htm* (accessed on 19/7/04).

Bakken, Frode (2002) *The commercialisation of libraries and archives*, speech given by Frode Bakken, Councillor and President of the Norwegian Libraries Association and Chief Librarian of Telemark's University Libraries on the occasion of the 2nd Assembly of European Regions (AER) Conference of European Regional Ministers for Culture and Education, Brixen, 18 October. Available at: *http://www.eblida.org/lobby/lobbying/gats/frode_aer.htm* (accessed on 19/7/04).

Barlow, Maude (2001) The last frontier, *Ecologist*, February: 1–17. Mirrored from: *http://www.theecologist.org/lastfrontier.html*, with permission of Managing Editor, Malcolm Trait. Available at: *http://www.ratical.org/co-globalize/lastfront.html* (accessed on 19/07/04).

Basso, Pietro (2003) *Modern Times, Ancient Hours: Working Lives in the Twenty-First Century*. London: Verso.

Batt, Chris (2001) People's Network, a news item, *Library Association Record*, 103 (6): 328.

BBC (British Broadcasting Corporation) (2001a) The WTO and the GATS, a transcript of BBC Radio 4 programme, *You and Yours*, 12.30–12.50 pm, 17 October. Available at: *http://www.wdm.org.uk/campaign/GATSyouandyours.htm* and also at: *http://attac.org.uk/attac/document/you-yours-who-gats.pdf?documentID=117* (accessed on 19/07/04).

BBC News (2001b) *Web publishers charge for content.* 20 July. Available at: *http://news.bbc.co.uk/1/hi/business/1447145.stm* (accessed on 19/7/04).

Beechey, Bronwen (1995) *Rally opposes privatisation of libraries.* Article posted on the *Green Left Weekly Home Page.* Available at: *http://www.greenleft.org.au/back/1995/195/195p6.htm* (accessed on 19/7/04).

Bellman, Christophe, Dutfield, Graham and Meléndez-Ortiz, Ricardo (eds) (2003) *Trading in Knowledge: Development Perspectives on TRIPS, Trade and Sustainability.* London: Earthscan.

Benjamin, Alison (2001) Read alert, *The Guardian (G2)*, 13 June: 4–5.

Bennahum, David S. (1995) The future of libraries, *Meme*, 1.06. Available at: *http://memex.org/meme1-06.html* (accessed on 19/7/04).

Bently, Lionel (2002) *Between a rock and a hard place: the problems facing freelance creators in the UK media market-place: a briefing document on behalf of the Creators' Rights Alliance.* London: Institute of Employment Rights.

Berne Convention for the Protection of Literary and Artistic Works: Paris Text (1971). Available at: *http://www.law.correll.edu/treaties/berne/overview.html* (accessed on 22/07/04).

Berne Convention for the Protection of Literary and Artistic Works (page last modified 3 June 2004). From Wikipedia, the free encyclopaedia. Available at: *http://en.wikipedia.org/wiki/Berne_Convention_for_the_Protection_of_Literary_and_Artistic_Works* (accessed on 19/07/04).

Bernier, Ivan (2003) *A comparative analysis of Chile, the U.S. and Singapore – U.S. Free Trade Agreements with particular reference to their impact in the cultural sector.* Available at: *www.screenquota.org/epage/upload/us%20chile%20singapore%20fta%20&%20culture%20by201.bernier.pdf* (accessed on 19/07/04).

Berry, John (1997) The popular quick fix: examining library credibility and principle, *Library Journal*, 122 (13): 6.

Berry, John W. (2002) *John W. Berry's (American Library Association's President) May 16 2002 letter to the USTR*. Available at: *http://www.ala.org/ala/washoff/WOissues/copyrightb/intlcopyright/berryltr.pdf* (accessed on 21/07/04).

Billington, James H. (2001) Humanizing the information revolution, *IFLA Journal*, 27 (5/6): 301–6.

Birch, Dave (1998) *An experiment in micropayments. We've taken real money! – Financial Times Virtual Finance Report*. Available at: *http://www.birches.org/dgwb/pubs/ftvfr/018mpayments306.pdf* (accessed on 21/07/04).

Blair, Tony (1999) *Speech to the CBI conference in Brighton*, 2 November. Available at: *http://www.number-10.gov.uk/public/news/features.feature_display.asp?id-680*.

Boseley, Sarah (2002) Cost-price drugs plan for poor countries, *The Guardian*, 28 November: 2.

Boseley, Sarah (2003a) Public outrage prompts ban on baby sex selection, *The Guardian*, 12 November. Available at: *http://www.guardian.co.uk/uk_news/story/0,3604,1082836,00.html* (accessed on 19/07/04).

Boseley, Sarah (2003b) Prescription for world's poorest stays unwritten, *The Guardian*, 20 February: 10.

Bowden, Russell (2000) The information rich and IFLA's information poor, *IFLA Journal*, 26 (4): 298–302.

British Columbia Library Association (BCLA) (undated:a) *Imagine a World without Libraries – it could happen* ...The British Columbia Library Association, Vancouver. Available at: *http://www.vcn.bc.ca/bcla-ip/globalization/wtothreat.html* (accessed on 20/03/04).

British Columbia Library Association (BCLA) (undated:b) *GATS and the Threat to Libraries*, British Columbia Library Association, Vancouver. Available at: *http://www.vcn.bc.ca/bcla-ip/globalization/gats.htm* (accessed on 20/03/04).

British Copyright Council (2001) *Intellectual property and human rights response to the sub-committee on Human Rights Resolution 2000/7* (ResolutionE/CN.4/SUB2/RES/2000/7). Available at: *http://www.britishcopyright.org/pdfs/policy/2001-005.pdf* (accessed on 22/07/04).

British Council (1999) *The Information Society, Public Libraries*. Available at: *http://www.google.com/search?q=cache:ON.../infosoc.htm+1964+Public+Library+Act&hl=e*.

Brooks, Libby (2001) I wasn't in the riot. I wasn't being violent, *The Guardian (G2)*, 19 September: 16–17.

Brown, Derek (2001) China joins the club, *Guardian*, 11 December. Available at: *http://www.guardian.co.uk/china/story/0,7369,617159,00.html* (accessed on 22/07/04).

Burge, Suzanne (1998) *Much pain, little gain: privatisation and UK governmental libraries*, paper given at 64th IFLA General Conference, 16–21 August. Available at: *http://www.ifla.org/IV/ifla64/187-139e.htm* (accessed on 19/7/04).

Byers, Stephen (2000) Speech to the Mansion House, 1 February. Available at: *http://www.dti.gove.uk/Minspeech/byers030200.htm*.

Byrne, Alex (1999) Freedom of access to information and freedom of expression in a pluralistic world, *IFLA Journal*, 25 (4): 223–31.

Byrne, Alex (2000a) Towards a world of free access to information and freedom of expression, *IFLA Journal*, 26 (4): 255–9.

Byrne, Alex (2000b) We would live in peace and tranquility and no one would know anything, *Australian Academic and Research Libraries*, 31 (3): September. Available at: *http://archive.alia.org.au/sections/ucrls/aarl/31.3/full.text/byrne.html* (accessed on 22/7/04).

Caffentzis, George (1997) Why machines cannot create value: or, Marx's theory of machines. In: *Cutting Edge: Technology, Information Capitalism and Social Revolution* (eds Jim Davis, Thomas A. Hirschl and Michael Stack). London: Verso.

Canadian Library Association (CLA) (1999) *Canadian Library Association Perspective on the World Trade Organisation Meetings*, approved by the Canadian Library Association Executive Council, November 1999. Available at: *http://www.cla.ca/about/wto.htm* (accessed on 19/7/04).

Capita Property Consultancy (2002) *Hackney Technology and Learning Centre completed*. Available at: *http://www.capita-pc.co.uk/cpc9CDE7F5D277F4CF7A785F23FBCCBA5E8_B5ABF4*. See also: *http://www.capitasymonds.co.uk/news/content/news_336.asp* (accessed on 22/07/04).

Chang, Ha-Joon (2003) Unfree Global Markets, *Le Monde Diplomatique*, August: 6–7.

Chartered Institute of Library and Information Professionals (UKCILIP) (1998) *Your Right to Know: Freedom of Information*. Available at: *www.la-hq.org.uk/directory/prof_issues/yrtk.html* (accessed on 19/07/04).

Chartered Institute of Library and Information Professionals (UKCILIP) (2003) *CILIP response to liberalising trade in services: a new consultation on the World Trade Organisation GATS negotiations*,

January. Available at: *www.cilip.org.uk/advocacy/responses/030203 .html* (accessed on 19/07/04).

Coates, Tim (2002) How to fix our libraries: are our public libraries living on borrowed time? *Guardian*, 18 May: 9.

Coates, Tim (2004) *Who's in Charge: a Libri Report*, April. Available at: *http://libri.org.uk* (accessed on 19/7/04).

Cohen, Nick (2000) *Cruel Britannia*. London: Verso Books.

Commission on Intellectual Property Rights (2002) *Integrating intellectual property rights and development policy: report of the CIPR*, 2nd edn. London: Commission on Intellectual Property Rights.

Commission on International Trade and Investment Policy (1999) Available at: *http://www.iccwbo.org/home/statements_rules/statements/ 1999/services_trade_liberalization.asp* (accessed on 22/07/04).

Committee on Copyright and Other Legal Matters (CLM), IFLA (2001) *The IFLA position on copyright in the digital environment*. Available at: *http://www.ifla.org/III/clm/p1/pos-dig.htm* (accessed on 19/07/04).

Committee on Copyright and Other Legal Matters (CLM), IFLA (2002a) *Limitations and exceptions to copyright and neighbouring rights in the digital environment: an international library perspective*. Available at: *www.ifla.org/III/clm/p1/ilp/htm* (accessed on 19/07/04).

Committee on Copyright and Other Legal Matters (CLM), IFLA (2002b) *Tips for TRIPS: a guide for libraries and librarians to the Agreement on Trade-Related Aspects of Intellectual Property Rights*. Available at: *www.ifla.org/III/clm/p1/tt-e.htm* (accessed on 21/07/04).

Committee on Copyright and Other Legal Maters (CLM), IFLA (2002c) *Report of CLM meeting: 2002 IFLA General Conference in Glasgow: walls come down for CLM in Glasgow!* Available at: *http:// www.ifla.org/III/clm/p1/glas02.htm* (accessed on 21/07/04).

Consultations on Services in the Cultural Sector (2000) Available at: *http://europa.eu.int/comm/avpolicy/extern/gats2000/concs_en.htm* (accessed on 21/07/04).

Cookson, Matthew (2002) Less books equals less library users, *Socialist Worker*, 8 June: 11.

Council Offices/Library Project, Hackney, London (undated). Available at: *http://www.millgroup.co.uk/printer-hackney.html* (accessed on 19/07/04).

Crane, Gregory (2001) Commercial digital libraries and the academic community, *D-lib Magazine*, 7 (1). Available at: *http://www.dlib.org/ dlib/january01/crane/01crane.html* (accessed on 22/07/04).

Crocker, Steve (1999) *The siren song of the Internet micropayments*, April. Available at: *http://www.cisp.org/imp/april-99/04-99/crocker.htm* (accessed on 22/7/04).

Culp, Eric (2004) Calls for longer working week grow strong in Germany, *The Business*, 11/12 July: 8.

D'Angelo, Ed (2004) *Barbarians at the gates of the public library: how postmodernism consumer capitalism threatens democracy, civil education and the public good*. Available at: *http://www.blackcrow.us/index.htm* (accessed on 19/7/04).

Danish National Library Authority and NAPLE (2002) *The Public Library in the Electronic World, Copenhagen*. Available at: *http://www.bs.dk/naple/naple_report.pdf* (accessed on 19/7/04).

Davies, Gillian (2002) *Copyright and the Public Interest*. London: Sweet & Maxwell.

Davis, Jennifer (2003) *Intellectual Property Law*, 2nd edn. Butterworths Core Text Series. London: LexisNexis, Reed Elsevier.

De Jonquieres, Guy (2001) Dealing in Doha: Osman Bin Laden has galvanised efforts to launch a new global trade round. But even if this week's WTO meeting succeeds, serious hurdles lie ahead, *Financial Times*, 6 November: 24.

De Jonquieres, Guy (2002) Supachai's mission: the WTO's new director-general aims to help poorer nations benefit more from international trade. But his appointment has caused some unease in the West, *Financial Times*, 2 September: 18.

De Jonquieres, Guy and Williams, Frances (2001) Moore spells out dangers of failure at WTO talks, *Financial Times*, 10/11 November: 13.

Delmas-Marty, Mireille (2003) Justice for law: international law favours market values, *Le Monde Diplomatique*, August: 2–3.

Denny, Charlotte (2001) Row as WTO lobbyists keep out poor: special report on globalisation, *The Guardian*, 3 September. Available at: *http://www.guardian.co.uk/business/story/0.3604.545795.00.html* (accessed on 22/7/04).

Deodhar, Satish Y. (2002) *Managing Trade in Educational Services: Issues for India's Response in WTO Negotiations*, IIMA Working Paper No. 2001/10/03. The paper was presented at the National Seminar on WTO and Allied Issues, Indian Institute of Foreign Trade, New Delhi, February 2002. Available at: *http://www.iimahd.ernet.in/~satish/wtoedu.pdf* (accessed on 22/7/04).

Department for Culture, Media and Sport (DCMS) (2000a) *Comprehensive and efficient – standards for modern public libraries:*

a consultation paper. Available at: *http://www.culture.gov.uk/libraries -pls-assess.pdf* (accessed on 22/07/04).

Department for Culture, Media and Sport (DCMS) (2000b) *Cash boost gets libraries up to speed on the Internet*, December. Available at: *http://www.culture.gov.uk/heritage/search.asp?name=/press/releases/he ritage/ 2000/dcms305*.

Derber, Charles (2003) *People before Profit: the New Globalisation in an Age of Terror, Big Money, and Economic Crisis*. London: Souvenir Press.

Deschamps, Christine (2002) Can libraries help bridge the digital divide? *NordInfo*. Available at: *http://www.nordinfo.helsinki.fi/publications/ nordnytt/nnytt4_01/deschampts.htm* (accessed on 21/07/04).

Dietz, A. (1994) *The artist's right of integrity under copyright law – a comparative approach*, 25 IIC 177 at 183.

Dodds, Anneliese (2001) GATS: higher education and public libraries, *Information for Social Change*, 14 (Winter 2001/02): 21–5. Available at: *http://libr.org/ISC* (accessed on 21/07/04).

Doehring, Greg (undated) *Increasing investment: income generation for survival or growth?* Available at: *http://www.lisa.wa.gov.au/pdf/ Increasinginvestmentpdstratdir2002-07.pdf* (accessed on 21/07/04).

Drahos, Peter and Braithwaite, John (2002) *Information Feudalism: Who Owns the Knowledge Economy?* London: Earthscan.

Drahos, Peter and Braithwaite, John (2003) Securing the knowledge empire, *Mute: Culture and Politics After the Net*, 27 (Winter/Spring): 16–17.

Edmonds, Diana (2003) Portfolio for success?, *Library and Information Update*, 2 (7): 50–1.

Edwards, Michael and Zadek, Simon (2003) Governing the provision of global public goods: the role and legitimacy of nonstate actors. In: *Providing Global Public Goods* (eds Inge Kaul et al.), pp. 200–24. New York: Oxford University Press.

Elliott, Larry and Denny, Charlotte (2002) UK wrecks cheap drugs deal, *Guardian*, 21 December: 2.

Ericson, Anders (2002) Privatising bit for bit, *Bok Og Bibliotek*, 69 (7): 18–19 (in Norwegian) (Anders Ericson interviews Ruth Rikowski about her work on the GATS and libraries). Available at: *http://www.frilanders.net/eget/bibliotek/rikowski.html* (accessed on 19/7/04).

Ericson, Anders and Bakken, Frode (2003) Free trade with library services? – no 'all clear' regarding GATS, *Information for Social*

Change, Summer, No 17. Available at: *http://www.libr.org/isc/articles/17-Ericson-Bakken.html* (accessed on 20/07/04). Reprinted in: *Link-Up: The Newsletter of Link: A Network for North–South Library Development*, 15 (3/4): 14–16. Translated into English by Anders Ericson. Originally published in Norwegian, in *Bok Og Bibliotek (BOB)*, 1, 200.

European Bureau of Library, Information and Documentation Associations (2000) *World Trade Organisation*. Available at: *http://www.eblida.org/wto/wto.htm*.

European Bureau of Library, Information and Documentation Associations (EBLIDA) (2002a) *EBLIDA statement on the WTO GATS negotiations: libraries and trade in services*. Available at: *http://www.eblida.org/position/GATS_Statement_Nov02.html*.

European Bureau of Library, Information and Documentation Associations (EBLIDA) (2002b) *GATS WTO General Agreement on Trade in Services, June*. Available at: *http://www.eblida.org/lobby/lobbying/gats* (accessed on 21/07/04).

European Bureau of Library, Information and Documentation Associations (EBLIDA) (2003a) *EBLIDA response to the EC consultation on WTO members' requests to the EC and its member states for improved market access to services, January*. Available at: *http://www.eblida.org/position/GATS_response_Jan03.htm* (accessed on 21/07/04).

European Bureau of Library, Information and Documentation Associations (EBLIDA) (2003b) EBLIDA GATS response, *Managing Information*, 10 January. Available at: *http://www.managinginformation.com/news/content_show_full.php?id=1076* (accessed on 21/07/04).

European Commission (EC) (2003) *Report on United States barriers to trade and investment*, Brussels, December. Available at: *http://trade-info.cec.eu.int/doclib/docs/2003/december/tradoc_115383.pdf* (accessed on 21/07/04).

Ezard, John (2004) British libraries could shut by 2020, *Guardian*, 28 April: 5.

Filkin, Geoffrey (2004) personal correspondence – letter dated 15 June, from the Department for Constitutional Affairs.

Fox, Megan (2001) Questia and the for-profit online library trend. *Simmons College Libraries Newsletter*, Spring 2001. Available at: *http://www.simmons.edu/libraries/LibNewsletterSpring2004.pdf* (accessed on 21/07/04).

Freedman, Des (2002) *Trade versus culture: an evaluation of the impact of current GATS negotiations on audio-visual industries.*

Available at: *http://www.isanet.org/noarchive/freedman.html* (accessed on 21/07/04).

Fritz, Thomas and Fuchs, Peter (undated) *GATS: public services under pressure to liberalize: the GATS negotiations in the WTO – a challenge for international civil society, Global Issue* – Paper 1. Heinrich Böll Stiftung. Published on the occasion of the WTO conference in Cancun. Available at: *http://www.boell.de/downloads/global/GIP%201% 20GATS_Eng1.pdf* (accessed on 21/07/04).

Froehlich, Thomas J. (2000) Intellectual freedom, ethical deliberation and codes of ethics, *IFLA Journal*, 26 (4): 264–72.

GATS and the Globalisation of NZ Education: Education Forum (2003) *Scoop Media*, 16 April. Available at: *http://www.scoop.co.nz/mason/ stories/ED0304/S00039.html* (accessed on 21/07/04).

GATS and Ontario Public Libraries (2002) Available at: *http://www .culture.gov.on.ca/english/culdiv/library/gats-faq.htm* (accessed on 20/07/04).

GATS and the threat to libraries. Available at: *http://www.vcn.bc.ca/ bcla-ip/globalization.gats.html* (accessed on 20/07/04).

GATSWatch (undated) *GATS Requests and Offers*. Available at: *http:// www.gatswatch.org/requests-offers.html* (accessed on 20/07/04).

George, Susan (1988) *Fate Worse than Debt*. London: Penguin/Grove Press.

Gervais, Daniel (2003) *The TRIPS Agreement: Drafting History and Analysis*, 2nd edn. London: Sweet & Maxwell.

Godrej, Dinyar (2002) 8 things you should know about patents on life, *New Internationalist*, 349, September: 9–12.

Goetz, Thomas (2004) The eagle is grounded: while America works to protect intellectual property, everyone else is innovating, *Wired*, 2 (February): 23–4.

Gould, Ellen (2004) *Update on the GATS negotiations and their implications for public sector libraries*, Prepared for the Canadian: Library Association, June.

Gray, John (2001) The era of globalisation is over: communism failed, but market liberalism then tried to impose its own utopia. The atrocities should mark the end of that crusade, *New Statesman*, 24 September: 25–7.

Grieshaber-Otto, Jim and Sanger, Matthew (2002) *Perilous Lessons: The Impact of the WTO Services Agreement (GATS) on Canada's Public Education System*. Ottawa: Canadian Centre for Policy Alternatives.

Guardian Editorial (2001) Power shifts in the WTO: developing countries flex their muscles, *Guardian*, 15 November: 23.

Guardian Editorial (2002a) Bush's bitter medicine: the poor need cheap drugs, not cheap talk, *Guardian*, 30 December: 15.

Guardian Editorial (2002b) Drug-price buster: Clare Short makes a difference, *Guardian*, 28 November: 25.

Guardian Editorial (2002c) Restocking the shelves: is it a disgrace to allow libraries to wither?, *Guardian*, 17 May: 19.

Guardian Editorial (2003) Across the great divide, *Guardian*, 10 December: 103.

Hamilton, Stuart (2002) Internet accessible information and censorship, intellectual freedom and libraries – a global overview, *IFLA Journal*, 28 (4): 190–7.

Haralambos, Mike and Holborn, Martin (2004) *Sociology: Themes and Perspectives*, 6th edn. London: HarperCollins.

Harding, James (2001) WTO protestors plan sea route to raid on Qatar, *Financial Times*, 11 December: 1.

Hefter, Laurence R. and Litowitz, Robert D. (undated) *What is intellectual property?* Available at: *http://usinfo.state.gov/products/pubs/intelprp/* (accessed on 20/07/04).

Hencke, David (2004) Treasury accused as cost of information soars, *Guardian*, 18 May: 1. Available at: *http://politics.guardian.co.uk/foi/story/0,9061,1219181,00.html* (accessed on 22/07/04).

Hogwood, Chris (2003) *Higher education in a changing world: Chris Hogwood reports on the South Africa Minister for Education's keynote address.* Available at: *http://www.acu.ac.uk/yearbook/ november2003/ 12-19.pdf* (accessed on 21/07/04).

House of Lords, Select Committee on Economic Affairs (2002), *Globalisation: Session*, 1st Report. London: Stationery Office.

Hunt, Fiona (1998a) *MAI fact sheet from British Columbia Library: what will the MAI do for libraries?* (BCLA Information Policy Committee). Available at: *http://www.libr.org/SRRT/docs/MAI_fact_sheet.html* (accessed on 20/07/04).

Hunt, Fiona (1998b) *What will the MAI do for Canada's libraries? Absolutely nothing! Read on for more information ...* Prepared for the Information Policy Committee, June. Available at: *http://www.vcn.bc.ca/bcla-ip/globalization/maifact.html* (accessed on 21/07/04).

Hunt, Fiona (2001a) The WTO and the threat to libraries, *Progressive Librarian: A Journal for Critical Studies and Progressive Politics in Librarianship*, Issue 18, Summer 2001. Reprinted in *Information for Social Change*, 14 (Winter 2001–2): 60–5. Available at: *http://libr.org/ISC* (accessed on 20/07/04).

Hunt, Fiona (2001b) Why the World Trade Organization is a threat to libraries, *American Libraries*, September. Available at: *http://libr.org/ GATS/Hunt-Sheketoff.html* (accessed on 20/07/04).

Hutton, Will (2004) Living on borrowed time: public libraries need to be properly managed, by people committed to the idea of public value – or they will die, *Sunday Observer*, 2 May.

India's Market-Opening Offer in the GATS Negotiations (2004) India Submits Cautious Services Offer, *Bridges Weekly Trade News Digest*, 8 (3), 28 January. Available at: *http://www.union-network.org/uniflashes .nsf/0/e59a76abcc16a48fc1256e2f00514d56?0* (accessed on 21/07/04).

Information Society (2001) World Trade Organisation and GATS, *Information Society*, Summer issue 02: 14–15.

Inoue, Yasuyo (2000) People, libraries and the JLA committee on intellectual freedom in libraries, *IFLA Journal*, 26 (4): 293–7.

Instant Library (2003) Portfolio for success, *Instant Library*, 14 July. Available at: *http://www.instant-library.com/News.html* (accessed on 20/07/04).

International Federation of Library Associations and Institutions (IFLA) (1999) *International Federation of Library Associations and Institutions Statement on Libraries and Intellectual Freedom*. The Hague. Available at: *http://www.ifla.org*.

International Federation of Library Associations and Institutions (IFLA) (2000) (revised 2001) *IFLA position on copyright in the digital environment*. Available at: *http://www.ifla.org/V/press/copydig.htm* (accessed on 20/07/04).

International Federation of Library Associations and Institutions (IFLA) (2001a) *The IFLA Position on WTO Treaty Negotiations, Committee on Copyright and Other Legal Matters (CLM), International Federation of Library Associations and Institutions*, Version I, February. Available at: *http://www.ifla.org/III/clm/p1/pos-wto.htm*.

International Federation of Library Associations and Institutions (IFLA) (2001b) *The IFLA position on the WTO Treaty negotiations, International Federation of Library Associations and Institutions*, Version II, September. Available at: *http://www.ifla.org/III/clm/p1/ wto-ifla.htm*.

International Federation of Library Associations and Institutions (IFLA) (2002) *The IFLA position on WTO treaty negotiations, Committee on Copyright and Other Legal Matters (CLM), International Federation of Library Associations and Institutions*, Version III, December. Available at: *http://www.ifla.org/III/clm/p1/pos-wto.htm* (accessed on 20/07/04).

International Trade Daily (2002) WTO requests for services liberalisation begin: U.S. targets 127 member countries, *International Trade Daily*, 5 July.

Jawara, Fatoumata and Kwa, Aileen (2003) *Behind the Scenes at the WTO: the Real World of International Trade Negotiations*. London: Zed Books.

Johnson, Jo (2004) Business hits at Chirac for not reforming 35-hour week, *Financial Times*, 16 July: 6.

Joy, Clare (2001) Trading away basic rights: the General Agreement on Trade in Services (GATS), *Information for Social Change*, 14 (Winter): 19–21. Available at: *http://libr.org/ISC* (accessed on 21/07/04).

Kaul, Inge and Mendoza, Ronald U. (2003) Advancing the concept of public goods. In: *Providing Global Public Goods* (eds Inge Kaul et al.), pp. 78–111. New York: Oxford University Press.

Kaul, Inge et al. (2003) How to improve the provision of global public goods. In: *Providing Global Public Goods* (eds Inge Kaul et al.), pp. 21–58. New York: Oxford University Press.

Kaushik, Atul (2003) The Indian experience in the field of IPRs, access to biological resources and benefit sharing. In: *Trading in Knowledge: Development Perspectives on TRIPS, Trade and Sustainability* (eds C. Bellmann, G. Dutfield and R. Meléndez-Ortiz), pp. 255–63. London: Earthscan.

Kay, John (2002) Copyright law has a duty to creativity, *Financial Times*, 24 October: 21.

Kelsey, Jane (2001) *The Implications of New Zealand's Commitments on Trade in Education and Research Services*. Available at: *http://www .teac.govt.nz/Report4/submissions110.pdf*.

Kennedy, Maev (2002) Readers deserting 'shabby' libraries: Audit Commission report shows visits have fallen by 17% in 10 years but more people use the service to access the Internet and study, *Guardian*, 17 May: 7.

Khor, Martin (2001) Present problems and future shape of the WTO and the multilateral trading system, *Third World Network, Briefing Paper 2*, September.

Khor, Martin (2002a) *Rethinking IPRs and the TRIPS Agreement*. Paper distributed at Commission on Intellectual Property Rights Conference, 'How intellectual property rights could work better for developing countries and poor people', London, 21–22 February 2002 (paper originally presented at an international seminar on 'Intellectual Property and Development: What future for the WTO TRIPS Agreement?' in Brussels, organised by Oxfam and other NGOs).

Khor, Martin (2002b) *Manipulation by tactics, conquest by drafts, rule through text: how the WTO produced its Anti-Development Agenda at Doha*. Paper distributed at Commission on Intellectual Property Rights Conference, 'How intellectual property rights could work better for developing countries and poor people', London, 21–22 February 2002.

Khor, Martin (2002c) *Intellectual Property, Biodiversity and Sustainable Development: Resolving the Difficult Issues*. London: Zed Books.

Kirkby Times (2003) New Labour lied to gain support for Iraq War, *Kirkby Times*. Available at: *http://www.kirkbytimes.co.uk/antiwaritems/ blair_lied.html* (accessed on 22/07/04).

Klein, Naomi (2001) *No Logo*. London: Flamingo.

Klein, Naomi (2003) *Librarianship as a revolutionary choice*, speech at the joint American Library Association/Canadian Library Association Conference, 24 June. Available at. *http://www.libr.org/Juice/issues/ vol6/LJ_6.16.html* (accessed on 20/07/04).

Krajewski, Markus (2002a) *Public services and trade liberalization – mapping the legal framework*. Part of this paper builds on Krajewski's research study 'Public services and the scope of GATS', written for the Center for International Environmental Law (CIEL) in June 2001. Available at: *http://www.ciel.org*.

Krajewski, Markus (2002b) *Public interests, private rights and the 'constitution' of GATS*. Paper for the workshop 'GATS: trading development?', Centre for the Study of Globalisation and Regionalisation, University of Warwick, 20/21 September.

Kynge, James (2001) China enters WTO dawn with mixed expectations, *Financial Times*, 11 December: 14.

Labour Left Briefing (2000) Twenty-five reasons to oppose PFI – excerpts from a news report from the Sheffield-based Centre for Public Services which reveals the political costs of the Private Finance Initiative (PFI) and Public Private Partnerships (PPP), *Labour Left Briefing*, July: 16–17.

Lambert, Jean (2002) *The General Agreement on Trade in Services (GATS): democracy, public services and government regulation*. Produced by Lifework; printed by Toptown Printers, Barnstaple.

LA Record news item (2000a) Best value – fear of documentation fever. *Library Association Record*, 102 (1): 7.

LA Record news item (2000b) Twenty-three steps to pleasing the DCMS (national standards for public libraries). *Library Association Record*, 102 (6): 303.

LA Record news item (2000c) Standards make hearts beat faster (public libraries). *Library Association Record*, 102 (8): 426.

LA Record news item (2000d) Best Value – is it a technical Tory trap? *Library Association Record*, 102 (9): 489.

LA Record news item (2000e) PFI library first. *Library Association Record*, 102 (10): 545.

LA Record news item (2001a) Hackney turns the corner – public libraries. *Library Association Record*, 103 (2): 67.

LA Record news item (2001b) More demands fall on staff: public library standards. *Library Association Record*, 103 (3): 131.

LA Record news item (2001c) Best Value – get radical, say inspectors. *Library Association Record*, 103 (3): 134.

LA Record news item (2001d) Focus on learning and ICT (Resource – the Council for Museums, Archives and Libraries). *Library Association Record*, 103 (7): 389.

LA Record news item (2001e) Another £6m for People's Network, New Opportunities Fund. *Library Association Record*, 103 (8): 461.

LA Record news item (2001f) Consultants move in (public libraries). *Library Association Record*, 103 (9): 515.

LA Record news item (2001g) Best Value – learn to love your BVI. *Library Association Record*, 103 (10): 594.

LA Record (2002) Appointments. *Library Association Record, Appointments Supplement*, 5 (1): 19.

LaRocque, Norman (2003) *GATS and the globalisation of NZ education*, education forum speech, 16 April. Available at: *http://www .scoop.co.nz/mason/stories/EDO304/S00039.htm* (accessed on 20/07/04).

Larson, Alan (2002) *Under Secretary Larson outlines U.S. policy on intellectual property rights*. Alan Larson, Under Secretary of State for Economic, Business and Agricultural Affairs, speaking before the Senate Committee on Foreign Relations, Washington, DC, 12 February. Available at: *http://usinfo.state.gov/topical/econ/ipr/larson12.htm* (accessed on 20/07/04).

Lashmer, Paul and Oliver, Richard (2000) Library standards hit all-time low, *Independent on Sunday*, 28 May: 8.

Lawson, Neal and Leighton, Daniel (2004) Burn the village to save the village, *New Statesman*, 29 March: 31–3.

Leadbeater, Charles (1999) *Living on Thin Air*. London: Viking, Penguin Group.

Leadbeater, Charles (2003) *Overdue: How to Create a Modern Public Library Service*, Laser Foundation Report. London: Laser Foundation.

Legrain, Philip (2001) Dump those prejudices: the left must learn to love the World Trade Organisation, *Guardian*, 12 July: 17.

Lessing, Lawrence (2002) Time to end the race for ever-longer copyright, *Financial Times*, 17 October: 21.

Levett, Shelagh (undated) *Partnership for investment: the PFI solution for Bournemouth Libraries*. Available at: *http://www.publicnet.co.uk/publicnet/fe031125.htm* (accessed on 20/07/04).

Libecon Newsletter (2004) Available at: *http://www.libecon.org* (accessed on 20/07/04).

Library Association of Ireland (2003) *Annual General Meeting, 2003*, Motions available at: *http://www.libraryassociation.ie/events/AGM2003_motions.rtf* (accessed on 22/07/04).

Lillington, Karlin (2001) Sentries at the gate: copyright is the Internet's new battleground. The outcome will decide how our culture develops, *Guardian Online*, 20 December: 1–3.

Locke, J. (1690) *Two Treaties of Government* (ed. P. Laslett). Cambridge: Cambridge University Press, 1988.

Lyman, Peter (1998) *The Dynamics of the Information Market, Beyond the Beginning: The Global Digital Library*. Available at: *http://www.ukoln.ac.uk/services/papers/bl/blri078/content/repor~t9.htm* (accessed on 20/07/04).

McInroy, Rob and Coult, Graham (2001) Lincolnshire libraries and the Internet – Graham Coult interviews Rob McInroy, *Managing Information*, 8 (10): 46–51.

MacKenzie, Jane (2002) The quiet storm, *The Big Issue*, 12–16 August: 10–11. Available at. *http://libr.org/ISC* (accessed on 20/07/04).

Managing Information news item (2003) Haringey libraries – a 'good' service, *Managing Information*, 10 (10): 10.

Mangeni, Francis (2003) Implementing the TRIPS Agreement in Africa. In: *Trading in Knowledge: Development Perspectives on TRIPS, Trade and Sustainability* (eds C. Bellman, G. Dutfield and Ricardo Meléndez-Ortiz), pp. 219–31, London: Earthscan.

Marsden, Christopher (ed.) (2000) *Regulating the Global Information Society*, Warwick Studies in Globalisation. London: Routledge.

Marx, Karl (1887) (1954 – reproduced text of English edition of 1887). *Capital: A Critique of Political Economy*, Vol. 1. London: Lawrence & Wishart.

Marx, Karl and Engels, Frederick (1848) *The Communist Manifesto*. Hardmonsworth: Penguin Books.

Marx, Karl and Engels, Frederick (undated) Theses on Feuerbach. In: *Selected Works in One Volume*. Moscow: Progress Publishers.

Menzies, Heather (1987) *The virtual library: kiosk or community?*, Canadian Library Association. Available at: *http://www.vcn.bc.ca/bcla-ip/globalization/clamenzies.html* (accessed on 20/07/04).

Meyer, Chris (2000) What's the matter? No longer does bigger, heavier, and more solid mean more value, *Business*, 2 (March): 193–8.

Millward, Debbie (1998) *Libraries as profit centres.* Available at: *http://www.sla.org/chapter/cwcn/wwest/v2n1/dminfo.htm* (accessed on 21/07/04).

Ministry of Foreign Affairs of Japan and Economic Affairs Bureau (2002a) *Japan's basic strategy for the WTO new round negotiations, October.* Available at: *http://www.mofa.go.jp/policy/economy/wto/round0210.html* (accessed on 20/07/04).

Ministry of Foreign Affairs of Japan (2002b) *Negotiating proposal on education services, March.* Available at: *http://www.mofa.go.jp/policy/economy/wto/educated0203.html* (accessed on 20/07/04).

Ministry of Foreign Affairs of Japan (2003c) *WTO services trade negotiations outline of Japan's initial offers, April.* Available at: *http://www.mofa.go.ip/policy/economy/wto/submit0304.html* (accessed on 20/07/04).

Monbiot, George (2000) *The Captive State: The Corporate Takeover of Britain.* London: Macmillan.

Monbiot, George (2003a) *The Age of Consent: A Manifesto for a New World Order.* London: Flamingo.

Monbiot, George (2003b) I was wrong about trade: our aim should not be to abolish the World Trade Organisation, but to transform it, *Guardian*, 24 June: 21.

Montagnon, Peter (2000) Market economy is 'set policy', *Financial Times*, 24 January: 10.

Morrison, Scott (2002) Lights go out at Stanford after tech bubble bursts, *Financial Times*, 4 December: 20.

Mougayar, Walid (2000) Aggregation nation: a nontrivial pursuit: turning information into electronic markets, *Business*, 2 (March): 253–8.

Naughton, John (2003) Intellectual property is theft. Ideas are for sharing, *Sunday Observer, Business*, 9 February: 6.

Neary, Michael and Rikowski, Glenn (2002) Time and speed in the social universe of capital. In: *Social Conceptions of Time: Structure and Process in Work and Everyday Life* (eds G. Crow and S. Heath), pp. 53–65. London: Palgrave.

Nehms, Rosemary (1997) *News libraries as profit centres – survey results*. Available at: *http://www.ibiblio.org/slanews/surveys/profit.html* (accessed on 22/07/04).

New Opportunities Fund (2001) *£50 million fuels learning revolution for all*. New Opportunities Fund Digitisation of Learning Materials Programme. Available at: *http://www.nof-digitise.org/launch.html*.

Nicholson, Denise (2002) The 'information-starved' – is there any hope of reaching the 'information super highway?', *IFLA Journal: Official Journal of the International Federation of Library Associations and Institutions*, 28 (5/6): 259–65.

Nicholson, Jennifer – see Australian Library and Information Association (2001).

Nilsson, Kjell (2003) *The IFLA/EBLIDA talks with the World Trade Organization and the European Commission about GATS and libraries, 18 December 2002 – report to the Executive Committee of EBLIDA*, 18 August. Available at: *http://libr.org/ISC*.

Non-Governmental Organisations (NGOs) (2001) *Re-Thinking TRIPS in the WTO: NGOs Demand Review and Reform of TRIPS at Doha Ministerial Conference*. Paper distributed at Commission on Intellectual Property Rights Conference, London, 21–22 February 2002, entitled 'How intellectual property rights could work better for developing countries and poor people'.

Oja Jay, Dru (2000) *Rethinking micropayments*. Available at: *http://www.dru.ca/micropayments/rethinking.html* (accessed on 20/07/04).

Okpaluba, Johnson (undated) *The Rome Convention: overview*. Available at: *http://www.rechten.unimas.nl/spinoza/iplib.rome1.htm* (accessed on 20/07/04).

Oppenheim, Charles (2003) The new copyright legislation: text of a talk given by Charles Oppenhem to the Aslib Northern Branch, *Managing Information*, 10 (7): 38–40.

Ormes, Sarah (1996) Public libraries corner: commercial partnerships in the public library: Sarah Ormes looks at the increase of net access in public libraries, *Ariadne*, 5 (September). Available at: *http://www.ariadne.ac.uk/issue5/public-libraries/* (accessed on 20/07/04).

Ott, Christopher (1999) Brain power for sale, *Vancouver Sun*, 12 August.

Oxfam (2001) *Q&A on Trade-Related Aspects of Intellectual Property Rights (TRIPS)*. Available at: *http://www.oxfamamerica.org/advocacy/art611.html* (accessed on 20/07/04).

Panagariya, Arvind (2003) International trade, *Foreign Policy*, November/December, pp. 20–30.

Panitchpakdi, Supachai (2002) World trade must not be tripped by drugs, *Financial Times*, 16 December: 21.

Pateman, John (2003) Review of 'Overdue: How to Create a Modern Public Library Service' by Charles Leadbeater, Laser Foundation, April 2003, *Information for Social Change*, 17. Available at: *http://libr.org/ISC* (accessed on 20/07/04).

Pedley, Paul (2003a) *Essential Law for Information Professionals*. London: Facet.

Pedley, Paul (2003b) An overview of the new copyright licensing agency licences, *Managing Information*, December, 10 (10): 52–3.

People's Network (2000) So, what is the People's Network? *People's Network Outline*, December. Available at: *http://www.peoplesnetwork/gov.uk/tow.index.html*.

Peterson, Luke Eric (2001) Watch out, the lawyers are coming! Big corporations have stumbled on a new way to frustrate governments whose regulations put a Dent in their profits, *New Statesman*, 9 July, pp. 21–22.

Piore, Adam (2001) From Seattle to Doha: the untold story of the Battle of Seattle is that a deal was lost not in the street, but behind closed doors. That bitter legacy looms over Doha, *Newsweek*, 12 November, CXXXVIII (20): 35–41.

Postone, Moishe (1996) *Time, Labour and Social Domination: A Reinterpretation of Marx's Critical Theory*. Cambridge: Cambridge University Press.

Potter, David (1999) Wealth creation in the knowledge economy of the next millennium, Third Millennium Lecture. Available at: *http://www.number10.gov.uk/output/Page3051.asp* (accessed on 22/7/04).

Private Libraries Association (1999) Available at: *http://www.the-old-school.demon.co.uk/pla.htm* (page hosted by Private Presses of the UK) (accessed on 20/07/04).

Professional Associations from the Cultural Milieu (2001) Final Declaration: First International Meeting of Professional Associations from the Cultural Milieu, 13 September. Available at: *http://www.cdc-ccd.org/Anglais/Liensenanglais/events/meeting/eng-declaration.doc* (accessed on 22/07/04).

Public Libraries Mobilising Advanced Networks (2003) *Funding and financial opportunities (Summary)*. Available at: *http://www.pulmanweb.org/DGMs/section2/FundingFinancial1.htm* (accessed on 20/07/04).

Pushpangadan, P. (2002) *Traditional Knowledge and Folklore – a benefit sharing model experimented in India*. Based on a paper presented at the conference organised by the Commission on Intellectual Property Rights at the Royal Society in London on 21–22 February 2002.

RAFI (1997) *Conserving Indigenous Knowledge: Integrating Two Systems of Innovation*. New York: Rural Advancement Foundation International and United Nations Development Programme.

Rao, M. B. and Guru, Manjula (2003) *WTO and International Trade*, 2nd edn. New Delhi: Vikas Publishing.

Red Pepper (2002) *Special issue on Education and the GATS*, November.

Regan, Bernard (2001) *Not for Sale: The Case against the Privatisation of Education*. London: Socialist Teachers Alliance.

Resource (2001a) *Response to the Department of the Environment, Transport and the Regions Consultation Paper – 'Working with others to achieve Best Value'*. Resource: The Council for Museums, Archives and Libraries, 25 May. Available at: *http://www.resource.gov.uk/news/*.

Resource (2001b) *Libraries get the green light for computer development*, Resource: The Council for Museums, Archives and Libraries, June. Available at: *http://www.resource.gov.uk/news/* (Resource now renamed – Museums, Libraries and Archives Council (MLA)).

Resource (2001c) *Resource announces £2.6m of grants from the Bill and Melinda Gates Foundation gift*. Resource: The Council for Museums, Archives and Libraries, July. Available at: *http://www.peoplesnetwork .gov.uk/news/pressreleasearticle.asp?id=107* (accessed 22/07/04) (Resource now renamed – Museums, Libraries and Archives Council (MLA)).

Resource (2001d) *Shh! – the library secret – is OUT: £4 million computer boost from lottery cash*. Resource, 30 August. (Resource now renamed – Museums, Libraries and Archives Council (MLA)).

Resource (2001e) *Local libraries – book to hook up to the Internet FREE. Over £3 million lottery input for computer power today* (Resource now renamed – Museums, Libraries and Archives Council (MLA)).

Revill, Jo (2003) 'No' to choosing your baby's sex, *Observer*, 9 November. Available at: *http://www.guardian.co.uk/genes/articles/ 0,2763,108115,00.html* (accessed on 22/07/04).

Rikowski, Glenn (2001a) Transfiguration: globalisation, the World Trade Organisation and the national faces of the GATS, *Information for Social Change*, 14 (Winter 2001/2): 8–17. Available at: *http://libr.org/ISC*. Also available at: *http://www.ieps.org.uk.cwc.net/ Rikowski2002.pdf* (accessed on 20/07/04).

Rikowski, Glenn (2001b) *The Battle in Seattle: Its Significance for Education*. London: Tufnell Press.

Rikowski, Glenn (2002a) Fuel for the living fire: labour-power! In: *The Labour Debate: An Investigation into the Theory and Reality of Capitalist Work* (eds Ana C. Dinerstein and Michael Neary), pp. 179–202. Aldershot: Ashgate.

Rikowski, Glenn (2002b) Schools: the great GATS buy. Available at: *http://www.ieps.org.uk.cwc.net/rikowski2002c.pdf* (accessed on 20/07/04).

Rikowski, Ruth (2000a) The essential bridge: a new breed of professional?, *Managing Information*, April, 7 (3): 40–5.

Rikowski, Ruth (2000b) The knowledge economy is here – but where are the information professionals? (Part 1), *Business Information Review*, 17 (3): 157–67.

Rikowski, Ruth (2000c) The knowledge economy is here – but where are the information professionals? (Part 2), *Business Information Review*, 17 (5): 227–33.

Rikowski, Ruth (2001) GATS: private affluence and public squalor? Implications for libraries and information, *Managing Information*, 8(10): 8–10. Available at. *http://www.libr.org/Juice/issues/vol4/LJ_4.46.htm#7* and at *http://www.attac.org.uk/attac/document/rikowski-gats-influence-squalor.pdf?documentID=119* (accessed on 20/07/04).

Rikowski, Ruth (2002a) The corporate takeover of libraries, *Information for Social Change*, 14 (Winter 2001/02): 25–60. Available at: *http://libr.org/ISC* (accessed on 20/07/04).

Rikowski, Ruth (2002b) The WTO, the GATS and the meaning of 'services', *Public Library Journal*, 17 (2): 48–50 (Part 1 of a two-part article based on a talk entitled 'The WTO/GATS Agenda for Libraries').

Rikowski, Ruth (2002c) Takeover by stealth?, *Public Library Journal*, 17 (3): 73–6 (Part 2 of a two-part article based on a talk entitled 'The WTO/GATS Agenda for Libraries').

Rikowski, Ruth (2002d) The capitalisation of libraries, *The Commoner: A Left-Activist e-Journal*, 14 (May). Available at: *http://www.commoner.org.uk* (accessed on 20/07/04).

Rikowski, Ruth (2002e) WTO/GATS agenda for libraries, *Focus: On International Library and Information Work – Journal for the International Library and Information Group*, 33 (2): 53–65.

Rikowski, Ruth (2002f) What does the future hold for our public libraries? *Information for Social Change*, Summer, 15: 55–60. Available at: *http://libr.org/ISC*. Also available at: *http://www.attac*

.org.uk/attac/document/rikowski-future-libraries.pdf?documentID=118 (accessed on 20/07/04).

Rikowski, Ruth (2002g) Feedback on globalisation and information issue of ISC, *Information for Social Change*, Summer, 15. Available at: *http://libr.org/ISC* (accessed on 20/07/04).

Rikowski, Ruth (2002h) Fringe meeting at IFLA Conference (2002) 'The profit virus: globalisation, libraries and education', *Link-Up: The Newsletter of LINK: A Network for North–South Library Development*, 14 (3): 17–19. Also available on library juice: *http://www.libr.org/juice/issues/vol5/lj_531.htm#2* (accessed at 20/07/04).

Rikowski, Ruth (2002i) IFLA Conference (2002) – Part 1: raising awareness about the GATS and 'Women's issues', *Information for Social Change*, 16 (Winter): 21–8. Available at: *http://libr.org/ISC* (accessed on 20/07/04).

Rikowski, Ruth (2002j) IFLA Conference (2002) – Part 2: report on meetings and demonstrations attended, overall impressions and a look towards the future, *Information for Social Change*, 16 (Winter): 29–36. Available at: *http://libr.org/ISC* (accessed on 20/07/04).

Rikowski, Ruth (2002k) Anti-globalisation websites, *Information for Social Change*, 16 (Winter): 56–8. Available at: *http://libr.org/ISC* (accessed on 20/07/04). Reprinted in: *Link-Up: The Newsletter of Link: A Network for North–South Library Development*, 15 (1), March (2003).

Rikowski, Ruth (2002l) Kommersialisering och privatisering – WTO/GATS agenda for bibliotek I ett engelskt perspektiv, *Bis (Bibliotek i Samhaelle)*, 3: 6–9 [article in Swedish: WTO/GATS Agenda for libraries, with special reference to public libraries in England, *Libraries in Society*]. Available at: *http://www.foreningenbis.org/Gats/gatsrr.html* (accessed on 22/07/04).

Rikowski, Ruth (2002m) IFLA 2002 Conference in Glasgow: a first-timers impression, *IFLA Journal: Special Issue on the Glasgow Conference*, 28 (5/6: Winter): 278–80. Available at: *http://www.ifla.org/V/iflaj/*.

Rikowski, Ruth (2002n) Fringe meeting at IFLA 2002 Conference – 'The profit virus: globalisation, libraries and education', *IFLA Journal: Special Issue on the Glasgow Conference*, 28(5/6: Winter): 341–2. Available at: *http://www.ifla.org/V/iflaj/news280506.pdf* (accessed on 22/07/04).

Rikowski, Ruth (2002o) Globalisation and libraries. In: *Globalisation*, report by House of Lords, Select Committee on Economic Affairs,

Session (2002–3) 1 Report, the Stationery Office, in *Volume of Evidence*, part 2, HL5-II – on CD ROM, pp. 360–71.

Rikowski, Ruth (2002p) *WTO/GATS agenda for libraries*. Talk prepared for ATTAC meeting on 30 April. Available at: *http://www.attac.org.uk/attac/document/rikowski-gats-agenda-libraries.pdf? documentID=120* (accessed on 22/07/04).

Rikowski, Ruth (ed.) (2002q) Globalisation and information, *Information for Social Change*, 14 (Winter 2001/2). Available at: *http://libr.org/ISC* (accessed on 22/07/04).

Rikowski, Ruth (2003a) Tripping over TRIPS? An assessment of the World Trade Organization Agreement on Trade Related Aspects of Intellectual Property Rights, focusing in particular on trade, moral and information issues, *Business Information Review*, 20 (3): 149–57. Available at: *http://www.sagepub.co.uk/PDF/JOURNALS/FULLTEXT/a039452.pdf_tripping+over+trips%3F&hl=en* (accessed on 21/07/04).

Rikowski, Ruth (2003b) TRIPS into the unknown: libraries and the WTO Agreement on Trade-Related Aspects of Intellectual Property Rights, *IFLA Journal: Official Journal of the International Federation of Library Associations and Institutions*, 29 (2): 141–51. Available at: *http://www.ifla.org/V/iflaj/ij.2.2003.pdf* (accessed on 21/07/04).

Rikowski, Ruth (2003c) Tripping along with TRIPS? The World Trade Organisation's Agreement on Trade-Related Aspects of Intellectual Property Rights, *Managing Information*, 10 (3): 10–12.

Rikowski, Ruth (2003d) The significance of WTO agreements for the library and information world, *Managing Information*, 10 (1): 43.

Rikowski, Ruth (2003e) Globalisation, libraries and information, *Relay: The Journal of the University College and Research Group of CILIP*, 55 (July): 11–12; and *Information for Social Change*, 17 (Summer). Available at: *http://libr.org/ISC* (accessed on 20/07/04).

Rikowski, Ruth (2003f) Library privatisation: fact or fiction? *Information for Social Change*, 17 (Summer). Available at: *http://libr.org/ISC* (accessed on 20/07/04).

Rikowski, Ruth (2003g) Value – the life blood of capitalism: knowledge is the current key, *Policy Futures in Education*, 1 (1): 163–82. Available at: *http://www.triangle.co.uk/pfie* (accessed on 22/07/04).

Rikowski, Ruth (2003h) *Value theory and value creation through knowledge in the knowledge revolution*. A dissertation submitted in partial fulfilment of the requirements of the University of Greenwich for the degree of MA by Research in Business. Included empirical research in knowledge management, interviews and focus groups.

Rikowski, Ruth (2004) On the impossibility of determining the length of the working day for intellectual labour, *Information for Social Change*, 19 (Summer). Available at: *http://libr.org/ISC*.

Rumsey, Sally (1999) Smart card people are happy people, *Ariadne*, 20 (June). Available at: *http://www/ariadne.ac.uk/issue20/tolimac* (accessed on 21/07/04).

Sahai, Suman (2003) Indigenous knowledge and its protection in India. In: *Trading in Knowledge: Development Perspectives on TRIPS, Trade and Sustainability* (eds Christophe Bellman, Graham Dutfield and Ricardo Meléndez-Ortiz), pp. 166–74. London: Earthscan.

Salgar, Ana M. H. (2003) Traditional knowledge and the biotrade: the Columbian experience. In: *Trading in Knowledge: Development Perspectives on TRIPS, Trade and Sustainability* (eds Christophe Bellman, Graham Dutfield and Ricardo Meléndez-Ortiz), pp. 184–9. London: Earthscan.

Schleihagen, Barbara (2002) Intellectual freedom and libraries: German perspectives, *IFLA Journal*, 28 (4): 185–9.

Seetharama, S. (ed.) (1998) *Libraries and Information Centres as Profit Making Institutions*. New Delhi: Vedham eBooks.

Seidelin, Susanne (2002) Intellectual freedom and libraries: international perspectives, *IFLA Journal*, 28 (4): 181–4.

Sharma, Vijender (2002) *WTO, GATS and the future of higher education in India*, January. Available at: *http://www.indowindow.com/akhbar/article.php?article=9&category=7&issue=15* (accessed on 21/07/04).

Sherwood, Bob (2002) Inventive employees could be rewarded royalties, *Financial Times*, 4 December: 1.

Shimmon, Ross (2001) Can we bridge the digital divide? What can the international library community do about the growing gap between those with access to ICT and those without, *Library Association Record*, 103 (11): 678–9.

Shirky, Clay (2000) *The case against micropayments*. Available at: *http://www.open2p2.com/pub/a/p2p/2000/12/19/micropayments.html?page=2* (accessed on 21/07/04).

Shiva, Vandana (2001) *Protect* or *Plunder? Understanding Intellectual Property Rights*. London and New York: Zed Books.

Short, Clare (2001) Making globalisation work for poor people, *Education International*, July, 7 (2): 17.

Shrybman, Steven (2000) *Information, commodification and the World Trade Organisation*. Paper presented at the 66th IFLA Council and

General Conference, Jerusalem, Israel, 13–18 August. Available at: *http://www.ifla.org/IV/ifla66/papers/176-148e.htm* (accessed on 20/07/04).

Shrybman, Steven (2001) *An assessment of the impact of the General Agreement on Trade in Services on policy, programs and law concerning public sector libraries.* Prepared for the Canadian Library Association, Canadian Association of University Teachers, Canadian Association of Research Libraries, Ontario Library Association, Saskatchewan Library Association, Manitoba Library Association, Industry Canada, British Columbia Library Association, Library Association of Alberta and National Library of Canada (Ontario, Canada), October. Available at: *http://www.caut.au/english/issues/trade/GATS.pdf* (accessed on 21/07/04).

Sibthorpe, Richard (2001) A new path to follow – Private Finance Initiative, *Library Association Record*, 103 (4): 236–7.

Sigurdson, Jon and Tagerud, Yael (eds) (1992) *The intelligent corporation: the privatisation of intelligence.* Available at: *http://www.taylorgraham.com/books/sigintcor.html* (accessed on 21/07/04).

Simmons, Sylvia (1999) Building a portal for the people, *Times Higher Education Supplement*, 24 September: 15.

Simmons, Sylvia (2000) Defenders of the public good, *Library Association Record*, 102 (1): 26–7.

Sinclair, Scott (2000) *GATS: How the WTO's new 'services' negotiations threatens democracy*, Movement for a Socialist Future website at: *http://socialistfuture.org.uk/globaleconomy/The%20Issues/gats.htm* (accessed on 21/07/04).

Smith, Adam (1994) [1776] *The Wealth of Nations: An Inquiry into the Nature and Causes.* New York: Modern Library.

Smith, J. and Moran, T. (2000) WTO 101: myths about the World Trade Organisation, *Dissent*, Spring: 66–70.

Smith, Nick (2000) *Copyright as a potential barrier to access to information.* Paper given at the IFLA General Conference, Jerusalem, August 2000. Available at: *http://www.ifla.org/III/clm/p1/israel00.pdf* (accessed on 20/07/04).

South Africa says No to WTO (2001) Gauteng Department of Economic Affairs Gauteng Anti-WTO protest, *Food First: Institute for Food and Development Policy*, 9 November. Available at: *http://www.foodfirst.org/progs/global/trade/wto2001/southafrica.html* (accessed on 20/07/04).

StorageTek (2001a) Making Net Profit – Executive Summary of the White Paper on Micropayments, *Industry News*, 17 April, 3 pages at: *http://nws.statedigital.net/cgi-mf/news.pI?news_id=116&exhibition_id=7*.

StorageTek (2001b) *Micropayments: Making Net Profits – A StorageTek perspective*, White Paper on Micropayments. Woking: Storage Technology Corporation UK.

Straw, Jack (2001) Globalisation is good for us: the best way to combat world poverty is to increase trade, *Guardian*, 10 September: 13.

Tapscott, Don (2000) Minds over matter: the new economy is based on brains, not brawn. The only thing that counts is smart, *Business*, 2 (March): 220–7.

Tebtebba Foundation (1999) *No to patenting of life! Indigenous peoples' statement on the TRIPS Agreement of the WTO*. Available from: *http://lists.essential.org/mai.not/msg00160.html*.

Torremans, Paul (2001) *Holyoak and Torremans Intellectual Property Law*, 3rd edn. London: Butterworths.

Trade Policy Directorate (2001) *General Agreement on Trade in Services*, 7 March.

Triggle, Nick (2002) Cover story: a new wave of hi-tech libraries is winning back the public in some cities, but updating the inside is not enough if the buildings are falling down, *Guardian Society*, 20 November: 10–11.

United Nations Conference on Trade and Development (UNCTAD) (1998) *World Investment Report 1998: Trends and Determinants*. New York and Geneva: UN.

Utkarsh, Ghate (2003) Documentation of traditional knowledge: People's Biodiversity Registers. In: *Trading in Knowledge: Development Perspectives on TRIPS, Trade and Sustainability* (eds Christophe Bellman, Graham Dutfield and Ricardo Meléndez-Ortiz), pp. 190–5. London: Earthscan.

Valauskas, Edward J. (1999) A review of privatisation, *Inspel*, 33 (1): 1–9.

W3C (undated) Micropayments overview. W3C Technology and Society Domain. Available at: *http://www.w3.org/Ecommerce/Micropayments* (accessed on 13/10/01).

Wainwright, Martin (2003) Libraries blamed for their own decline, *Guardian*, 18 August: 26.

Ward, Suzanne M. (1997) Starting and managing fee-based information services in academic libraries, *Foundations in Library and Information Science*, 40.

Watkins, Kevin (2002) Main development from WTO talks is a fine line in hypocrisy, *Guardian*, 26 September: 19.

Watkins, Kevin (2003) Countdown to Cancun, *Prospect*, August: 28–33.

Watson, Angela (2001) *Best returns: Best Value guidance for local authorities in England*, 2nd edn, July. Available at: *http://www.la-hq .org.uk/directory/prof-issues/br.html* (accessed on 21/07/04).

Webb, Sylvia and Winterton, Jules (2003) *Fee-based Services in Library and Information Centres*, 2nd edn (Aslib Know How Guides). London: Europa Publishers.

Webster, Frank and Dempsey, Lorcan (an exchange) (1999a) Virtual library – false dawn? *Ariadne*, 20. Available at: *http://www.ariadne.ac .uk/issue20/public-libraries*. Also available at: *http://www.uk.oln .ac.uk/services/papers/ukoln/dempsey-1999-01/*. A condensed version of this exchange appeared in *Library Association Record*, 101.

Webster, Frank (1999b) *Public libraries in the information age*, October. Available at: *http://www.librarylondon.org/localgroups/camden/ pdfdocs/Webster.pdf* (accessed on 21/07/04).

Webster, Frank (2002) *Theories of the Information Society*, 2nd edn. London: Routledge.

Weeraworawit, Weerawit (2003) International legal protection for genetic resources, traditional knowledge and folklore challenges for the intellectual property system. In: *Trading in Knowledge: Development Perspectives on TRIPS, Trade and Sustainability* (eds Christophe Bellman, Graham Dutfield and Ricardo Meléndez-Ortiz), pp. 157–65. London: Earthscan.

Weiss, Helen (2000) Tracking usage patterns: how management information systems can help librarians adapt commercial marketing techniques to revolutionise their service, *Library Association Record*, 102 (8: August): 448–9.

Welch, Rob (2000) Knowledge management in a deconstructing economy: treating KM as another fad ignores its key role in the new economy, *Knowledge Management*, May: 10.

Wesselius, Eric (2003) Driving the GATS juggernaut, *Red Pepper*, January. Available at: *http://www.globalpolicy.org/socecon/bwi-wto/ wto/2003/01gats.htm* (accessed on 20/07/04).

White Paper on Open Government, Cm 2290, HMSO. Referenced in: *Essential Law for Information Professionals* by Paul Pedley (2003). London: Facet, p. 123.

Whitfield, Dexter (2001) *Public Services and Corporate Welfare.* London: Pluto Press.

Whitney, Paul (2000) *Libraries and the WTO.* Notes for a presentation to the 66th IFLA General Conference, Jerusalem, Israel. August 2000. Available at: *http://www.ifla.org/III/clm/p1/whitney.pdf* (accessed on 20/07/04).

Whitney, Paul (2003) Notes for an update on libraries and international trade treaties, *World Library and Information Congress*, 69th IFLA General Conference and Council, 1–9 August. Available at: *http://www.ifla.org/IV/ifla69/papers/201e-Whitney.pdf* (accessed on 20/07/04).

Wild, Joff (2002) Digging for hidden treasure in R&D, *Financial Times*, 23 December: 10.

Williams, David (2002) Browse but don't borrow: many university libraries either do not allow the public to borrow books or charge them for the privilege, but how does this square with lifelong learning?, *Guardian Education*, 8 October: 14.

Williams, Frances (2002a) Russian commitment speeds talks on WTO entry, *Financial Times*, 19 December: 7.

Williams, Frances (2002b) WTO minnows cry foul on mediation, *Financial Times*, 24 October: 8.

Williams, Frances (2002c) Early trade talks are top priority, says new WTO chief, *Financial Times*, 3 September: 8.

Williams, Frances (2003a) Hopes revive for talks on alternatives to patents, *Financial Times*, 1 October: 7.

Williams, Frances (2003b) Geneva battle resumes on WTO accord, *Financial Times*, 10 June: 6.

Williams, Frances (2004) World trade talks on services markets 'may last years', *Financial Times*, 6 July: 9.

Worden, Scott (1998) *Micropayments and the future of the Web.* Cambridge, MA: Harvard University. Available at: *http://cyber.law .harvard.edu/fallsem98/final_papers/worden.html* (accessed on 20/07/04).

World Development Movement (WDM) (2003a) *GATS: From Doha to Cancun*, 25 August. Available at: *http://www.wdm.org.uk/cambriefs/ gats/gatscancunupdate.htm* (accessed on 20/07/04).

World Development Movement (WDM) (2003b) *Stop the GATSastrophe!: GATS Campaign,* Available at: *http://www.wdm.org.uk/campaign/GATS.htm* (accessed on 20/07/04).

World Intellectual Property Organisation (WIPO) (2001) *Collective management of copyright and related rights,* August. Available at: *http://www.wipo.org/about-ip/en/about_collective_mngt.html* (accessed on 21/07/04).

World Intellectual Property Organisation (WIPO) and News Report (2003) Study takes critical look at benefit sharing of genetic resources and traditional knowledge, *Managing Information,* 11 (2): 20.

World Trade Organisation (WTO) (1994) *General Agreement on Trade in Services (GATS): Uruguay Round Agreement.* Available at: *http://www.wto.org/english/docs_e/legal_a/26-gats_01_e.htm* (accessed on 21/07/04).

World Trade Organisation (WTO) (1995) *TRIPS – Text of the Agreement on Trade-Related Aspects of Intellectual Property Rights, Annex IC of WTO.* Available at: *http://www.wto.org/english/tratop_e/trips-e/t_agm0_e.htm* (accessed on 21/07/04).

World Trade Organisation (WTO) (1999) *Labour issue is 'false debate', obscures underlying consensus. WTO Chief Michael Moore tells unions.* World Trade Organisation, Press Release, press/152, 28 November. Available at: *http://www.wto.org/english/news_e/press99_e/pr152_e.htm* (accessed on 21/07/04).

World Trade Organisation (WTO) (undated:a) *Overview: the TRIPS Agreement: a more detailed overview of the TRIPS Agreement.* Available at: *www.wto.org/english/tratop_e/trips_e/intel2_e.htm* (accessed on 20/07/04).

World Trade Organisation (WTO) (undated:b) *Trading into the Future: the introduction to the WTO. The Agreements: intellectual property, protection and enforcement.* Available at: *http://www.enyox.com/dev/unido-tcb/upload/files/CMSEditor/WTO_Trading_into_the_future.pdf* (2nd edn, 2001) (accessed on 21/07/04).

World Trade Organisation (WTO) (undated:c) *Trade policy reviews: brief introduction – overseeing national trade policies: the TRM.* Available at: *http://www.wto.org/english/tratop_e/trp_e/tpr_e.htm* (accessed on 21/07/04).

World Trade Organisation (WTO) (undated:d) *TPR: Introduction and objectives.* Available at: *http://www.wto.org/english/thewto_3/whatis_e/eol/e/wto08/wto8_4.htm* (accessed on 21/07/04).

Writers' Guild of America, West (undated) *http://www.wga.org* (accessed on 21/07/04).

Yap, Derek (1998) *Selected Internet resources for information on the MAI, Prepared for the BCLA: Information: Policy Committee*, May.

Yushkiavitshus, Henrikas (2000) Intellectual freedom in libraries in Eastern Europe, *IFLA Journal*, 26 (4): 288–92.

Zageman, Bertam (undated) *GATS and water*. Available at: *http://www.gatswatch.org/GATSandDemocracy/water.html* (accessed on 20/07/04).

For links to readings about the implications of GATS on public libraries throughout the world, see GATS and public libraries website at: *http://libr.org/gats/*.

Index of authors

Index of places and organisations

Index of subjects

TRIPS, 235–7, 240, 244, 245,
246–54, 267–8, 271, 279–84,
305
water privatisation, 49, 80
WTO, 1–2, 21–3, 25–6, 80–1, 283
digital divide, 79–80, 118, 119,
121–2, 150, 274
digital value, 326
direct payments, 121

economic rights – *see* copyright
education services, 51, 60, 99–100,
182
Canada, 62, 67
India, 81–3
Japan, 71
New Zealand, 77–8
South Africa, 83–4
UK, 133, 153, 176–7
efficiency in library services, 111,
139
electronic library services, 92, 111,
122, 125–6, 176, 303
see also People's Network
English language, dominance of, 11,
280
ethics, 262–3, 279, 318
see also morality
Euro (currency), 123
evolution:
capitalism, 3, 304, 334–5
social systems, 291, 295, 298–9,
312–13, 334
see also Darwinism
exchange value, 134, 308–10
exemptions from GATS, 40, 64, 70,
73, 82, 164, 168, 172, 174, 175
expansion:
capital, 13
value, 310

exploitation:
in developing world, 239–40, 267,
272
of labour, 57, 134, 304, 311–12,
316

fee-based library services, 114–15,
117
folklore – *see* traditional knowledge
free access to information, 93, 176
222, 224, 226, 228, 256, 258,
259–63, 272
free flow of information, 12, 98, 99,
119–20, 121, 222–3, 225, 228,
256–7, 259–66
free trade – *see* trade liberalisation
free trade agreements (bilateral and
multilateral), 95–6
freedom of expression, 222, 225–6,
258, 260–3
freedom of information, 99, 225–6,
256, 258, 259, 264–6
Freedom of Information Act, 264–5
functionalism, 14
funding of public libraries, 115
future of public libraries, 103–9

GATS, 35–47, 49–97, 103–60,
161–84, 306
articles about, 91
audio-visual industry, 96–7
barriers to trade, 86, 121, 124,
148, 164, 170
'bottom-up' aspect, 39
categorisations, 57–9
CILIP statement, 92–4
commercialisation of public
services, 43–7
commodification, 55, 304, 307,
312, 316, 320, 326–7, 335